SEVENTH EDITION

A Resource Guide for Elementary School Teaching

Planning for Competence

Patricia L. Roberts

Richard D. Kellough

Kay Moore

California State University, Sacramento

Boston Columbus Indianapolis New York San Francisco Upper Saddle River
Amsterdam Cape Town Dubai London Madrid Milan Munich Paris Montreal Toronto
Delhi Mexico City Sao Paulo Sydney Hong Kong Seoul Singapore Taipei Tokyo

Senior Acquisitions Editor: Kelly Villella Canton
Editorial Assistant: Annalea Manalili
Vice President, Director of Marketing: Quinn Perkson
Senior Marketing Manager: Darcy Betts
Production Editor: Gregory Erb
Editorial Production Service: S4Carlisle Publishing Services
Manufacturing Buyer: Megan Cochran
Electronic Composition: S4Carlisle Publishing Services
Photo Researcher: Annie Pickert

Credits and acknowledgments borrowed from other sources and reproduced, with permission, in this textbook appear on appropriate page within text.

Library of Congress Cataloging-in-Publication Data
Roberts, Patricia, 1936-
  A resource guide for elementary school teaching : planning for competence/Patricia L. Roberts,
  Richard D. Kellough, Kay Moore. — 7th ed.
    p. cm.
  Includes bibliographical references and index.
  ISBN 978-0-13-703946-3
  1. Elementary school teaching.   2. Competency based education.   I. Kellough, Richard D.
(Richard Dean) II. Moore, Kay. III. Title.
  LB1555.K39 2011
  372.1102—dc22   2010002204

Printed in the United States of America

10 9 8 7 6 5 4 3 2 1 BRG 14 13 12 11 10

www.pearsonhighered.com

ISBN-10:   0-13-703946-8
ISBN-13: 978-0-13-703946-3

About the Authors

Patricia L. Roberts joined the faculty of the School of Education at California State University, Sacramento, where she taught courses in children's literature, reading, and language arts, and served as coordinator of Teacher Education in Elementary Education and associate chair and chair of the Department of Teacher Education. In addition, Dr. Roberts is the author and co-author of more than twenty teacher resource books and texts, including *A Guide to Developing Interdisciplinary Thematic Units,* Fourth Edition (with R. D. Kellough). Her current research centers on teaching curriculum content and multicultural literature for children. Dr. Roberts, an invited biographee in *Who's Who in America* and *Who's Who in the World,* is the recipient of the Distinguished Alumnus of the Year award from the University of the Pacific and the California State University's Award of Merit for Teaching. The Award of Merit is given for a superior teaching record and outstanding service to the institution and to the community. Additional recognitions include listings in *International Who's Who of Intellectuals, Who's Who in American Education, Two Thousand Notable American Women, The World Who's Who of Women, The Directory of Distinguished Americans, International Directory of Distinguished Leadership, The International Who's Who of Contemporary Achievement,* and online *Cambridge Who's Who Registry Among Executive and Professional Women.*

Richard D. Kellough, professor emeritus, is author and co-author of more than fifty textbooks, including *A Primer for New Principals: Guidelines for Success; A Resource Guide for Teaching K–12; Teaching Young Adolescents: A Guide to Methods and Resources; Secondary School Teaching: A Guide to Methods and Resources; Your First Year of Teaching: Guidelines for Success;* and *Science K-8: An Integrated Approach,* as well as numerous journal articles. A member of several prominent organizations, Dr. Kellough has been elected to the Phi Sigma Society, the Botanical Society of America, and the American Bryological Society. His many recognitions include recipient of the Outstanding Biology Teacher Recognition Award (State of California) from the National Biology Teachers Association, being named a National Science Foundation Research Fellow at the University of California, Davis, as well as listings in *The International Authors and Writers Who's Who, Leaders in Eco Education, Men of Achievement* (Volume I), *Dictionary of Educational Biography* (Volumes 9 and 10), and *Leaders in Education.*

Kay Moore is a professor at California State University, Sacramento, in the Department of Teacher Education. Professor Moore teaches courses in literacy and social studies for preservice teachers and undergraduate and graduate classes in juvenile literature. She has served as associate chair of her department and director of the Liberal Studies Program. A former elementary classroom teacher for ten years, she was honored as El Dorado County (California) Teacher of the Year for 1985. She served as president of the California Reading Association (CRA) from 1994 to 1995 and received the John Martin Award for exemplary service to that organization. She returned to the CRA Board as the editor of *The California Reader* (2007–2010). For her numerous contributions to the literacy field, Professor Moore was inducted into the California Reading Hall of Fame in 2007. She is the author of two juvenile books published by Scholastic, *If You Lived at the Time of the Civil War* (1994) and *If You Lived at the Time of the American Revolution* (1997). With Linda Wells, she created the story coloring book, *The Night Before Christmas, 1849.* A contributor to the CRA publication, *Building Literacy: Making Every Child a Reader,* she has also designed activities for the California Young Reader Medal activities book for the last eight years.

Brief Contents

Contents

PART 3   EFFECTIVE INSTRUCTION, TEACHER ASSESSMENT, AND PROFESSIONAL DEVELOPMENT   181

CHAPTER 8   What Do I Need to Know to Use Teacher Talk and Questioning as Instructional Tools?   182

CHAPTER 9   What Guidelines Assist My Use of Demonstrations, Thinking, Inquiry Learning, and Games?   206

*To assist the precredentialed teacher in preparing to take a teacher test, we have placed a target bullet (•) by selected word entries in the subject index. The target bullet indicates the subject matter (based on content analysis of Praxis II and other teacher tests) that we suggest be reviewed to get ready to take an upcoming teacher test for licensing and credentialing. The target bullets stand for Target Topics for Teacher Tests (TTTT) and provide a ready visual reference for content areas to study.

NOTE: Every effort has been made to provide accurate and current Internet information in this book. However, the Internet and information on it are constantly changing, so it is inevitable that some of the Internet addresses listed in this resource guide will change. If URLs have typographical errors, please notify the editor so that corrections can be made in future editions. One factor that may affect changes in addresses is that Internet protocol (IP addresses) specialists have indicated that the availability of IP addresses may be depleted by 2012. If the addresses run out, educators who need access may have to purchase from those who have unused ones, and thus, addresses may change.

Preface

Welcome to the seventh edition of *A Resource Guide for Elementary School Teaching: Planning for Competence*. We have kept our goal and the original purpose of this resource guide, which is to provide a practical guide for college or university students who are preparing to become competent elementary schoolteachers. The essence of the purpose is reflected in the subtitle, *Planning for Competence*. Other readers who may find this revised guide useful are first- and second-year teachers, and experienced ones who want to continue developing their teaching skills as well as curriculum specialists who lead teaching workshops and summer school courses, and school administrators who want a current, practical, and concise reference of methods, guidelines, and resources for teaching in the elementary school.

NEW TO THIS EDITION

The research for this seventh edition was intense due to the interest in education and technology, state and national standards, high-stakes testing, state teacher tests, and the effect of the last presidential election on education and the changes in the No Child Left Behind Act. As part of its preparation, we wanted a book that would reflect current trends and instructor and student comments and support the following new features:

- **Updated Application Exercises.** All exercises provide planning for competence in elementary school teaching. Updated materials are included, such as creating a rubric, preparing a résumé, and engaging in cooperative and collaborative work, a skill often found on student teaching evaluations. Each exercise assists teacher candidates in using their knowledge about teaching and learning in the elementary school.
- **Interactive Focus.** This is an interactive book where there is an emphasis on the beginning teacher working cooperatively and collaboratively using interactive exercises with others in a group, just as he or she would work with other members of an elementary school faculty team. We believe that one who is learning how to teach for the first time needs a great deal of interaction and support from others. This book's

approach addresses the concern of the Deputy Executive Director of the National Staff Development Council, Joellen Killion:

> "One of the things we've been nervous about with online learning is that it could set us back decades where . . . teachers . . . sit alone in front of their computers, answering questions in isolation." (Technology Counts, *Education Week*, March 29, 2009, 28: 26, p. 24).

- **Updated Chapters.** All chapters have been updated and polished with new illustrations in the presentations, including a photo of the newly named Barack Obama Elementary School to reflect Obama's historic election as America's president and new Choices for Differentiated Self-Instruction.
- **New Content on Diversity.** There is new content on multicultural and global education, English language learners (ELLs), and a culturally responsive classroom. Specifically, you will find more coverage of ELLs in Chapter 2, multicultural and global education in Chapter 5, and culturally responsive classrooms in Chapter 4.
- **New Content on Technology.** Also, the inclusion of integrated technology throughout the book offers ways that teachers present information in the elementary school, and often, highlights selected Internet websites that are useful to elementary schoolteachers.
- **Teaching Vignettes with Integrated Technology.** There are teaching vignettes, *Looking at Teachers I* in chapter beginnings and *Looking at Teachers II* in chapter endings, with current insights regarding different grade levels in elementary school teaching. All vignettes, which are springboards for class discussion, integrate technology use. About half of these vignettes now focus on English language learners. Additionally, half of the chapter-ending vignettes now form the basis for questions in the Teacher Tests Study Guide at the back of the book. These are short-response-type questions that will help teacher candidates prepare to take their state teacher tests.
- **Self-Check Reflection Guides.** These evaluative guides provide an opportunity for professional reflection through a Midpoint Self-Evaluation (after Chapter 6) for teacher candidates that relates to the content and

competency development addressed in the first six chapters. After completing Chapter 11, there is a Final Self-Evaluation for teacher self-evaluation and professional growth and development related to the content and competency development for Chapters 7–11. Both reflective self-evaluations are in Appendix B. These self-evaluations are a valuable basis for a prelicensed teacher's self-assessment, self-reflection, and continued professional growth and development.

UNIQUE FEATURES

- **Matrix Inside Front Cover: Connection of This Book to INTASC Principles and NBPTS Standards.** This information is to help teacher candidates prepare for taking teacher tests by providing content related to the principles of the Interstate New Teacher Assessment and Support Consortium **(INTASC)** and to the standards of the National Board for Professional Teaching Standards **(NBPTS).** The principles and standards are seen in the matrix inside the front cover of this resource guide. All chapters, with new illustrations, contain material in them that connects with the subject matter that precredentialed teachers are usually tested on through teacher tests—these are the areas of management, assessment of learning, curriculum and instruction, assessment of teaching, and professional development. An overview of the connection between the content in this book and the subject matter often presented on teacher tests and noted in professional standards and principles is shown concisely in this matrix for the interested reader.

- **Chapter-Opening Visual Organizers.** These graphics serve as advance organizers, documented by research for value in meaningful learning, and provide a guide to chapter study. They mentally prepare readers for the study of the material in the chapter by providing them with a conceptual arrangement of what is to be learned.

- **Chapter Objectives.** These objectives at the front of each chapter provide a description of what the reader should be able to do upon completing the reading of the chapter and after completing the related application exercises, interacting with the end-of-chapter activities.

- **Key Terms in Bold.** This book's collection of key terms is shown in bold in the main narrative and defined in the glossary at the back of the book.

- **Exemplary Schools and Programs.** So readers can learn and read about or visit exemplary schools and programs online, several are recognized and identified by name and, where appropriate, by URLs. These schools are supported by committed teachers, administrators, parents, and community representatives who struggle daily, year after year, to provide children with a quality education. They continue their struggle in spite of the commissions, authors, and politicians who strongly criticize what they perceive as the failures of public school education, and we wanted to recognize these schools in this book.

- **Unique Subject Index with Bullets That Identify Target Topics for Teacher Tests (TTTT).** The subject index is a special feature because it is not only an alphabetical list to facilitate reference to topics in this book but it is also a visual guide for precredentialed and prelicensed teachers since bullets identify topics often targeted and found on state teacher tests. In this subject index, the bullets are located beside selected word entries that reflect the teacher test material. This visual aid of bullets provides a way to quickly identify the topics in the index that we suggest be reviewed when preparing for licensure exams.

- **End-of-Chapter Bibliographies.** There are succinct end-of-chapter bibliographies that support the specific content in each chapter. We include these because the specific bibliographies at the end of the chapters are time-efficient for the busy teacher or teacher candidate trying to find resources or follow up material about a chapter topic.

- **Chapter Summaries and Extending Competency Sections.** All chapters close with a summary and a section titled *Extending My Competency* that serves as an additional informational source for precredentialed elementary teachers who are getting ready to take upcoming teacher tests. This section will lead the reader to further practice and planning for competence through the following features:

  Feature One: With Discussion . . . This component invites precredentialed and prelicensed teachers to read and respond to discussion questions at the end of the chapters so that they can *actively rehearse/practice* their responses to questions that might be asked of them by a colleague, a parent, a community member, or another educator. Through the questions, they might be asked to explain content, theory, related research, or identify techniques or strategies; they might be asked to make connections between topics in this resource guide or be asked to relate an experience that they have had to a topic in a chapter; additionally, they might be asked to react to the subject matter or to situations or explain a point of view about a current trend, issue, or problem happening in education.

  Feature Two: With Video . . . This component invites readers to review their knowledge of selected key content presented in each of the chapters by viewing a teaching video on online methods site www.MyEducationLab.com. Click on our book icon and the link that is indicated.

Feature Three: With Portfolio . . . This component invites precredentialed teachers to begin a portfolio to assist them in self evaluation, in assessing their teaching, in self-reflection, in continuing professional growth and development, and, if appropriate for their state, in documenting their competence for certification and licensing regulations. Assistance with Portfolio Builders can be found on our book's site at www.MyEducationLab.com.

- **End of Chapter and Appendixes.** At the back of each chapter, *With Readings* is a section of references, both classic and current, that forms a useful target bibliography about the content for the chapter; another section, *With Notes,* documents the chapter sources. At the back of the book, there is an *Appendix A, Teacher Tests Study Guide,* that provides short-answer essay questions and hints for responses helpful when preparing to take teacher tests. There is also *Appendix B, Self-Check Reflection Guides,* useful for teacher reflection. Further, there is a *Glossary, Children's Book Titles Index, Authors and Illustrators Index,* and *Name Index.* The *Subject Index with Target Topics for Teacher Tests (TTTT),* as we mentioned earlier, is a special feature and unique index because it assists a precredentialed teacher in preparing for taking a Praxis II exam or other teacher test and closes the book.

OUR BELIEFS: HOW AND WHERE THEY ARE REFLECTED IN THIS RESOURCE GUIDE

In the preparation of this text, we saw our task *not* as making the teaching job easier for you—effective teaching is never easy—but as improving your teaching effectiveness and providing relevant guidelines and current resources. You may choose from these resources and build upon what works best for you. Nobody can tell you what will work with your students; you will know them best. We do share what we believe to be the best of practice, the most useful of recent research findings, and the richest of experiences. The highlighted statements that follow in italics present our beliefs and explain how they are included in this resource guide.

The best learning occurs when the learner actively participates in the process, which includes having ownership in both the process and the product of the learning. Consequently, this resource guide is designed to engage you in "hands-on" and "minds-on" learning about effective teaching. For example, rather than simply finding a chapter devoted to an exposition of the important topic of cooperative learning, in each chapter you will become involved in cooperative and collaborative learning. In essence, via the application exercises found in every chapter, you will practice cooperative and collaborative learning, talk about it, practice it some more, and finally,

through the process of doing it, learn a great deal about it. This resource guide *involves* you in preparation for being a valuable elementary school faculty member.

The best strategies for learning about teaching are those that model the strategies used in exemplary teaching of children. As you will learn, integrated learning is the cornerstone of effective teaching for the twenty-first century, and that is a premise upon which this resource guide continues to be designed.

To be most effective, any teacher, regardless of grade level and subject, must use an eclectic style in teaching. Rather than focusing your attention on particular models of teaching, we emphasize the importance of an eclectic model—that is, one in which you select and integrate the best from various instructional approaches. For example, there are times when you will want to integrate technology or use an implicit, social-interactive, or student-centered approach (perhaps through project-based learning), and there are other times when you will want to use a systematic explicit expository approach (perhaps by brief lecturing). This resource guide provides guidelines that will help you not only to decide which approach to use at a particular time, but also ways to develop your skill in using specific approaches.

Learning should be active, pleasant, fun, meaningful, and productive. Our desire is, as it always has been, to present this text in an enthusiastic, positive, and cognitive-humanistic way, in part by providing rich experiences in cooperative and collaborative learning. How this is done is perhaps best exemplified by the active applications that are the learning exercises found throughout this book. Some new application exercises have been added to ensure that you become an active participant in learning the methods and procedures that are most appropriate in facilitating the learning of the active, responsible children present in today's elementary schools.

Teaching skills can be learned. You realize that in medicine, certain knowledge and skills must be learned and developed before the student physician is licensed to practice alone with patients. In law, certain knowledge and skills must be learned and developed before the law student is licensed to practice in a courtroom. So it is in education: in teacher preparation, knowledge and skills must be learned and developed before the teacher candidate is licensed to practice the art and science of teaching children. We would never consider allowing just any person to treat our child's illness or to defend us in a legal case; the professional education of teachers is no less important! Receiving professional education in how to reach children is absolutely necessary, and certain aspects of that education must precede any interaction with children if teachers are to become truly accomplished professionals.

ORGANIZATION OF THIS BOOK: AN OVERVIEW

Competent elementary school teaching is a kaleidoscopic, multifaceted, eclectic process. When preparing and writing a resource guide for use in elementary teacher preparation, by necessity, one must separate that total kaleidoscopic view into separate views, which is not always possible to do in a way that makes the most sense to everyone using the book. However, we believe that there are *developmental components involved in becoming a competent teacher*. Thus, this book is organized around those components: (a) why, (b) what, and (c) how and how well. Each of the three parts of this resource guide clearly reflects one of these three components. Each part is introduced with the chapters of that part and some reflective thoughts relevant to topics addressed in its chapters. The visual graphic that follows in this preface illustrates how these three developmental elements are divided.

```
+-----------------------+  +-----------------------+
|         Why?          |  |         What?         |
|   Elementary School   |  | Planning for Curriculum|
|  Teaching and Learning|  |    and Instruction    |
|         Part I        |  |        Part II        |
+-----------------------+  +-----------------------+

      +-----------------------------+
      |   Planning for Competency   |
      +-----------------------------+

   +-------------------------------------+
   |         How and How Well?           |
   | Effective Instruction, Teacher      |
   | Assessment, and Professional        |
   | Development                         |
   |              Part III               |
   +-------------------------------------+
```

These components match the major subject material that the teacher tests usually contain:

Resource Guide Components	Teacher Tests
Who?	Planning for Management
What?	Planning for Curriculum and Instruction
How and How Well?	Planning for Effective Instruction; Planning for Teacher Assessment and Professional Development

Part I: Elementary School Teaching and Learning

To better reflect the *why* component—the reality and challenge of elementary school teaching today—Part I underwent substantial reorganization and updates for this edition. Chapters 1 and 2 are, we believe, better organized with figures and more focused in the overview of elementary schools and elementary learners, including ELLs. Chapter 1 presents an important overview of the reality and the challenge of teaching grades in an elementary school today. It mentions high stakes testing and the No Child Left Behind Act. Chapter 2 considers the students and developments in cognitive learning theory that enhance and celebrate the differences in students and their styles of learning. *Regardless of gender, social or physical abilities, and ethnic or cultural characteristics, all students must have equal opportunity to participate and learn in the classroom.* This belief is reflected throughout this resource guide. Chapter 3, devoted to the behaviors of a classroom teacher relates mainly to the topic of management, including information on the culturally responsive classroom. This chapter reflects the expectations, responsibilities, and classroom behaviors that are characteristic of competent elementary schoolteachers. Chapter 4, strengthened by new illustrations and organization, focuses on the classroom learning environments. Because a teacher must have the students' attention to effectively implement any instructional plan, guidelines for establishing and maintaining a supportive environment for learning are also presented in Chapter 4.

Part II: Planning for Instruction

To reflect the planning, or *what*, component, Part II includes three chapters that are now stronger with new illustrations and organization. Related to the important guideline, *effective teaching is performance-based and criterion-referenced*, Chapter 5 addresses planning and selecting the content of the curriculum. It has information about standards that have been developed for different subject areas of the elementary school curriculum and about the high-stakes testing that often accompanies curriculum standards. The section on preparing and using instructional objectives emphasizes the relationship of objectives to assessing learning and planning instruction. Chapter 5 also has updated material about issues related to a teacher's rationale for selecting materials, district material selection, and reconsideration policies, and the difference between a challenge and censorship; it now includes an action plan related to censorship. Chapter 6 is about assessing what students know or think they know before, during, and after the instruction to assist teachers in further planning of instruction. In addition to the use of portfolios, scoring guides and rubrics, checklists, performance assessment, and students' self-assessment, the chapter provides practical guidelines for parent-teacher collaboration and for marking and grading. There is an emphasis on how a teacher can interpret test results, a way to report results, and ways to communicate results to parents or guardians interested in the student's achievement. Chapter 7 presents instructional planning as a three-level and seven-step process, and introduces the topics of activity planning, lesson planning, and unit planning. Also, this chapter provides the theoretical considerations for the selection of instructional strategies.

Part III: Strategies, Effective Teaching, and Professional Development

For this edition, the *how* and *how well* component, Part III, now includes four chapters. Chapter 8 provides guidelines and resources for the use of teacher talk and questioning, with enhanced emphasis on the encouragement and use of children's questions. Chapter 9 emphasizes various ways of grouping children for instruction, using assignments, ensuring equity in the classroom, using project-centered teaching, and writing across the curriculum. Some classic references apply, such as the early writing by G. Polya about his method of problem solving based on classroom experience in *Induction and Analogy in Mathematics* (Princeton, NJ: Princeton University Press, 1954).

Chapter 10 provides guidelines and resources for the use of demonstrations, teaching of thinking, use of inquiry learning, and educational games. Chapter 11 focuses your attention on the *how well* component and mainly reflects how the teacher is doing. This chapter emphasizes the assessment of teaching effectiveness and guidelines for ongoing professional development. It also contains a culminating peer teaching application exercise, which is a performance-assessment-type final examination for the course or program for which this book is being used. Also in Chapter 11 are other popular items—guidelines for student teaching, finding a teaching position, writing a résumé, and engaging in ongoing professional development.

SUPPLEMENTARY MATERIALS

The following ancillaries are available to instructors for download from the password-protected Pearson Instructor Resource Center (IRC) at www.pearsonhighered.com/irc. Contact your Pearson representative or call faculty service at 1-800-526-0485 for assistance.

- **The Instructor's Manual** provides instructors with a variety of useful resources, such as assessments, chapter overviews, teaching strategies, and ideas for classroom activities, and discussions.

PEARSON myeducationlab

The Power of Classroom Practice

"Teacher educators who are developing pedagogies for the analysis of teaching and learning contend that analyzing teaching artifacts has three advantages: it enables new teachers time for reflection while still using the real materials of practice; it provides new teachers with experience thinking about and approaching the complexity of the classroom; and in some cases, it can help new teachers and teacher educators develop a shared understanding and common language about teaching. . . ."[1]

As Linda Darling-Hammond and her colleagues point out, grounding teacher education in real classrooms—among real teachers and students and among actual examples of students' and teachers' work—is an important, and perhaps even an essential, part of training teachers for the complexities of teaching in today's classrooms. For this reason, we have created a valuable, time-saving website—MyEducationLab—that provides you with the context of real classrooms and artifacts that research on teacher education tells us is so important. The authentic in-class video footage, interactive skill-building exercises and other resources available on MyEducationLab offer you a uniquely valuable teacher education tool.

MyEducationLab is easy to use and integrate into both your assignments and your courses. Wherever you see the MyEducationLab logo in the margins or elsewhere in the text, follow the simple instructions to access the videos, strategies, cases, and artifacts associated with these assignments, activities, and learning units on MyEducationLab. MyEducationLab is organized topically to enhance the coverage of the core concepts discussed in the chapters of your book. For each topic on the course you will find most or all of the following resources:

Connection to National Standards

Now it is easier than ever to see how your coursework is connected to national standards. In each topic of MyEducationLab you will find intended learning outcomes connected to the appropriate national standards for your course. All of the Assignments and Activities and all of the Building Teaching Skills and Dispositions in MyEducationLab are mapped to the appropriate national standards and learning outcomes as well.

Assignments and Activities

Designed to save instructors preparation time, these assignable exercises show concepts in action (through video, cases, or student and teacher artifacts) and then offer thought-provoking questions that probe your understanding of theses concepts or strategies. (Feedback for these assignments is available to the instructor.)

Building Teaching Skills and Dispositions

These learning units help you practice and strengthen skills that are essential to quality teaching. First you are presented with the core skill or concept and then given

---

[1]Darling-Hammond, L., & Bransford, J., Eds. (2005). *Preparing Teachers for a Changing World.* San Francisco: John Wiley & Sons.

an opportunity to practice your understanding of this concept multiple times by watching video footage (or interacting with other media) and then critically analyzing the strategy or skill presented.

Video Examples

These video clips showing classroom footage and real teachers exemplify themes, approaches, and issues related directly to the topic.

IRIS Center Resources

The IRIS Center at Vanderbilt University (http://iris .peabody.vanderbilt.edu—funded by the U.S. Department of Education's Office of Special Education Programs OSEP) develops training enhancement materials for pre-service and in-service teachers. The Center works with experts from across the country to create challenge-based interactive modules, case study units, and podcasts that provide research-validated information about working with students in inclusive settings. On your MyEduca-tionLab course we have integrated this content where appropriate to enhance the content coverage in your book.

Teacher Talk

This feature links to videos of teachers of the year across the country discussing their personal stories of why they teach. This National Teacher of the Year Program is sponsored by the Council of Chief State School Offi-cers (CCSSO) and focuses public attention on teaching excellence.

General Resources on Your MyEducationLab Course

The *Resources* section on your MyEducationLab course is designed to help you pass your licensure exam, put together an effective portfolio and lesson plan, prepare for and navigate the first year of your teaching career, and understand key educational standards, policies, and laws. This section includes:

- **Licensure Exams:** Access guidelines for passing the Praxis exam. The *Practice Test Exam* includes practice questions, *Case Histories*, and *Video Case Studies*.
- **Portfolio Builder and Lesson Plan Builder:** Create, update, and share portfolios and lesson plans.
- **Preparing a Portfolio:** Access guidelines for creating a high-quality teaching portfolio that will allow you to practice effective lesson planning.
- **Licensure and Standards:** Link to state licensure standards and national standards.
- **Beginning Your Career:** Educate yourself—access tips, advice, and valuable information on:
  - *Resume Writing and Interviewing:* Expert advice on how to write impressive resumes and prepare for job interviews.

- *Your First Year of Teaching:* Practical tips to set up your classroom, manage student behavior, and learn to more easily organize for instruction and assessment.
- *Law and Public Policies:* Specific directives and requirements you need to understand under the No Child Left Behind Act and the Individuals with Disabilities Education Improvement Act of 2004.
- **Special Education Interactive Timeline:** Build your own detailed timelines based on different facets of the history and evolution of special education.

Visit *www.myeducationlab.com* for a demonstration of this exciting new online teaching resource.

ACKNOWLEDGMENTS

We would never have been able to complete this edition had it not been for the valued help of numerous people—former and current students and teachers in our classes who have shared their experiences with us; administrators and colleagues who have debated with us about impor-tant issues in education; and authors and publishers who have graciously supported this book. To each we offer our warmest thanks, especially J. Smith, education administra-tor, who developed www.teachertube.com., a valuable source for the teachers we know, and to L. A. Packard, teacher, for her illuminating teaching suggestions.

Although we take full responsibility for any errors or omissions in this resource guide, we are deeply appre-ciative to others for their recent cogent reviews and educational insight in the development of this edition. We continue to respond to the many reviewers and users and students who have used this resource guide and we have made changes as a result of their feedback. Their positive words, some of which we share here, have given us additional insight in writing this latest edition:

" . . . *Application Exercises—a nice selection from which to choose . . . I appreciate that they are included.*"

"*It is those exercises (application exercises) that are most valuable to the way that I structure my course and that my students have also commented on being most valuable.*"

"*These (application exercises) are a highlight of this text to me, and it is very helpful in teaching undergraduates that they are separate sheets that are perforated.*"

"*I have been highly satisfied with the book and my students have had favorable responses to the text.*"

Also, those who have provided current reviews for our latest edition, for which we are deeply grateful, are as follows: Michele Jolivette, Truman College; Christina Siry,

Manhattanville College; and Nancy L. Slattery, Illinois State University.

Further, we want to express our deepest admiration and appreciation to the highly competent professionals at Pearson with whom we have had a professional relationship for many years. We especially thank Editorial Assistant, Annalea Manalili, for her valuable assistance and ongoing cheerfulness, Megan Cochran for her pleasant words, and Paul Smith, Vice President, Editor in Chief, Education, for leading the way. They made writing this Seventh Edition doable.

Although it is very difficult to predict what the children of today will really need to know to be productive citizens in the middle of this century, we do believe they will always need to know how to learn, how to read, how to communicate effectively, and how to think productively. We believe that young people need skills in how to gain knowledge and how to process information, and they need learning experiences that foster effective communication and productive, cooperative behaviors. We hope all children will feel good about themselves,

about others, and about their teachers, schools, and communities. This resource guide continues to emphasize the importance of helping students to develop these skills, feelings, and attitudes.

The appropriate teaching methods for reaching these goals are those that incorporate thoughtful planning, acceptance of the uniqueness of each individual, honesty, trust, sharing, risking, collaboration, communication, and cooperation. Also, we believe children best learn these skills and values from teachers who model the same. This resource guide continues to be faithful to that hope and to that end.

We dedicate this book to our families and are indeed indebted and grateful to all the people in our lives, now and in the past, who have interacted with us and reinforced what we have known since we began our careers as teachers: Teaching is the most rewarding profession of all.

P. L. R.
R. D. K.
K. M.

PART 1

Elementary School Teaching and Learning

Michael Sohn/AP Images

Stan Honda/AFP/Getty Images

1

What Do I Need to Know About Today's Elementary Schools?

Visual Chapter Organizer and Overview

The Elementary School: Getting to Know It

> Primary and Elemiddle Schools
> Magnet Schools and Charter Schools
> Orientation Meetings for Teachers
> School Schedules
> Subjects of the Curriculum
> Team Teaching
> Looping

The Fundamental Characteristic of Exemplary Elementary School Education

> Teachers and Commitment
> Teachers and Reflective Decision Making
> The Effective Principal
> Commitment to Helping All Children Succeed in School

Ways to Connect with Home, Community, and School

> Home and School Connections
> Service Learning and Place-Based Education
> Telecommunications Networks
> Professional Resources File

The Emergent Overall Picture

> Key Trends and Practices Today
> No Child Left Behind Act
> Curriculum Standards and High-Stakes Testing
> Problems and Issues That Trouble the Nation's Schools

LOOKING AT TEACHERS I

Integrated Technology, Computer Sources

At the East End Community School (an Expeditionary Learning School, Portland, Maine), two teachers introduce second-graders who had been studying ocean habitats to expeditionary learning by asking the owner of a local floating restaurant to talk to the students about a problem at the restaurant. An Expeditionary Learning School involves students in study/research to create products beyond the classroom. At the restaurant, it seems that youngsters got bored waiting for their food to be served. The owner asked the students if they could create an activity book to keep young customers interested until

their food was ready and brought to their table. To respond to this, the teachers and second-graders did the following:

- Looked at activity books as models; discussed form and function of an activity book; discussed possible content and activities
- Increased their knowledge by spending a day on a lobster boat, interviewed the captain, visited a lobster market, met with a chef, and took notes to record the information they had gained

- Read additional books and located computer sources about ocean habitats and lobsters, and decided the activity book would include the students' understanding of ocean habitats, life cycles, and systems they had studied
- Developed the book and refined students' writing skills
- Added new vocabulary as students wrote drafts for the pages on paper and computer word programs

The end result of the students' expeditionary learning was their successful creation of an authentic product for a popular local restaurant in their city.

A Focus on English Language Learners

English language learners (ELLs) can be asked to respond to a problem (just as the second-graders mentioned previously were asked by the owner of a local restaurant to create an activity book to keep young customers interested until their food was ready and brought to their table). ELLs can explore a similar request and discover multiple ways to make meaning and also use art/music as a part of their language acquisition/literacy. They can learn and flourish in responding to a community member's request that helps them focus on thinking and understanding (Buhrow and Garcia, 2006). Further, to begin building a community of learners, Vaughn, Bos, and Schumm (2007) mention that a teacher displayed a picture of each student in the classroom. Fastened to each were lists of strengths identified by the student and the teacher. The lists were helpful as students were encouraged to acknowledge the skills of one another during the school day, and when they discovered new ways their peers were special, they could add the ways to the list attached to the student's picture. Acknowledging ways other students are special is an appropriate classroom activity for any elementary grade level.

First day of school jitters ever in your thoughts? Or just interested in what the first day of school might be like for both teachers and students? If so, listen to Sarah Jane Hartwell saying, "I hate my new school" in *First Day Jitters* (Watertown, Massachusetts: Charlesbridge Publishing, 2000) written by J. Danneberg and illustrated by J. Love. It is the first day of school and Sarah does not want to go. Why? She says that she doesn't know anybody and that school will be hard, and she hides in her bed under the covers. The family's white cat and brown terrier are by her bed and look concerned when she says she feels sick. Mr. Hartwell cajoles Sarah into eating breakfast, gives her a lunchbox, and drives her to her new school where Mrs. Burton, the school principal, meets Sarah at the car and walks with her to her classroom. There, Mrs. Burton introduces her to the students in the class as their . . . new teacher, Mrs. Sarah Jane Hartwell. With this ending, a listener or reader may be surprised to learn that the one who has the jitters is the teacher. If this story appeals to you, take time to locate this book in the library or bookstore or find similar stories to read to your class on the first day of school.

Putting first-day apprehensions aside for the moment (we are sure you'll be successful because you are intent on developing your competencies), we want to welcome you to the exciting world of elementary school teaching. Whether you are starting your first career or in the process of beginning a new and different career, this resource guide is for you—it is written for anyone interested in elementary school teaching, including first-day concerns, and for starting the journey toward becoming a professional teacher of children in kindergarten through grade six.

If you are now in a program of teacher preparation, then it is possible that near the completion of the program, you will be offered your first teaching contract. When that happens, you will be excited—eager to sign the contract and to begin your new career. But after the initial excitement, you will have time to reflect. Many questions will then begin to surface. You undoubtedly will ask: What grade(s) will I have? What preparation will I need to make? Will I be a member of a teaching team?

Other questions may come to your mind: How can I prepare for students I have never met? What school and district policies do I need to learn? What support services will I have? What standardized tests are given, when will they be given, and how shall I prepare students for them? What reading, mathematics, social studies, and science programs will I be using? Where and how do I obtain classroom supplies? What are my extracurricular responsibilities? Is there a school dress code for students? How shall I contact parents? How often will I be evaluated and by whom? Will there be an orientation for new teachers? And—how do I get answers to my questions?

To guide you through this initial experience, and to help answer some of the questions you might have now and in the future, the information presented in this book about schools, students, teachers, administrators, and parents and guardians offers a basic glimpse into today's world of elementary school teaching. This active world is so complex that few authors can say everything that needs to be said to every teacher. But we must begin somewhere and this chapter, with the visual chapter organizer that serves as a preview before reading the chapter, is our beginning.

CHAPTER OBJECTIVES

Specifically, on completion of this first chapter, you should be able to:

1. Describe two or more essential characteristics of exemplary elementary school education.
2. Describe two or more current trends, problems, and issues in American public elementary school education.
3. Describe the significance of home, school, and community connections to a child's education and of efforts being made by elementary school educators to enhance the connections to a child's education among the home, school, and local and global communities.
4. Reflect on your own elementary school experiences and reflect on which experiences would help you make certain decisions as a teacher in your classroom.
5. Identify one or more reasons other teacher candidates have selected teaching as a career goal and identify one or more personal/professional characteristics that make an effective teacher.

THE ELEMENTARY SCHOOL: GETTING TO KNOW IT

The elementary school usually enrolls children between the ages of 5 and 11; converting these ages to what traditionally have been known as "grades," we recognize grades kindergarten through six (K–6).

Primary and Elemiddle Schools

In some places, the elementary school is a primary school, with grades K–3 or K–4, followed by a middle school, and then a high school with grades nine through twelve. In other places, the elementary school grade ranges are K–8. Because it houses children of both elementary and middle school age, a K–8 school is referred to sometimes as an *elemiddle school*. The K–8 elementary schools ordinarily are followed by a four-year high school. The K–6 elementary schools are usually followed by a three-year junior high school or a middle school followed by a three-year senior high school. However, a K–6 elementary school with a two-year middle school and a four-year high school is not uncommon.

Magnet and Charter Schools

Whatever elementary grade you are hired to teach, you will want more information: What will the schools be like? What will the students be like? What will their parents or guardians be like? If it is a multiple school district, to which school will I be assigned? Will it be a traditional school or a **magnet school,** that is, a school that focuses on a particular academic or philosophical area? For several examples, Capitol Hill Magnet School (St. Paul, Minnesota) provides a program for gifted and talented children in grades 1–8; at John Stanford International School (Seattle, Washington), students in grades 1–5 receive global curriculum topics, have a multi-language library, a dual-language immersion program, and service from a Bilingual Orientation Center for English language learners; at Phalen Lake Elementary (St. Paul, Minnesota), a Hmong Studies magnet school, faculty members link Hmong culture and history into the core curriculum at each grade since the student body is nearly two-thirds Hmong; at High Peaks Core Knowledge Elementary School (Boulder, Colorado), the Core Knowledge Curriculum is at the center;[1] at Irwin Avenue Elementary School (Charlotte, North Carolina), the focus is on the philosophy of open education, and at North Las Vegas Middle School (Nevada), a NASA Explorers school, one focus is the Civil Air Patrol enrichment program led by an aerospace education teacher who makes arrangements for the students to have live video sessions with the International Space Station.[2]

Here are some of the other possibilities. The school where you are assigned could be an **expeditionary learning school** involving students in study/research to create products beyond the classroom or a **charter school,** an autonomous education entity operating under a charter or contract that has been negotiated between the organizers, who create and operate the school, and a sponsor, who oversees the provisions of the charter.[3] As an example of a recent charter school, a state teachers' union and the district's teachers' association have created the Humane Education Charter School (Sacramento, California) that aims to reduce violence through the teaching of respect, compassion, responsibility, and community service for children in grades K–6. Further, the school to which you are assigned could be an extended-day school, a school that offers an after-school period, and often, a homework-help time with volunteer tutors, or a **full-service community school,** a school that serves as a center for education and various health, social, and cultural services under one roof.[4]

Orientation Meetings for Teachers

As a beginning teacher, you will be expected to participate in an orientation meeting for teachers. Some school districts begin the academic year with a districtwide orientation, and others schedule on-site orientations at each school. Some districts do both, with perhaps a districtwide meeting in the morning followed by on-site meetings in the afternoon. Of course, the scheduling and planning of orientation meetings will vary district by district and from school to school. The objectives for all orientation meetings, however, should be similar. As a new teacher, you will be encouraged by district personnel to meet several responsibilities. For example, you will be asked to become familiar with the district's or school's written statement of its unique beliefs and goals—its **statement of mission** (or philosophy or vision)—and what the statement means to the people affiliated with the school or district. Selected elements of various mission statements are shown in Figure 1.1.

School Schedules

School schedules vary from state to state, from district to district, and from school to school. Many school years begin in late August or early September and continue through late May or mid-June. Other schools operate on a year-round schedule with the school year beginning in August and ending in June or July.[5] In a school with year-round education (YRE), a teacher might teach for three consecutive months followed by a month off, then for another three months on and then a month off, and so on, throughout the year, or one might teach in a 45/15 program, which refers to a yearlong schedule of 9 weeks

- Prepare each child for the future and working together for a better world.
- Create a desire for learning.
- Assist children as they develop responsibility and respect for themselves and others and for the environment.
- Support children as they function independently and develop moral/ethical behavior (tolerance, cooperation) and their communication skills.
- Assist children in critical thinking and creativity.
- Support children in developing an appreciation for the American heritage and the heritage of diverse cultures.
- Assist children in participating as citizens in our representative democracy.[6]

Figure 1.1
Selected elements of school mission statements.

(45 days) of school followed by 3 weeks (15 days) off. Another example of an alternative schedule is the modified year-round schedule, which involves teaching for nine weeks, then being off two weeks.

In most places in the United States, the school year is still approximately 180 days out of a 365-day calendar year. Some schools, however, such as the Brooks Global Studies Extended-Year Magnet Elementary School in Greensboro, North Carolina, have extended their school year to a longer time such as 210 days and are called **extended-year schools.** Not to be confused with the extended-year school is the extended-day school. Fletcher-Maynard Academy (Cambridge, Massachusetts), for example, is a public elementary/middle school with an eight-hour extended school day program.

Some schools are in session fewer than five days per week, usually four days.[7] Most schools that are on a four-day week are small rural schools, often including grades K–12, where the children spend several hours each day riding the school bus. Schools on a four-day week usually go longer each day, such as from 8 a.m. until 4 p.m., with Monday or Friday off. Still other schools have a four-day week with only teachers attending on Fridays for preparation time.

After being assigned to a school and becoming familiar with the campus, you should turn your attention to all of the available school schedules for playground duty, lunch, bus duty, the library, special programs, and special days. The school day usually begins about 8:00 a.m. and lasts until 3:00 p.m. In schools that are crowded, beginning and ending times may be staggered, and some students and teachers may start as early as 7:30 a.m. and leave at 2:30 p.m. Others may begin at 9:00 a.m. and continue until 4:00 p.m. District and state laws vary. But they generally require that teachers be in the classroom no later than fifteen minutes prior to the start of school and remain in the classroom no less than fifteen minutes after the dismissal of the children.

Subjects of the Curriculum

The time spent daily on each subject taught will vary with grade level and may be dictated by adopted program, state law, or district policy, but for each grade, the curriculum plans should include lessons for multiple subjects.

English/reading/language arts/technology (also known as **literacy,** which currently connotes a wide range of abilities and competencies needed for the twenty-first century) and mathematics, science, social science/history/geography constitute the **core curriculum.** These subjects are often accompanied by art, music, physical education, health, and sometimes, foreign language. In some schools and in some grades, not all of these subjects are taught every day, nor are they always all taught in one classroom by just one teacher.

Although studies demonstrate that the early study of a second language provides cognitive benefits, gains in academic achievement, and positive attitudes toward diversity, the study of a second or foreign language, unfortunately, is not a part of the curriculum for very many elementary schools.[8] In some elementary schools, however, such as Sunset Elementary School (Miami, Florida), foreign language study is a significant component of the core curriculum.[9]

The choice of language offered by elementary schools varies, of course, depending to some extent on the community, the availability of teachers, and the extent to which the program can be sustained for several years.[10] Generally, elementary school foreign language programs fall within a spectrum of types. At one end are **total immersion programs,** in which all of the classroom instruction is in the target foreign language. At the other end of the spectrum are foreign language experience (FLEX) programs, where classes may meet only a few times a week, and the goal is to introduce children to one or more foreign languages and cultures rather than to develop proficiency in the use of a target foreign language. Somewhere in the middle on the spectrum are foreign language in the elementary school (FLES) programs, which focus mostly on cultural awareness and developing listening and speaking skills in a target foreign language. FLES programs follow the natural sequence of language learning: understanding, speaking, reading, and writing. For young children, a typical FLES lesson would include physical activities such as songs, rhymes, games, and playacting with puppets.[11] In addition to the specialized skills of the subjects mentioned previously, students learn other, more general skills as components of the elementary school curriculum. These include critical thinking skills, socialization skills, and organizational and study skills.

Team Teaching

Traditionally, elementary schoolteachers have taught their groups of children in their self-contained classrooms for most of the school day while fairly isolated from other teachers and school activities—not unlike the parallel play of preschool children, that is, playing side by side, but not together. In some schools, that is still the case. Increasingly, however, elementary school teachers are finding themselves members of a collaborative **teaching team** in which several teachers work together to reflect, plan, and implement a curriculum for a common cohort of students. This type of team teaching may comprise only a few teachers, for example, all second-grade teachers of a particular elementary school, or the teachers who teach the same cohort of sixth-grade children in English/reading/language arts and in social studies/history/geography at the same or another school. They may meet periodically to plan a curriculum and learning activities around a common theme.

Sometimes, teaching teams comprise one teacher each from the four areas of the core curriculum. In addition to teachers of the core subjects, specialty-area teachers may be part of the team, including teachers of foreign language, physical education, the arts, and even special education teachers, school counselors, and specialty personnel who work with at-risk students. Because the core and specialty subjects cross disciplines of study, these teams are commonly called interdisciplinary teaching teams, or simply **interdisciplinary teams.**

CHOICES FOR DIFFERENTIATED SELF-INSTRUCTION

To begin your own differentiated self-instruction with this book, you can vary the level and pace of your learning with the following suggestions:

- If you are interested in increasing the level of your knowledge about English language learners (ELLs) *right now*, then turn to Chapter 2 where you can find more about the nature of learners. Also, *Looking at Teachers I* in each chapter has a pinpoint focus on diverse learners.

- If you want to pick up your pace about creating lesson plans, then turn ahead to Chapter 5, where you can find planning for objectives, instructions, standards, state/district documents, and sequencing content.

- If you are ready to learn more about assessment choices, read Chapter 6 and Figure 6.4, Sample Scoring Guide/Rubric for Assessing Student Writing, *right now* and then turn to Application Exercise 6.1, Preparing Assessment Items, Application Exercise 6.2, Preparing a Rubric, and Application Exercise 9.1 to see its accompanying Peer and Self-Assessment Rubric.

- If you are interested in diversity and multicultural and global education, read about teaching in diverse classrooms (Chapters 1 and 11), connections among multicultural history, social change and America's laws, and worldwide communication via Internet (Chapter 7).

- To learn more about writing a statement of your own emerging teaching style that will turn into your philosophy of education, turn to Application Exercise 3.3 in Chapter 3. This material will help you record insights about where you stand philosophically as you interact with educational issues, nature of learners, curriculum content, and assessment. Later, referring to these insights, you can write your philosophy statement and it will help you prepare for a future interview for a teaching job.

- If you are asked to prepare a teaching portfolio at this time, take a look at the Portfolio Builders in www.myeducationlab.com.

Looping

In some schools, a teacher or a team of teachers remains with the same cohort of elementary children for two or more years, a practice known as **looping** (also referred to as *multiyear grouping, multiyear instruction, multiyear placement, persistent teams*, and *teacher–student progression*). Although the practice of looping is not new, in recent years there has been renewed interest in it because of the positive findings related to young children from recent research studies. Positive findings indicate that the benefits of looping include improved student–teacher relationships, more efficient instruction, better learning, improved attendance, fewer referrals to special education programs, and improved student behavior.[12] Perhaps the positive findings can be summarized as being the result of an effective teacher (or teaching team) getting to know a group of children well and being able to remain with that group longer than one school year, rather than starting all over again in a year with an entirely different group of children.

Inside your own busy classroom, you will be learning the names of your students, making decisions, following your detailed instructional plans, and keeping one eye on the clock for a day or two—a behavior that helps you observe the schedule for recess, lunch, coordination with other teachers, and dismissal at the end of the school day. You will find that the changes in scheduling may vary from year to year at a particular school. For example, Figures 1.2a and 1.2b present sample teacher schedules that reflect some of the variety you will find for different grades at different schools.

THE FUNDAMENTAL CHARACTERISTIC OF EXEMPLARY ELEMENTARY SCHOOL EDUCATION

Wherever and however the students are housed, whatever the schedules, and regardless of other practices, in the end, it is the dedication and commitment to students and the involved adults' understanding of students that is the incisive element. Thus, it is everyone at school—the teachers, administrators, office staff, bus drivers, cooks, grounds crew, security staff, custodial staff, and support personnel—who reflect the fundamental characteristic of

8:25–8:55	Expeditionary learning circle Attendance, flag salute, patriotic song, community song, calendar, weather, expeditionary learning discussion and business
8:55–9:15	Spelling activities
9:15–10:05	Reading activities
10:05–10:35	Math block
10:35–10:45	Recess
10:45–12:10	Language arts block (reading, writing, grammar, speaking related to expeditionary learning project) Computer and library (Wed. 11:00–12:05)
12:10–12:50	Lunch
12:50–1:45	Language arts continued (teacher read-aloud, independent reading, cursive instruction)
1:45–2:00	Recess
2:00–3:25	Integration of social studies, science, art Physical education (Thurs. 2:00–2:40)

Figure 1.2a
A second-grade class schedule.
(*Source:* Based on opening vignette, *Looking at Teachers I* in Chapter 1)

7:10–8:10	Teacher-parent conferences
8:15–8:45	Total school assembly (flag salute, announcements, songs)
8:45–9:15	Spelling in homeroom class
9:15–10:00	Music, art, and physical education (alternating every third day)
10:00–10:10	Bathroom break; class change
10:30–11:30	Group 1—language arts; Group 2—math; Group 3—science and social studies
11:30–11:35	Change back to homeroom class
11:35–12:00	Oral/silent reading in homeroom class
12:00–12:25	Lunch
12:25–12:40	Recess
12:40–12:45	Class change
12:45–1:45	Group 1—science and social studies; Group 2—language arts; Group 3—math
1:45–2:40	Reading in homeroom class
2:40–2:45	Clean up and dismissal
2:45–3:30	Tutoring
3:40–5:00	Teacher-parent conferences

Figure 1.2b
A fifth-grade schedule.
(*Source:* Based on ending vignette, *Looking at Teachers II*, Chapter 1)

exemplary elementary school education. This characteristic, as we see it, is to celebrate and build on the diverse nature and needs of students, a concept that is the essence of Chapter 2.

Teachers and Commitment

Elementary schoolteachers represent myriad individual personalities that are perhaps impossible to capture in generalizations. Let us imagine that a teaching colleague mentions that Charles Burger, in Room 17, is a "fantastic teacher," "one of the best teachers in the district," "super," and "top-notch." What might be some of the characteristics you would expect to see in Charles' teaching behaviors? (Teacher responsibilities and behaviors are the topic of Chapter 3.)

You can expect Charles to (a) be understanding of the school's stated mission and committed to it; (b) know the curriculum and how best to teach it; (c) be enthusiastic, motivated, and well organized; (d) show effective communication and interpersonal skills; (e) be willing to listen to the students and to risk trying their ideas; and (f) be warm, caring, accepting, and nurturing toward all students.

Elementary school students need teachers who are organized and who know how to establish and manage an active, supportive learning environment (the topic of Chapter 4), even with its multiple instructional demands. Students respond best to teachers who provide leadership and who enjoy their function as role models, advisers, mentors, and reflective decision makers.

Teachers and Reflective Decision Making

During any school day, whether you are a teacher of kindergarten children or a teacher of sixth-graders, you will make hundreds of nontrivial decisions. Some of the decisions are made instantaneously. Other decisions are made in preparation for the teaching day. During one school year, a teacher literally makes thousands of decisions—some of which can and will affect the lives of that teacher's students for years to come. This is, indeed, an awesome responsibility.

Initially, of course, you will make errors in judgment, but you also will learn that children can be amazingly resilient and that there are experts available who can guide you to help ensure that the children are not damaged by your mistakes. You can learn from your errors. Keep in mind that the sheer number of decisions you make each day will mean that not all will be the best decisions that could have been made had you had more time and better resources for planning.

Good Teaching Is as Much an Art as It Is a Science

Although pedagogy is based on scientific principles, good classroom teaching is as much an art as it is a science. Few

rules apply to every teaching situation. In fact, decisions about the selection of content, instructional objectives and materials, teaching strategies, a teacher's response to student misbehavior, and the selection of techniques for assessment of the learning experiences are all the result of subjective judgments. While many decisions are made at a somewhat unhurried pace when you are planning for your instruction, many others will be made intuitively and quickly. Once the school day has begun, there is rarely time for making carefully thought-out judgments. At your best, you base your decisions on your teaching style, which in turn is based on your knowledge of school policies, pedagogical research, the curriculum, and the unique characteristics of the students in your charge. You will also base your decisions on common sense and reflective judgments. The better your understanding and experience with the students, the curriculum, and the school's environment and policies, and the more time you give for thoughtful reflection, the more likely it will be that your decisions will result in the students meeting the learning targets and educational goals. (More about learning targets and educational goals is discussed in Chapter 5.)

You will reflect on, conceptualize, and apply understandings from one teaching experience to the next. As your understanding about your classroom experiences accumulate, your teaching will become more routine, predictable, and refined. The topic of reflective decision making is presented more fully in Chapter 3; for now, to extend your awareness of the reality of elementary school teaching with others in a cooperative and collaborative way, do Application Exercise 1.1 and Application Exercise 1.2.

The Effective Principal

The principal can make a difference. As a new or visiting member of the faculty, one of your tasks is to become familiar with the administrative organization of your school and district. One person significantly responsible for the success of any school is the principal. From your point of view, what seem to be the characteristics of an effective elementary school principal? Perhaps foremost are the principal's vision of what a quality school is and the drive to bring that vision to life. In our view, school improvement is the effective principal's constant theme.

Through personal skills in instructional leadership, the principal establishes a climate in which teachers and students share the responsibility for determining the appropriate use of time and facilities. Because exemplary elementary school educators believe in the innate potential of every child, instead of lowering standards and expectations, they modify the key variables of time, grouping, and instructional strategies to help each child achieve quality learning (as you'll see in Chapter 8), a task nearly impossible to do without a supportive, knowledgeable, positive, and forward-thinking school principal.[13]

In addition to the school principal, there sometimes is an assistant or vice principal, especially for larger schools. This person has specific responsibilities and oversight functions, such as student activities, school discipline and security, transition programs, and curriculum and instruction. Sometimes teachers who are mentors, grade-level leaders or department chairs, or designated team leaders may also be responsible for administrative functions. But the principal is (or should be) the person with the final responsibility for everything that happens at the school. Whereas principals used to debate whether they were leaders or managers, today there is no debate—to be most effective, the principal must be both.[14]

Commitment to Helping All Children Succeed in School

In any school, there are students who have a high probability of dropping out. *At risk* is the term used by educators when referring to those students. Researchers have identified five categories of indicators that cause a child to be at risk: (a) academic failure—exemplified by low marks and grades, absences from school, low-self-esteem; (b) family instability—often identified by divorce, moving, separation; (c) family socioeconomic situation—exemplified by lack of education, low income, and negativism; (d) family tragedy—identified by health problems or parent/guardian illness or death; and (e) personal pain—exemplified by drugs, physical and psychological abuse, or suspension from school.[15] Many children at any one time have risk factors from more than one of these categories. Although some schools have a higher percentage of children at risk than do others, it has been estimated that by the year 2020 and without intervention, the majority of students in the public schools in the United States will be at risk. As part of intervention, however, it seems that improving and building school partnerships with culturally and linguistically diverse families helps lift the achievement of their children. One example is the Parent Partnership for Achieving Literacy (PAL) program, where teachers improve their knowledge of the culture, strengths, and needs of the children and families and where parents understand the expectations of the teachers and schools through PAL workshops, meetings, and e-mailings.[16]

APPLICATION EXERCISE 1.2

Dialogue with a Teacher Candidate

Instructions: The purpose of this activity is to identify reasons other teacher candidates have selected teaching as a career goal and to identify one or more personal professional characteristics that make an effective teacher. Select one teacher candidate, and on the back of this page of questions, record that person's responses to the following questions in one column, while that person records your responses to the same questions in a second column. Please work together cooperatively and collaboratively. Use some of the information to introduce your teacher candidate to the group. Share other responses with your group. (*Note to instructor:* This application could be used during the first week of your school term as an icebreaker.)

Date of interview _____   Name of interviewee _____

Questions to ask:

1. Why and when did you select elementary school teaching as a career?

2. What do you plan to do during the summer if you are free from teaching in a 9-month school?

3. Why would you like to teach/not teach in a year-round school?

4. What other teachers are there in your family?

5. What is your favorite grade level?

6. Favorite subject?

7. To what extent do you plan to help your school have a safe, supportive learning environment?

8. What are your future plans? A lifetime career as a classroom teacher?

9. Will you consider moving into a specialty or an administrative position?

10. Would you like to be a famous educator? In what way?

11. If you could change the way you were taught in school, what would you change?

12. How would you describe your current feelings about being an elementary teacher? What specifically are you most looking forward to during this program of teacher preparation?

13. What person and professional characteristics do you feel you have that would make you an effective teacher?

14. Why are you proud to be a teacher candidate? A candidate who represents your ethnic group?

15. Since we realize that teachers should give clear directions to students to be easily understood, what clear directions can you give me, if I keep my eyes shut, to navigate around this room to the exit door in case of fire?

First Column	*Second Column*
Other candidate's responses	My responses

Today's movement to transform schools into caring and responsive learning environments has as its sole purpose that of helping all children, especially those at risk, make the transitions necessary to succeed in school and in life. The future of our nation and, indeed, our world, might rest heavily on the success of this movement

Responsive Practices for Helping All Children Succeed in School

Becase of the enormous diversity of students in the classroom, the advantage of using a combination of practices concurrently is usually greater in helping all children succeed in school than is the gain from using any singular practice by itself. Four significant approaches that have helped students make successful transitions are (a) the reorganization of schools (such as moving sixth-graders to a middle-level school), (b) the restructuring of school schedules (such as YRE and extended school days), (c) **culturally responsive teaching** that teaches to the strengths, experiences, and performance styles of diverse students, and (d) the Parent Partnership for Achieving Literacy (PAL) program mentioned earlier in this chapter.

Other important responsive practices (including attitudes) are the following:

- Sharing with all teachers and staff the perception that all children can learn when they are given adequate support, although not all students need the same amount of time to learn the same thing
- Maintaining high, although not necessarily identical, expectations for all students
- Paying personalized attention, being an adult advocate, and creating scheduling and learning plans to help students learn in the manner by which they best learn (Research clearly points out that achievement increases, students learn more, and students enjoy learning and remember more of what they have learned when individual learning styles and capacities are identified and accommodated; learning style traits are identified and accommodated; learning style traits are known that significantly discriminate among students who are at risk of dropping out of school and students who perform well, as discussed in Chapter 2)
- Engaging parents and guardians as partners in their child's education
- Spending extra time and guided attention on basic skills, such as those of thinking, writing, and reading, rather than on rote memory
- Using specialist teachers, smaller student cohorts, and smaller classes
- Engaging in **peer tutoring** and **cross-age coaching**
- Paying particular attention to the development of coping skills.

These responsive practices are repeated and discussed throughout this resource guide. Another responsive practice in promoting the success of all children is making connections among the home, school, and local and global communities, as discussed next.

WAYS TO CONNECT WITH HOME, COMMUNITY, AND SCHOOL

It is well known that family members' involvement in and support for their child's education can have a positive impact on that child's achievement at school. For example, when parents, guardians, or siblings of at-risk students get involved, the child benefits from more consistent attendance at school, more positive attitudes and actions, better grades, and higher test scores.[17] Further, in recognition of the positive effect that parent and family involvement has on student achievement and success, the National PTA has published National Standards for Parent/Family Involvement Programs (Chapter 5).[18]

Home and School Connections

At times, teachers develop their own personal family-involvement programs as well as approaches to help students find connections to others and to feel themselves members of many groups—intimate groups, community groups, and a world group.[19] At other times, schools have adopted formal policies about home and community connections. These policies usually emphasize that parents and guardians should be included as partners in the educational program and that teachers and administrators will inform parents and guardians about their child's progress, about the school's family involvement policy, and about any programs in which family members can participate. Some schools are members of the **National Network of Partnership Schools** (2000), and efforts to foster family and community involvement are as varied as the schools and the people who participate. These efforts include (a) use of technology such as using the school's web page on the Internet to show student–teacher–parent/guardian contracts and assignment calendars; (b) electronic software, hardware, workshops, and newsletters for family members to help their children;[20] (c) involvement of community leaders in the classroom as mentors, aides, and role models;[21] (d) home visitation programs; (e) homework hotlines; (f) personal notes home and regular phone calls about a student's progress, both expressing concern and praising students;[22] and involvement of students in service learning.[23] One of your tasks as a visiting or new teacher will be to discover the extent and nature of your school's efforts to involve family and community representatives in the education of the children. Educators increasingly are looking at service learning/place-based education as a means of helping young people connect learning with life. If you are interested in service learning, discussed next, you may review information for writing grants for successful projects that could help the elderly, military personnel, patients in hospitals, and others in *Helping Kids Help: Organizing Successful Charitable Projects* (Zephyr, 2007) by R. Heiss.

Service Learning and Place-Based Education

In service learning, students learn and develop their social skills in active participation linked to place-based education and thoughtfully organized and curriculum-connected experiences that meet community needs.[24] To support place-based learning, community members, geographic features, buildings, monuments, historic sites, and other places in a school's geographic area constitute some of the richest instructional laboratories that can be imagined.

To take advantage of this accumulated wealth of resources, as well as to build school-community partnerships for service learning, you are advised to begin your file of community resources once you are hired by a school district. For instance, you might include files about the skills of the students, parents, guardians, or other family members, noting which ones could be resources

Jeff Greenberg/Photoedit

for a study occurring in your classroom. You might also include files about various resource people who could speak to the students about what other communities of teachers, students, and adult helpers have done.

Telecommunications Networks

Teachers who want to guide their students toward becoming autonomous thinkers, effective decision makers, and lifelong learners and to make their classrooms more student-centered, collaborative, interdisciplinary, and interactive, are increasingly turning to telecommunication networks and the global community. Webs of connected computers allow teachers and students from around the world to teach each other directly and gain access to quantities of information previously unimaginable. Students using distance learning and networks learn and develop new inquiry and analytical skills in a stimulating environment and gain an increased appreciation of their role as world citizens. As you will discover, the use of technology is shown in each chapter's narrative throughout this resource guide. Further, www.myeducationlab.com has additional content to help you broaden your knowledge base about today's elementary schools.

Professional Resources File

Now is a good time to start your professional resources file on a computer file, on index cards, or on the *For Your Notes* pages in this book, and then maintain it throughout your study. Note that to help you begin your file, many resource ideas and sources are mentioned and listed throughout this book.

THE EMERGENT OVERALL PICTURE

Certainly, no facet of education receives more attention from the media, causes more concern among parents, guardians, and teachers, or gets larger headlines than that of a decline—either factual or fanciful—in students' achievement in the public schools. Reports are issued, polls taken, debates organized, and blue-ribbon commissions formed. Community members write letters to newspapers about it, news editors devote editorial space to it, television anchors comment about it, politicians use it to grab camera time, and documentaries and specials focus on it in full color. We read headlines such as "States Press Ahead on 21st Century Skills," "U.S. Urban Students Found to Be Middling vs. Foreign Peers," and so on. We are not positive about this, but we think this current interest has never been matched in its political interest and participation, and it has affected and continues to affect both the public schools and the programs in higher education that are directly or indirectly related to teacher preparation and certification.[25] Here are R. D. Kellough's words about your possible input in this:

> Many schools provide new teachers with a planned program of new-teacher induction and mentoring. If your school does not provide a program, you will need to assert yourself and build a network of supporters.[26]

In response to this interest, educators, corporate and small-business businesspersons, and politicians have acted. Around the nation, their actions have resulted in support for the following:

- Developing/refining of curriculum standards
- Restructuring schools for more curriculum options
- Emphasizing education about cultural diversity and ways of teaching English language learners
- Emphasizing support for students as they connect what is being learned with real life and connect between curriculum subjects and academics and vocations
- Emphasizing raising test scores, reducing school dropout rates, increasing instructional times, questioning high-stakes testing (which is covered in more detail in later chapters) and its required/forced suitability for every student
- Emphasizing rewards to high-performing schools as well as focusing on low-performing schools
- Forming school-home-community connections
- Helping students make effective transitions from one level of schooling to the next and from school to life
- Restructuring the former No Child Left Behind Act and some of its core tenets of standards and accountability for all student groups, improving school safety and reducing drug use, maintaining quality of effective teachers, and interacting with parents and innovative learning programs
- Changing standards for teacher certification

With regard to changes in standards, model standards were prepared and released by the Interstate New Teacher Assessment and Support Consortium (INTASC, 1992), a project of the Council of Chief State School Officers (CCSSO), in a document titled *Model Standards for Beginning Teacher Licensing and Development.* These model standards describe what prospective teachers should know and be able to do to receive a teaching license. Representatives of at least thirty-six states and professional associations—including the National Education Association (NEA), the American Federation of Teachers (AFT), the American Association of Colleges for Teacher Education (AACTE), and the National Council for the Accreditation of Teacher Education (NCATE)—make up the group. The standards are performance-based and revolve around a common core of principles of knowledge and skills that cut across disciplines. These INTASC standards[27,28] were developed to be compatible with those of the National Board for Professional Teaching Standards (NBPTS). You'll see a recap of these standards and principles inside the front cover of this book and how they correlate with the chapters you'll be reading.

Key Trends and Practices Today

For your quick review, we list several major trends and practices current in today's educational scene in Figure 1.3. However, also in the current educational scene are specific main features of the No Child Left Behind Act (an act perhaps renamed or reconfigured by the time you read this) that are discussed in the following section.

No Child Left Behind Act

Related to today's elementary schools, some teachers, both precredentialed and credentialed, are wondering about the current No Child Left Behind (NCLB) initiative and what future changes will mean for their classrooms. Some teachers wonder how the changes made by our Congress will affect their schools, districts, and states, and they talk about national or local standards-based reform. Others discuss the underfunding of NCLB, the flaws seen in the implementation of the standards, and address testing and accountability provisions. Still others are concerned about giving students in low-performing schools a genuine opportunity to transfer to much better ones. By the time you read this, there will probably be a reauthorization bill by Congress that will provide funding for a revised NCLB with support for electronic data, national/local standards linked to high-quality assessments, testing for all students and teachers, and perhaps a viable transfer option for low-income students to attend high-quality schools.

The initial NCLB Act required, among other things, the states to test students' level of mastery of basic educational skills (e.g., third-grade students should demonstrate their abilities to read), and currently educators are feeling increased pressure to raise students' scores on tests. Considering all of this, it seems that a key word that describes the emphasis in the act is *accountability.* Accountability is addressed in standards for all student groups, in standards to improve school safety and reduce drug use, in the quality of effective teachers, and in increased interaction with parents. Related to this, you'll find interested educators discussing the following several concerns:

- *Concern: Funding.* When some educators were asked *What is the estimated cost of NCLB's goal of making all students academically proficient in six years?* their response suggested that the cost would vary from state to state depending on the makeup of the student population, the local cost of living, and the level of the performance standard adopted. However, as a

- Title I school improvement grants to help finance interventions for low-performing schools struggling to meet the goals of the No Child Left Behind Act

- Interest in national standards for local and state education data so that comparisons across districts can be made related to student assessment data and budget data; improving tests to measure higher-order thinking skills

- Recruit, prepare, retain, and reward teachers with scholarships for undergraduate, graduate, and alternative certification of teachers; funding to pay bonuses to teachers who are mentors or work in hard-to-staff schools in urban or rural areas

- Funding for preschool and K–12 programs, for teacher training, and development of preschool programs

- Support for charter schools and school choice; possible tax credit for students who perform hours of community service

- Funding for the Institute of Education Sciences for research, development, and dissemination of promising practices

- Support for the Teacher Incentive Fund to help districts finance pay-for-performance programs for teachers and principals along with inclusion of noninstructional personnel such as counselors, custodians, and food-service workers to take part in the pay systems; interest in developing systems through collective bargaining process or through a majority of teachers to approve systems in non-bargaining areas

- Support for reading programs, including the Striving Readers Program, Adolescent Literacy programs, and Early Literacy Grants; a demonstration program that would allow districts to test strategies to improve students' reading comprehension

- State grants for special education, career and technical education, and education technology to help districts integrate technology in the classroom; competitive grants program for feeder middle schools and their linked high schools to lower the dropout rate

- Promotion of innovative programs such as residency programs to recruit new teachers, reforming teacher certification or licensure requirements, alternative certification, and tenure reform

Figure 1.3
Key trends and practices in today's elementary schools.

coast-to-coast estimate, they predicted the state of New York would need an estimated increase of 129 percent in Federal Title I aid and California would need an estimated increase of 547 percent.

- *Concern: Flaws in Testing and Standards.* It seems there are three camps of educators announcing their concerns about testing and standards used by states to measure student achievement. In *camp 1,* some educators advocate a national test and national standards to help achieve international competitiveness and stop any watering down/dilution of these materials. It seems some states have failed to develop clear content standards for what students should know and be able to do and they also lack multiple standards for all segments of the total student group. In addition, some states have poor-quality assessment tests. In *camp 2,* other educators advocate that better quality can be achieved by using thousands of local measures—homework, papers, and teacher-created tests—that vary from district to district. However, critics point out

that such measures cannot be compared with one another and that students would be held to different standards, and thus measured by different educational yardsticks, but would still have to compete for similar jobs and the same colleges. In *camp 3,* still other educators are suggesting that there should be a national databank of locally developed test items to make an open-source testing system. They propose that a panel of educators create a pool (or core) of short-answer, problem-solving items, and essay test items to reflect national standards. States would then draw from the pool to revise their testing programs.

- *Concern: Flaws in Transferring to Better-Performing Schools.* Additional financial incentives are needed to encourage high-performing schools to accept transfers by low-income students. Concerned educators point out that low-income students can perform at high levels if given the right environment and they need a genuine opportunity to attend economically and racially integrated schools such as those in interdistrict integration programs. In another coast-to-coast note of interest, interdistrict integration programs have been initiated on both coasts—in Rochester, New York, and East Palo Alto, California. Both programs provide funds giving choice to students in persistently failing or dangerous schools so they can attend adequate, safe schools of choice.

- *Concern: Increasing Accountability.* Today's account-ability for NCLB supports a different kind of assess-ment in the classroom, as demonstrated by various elementary schools. Recognition for schools increasing accountability in assessment and other NCLB areas is acknowledged through the No Child Left Behind Blue Ribbon Schools Program. For example, King William Charles Lunalilo Elementary School, with principal Dean Nakamoto, was selected and recognized as a Blue Ribbon school (along with two other Hawaiian public schools) and received a NCLB Blue Ribbon School award in 2005.

- *Concern: Overall Impact.* The Center on Education Policy (Washington, DC) has these concerns: it seems schools spend more time on reading and math at the expense of other subjects, that students are taking more tests than before, and funds are inadequate to carry out educational responsibilities. We urge you to keep up with the current information about what is happening to the NCLB Act by going to www.ed.gov/nclb/landing.jhtml.

To further increase accountability at older grade levels, artificial intelligence software presents students with prob-lems, keeps track of their responses, and designs an indi-vidualized learning program that emphasizes instruction and testing in areas where each student needs it most. Here are two examples:

Example 1: READ 180 (http://teacher.scholastic.com/products/read180/) is reading software for students in grades 4–12 who are reading below grade level. The software assesses the students' reading skills while creating exercises that reinforce those skills. To accompany the software, the teachers teach group reading and skills lessons and introduce high-interest, low-reading-level books. The students then rotate through three computer learning stations with com-puter lessons, and the software calculates each student's skill levels in decoding, vocabulary, and other reading areas. The lessons help the students learn basic reading skills by providing each student with an individualized set of lessons that emphasize some needed skills.

Example 2: Lightspan, Inc. (www.edutest.com), merged with Plato Learning, Inc., has a series of testing software, EduTest, that helps teachers design assessments based on the statewide basic skills demanded by the NCLB Act. In Florida as an example, the Department of Education requires the Florida Comprehension Assessment Test (FCAT), but this test has been failed by tens of thousands of students. To offset this, Florida made available Lightspan's EduTest tutorial software program to prepare for the FCAT in schools in at-risk areas. The software has easy-to-read profiles so teachers can see who is making progress and who needs immediate help, and this makes a difference in preparing for the test. In support of this, a principal at one elementary school in Jacksonville reported that the software pushed the school's scores up and out of the at-risk range and thus made a difference in the students' FCAT scores.

Curriculum Standards and High-Stakes Testing

Indeed, curriculum standards define what students should know and be able to do, and high-stakes testing is the result of test developers using both state and national standards, accessible on the Internet (www.statestandards.com), for guidance in developing stan-dardized tests for students.

High-stakes testing also refers to the tests being used at various grade levels to determine student achieve-ment, promotion, and rewards to schools and even to individual teachers and students. In about half of the fifty states, some tests may be a requirement to graduate from high school. More will be said about this when standards are discussed in Chapter 5.

You may be interested to know that students with access to computers can practice and prepare online for the state-mandated standardized tests. In schools with the required computer technology and with the appropriate number of computers to provide access time to individ-ual students, selected software programs can help students prepare for the tests.

Two such programs are homeroom.com, a division of The Princeton Review, and, as mentioned previously, EduTest (www.edutest.com). Proponents of such online preparation argue that a major advantage is the immedi-ate scoring of practice testing with feedback about each student's areas of weakness, thereby providing the teacher with information necessary for immediate reme-diation. If their arguments are accurate, then it would seem that students of such technology-rich schools would clearly be at an advantage over students in schools where this technology is not available. It would follow that the district and government agencies that mandate the stan-dards and specific assessment practices should provide avenues and tools to ensure equity and success for all students toward reaching the expected learning outcomes within the designated learning time. To keep up to date with information about this issue of high-stakes testing and others, use your national professional associations as sources. For their Internet addresses, see Figure 1.4.

AAE: Association of American Educators, 27405 Puerta Real, Suite 230, Mission Viejo, CA 92691 (www.aaeteachers.org/)

AFT: American Federation of Teachers, AFL-CIO, 555 New Jersey Avenue, NW, Washington, DC 20001 (www.aft.org)

NAPE: National Association of Professional Educators, Suite 300., 900 17th Street, Washington, DC 20006 (www.teacherspet.com/napeindx.htm)

NEA: National Education Association, 1201 16th Street, NW, Washington, DC 20036-3290 (www.nea.org)

Figure 1.4
National Professional Associations for Teachers.

Problems and Issues That Trouble the Nation's Schools

Major problems and issues that plague our nation's schools, in addition to those discussed earlier related to NCLB, are mentioned in Figure 1.5. Some of these are discussed in subsequent chapters (see index for topic locations). Perhaps you and members of your class can identify other problems to add to this list of issues faced by our nation's educators.

Another example of a problem/issue is that of traditional instruction versus dialogue and exploring ideas with students. When compared with traditional instruction—one of the characteristics of exemplary instruction in today's classrooms—the teacher's encouragement of dialogue, discussion, and exploring ideas among students will be discussed throughout this guide and especially in Chapter 7. As mentioned in the preface to this book, modeling the very behaviors we expect of teachers and students in the classroom is a constant theme throughout this book.

Related to Achievement

- A demand for test scores and statistics that can be used to judge schools, with a concomitant controversy over the concept of grading schools and publishing the reports; Continuing controversy over standardized norm-referenced testing;[29] Controversy over the inclusion/exclusion of certain children from state mandatory testing

Related to Content

- Continuing disputes over books and their content; Long-running arguments about morality, sexuality education, and values; Controversy created by the concept of teaching less content but teaching it better; Dispute over the need for the development of a national curriculum with national assessment;[30] Identification and development of programs that recognize, develop, and nurture talents in all youth at all levels of education;[31] Teaching and assessing for higher order thinking skills

Related to Grouping

- Continued disagreement over use of traditional ability grouping or curriculum tracking

Related to Schools and Teachers

- Low teacher salaries when compared with other college-educated workers;[32] Retention in grade versus social promotion;[33] Scarcity of multicultural teachers to serve as role models for minority children;[34] School security and the related problems of crime, drugs, violence, and weapons on school campuses and in school neighborhoods;[35] School populations that are too large;[36] Sexual harassment of students;[37] Shortage of male teachers, especially in the elementary schools;[38] School buildings that are old and desperately in need of repair and updating

Related to Students At Risk and Teachers

- Shortage of qualified teachers, especially in certain disciplines and in schools with high percentages of children at risk; The number of students at risk of dropping out of school; The education of teachers to work effectively with children who may be too overwhelmed by personal problems to focus on learning and to succeed in school, especially when charged fees for course materials;[39] The expectation that teachers should teach more and with improved results to a population of students, some at risk, that has never been more diverse or demanding

Figure 1.5
Problems and issues that trouble the nation's teachers and schools.

LOOKING AT TEACHERS II

Integrated Technology, Lesson-Related Sites

Rachel is a fifth-grade teacher in a low socioeconomic school within a moderately large city on the East Coast of the United States. The thirty-four students in her class include ten limited English speakers and ten with identified learning problems. Some of the children have skills as low as those equivalent to first grade. In any given week, Rachael recycles newspapers and sells snacks to help pay for field trips because the school and the children cannot. On a typical school day recently, Rachael began her work at 7:10 a.m. with three parent conferences. The children arrived and school began at 8:15 and ran until 2:45 p.m. Rachel then tutored children until 3:30, conducted four more

parent conferences, straightened her classroom and readied a few things for the next day, and went home at 6:30 p.m. She had dinner, planned lessons, and searched for motivational ideas on lesson-related websites (www.teachertube.com provided videos of projects in categories such as *reading*, and http://gallery .carnegiefoundation.org had multimedia presentations of classroom teaching).

Rachel then read and marked papers for two hours before retiring for the night. For your review, this teacher's busy school day was shown in one of the elementary teachers' schedules you read earlier in this chapter.

SUMMARY

In beginning to plan for developing your teaching competencies, you have read an overview about the characteristics of education in today's elementary school, including the similarities and differences in schools that have grades K–6, the characteristics of some of the adults who work there, and some of the trends and practices, such as those exemplified by current national and state standards as well as the No Child Left Behind Act. You realize that there are problems and issues that continue to concern our nation's schools. The knowledge will be useful in your assimilation of the content explored in the chapters that follow, beginning in the next chapter with the characteristics of elementary schoolchildren, how they learn, and strategies to work effectively with them. You'll note that you can begin to extend your professional competencies in the section that follows, beginning with a discussion about an exemplary elementary school.

What's to Come. Despite the many blue-ribbon commissions, writers, and politicians who vilify facets of public school education, thousands of dedicated teachers, administrators, parents, and members of the community struggle daily, year after year, to provide students with a quality education.[40] Throughout the chapters of this book, selected exemplary schools and school programs are recognized and identified by name.

Additionally, at the end of Chapter 2, about the nature of elementary learners, you'll be asked to continue extending your competencies in several ways—including through discussion, by observing a video to focus on selected learners, and other interactions.

EXTENDING MY PROFESSIONAL COMPETENCY

With Discussion

Exemplary Elementary School. Would I be able to explain a way to recognize an exemplary elementary school? What does school size have to do with an exemplary school? **To do:** Briefly research the topic of exemplary schools with materials you can access from Northwest Regional Educational Laboratory, Portland, Oregon (http://educationnorthwest.org.) After your research, describe at least three characteristics you would expect to find in an exemplary school. Explain why you have selected those particular characteristics to someone in your group.

With Video

Video Activity: Nature of an Elementary School. How can I explain the nature of a school to a colleague?

myeducationlab

Go to the Video Examples section of Topic #15: Collaborating with Colleagues and Families in the MyEducationLab for your course to view the video entitled "Involving Parents."

View the video with a colleague and take notes about (a) the principal, (b) the principal's agenda you infer, (c) the dedication and commitment to students by the teachers on this faculty that you can ascertain, and (d) the faculty's inclusion of the role of parents in their children's learning. Discuss your notes. Your discussion will reflect your insight into the nature of this school (through words and actions of the principal, teachers, parents, students you view), and that in turn will give you clues about the nature of what might happen in a classroom in this school. View the video again if needed.

With Portfolio

Portfolio Planning. How can I begin my professional portfolio and show my knowledge of today's elementary schools in connection with Principle 5 of INTASC and Standards 3 and 4 of NBPTS as seen on the inside of the front cover of this book? **To do:** To start your portfolio, you can develop and write a one- or two-page paper explaining your knowledge of the nature of today's elementary schools. Label your paper as Today's Elementary Schools. After reading and interacting with Chapter 1 in this resource guide, you can state how you have developed your competency in this chapter's following objectives:

- I can describe two or more essential characteristics of exemplary elementary school education.
- I can describe two or more current trends, problems, and issues in American public elementary school education.
- I can discuss the significance of home, school, and community connections to a child's education and of efforts being made by elementary school educators to enhance the connections to a child's education among the home, school, and local and global communities.
- I can return to the beginning of this chapter to review the remaining objectives.

Now, place your paper in your portfolio folder or in your computer file. Note that your teacher education program may require an electronic teaching portfolio at the completion of your student teaching, and this can be a beginning for you.

With Teacher Tests Study Guide

Teacher Tests for Future Licensing and Certification. If I wanted to prepare for taking a state teacher test to qualify for my teaching certificate/license and review my knowledge about the nature of today's elementary schools, how could I begin? **To do:** To support you as you prepare for teaching, you will find constructed response-type questions similar to those found on state tests for teacher licensing and certification in Appendix A of this book, the Teacher Tests Study Guide. The question about this chapter and today's elementary schools is linked to the classroom vignette found in *Looking at Teachers II*, Chapter 1. Write your response to the question and, if you wish, discuss it with another teaching candidate. If appropriate, use one or two of your colleague's suggestions to help you change your response to the question. Place your response in a Teacher Tests Study Guide folder or type/scan into a computer file. Plan to review and reread for study purposes before taking a scheduled teacher test for licensing and credentialing.

With Target Topics for Teacher Tests (TTTT)

If I wanted to start early and prepare for taking a state teacher test and review subject matter content about teaching in today's elementary schools, how could I begin? **To do:** Consider reviewing Target Topics for Teacher Tests (TTTT) in the subject index. Select the key words for this chapter in the visual organizer at the front of this chapter, or find words in bold in the narrative, or in the headings throughout the chapter. Find the key words in which you are interested in the subject index. To assist you as you prepare to take a teacher test, bullets (•) have been placed by selected word entries in the subject index and indicate Target Topics for Teacher Tests. The bullets highlight the core subject matter you are searching for related to this chapter—such as elementary schools, exemplary schools, home and school connections, trends, and other terms—that the authors suggest be reviewed in preparation for taking a teacher test similar to your state's test or to Praxis II Principles of Learning and Teaching exam.

WITH READING

Barley, Z. A., and Beesley, A. D. (2007). Rural School Success: What Can We Learn? *Journal of Research in Rural Education, 221*, 1–16.

Brandt, R. S. (Ed.). (2000). *Education in a New Era.* Alexandria, VA: Association for Supervision and Curriculum Development.

Buckley, F. J. (2000). *Team Teaching: What, Why, and How?* Thousand Oaks, CA: Sage.

Cawelti, G. (2000). Portrait of a Benchmark School. *Educational Leadership, 57*(5), 42–44.

Buhrow, B., and Garcia, A. U. (2006). *Ladybugs, Tornadoes, and Swirling Galaxies: English Language Learners Discover Their World through Inquiry.* Portland, ME: Stenhouse Publishers.

Costa, A. L., and Garmston, R. J. (2002). *Cognitive Coaching: A Foundation for Renaissance Schools.* Norwood, MA: Christopher-Gordon.

Dufresne, J. (2005). Keeping Students and School Safe. *Reclaiming Children and Youth, 14*(2), 93.

Green, D. G. (2006). Welcome to the House System. *Educational Leadership, 63*(7), 64–67.

Hall, G. E., and Hord, S. M. (2001). *Implementing Change: Patterns, Principles, and Potholes.* Boston: Allyn & Bacon.

Jennings, J., and Rentner, D. S. (2006). Ten Big Effects of the No Child Left Behind Act on Public Schools. *Phi Delta Kappan, 88*(2), 110–113.

Levy, S. (2008). The Power of Audience. *Educational Leadership 66*(3), 75–79.

Lubker, B. B., Bateman, F., and Vizoso, A. (2005). Medical Advances and Increased Survival: Continuing Effects on

School-Aged Population. *Delta Kappa Gamma Bulletin, 71*(3), 5–13.

Manno, B. V., Finn, C. E., Jr., and Vanourek, G. (2000). Beyond the Schoolhouse Door: How Charter Schools Are Transforming U.S. Public Education. *Phi Delta Kappan, 81*(10), 736–744.

Murphy, J., and Meyers, C. V. (2007). *Turning Around Failing Schools*. Thousand Oaks, CA: Corwin Press.

Nichols, S. L., and Berliner, D. C. (2008). Why Has High-Stakes Testing So Easily Slipped into Contemporary American Life? *Phi Delta Kappan, 89*(9), 672–676.

Pass, S., White, J., Owens, E., and Weir, J. (2006). Bringing Cultures into the Classroom: An Invitation to Families. *Social Studies and the Young Learner, 19*(2), 16–18.

Penuel, W. R., and Riel, M. (2007). The "New" Science of Networks and the Challenge of School Change. *Phi Delta Kappan, 88*, 611–15.

Potts, A. (2006). Schools as Dangerous Places. *Educational Studies, 32*, 319–330.

Powell, W. (2000). Recruiting Educators for an Inclusive School. In W. Powell and O. Powell (Eds.). *Count Me In: Developing Inclusive International Schools*. Washington, DC: Overseas Advisory Council.

San Antonio, D. M., and Salzfass, E. A. (2007). How We Treat One Another in School. *Educational Leadership, 64*, (8), 32–38.

Shariff, S. (2005). Cyber-dilemmas in the New Millennium: School Obligations to Provide Student Safety in a Virtual School Environment. *McGill Journal of Education, 40*, 467–487.

Swann, P. A. (2006). Got Web? Investing in a District Website. *School Administrator, 63*(5), 24.

Vaughn, S., Bos, C. S., and Schumm, J. S. (2007). *Teaching Students Who Are Exceptional, Diverse, and at Risk*. Boston: Allyn & Bacon.

Zmuda, A., Kuklis, R., and Kline, E. (2004). *Transforming Schools: Creating a Culture of Continuous Improvement*. Alexandria, VA: Association for Supervision and Curriculum Development.

WITH NOTES

1. If you want to read more about student work culminating in a genuine product, see S. Levy's The Power of Audience, *Educational Leadership, 66*(3), 75–79 (2008). For more on the Core Knowledge Curriculum, contact the Core Knowledge Foundation, 801 E. High Street, Charlottesville, VA 22902, (800) 238-3233, or visit the High Peaks Core Knowledge Elementary School at http://schools.bvsd.org/hp/index.php.

2. Read more about John Stanford International School (Seattle, WA) at www.jsisweb.com. Learn more about Phalen Lake's change to Hmong magnet school at www.phalenlake.spps.org. Read about North Las Vegas students who link up with astronauts in space at http://lasvegassun.com/news/2009/jan/10/north-las-vegas-students-link-astronauts/ or about students at Lincoln Elementary (Jamestown, North Dakota) who have a webcam conference with Johnson Space Center in Houston, Texas. (NASA in the classroom) at http://www.encyclopedia.com/doc/1G1-191860391.html. See also M. A. Dunn, Staying the Course of Open Education, *Educational Leadership, 57*(7), 20–24 (April 2000).

3. Contact the Center for Education Reform at (800) 521-2118 for a copy of the National Charter School Directory. See the Charter School home page via the United States Charter School website at www.uscharterschools.org/pub/uscs_docs/index.htm.

4. As an example, grades K–9 in San Diego School District (CA) have an Extended School Day Program; Read S. Maguire, A Community School, *Educational Leadership, 57*(6), 18–21, (March 2000).

5. K. Rasmussen, Year-Round Education, *Education Update, 42*(2), 1, 3–5 (March 2000).

6. Review complete school mission statements at these sites: For Julian Harris Elementary School (Decatur, AL, K–5), www.dcs.edu/webpages/JHarris; Sierra Oaks Elementary School (Sacramento, CA, K–5), www.sanjuan.edu/SierraOaks.cfm?subpage=12177; See also San Juan Unified School District website, www.sanjuan.edu/Academics.cfm?subpage=544; Skyview School (Prescott, AZ, K–8), www.skyviewschool.org; Whittier School (Chicago, K–6), http://whittierschool.org; and Woodland Hills Elementary School (Lawton, OK, K–6), http://lawtonps.org/schools/WoodlandHills/. See also G. Wiggins and J. Mctighe, *Schooling by Design: Mission, Action & Achievement* (Alexandria, VA: Association for Supervision and Curriculum Development, 2007).

7. A. P. Barker, Making a Big School "Small," *Educational Leadership, 63*(8), 76–77 (2006).

8. *Standards for Foreign Language Learning: Preparing for the 21st Century* from the American Council on the Teaching of Foreign Languages (ACTFL) at www.actfl.org; See also H. Leaman, One World, Many Languages: Using Dual-Language Books, *Social Studies and the Young Learner 21*(1), pp. 29–32 (September/October 2008).

9. Sunset Elementary School is an international studies magnet school with language/culture programs of study in cooperation with Spain and other countries. See the school's website at http://sunset.dadeschools.net.

10. *Ibid.*, see note 9.

11. *Ibid.*, see note 9.

12. J. Grant, I. Richardson, and C. Pforsten, In the Loop, *The School Administrator, 56*(1), 30–33 (January 2000).

13. R. D. Kellough, *A Primer for New Principals: Guidelines for Success* (Lanham, MD, Rowman & Littlefield, 2008), pp. 11–38; See G. Hoachlander, M. Alt, and R. Beltranena, *Leading School Improvement: What Research Says* (Atlanta, GA: Southern Regional Education Board, 2001).

14. W. Norton and J. J. Flessa, A Job Too Big for One: Multiple Principals and Other Nontraditional Approaches to School Leadership, *Educational Administration Quarterly, 42*, 518–550 (2006).

15. P. L. Tiedt and I. M. Tiedt, *Multicultural Teaching: A Handbook of Activities, Information, and Resources*, 6th ed. (Boston: Allyn & Bacon, 2002).

16. You can visit the home page of the National Institute on Education of At-Risk Students at www.ed.gov/offices/OERI/AT-RISK. See also B. A. Morrongiello and D. R. Snow and evidence-based approaches in *Classroom Strategies for Helping At-Risk Students* (Alexandria, VA: Association for Supervision and Curriculum Development, 2005);

M. W. Colombo, Building School Partnerships with Culturally and Linguistically Diverse Families, *Phi Delta Kappan, 88*(4), 314–318 (2006). Also see G. Gay, *Culturally Responsive Teaching: Theory,* (2006) *Research & Practice* (New York: Teachers College Press, 2000), p. 29; and R. S. Charney, Teaching Children to Care (Northeast Foundation for Children: *Responsive Classroom Newsletter, 142,* 2002), pp. 1–11.

17. Y. M. Wittreich, E. F. Jacobi, and I. E. Hogue, *Getting Parents Involved: A Handbook of Ideas for Teachers, Schools and Communities* (Norwood, MA: Christopher-Gordon, 2003); H. L. Hodgkinson, *Leaving Too Many Children Behind: A Demographer's View on the Neglect of America's Youngest Children* (Washington, DC: Institute for Educational Leadership, 2003).

18. PTA's national standards are available from National PTA, 541 N. Fairbanks Court, Suite 1300, Chicago, IL 60611-3396; phone: (312) 670-6782 or (800) 307-4PTA; fax: (312) 670-6783.

19. R. J. Nistler and A. Maiers, Stopping the Silence: Hearing Parents' Voices in an Urban First-Grade Family Literacy Program, *The Reading Teacher, 53*(8), 670–680 (May 2000).

20. Wittreich, Jacobi, and Hogue; see note 17.

21. Harold Reutter, "Back in the Classroom: Community Leaders Become Principals for a Day," retrieved from www.theindependent.com/articles/2008/10/08/import/2008/008-archive9.txt.

22. Wittreich, Jacobi, and Hogue; see note 17.

23. A. C. Berg, A. Melaville, and M. J. Blank, *Community and Family Engagement: Principals Share What Works* (Washington, DC: The Coalition for Community Schools, 2006).

24. S. H. Billig, Research on K–12 School-Based Service Learning: The Evidence Builds, *Phi Delta Kappan, 81*(9), 658–664 (May 2000).

25. L. Sosniak, The 9% Challenge: Education in School and Society, *Teachers College Record;* retrieved from www.tcrecord.org/Content.asp?Contentid=10756.

26. R. D. Kellough, *Your First Year of Teaching: Guidelines for Success,* 5th ed. (Pearson/Allyn & Bacon/Merrill, 2009), Prologue.

27. For copies of the INTASC document, contact CCSSO, One Massachusetts Avenue, NW, Suite 700, Washington, DC, 20001-1431, phone (202) 336-7000; www.ccsso.org.

28. Access the standards at www.nbpts.org/the_standards. You may want to review C. Danielson's Framework for Teaching in J. Cooper's *Classroom Teaching Skills,* 7th ed. (New York: Houghton-Mifflin, 2003).

29. S. Brookhart, C. Moss, and B. Long, Formative Assessment that Empowers, *Educational Leadership 66*(3), 52–57 (December 2000).

30. S. Ohanian, Goals 2000: What's in a Name? *Phi Delta Kappan, 81*(5), 233–255 (January 2000).

31. R. J. Marzano, D. J. Pickering, and J. E. Pollock, *Classroom Instruction That Works: Research-Based Strategies for Increasing Student Achievement* (Alexandria, VA: Association of Supervision and Curriculum Development, 2001).

32. J. Blair, Honored Teachers Want More Pay and Respect, *Education Week, 19*(36), 11 (Nov. 8, 2008).

33. A. Berlin, Social Promotion or Retention? *Education Week,* pp. 28–29, 30 (October 2008). Also see S. M. Brookhart, *Grading* (Upper Saddle River, N.J: Merrill Prentice Hall, 2004).

34. R. M. Ingersoll, The Teacher Shortage: Myth or Reality? *Pi Lambda Theta Educational Horizons, 81*(3), 146–152 (Spring 2003).

35. For warning signs exhibited by troubled children, download free material *Early Warning-Timely Response: A Guide to Safe Schools* (National Association of School Psychologists), from http://cecp.air.org/guide/guide.pdf.

36. Research indicates that elementary schools with fewer than 400 students are equal to, and often superior to larger ones on most measures. See School Size, School Climate, and Student Performance (Portland, OR, Northwest Regional Educational Laboratory) by K. Cotton, retrieved from www.apexsql.com/_brian/schoolsizematters.pdf.

37. N. Cambron-McCabe et al., *Public School Law: Teacher's and Student's Rights,* 5th ed., and *Legal Rights of Teachers and Students* (both Boston: Allyn & Bacon, 2004).

38. J. Shen, G. L. Wegenke, and V. E. Cooley, Has the Public Teaching Force Become More Diversified? National and Longitudinal Perspectives on Gender, Race, and Ethnicity, *Pi Lambda Theta Educational Horizons,* pp. 112–129 (Spring 2003); See also U.S. Department of Education, National Center for Education Statistics, *The Condition of Education* (2005) at http://nces.ed.gov/programs/coe/School%20Size%20Matters.pdf.

39. D. de Vise, Montgomery to Revisit Some School Fees, retrieved from www.WashingtonPost.Com/wp-dyn/content/article/2008/09/11/AR2008091103342.html; Positive findings about education are noted in *Do You Know the Good News about American Education?* (Center on Education Policy and American Youth Policy Forum, 2000), retrieved from www.cep-dc.org/index.cfm?fuseaction=Feature.showfeature&featureID=11.

40. *Ibid,* see note 39.

2

The Nature of the Challenge: What Do I Need to Know About Elementary Learners?

Bob Daemmrich Photography

Visual Chapter Organizer and Overview

Dimensions of the Challenge
The Classroom in a Nation of Diversity

Supporting the Challenge: Learning Modalities, Learning Styles, Learning Capacities, and Implications for Teaching

Learning Modalities
Learning Styles
The Three-Phase Learning Cycle
Learning Capacities: The Theory of Multiple Intelligences

Meeting the Challenge: Recognizing and Providing for Student Differences

Instructional Practices That Provide for
    Student Differences: General Guidelines
Developmental Characteristics of Children
    of Particular Age Groups
Recognizing and Working with Students
    with Special Needs

LOOKING AT TEACHERS I

Integrated Technology, Internet

In a sixth-grade classroom, the teacher led a discussion about ancient Greece's democracy, about participating in representative government, and why lack of money does not prevent someone from being able to run for political office. The teacher was challenged by a student with, "Well, then, why don't you prove it?" The teacher accepted the challenge and agreed to run for office on one condition. The condition was that the students (with their parents' permission) would organize and run the teacher's campaign.

With the students' organization, the teacher campaigned for a seat in the U.S. House of Representatives and won her party's nomination locally, but received less than 31 percent of the votes in the general election. This entire experience is narrated in *Ms. Cahill for Congress:*

One Fearless Teacher, Her Sixth-Grade Class, and the Election That Changed Their Lives Forever (New York: Ballantine/Random House, 2008) by T. Cahill and L. Gross. This narration gives insight into the nature of the sixth-grade learners, the students' participation during the year, and the lessons they learned during the election process. To integrate technology further, possibilities include asking teams of students to become specialists on specific Internet sites and start a chronicle of student-recorded log entries about the sites to collect comprehensive data useful in a campaign in representative government. Also, clips can be downloaded for free with no copyright restrictions about current events and public policy debates through C-SPAN Classroom at www.cspanclassroom.com.

A Focus on English Language Learners

As part of this election that changed the sixth graders' lives, time could always be scheduled for students to use language to persuade or elaborate in small groups or a large group. If you are doing this in your class, talk about the word *persuasion* and its meaning of trying to convince someone that he or she really needs or wants something. As an activity, each student can select from a box a square of paper with an item (perhaps new traffic cameras at busy street corners) drawn on it. Ask

them to pair together and take an allotted amount of time (perhaps set a timer for four minutes) to think about the item. Give each student in a pair four minutes to persuade the other student that he or she really needs or wants the item. The second student, who is listening, gets four minutes to ask questions about the item. Have students switch roles. Then, ask for a show of hands to see how many students think they really need or want the item (Vaughn, Bos, and Schumm, 2007).

CHAPTER OBJECTIVES

Specifically, upon completion of this chapter, you will be able to:

1. Explain one or more examples of children's diversity, their learning styles, learning modalities, and learning capacities (multiple intelligences).
2. Explain the importance of multicultural education and providing for student differences.
3. Give one or more examples of developmental characteristics of children in different age groups, some implications for instruction, and how positive

character development could impact the classroom.
4. Give examples of working with students who have special needs, that is, common English language learners, gifted students, children who take more time but are willing to try, recalcitrant learners, and abused children, and identify one or more key characteristics of productive teaching for them.
5. Generate thoughts about the grade level or age of students you might prefer to teach.

The bell rings, and the children enter your classroom, a kaleidoscope of personalities, all idiosyncratic, each a packet of energy, with different focuses, experiences, dispositions, learning capacities, and differing proficiencies in the verbal and written use of the English language; in other words, all different challenges. One of the challenges you'll understand is providing a wealth of opportunities for developing proficiency in the English language, as can be supported with *Water Dance* (Voyager Books, 2002) by T. Locker. Locker focuses on literary devices as he discusses the natural water cycle. Indeed, presenting literary devices such as a haiku-like narrative (. . . I float . . . I drift), a faux-riddle format (. . . that I am one thing . . . that I am many) and anthropomorphism (. . . I am the rain), through a children's book such as this one is just one part of the challenging profession of elementary school teaching. For instance, it's very challenging for a teacher to want to know children's literature well enough to be able to link a read-aloud children's book to a topic of study in which the students are engaged (e.g., the water cycle). We give you an example of this in this chapter's ending vignette, *Looking at Teachers II*. Another challenge, the biggest, is to understand and to teach 30 or so unique individuals, all at once, and to do it for 6 hours

a day, 5 days a week, 180 or more days a year! Indeed, what an educational adventure it is today, to be an elementary teacher, whether you are teaching five-year-olds in kindergarten or eleven- or twelve-year-olds in the sixth grade.

To prepare yourself for this challenge, consider the information provided in this chapter about the diverse characteristics and needs of elementary schoolchildren—for it is well known that their academic achievement is greatly dependent on how well their other developmental needs are understood and satisfied.

DIMENSIONS OF THE CHALLENGE

At any age, children differ in many ways—ambitions, aptitudes and talents, attitudes, hopes and dreams, experience, home life, ideals, interests, intellectual ability, language skills, learning capacities, motor ability, needs, physical characteristics, and social skills. Having long recognized the importance of these individual differences, educators have made many attempts to develop systematic programs of individualized, differentiated, and personalized instruction. For instance, in the

1920s, there were the programmed workbooks of the Winnetka Plan. The 1960s brought more plans, such as IPI (Individually Prescribed Instruction), IGE (Individually Guided Education), and PLAN (Program for Learning in Accordance with Needs). Later, the 1970s saw the development and growth in popularity of individual learning packages and the Individualized Education Program (IEP) for students with special needs. Although some of these efforts did not survive the test of time, others met with more success; some have been refined and are still being used. Today, for example, some schools report success using personalized learning plans and differentiated instruction for all students, not only those with specific needs.[1]

Personalized learning reflects the point of view that all persons learn in their own ways and at individual rates and are influenced by learning styles and learning capacities, modality preferences, information-processing habits, motivational factors, and physiological factors. Also, interests, background, innate and acquired abilities, and a myriad of other influences shape how and what a person will learn. From any particular learning experience, no two people ever learn exactly the same thing. Within the concept of personalized learning, however, is the teacher's insight in selecting developmentally appropriate strategies, including scaffolding that is a supporting system for learning, and adjusting instruction accordingly to meet the needs of individual students, especially ELLs and English-speaking students with learning problems. This selection of adjusting strategies and instruction is referred to as **differentiated** or **tiered instruction** that includes, for some students, direct instruction, interest centers, specific roles in groups, and activities that target learning styles—and for other students, independent assignments, working in pairs, teams, or small groups, self-selection of groups for study, and student choice for activities.

The Classroom in a Nation of Diversity

Central to the challenge is the concept of multicultural education, the recognition and acceptance of students from a variety of backgrounds. The goal of this concept is to provide schooling so that all children—male and female students, students with special needs, English language learners, and students who are members of diverse racial, ethnic, and cultural groups—have equal opportunity to achieve academically. In the overview of J. Hill and K. Flynn,

> [Since 2000], almost half a million children under the age of 5 were being raised in homes where no English was spoken at all. At least 125,000 of these children were likely to need special help in preschool and kindergarten to learn to speak and read English. If they do not get that help in their early years (and often they do not), it will be up to our

elementary school teachers to teach academic content as well as proficiency in English.[2]

The variety of individual differences among students requires that teachers use teaching strategies and tactics that accommodate those differences. To most effectively teach a diverse group of students, you need the skills shown in Figure 2.1.

The last two skills are the main topics of this chapter. To help you meet the challenge, a wealth of information is available. As a licensed teacher, you are expected to know it all, or at least to know where you can find all necessary information, and to review it when needed. Certain information you have stored in memory will surface and become useful at the most unexpected times. While concerned about all students' safety and physical well-being, you will want to remain sensitive to each child's attitudes, values, social adjustment, emotional well-being, and intellectual development. You must be prepared not only to teach one or more subjects, but also to do it effectively with children of different cultural backgrounds, diverse linguistic abilities, and different learning styles, as well as with students who have been identified as having special needs because of handicapping conditions. It is, indeed, a challenge! The statements that follow make this challenge even more clear:

- The United States has an increasing ethnic, cultural, and linguistic diversity that is affecting schools all across the country, not only in the large urban areas, but also in suburbs and small rural communities.
- The United States truly is a multilingual, multiethnic, multicultural nation. Considering children ages five through seven, approximately one out of every six speaks a language other than English at home. Many of these children have only limited proficiency

---

A Diverse Classroom

- Establish a classroom climate in which all students feel welcome and safe and in which they can learn and are supported in doing so (see Chapter 4).
- Develop techniques that emphasize cooperative and social-interactive learning and that deemphasize competitive learning (see Chapter 10).
- Build on students' learning styles, capacities, and modalities (this chapter).
- Develop strategies and techniques that have proven successful for students with specific differences (this chapter).

Figure 2.1
Effective teaching in a diverse classroom.

in the English language (i.e., conversational speaking ability only).

- In many large school districts, as many as one hundred languages are represented with as many as twenty or more different primary languages found in some classrooms.
- The traditional two-parent, two-child family now constitutes only about 6 percent of U.S. households. Approximately one-half of the children in the United States will spend some years being raised by a single parent. Many children go home after school to places devoid of any adult supervision. And, on any given day, tens of thousands of children are homeless—that is, they have no place at all to call home.
- By the middle of this century, the nation's population is predicted to reach 383 million, a population boom that will be led by Latinos and Asian Americans.
- Also by mid-century, minority youths in the school-age population throughout the United States will average close to 40 percent.[3]

The overall picture that emerges is a rapidly changing, diverse student population that challenges teaching skills. Teachers who traditionally have used direct instruction (see Chapter 7) as the dominant mode of instruction have done so with the assumption that their students were relatively homogeneous in terms of experience, background, knowledge, motivation, and facility with the English language. However, no such assumption can be made today. As a classroom teacher for the twenty-first century, you must be knowledgeable and skilled in using teaching strategies that recognize, celebrate, and build upon the cultural, ethnic, and linguistic diversity of the classroom, the community, and the nation. The emerging picture of education you face is your challenge.

SUPPORTING THE CHALLENGE: LEARNING MODALITIES, LEARNING STYLES, LEARNING CAPACITIES, AND IMPLICATIONS FOR TEACHING

Classroom teachers who are most effective are those who adapt their teaching styles and methods to their students, using approaches that interest the children, that are neither too easy nor too difficult, that match the students' learning styles and learning capacities, and that are relevant to the children's lives. This adaptation process is further complicated because each child is different from every other one. All do not have the same interests, abilities, backgrounds, or learning styles and capacities. As a matter of fact, not only do children differ from one another, but each child can change to some extent from one day to the next. What appeals to a child today may not have the same appeal tomorrow. Therefore, as the

teacher, you need to consider both the nature of children in general (for example, methods appropriate for a particular group of children in second grade are unlikely to be the same as those that work best for a group of sixth-graders) and each child in particular. For example, second-graders learn primarily from positive feedback while sixth-graders can process negative feedback and learn from their mistakes. As a student of a teacher preparation program, you probably have already experienced a recent course in the psychology of learning; what follows is merely a brief synopsis of knowledge about and relevant to today's teaching and learning.

Learning Modalities

Learning modality refers to the *sensory portal* (or input channel) by which a person prefers to receive sensory reception (modality preference), or the actual way a person learns best (modality adeptness). Some children prefer learning by seeing (a *visual modality*); others prefer learning through instruction from others (through dialogue), an *auditory modality*; while others prefer learning by doing and being physically involved, the *kinesthetic modality,* and by touching objects or using manipulatives, the *tactile modality.* A person's modality preference is not always that person's modality strength. The modality strength can be determined by a teacher who observes children carefully, but this primary strength can also be mixed and it can change as the result of experience and intellectual maturity. The way a child learned best when in the first grade, for example, is not necessarily the child's modality strength now that the same child is in the fourth grade. As one might suspect, modality integration (i.e., engaging more of the sensory input channels, using several modalities at once or staggered use) has been found to contribute to better achievement in student learning. We return to this concept in Part II of this resource guide.

Because many children have neither a preference nor strength for auditory reception, elementary schoolteachers should severely limit their use of the lecture method of instruction, that is, of placing too much reliance on formal teacher talk (discussed in Chapter 8). Furthermore, instruction that uses a singular approach, such as auditory (e.g., talking to students), deprives students who learn better another way—the kinesthetic and visual learners.

If a teacher's verbal communication conflicts with the teacher's nonverbal messages, children can become confused, and this, too, can affect their learning. And when there is a discrepancy between what the teacher says and what that teacher does, the teacher's nonverbal signal will be sending the strongest message every time. Actions do speak louder than words![4] A teacher, for example, who has just finished a lesson on the conservation of energy and does not turn off the room lights upon leaving the classroom for lunch, has, by inappropriate modeling behavior, created cognitive dissonance (disequilibrium) and sabotaged the real purpose for the lesson. For another example, cognitive dissonance is created by a teacher who asks children to not interrupt others when they are on task, but who repeatedly interrupts children when they are on task. This teaching behavior confuses children with the teacher's contradictory words and behavior. A teacher's job is not that of confusing children. As a general rule, most elementary school students prefer and learn best by touching objects, by feeling shapes and textures, by interacting with each other, and by moving things around. In contrast, learning by sitting and listening is difficult for many of them.

Learning modalities traits are known that significantly discriminate between students who are underachieving and at risk of not finishing school (discussed in Chapter 1) and students who perform well. Students who are underachieving and at risk need (a) frequent opportunities for mobility, (b) options and choices, (c) a variety of instructional resources, environments, and sociological groupings, (d) to learn during late morning and afternoon, rather than in the early morning, (e) informal seating rather than wooden, steel, or plastic chairs, (f) low illumination, and (g) tactile/visual introductory resources reinforced by kinesthetic (e.g., direct experiences and whole-body activities)/visual resources, or introductory kinesthetic/visual resources reinforced by tactile/visual resources.[5] As an example, at one problem school, after discovering that nearly two-thirds of its students were either tactile or kinesthetic learners, teachers and administrators grouped the students according to their modality strengths and altered the reading instruction schedules every three weeks so that each group of students had opportunities to learn at the best time of day. As a result, student behavior, learning achievement, and attitudes improved considerably.[6]

Regardless of grade level and subject(s) you intend to teach, you are advised to use strategies that integrate the modalities. Well-designed, thematic units (discussed in Chapter 7) and project-based learning incorporate modality integration. In conclusion, then, when teaching any group of students of mixed learning abilities, mixed modality strengths, mixed language proficiency, and mixed cultural backgrounds, for the most successful teaching, the integration of learning modalities is a must.

Learning Styles

Related to learning modality is **learning style,** which can be defined as independent forms of knowing and processing information. While some elementary school-children may be comfortable with beginning their learning of a new idea in the abstract form (e.g., visual or verbal symbolization), most need to begin with the concrete approach (e.g., learning by actually doing it and using manipulatives, as shown by the Learning Experiences Ladder later in this text). Many students prosper while working in groups, while others do not and prefer to work alone. Some are quick in their studies, whereas others are slow and methodical and cautious and meticulous. Some can sustain attention on a single topic for a long time, becoming more absorbed in their study as time passes. Others are slower starters and more casual in their pursuits, but are capable of shifting with ease from topic to topic, and from subject to subject. Some can study in the midst of music, noise, or movement, whereas others need quiet, solitude, and a desk or table. The point is this: learners vary not only in their skills and preferences in the way knowledge is received, but also in how they mentally process that information once it has been received. The latter is a person's style of learning. Learning style is not an indicator of intelligence, but rather an indicator of how a person learns.

Classifications of Learning Styles

Although there are probably as many types of learning styles as there are individuals, two major differences in how people learn are in how they perceive situations and how they process information.[7] On the basis of perceiving and processing and earlier work by Carl Jung on psychological types,[8] Bernice McCarthy identifies the following four major learning styles:[9]

1. The *analytic learner* perceives information abstractly and processes it reflectively. The analytic learner prefers items in sequence, needs details, and values what experts have to offer. Analytic learners do well in traditional classrooms.
2. The *commonsense learner* perceives information abstractly and processes it actively. The commonsense learner is pragmatic and enjoys hands-on learning. These learners sometimes find school frustrating unless they can see immediate use to what is being learned. In the traditional classroom, the commonsense learner is likely to be a learner who is at risk of not completing school, of dropping out.
3. The *dynamic learner* perceives information concretely and processes it actively. The dynamic learner also prefers hands-on learning and is excited by anything new. These learners are risk takers and are frustrated by learning if they see it as being tedious. In a traditional classroom, the dynamic learner also is likely to be an at-risk student.
4. The *imaginative learner* perceives information concretely and processes it reflectively. Imaginative learners learn well by listening and sharing with others, integrating the ideas of others with their own experiences. They often have difficulty

adjusting to traditional teaching, which depends less on classroom interactions and students' sharing and connecting of their prior experiences. In a traditional classroom, the imaginative learner is likely to be an at-risk student.

The Three-Phase Learning Cycle

To understand conceptual development and change, researchers in the 1960s developed a Piaget-based theory of learning where students are guided from concrete, hands-on learning experiences to the abstract formulations of concepts and their formal applications. Their theory became known as the three-phase learning cycle.[10] Long a popular strategy for teaching science, the learning cycle can be useful in language arts and other disciplines as well.[11]

The three phases of the learning cycle are as follows:

1. The *exploratory hands-on phase*, where students can explore ideas and experience assimilation and disequilibrium that lead to their own questions and tentative answers.
2. The *invention* or *concept development phase*, where, under the guidance of the teacher, students invent concepts and principles that help them answer their questions and reorganize their ideas; that is, the students revise their thinking to allow the new information to fit.
3. The *expansion* or *concept application phase*, another hands-on phase where the students try out their new ideas by applying them to situations that are relevant and meaningful to them. During application of a concept, the learner may discover new information that causes a change in the learner's understanding of the concept being applied.

You'll see, as discussed further in Chapter 9, that the process of learning is cyclical.[12] There have been more recent interpretations or modifications of the three-phase cycle, such as McCarthy's 4MAT.[13] With the 4MAT system, teachers employ a learning cycle of instructional strategies to try to teach to each student's learning style. As stated by McCarthy, in the cycle:

> learners sense and feel, they experience, then they watch, they reflect, then they think, they develop theories, they try out theories, then they experiment. Finally, they evaluate and synthesize what they have learned in order to apply it to their next similar experience. They get smarter. They apply experience to experiences.[14]

And during this process, they are likely to be using all four learning modalities.

The *constructivist learning theory* suggests that learning is a process involving the active engagement of learners who adapt the educative event to fit and expand their individual worldview (as opposed to the behaviorist pedagogical assumption that learning is something done to learners)[15] and to accentuate the importance of student self-assessment. In support of that theory, some variations of the learning cycle include a fourth phase of assessment. However, because we believe that assessment of what students know or think they know should be a continual process that permeates all three phases of the learning cycle, we reject any treatment of assessment as a self-standing phase.

Learning Capacities: The Theory of Multiple Intelligences

In contrast to the concept of learning styles, Gardner introduced what he called *learning capacities* exhibited by individuals in differing ways.[16] Originally, and sometimes still, referred to as *multiple intelligences*, or ways of knowing, capacities thus far identified are:

- *Bodily/kinesthetic*. Ability to control and maneuver one's body in such events as athletics, dance, and drama
- *Interpersonal*. Ability to understand people and relationships
- *Intrapersonal*. Ability to assess one's emotional life as a means to understand oneself and others
- *Logical/mathematical*. Ability to handle chains of reasoning and to recognize patterns and orders, to work with numbers
- *Musical*. Ability to perceive pitch, rhythm, sounds, tones, and variations of these; the ability to sing or play a musical instrument
- *Naturalist*. Ability to draw on materials and features of the natural environment to solve problems or fashion products
- *Verbal/linguistic*. Ability to learn and recognize distinctions among words, sounds, and language
- *Visual/spatial*. Ability to perceive images and to manipulate the nature of space, such as through architecture, mime, or sculpture

As discussed earlier, and as implied in the presentation of McCarthy's four types of learners, many educators believe that many students who are at risk of not completing school are those who may be dominant in a cognitive learning style that is not in synch with traditional teaching methods. Traditional methods are largely of McCarthy's analytic style: information is presented in a logical, linear, sequential fashion. Traditional methods also reflect three of the Gardner types: verbal/linguistic, logical/mathematical, and intrapersonal. Consequently, to better synchronize methods of instruction with learning styles, some teachers and schools, such as Essex Modern Languages Elementary Magnet School (Akron, Ohio) have restructured the curriculum, instruction, and assessment around Gardner's learning capacities[17] or around Sternberg's Triarchic Theory.[18] Sternberg identifies metaphors for the mind and intelligence (anthropological, biological, computation, epistemological, sociological, and systems) and proposes a theory of intelligence consisting of three elements: analytical, creative, and practical.[19]

The classroom vignette in the *Looking at Teachers II* section at the end of this chapter shows one way to put the theory of multiple intelligences and multilevel instruction into practice in a classroom. Classrooms in several schools are built on this concept. For example, you can learn about the Enota Multiple Intelligences Academy (Gainesville, Georgia) at www.edutopia.org/multiple-intelligences-immersion-enota-video, and www.gcssk12.net/eesweb/index.asp, and the New City School (St. Louis, Missouri) at www.newcityschool.org. From the preceding information about multiple intelligences and learning styles, you will realize at least two facts:

1. **Intelligence is not a fixed or static reality, but can be learned, taught, and developed.** Both you and your students must understand that intelligence is not a fixed entity, but a set of characteristics that, through a feeling of "I can" and with proper coaching, can be developed. When children understand that intelligence is incremental, something that is developed through use over time, they tend to be more motivated to work at learning than when they believe intelligence is a fixed entity.[20]
2. **Children learn and respond to learning situations in different ways.** A child may learn differently according to the situation or according to the child's ethnicity, cultural background, or socioeconomic status.[21] A teacher who for all students uses only one style of teaching, or who teaches to only one or a few styles of learning, day after day, is shortchanging those students who learn better another way. As emphasized by Rita Dunn, when children do not learn the way we teach them, then we must teach them the way they learn.[22]

MEETING THE CHALLENGE: RECOGNIZING AND PROVIDING FOR STUDENT DIFFERENCES

As a part of the expectations, responsibilities, and facilitating behaviors of an elementary school teacher, what measures could be taken to improve learning assistance for children in your classroom who will need special support in their educational activities? One of your concerns related to this may be a realization that your district may not have all of the funds to purchase special

technology for the students and another may be to determine ways to provide those students, in the best way that you can, with some ability and instruction to seek and retrieve information. In some areas, there might be an adaptive center for students with special needs in your school or district or a special education resource teacher that you can meet with to discuss your concerns.

Interest in improving learning assistance for students with special needs was a focus of the President's Committee of Advisors on Science and Technology on the Use of Technology to Strengthen K–12 Education in the United States (1997). This committee recommended that special attention should be given to technology use by students who have special needs. In support of this interest, first you may want to review some of the information about available assistive technologies for special needs students by reading a current source on technologies for adaptive assistance that has been recommended to you.[23] Second, you may want to assist your students in becoming productive members of the learning process regardless of their special needs or impediments by finding lessons and activities in the special education section (with downloads of freeware) through one of your favorite sites or through The Education World website at www.educationworld.com/. Third, you may want to become familiar with some of the current technology by reviewing these additional resources or discussing technology with a special education resource teacher in your district:

- To provide learning services to deaf and hearing impaired students, consider a program that translates text into American Sign Language characters on a computer screen that the resource teacher recommends, or a program called Signing Avatar.
- To assist students who are challenged physically, you may want to become familiar with a multisensory approach to reading similar to the *Kurzweill Scan and Read* program. To do this, research any zoom text-screen magnification program, any screen reader for the blind that is designed to read the Web, any keyboard with large print and raised keys, and the use of track balls, joysticks, and voice recognition computers.
- For students with visual impairments, investigate the value of *pwWebSpeak*, a web browser for those who want to access the Internet in a nonvisual or combined auditory/visual way, and the value of a speech output system interfaced with a screen reader and a Braille display.
- For students who need additional learning opportunities with technology, review the National Education Technology Plan (U.S. Department of Education), at http://edtechfuture.org.

- For teaching students who will benefit from your knowledge about resources on their learning styles, see:
  - ERIC link to multiple intelligences resources at www.indiana.edu/~reading/ieo/bibs/multiple.html
  - Howard Gardner's Project Zero website at http://pzweb.harvard.edu/
  - Resources on learning styles at www.d.umn.edu/student/loon/acad/strat/lrnsty.html

Supported by resources such as the ones mentioned, research and practical experience have contributed to a variety of instructional techniques that make a difference. First consider the following general guidelines, most of which are discussed in further detail in later chapters in this book.

Instructional Practices That Provide for Student Differences: General Guidelines

To provide learning experiences that are consistent with what is known about ways of learning and knowing, especially for English language learners and students with learning problems, consider the recommendations that follow and refer to them during the planning or preactive phase of your instruction:

- As frequently as is appropriate, and especially for skills development, plan the learning activities so they follow a step-by-step sequence from concrete to abstract.
- Collaboratively plan with students challenging and engaging classroom learning activities and assignments.
- Concentrate on using student-centered instruction by using project-centered learning, discovery and inquiry strategies, simulations, and role play (scaffolding).

- Maintain high but not necessarily identical expectations for every student. Establish standards and teach toward them step-by-step without wavering.
- Make learning meaningful by integrating learning with life (prior knowledge), helping each child successfully make the transitions from one level of learning to the next, one level of schooling to the next.
- Provide a structured learning environment with regular and understood procedures.
- Provide ongoing and frequent monitoring of individual student learning (additional scaffolding).
- Provide variations in meaningful assignments that are based on individual student abilities and interests (adjust the instruction).
- Use explicit instruction to teach the development of skills for thinking and learning (speak clearly, concisely, and sometimes slowly).
- Use reciprocal peer coaching and cross-age tutoring (perhaps native language peers).
- Use multilevel instruction.
- Use interactive computer programs and multimedia.
- Use small-group and cooperative learning strategies.

Developmental Characteristics of Children of Particular Age Groups

After many years of experience and research, specialists have come to accept certain precepts about children of particular ages, regardless of their individual genetic or cultural differences.[24,25] Before going further, begin Application Exercises 2.1 and 2.2.

APPLICATION EXERCISE 2.1

Obtaining Personal Insight Regarding the Age or
Grade Level That I Might Prefer to Teach

Instructions: Because of the age and developmental diversity of children in grades K–6, the purpose of this exercise is to challenge you to begin thinking about the grade or age level at which you might prefer to teach. However, we realize that the best way to fairly decide on an optimum grade level is to actually experience teaching it. Though a grade level may look challenging on paper, in this exercise, we want to point out that a particular grade level may actually be a good classroom experience for you. To begin to do this, you are asked to consider separately the category of cognitive development for ages 5–6, for ages 7–8, and for ages 9–14 in the material that follows.

1. Use a list of developmental characteristics of children from the material that follows, or from your favorite source or from a reference that your instructor suggests. As you read through it, mark a plus or minus sign after each numbered item, depending on the extent to which that item matters to you. A plus (+) means it matters a lot and a minus (–) means it does not matter to you. (You will have to number items if you are using unnumbered material.)

2. After reading and marking all items with either a plus or a minus, then identify the percentage of minus signs for each category. To do this, complete the calculations as follows: For the category of cognitive development for ages 5–6, in the material that follows, there are 15 items. Dividing the number of plus signs that you gave for these by the number 15 provides the percentage of plus signs given for that category. Subtracting that percentage number from 100 provides the percentage of minus signs for the category.

3. Continue for each of the other two categories, ages 7–8 with its 17 items and ages 9–14 with 10 items. Place the percentages in the blanks:

   Ages 5–6 percentage plus signs = _____

   Ages 7–8 percentage plus signs = _____

   Ages 9–14 percentage plus signs = _____

   The category that received your highest percentage of plus signs is ages _____. Would you concur that you have a preference toward teaching at this level? Yes or no? (circle one). Explain why or why not.

4. Compare and discuss your results of this exercise with those of your classmates in cooperative groups. What generalizations, if any, can be made from your individual results and collective discussion?

Cognitive Development of Children, Ages 5 and 6, Usually K and Grade 1

_____   1. Asks questions; has beginning intellectual and academic skills

_____   2. Has basic skills of reading

_____   3. Aware of meanings for symbols

_____   4. Writes words

_____   5. Has increased vocabulary

_____   6. Has a rate and learning manner that may vary widely from peers

_____   7. Likes to act out stories

_____   8. Involves himself or herself physically and mentally while reading

_____   9. Becoming more literal and factual, but still believes in figures (or pretends to believe in) such as Santa Claus, Easter Bunny, and Tooth Fairy

_____   10. Interested in numbers and does simple problems

_____   11. Difficulty with concepts of time and space

_____   12. Can and does memorize number facts

_____   13. Interested in parents' past

_____   14. Needs a great many concrete examples before developing more abstract concepts

_____   15. Tends not to be able to connect with concepts of time and space and sequences of large numbers and historical time

Cognitive Development of Children, Ages 7 and 8, Usually Grades 2 and 3

_____   1. Is actively curious; displays a longer attention span

_____   2. Plays and stays at a task or project for longer period of time

_____   3. Displays wide differences in abilities

_____   4. Interested in conclusions and logical ends

_____   5. Aware of community and world

_____   6. Listens to adult conversations sometimes

_____   7. Increasingly aware of money, property, ownerships, possessions

_____   8. Explores the unfamiliar

_____   9. Interested in the workings of such things as mechanisms, the human body, and so on

_____   10. Reads with greater regard for meaning by ages 7 and 8

_____   11. Enjoys reading by age 8; favorites are comic books, books with humor, fairy tales, and adventure stories

_____   12. Expresses himself or herself poetically; often with a sense of humor

_____   13. Increases a sense of time in terms of months and years

_____   14. Conscious of work people do

_____   15. Interested in other time periods, in trips to unfamiliar places

_____   16. Enjoys bartering, swapping, and starting collections

_____   17. Plays games, sends and receives correspondence

Cognitive Development of Children, Ages 9–12, Usually Grades 4–6

_____ 1. Can be egocentric; displays an increased ability to convince others

_____ 2. Displays imaginative powers

_____ 3. Exhibits independent, critical thoughts

_____ 4. Interested primarily in activities outside of school

_____ 5. Able to reason, judge, and apply experiences

_____ 6. Has willingness to learn what he or she considers to be useful

_____ 7. Experiences the phenomenon of metacognition, that is, the ability to think about one's thinking and to know what one knows and does not know

_____ 8. Enjoys using skills to solve real-life problems

_____ 9. Prefers active to passive learning experiences

_____ 10. Favors interaction with peers during learning activities

APPLICATION EXERCISE 2.2

Conversation with a Classroom Teacher

Instructions: The purpose of this exercise is to interview one or more elementary school teachers to identify one or more characteristics of productive teaching, perhaps one who is relatively new to the classroom and one who has been teaching for ten years or more. Use the following questions. You may duplicate blank copies of this form. Share the results with others in your class.

1. Name and location of school _____

   _____

2. Grade span of school _____

   _____

3. Date of interview _____

4. Name and grade level (and/or subject) of interviewee _____

   _____

5. In which area(s) of the school's curriculum do you work? _____

   _____

6. Why did you select teaching as a career? _____

   _____

   _____

   _____

7. Why are you teaching at this grade level? _____

   _____

   _____

   _____

8. What preparation or training did you have? _____

   _____

   _____

   _____

9. What advice about preparation can you offer? _____

   _____

   _____

   _____

   _____

   _____

10. What do you like most about teaching? _____

    _____

    _____

    _____

11. What do you like least about teaching? _____
_____
_____
_____

12. What is the most important thing to know to be an effective classroom teacher (i.e., what is the key characteristic of productive teaching)? _____
_____
_____
_____

13. How do you use technology in your classroom?_____
_____

14. What other specific advice do you have for those of us entering teaching at this level?
_____
_____
_____
_____
_____
_____
_____
_____
_____
_____
_____
_____
_____
_____
_____
_____
_____
_____
_____
_____
_____
_____
_____
_____
_____
_____
_____
_____
_____
_____
_____
_____
_____

Recognizing and Working with English Language Learners

English language learners, or ELLs, are sometimes referred to as limited English proficient (LEP) children. They are students whose English proficiency is not developed to the point where they can profit fully from English instruction. They differ from language minority students (i.e., children whose native language is other than English no matter how proficient) and in recent years have been given instruction mainly in the schools of California, Texas, New York, Florida, Illinois, and New Jersey. However, almost all the states have experienced increases in ELLs, and the schools are working hard to get resources to serve these newcomers to their states. As of the last U.S. census, the largest percent of children in immigrant families have origins in Mexico (40 percent), in the Caribbean (10 percent), and in East Asia (11 percent). These children are affected by factors that help shape their academic performance as English language learners: the language used in the home, the economic characteristic of being in a family with income often below the federal poverty level, and sometimes, the social characteristics of being in a family with limited formal education and an ethnic/racial minority status.

To the extent possible, it appears that implementation of evidence-based practices can enhance the academic engagement and learning of ELLs. We know that the strategic inclusion of the student's native language in the classroom can increase overall language and academic learning along with other factors that can improve the effectiveness of learning: screening for learning problems, close monitoring, small-group intervention, varied vocabulary instruction, peer-assisted learning opportunities, and culturally knowledgeable and bilingual teachers.

Students identified as ELLs also benefit from increased academic learning time, lower student–teacher ratios, and parent involvement. They may be placed in instruction with effective teaching strategies that (1) activate prior knowledge and (2) activate language (e.g., word similarities). While there is no single, universally accepted way to activate prior knowledge, some teachers begin this instruction by asking students to talk and write about their previous literacy experiences. With this approach, teachers can encourage students who have difficulty writing in English to write their answers in their native language. Native-language peers can help translate their comments into English. By activating prior knowledge, a teacher can discover a child's interests (perhaps a child likes reading about his or her country of origin) and include that interest (reading about the country) along with writing to sustain the child's interest and facilitate his or her language learning. In this setting, teachers could encourage students to connect further with their own prior historical knowledge of their country by reading several books and sharing their points of view on events and figures in world history with the rest of the students. Using instruction to activate language word similarities, a student's native language can be used to find an equivalent to a new word in a second language (e.g., English). For instance, Spanish-speaking students can compare English words (such as *angles*) to the students' native-language equivalents (*angulos*), and this invites the students to use something they already know, reinforcing their learning. As a classroom teacher, you will need to accumulate information and skills specific to teaching ELLs in your classroom, and perhaps can begin with specialized strategies such as those previously discussed to enhance the learning of all students.

Generally speaking, teaching ELL students can also include the use of the ELL cluster model or structured English immersion (SEI). The ELL cluster model is similar to the sheltered instruction approach, where language skills and content are taught concurrently. The class is taught in English, and aides who speak the ELLs' native languages assist.

In the structured English immersion program, you often are responding to a state requirement (as in Arizona, California, Massachusetts, and other states) to teach students the English language quickly so they can be more successful in school. To do this, when teaching a child with English language needs, you maximize instruction in English as the main content and use and teach English with brief targeted lessons at a level approximate to the abilities of the ELLs in the group. An average day of instruction usually includes lessons in listening skills, pronunciation, verb tense, grammar skills, and sentence structure (often 20 minutes each). There are lessons in math, science, social studies, and physical education (about 40 minutes each) along with vocabulary (30 minutes) and English reading and writing (60 minutes).

As an example of results in an ongoing sheltered English immersion program, the George Washington Elementary School (Madera, California), enrolls over 500 ELLs in grades K–6 and found that after one year of SEI, the school gained almost 30 points on state tests, and English language growth tripled in all grades. Further, almost 50 percent of the intermediate-grade students advanced to the next level of proficiency or met the criteria for being fully English proficient. Much research has been done on ELL students. You may want to find relevant articles about teaching ELLs to increase your view on this topic. We suggest reading the themed issue in *Educational Leadership* (66, 7, April 2009) about English language learners and searching www.ASCD.org.

Recognizing and Working with Other Students with Special Needs

Students with special needs (also referred to as *exceptional students* and *students with disabilities*) include those with conditions or impairments in any one or more of the following categories: autism, emotional, hearing, language or speech, mental retardation, orthopedic, traumatic brain injury, visual, other health impairment, or specific learning problems. To the extent possible, exceptional students must be educated with their peers in the regular classroom. Public Law 94-142, the Education for All Handicapped Children Act (EACH) of 1975, mandates that all children have the right to a free and appropriate education and to nondiscriminatory assessment. Recent amendments to this act have renamed the act to Individuals with Disabilities Education Act (IDEA, PL 101-476, 1990) and normalized the educational environment for students with disabilities to the *least restrictive environment* that is as normal as possible for these students (PL 105-17, 1997). The U.S. Supreme Court has made recent rulings affecting IDEA:[26] a district must provide catheterization or one-on-one nursing service to a student who needs it to attend school; parents are entitled to reimbursement for private school tuition/expenses if courts determine the parents' placement of the child is appropriate; a district may not suspend a violent/disruptive child with disabilities for more than ten days without due process as stated in IDEA; the party seeking due process bears the burden of proof; and parents winning legal disputes over a child's education plan are not authorized to be reimbursed for cost of experts or other non-lawyer consultants.

Students identified as having special needs may be placed in the regular classroom for the entire school day, called *full inclusion.*[27] Those students may also be in a regular classroom for the greater part of the school day, called partial inclusion, or only for designated periods. While there is no single, universally accepted definition of the term, inclusion is the concept that students with special needs should be integrated into general education classrooms regardless of the extent to which they can meet traditional academic standards. As to this concept, teacher candidates who have interviewed classroom students found that students today consider it right and natural for students with learning and behavioral difficulties to be in their classes and that they can easily adjust to co-teaching but sometimes are puzzled by the entry and exit of those who leave the class for resource rooms.[28] This term, *inclusion*, has largely replaced the use of an earlier and similar term, *mainstreaming*. As a classroom teacher, you will need information and skills specific to teaching learners with special needs in your classroom, and perhaps, consider specialized adaptations and strategies that can be used to enhance the learning of all students.

Generally speaking, teaching students who have special needs requires more care, better diagnosis, greater skills, more attention to individual needs, and an even greater understanding of the students. The challenges of teaching students with special needs in the regular classroom are great enough that to do it well, you will need specialized education beyond the general guidelines presented here. At some point in your teacher preparation, you should take one or more courses in working with the learner with disabling conditions who is included in the regular classroom.

When a child with special needs is placed in your classroom, your task is to deal directly with the differences between this student and other students in your classroom. To do this, you should develop an understanding of the general characteristics of different types of learners with special needs, identify the child's unique needs relative to your classroom, and design lessons that teach to different needs at the same time, called multilevel instruction, or multitasking, as exemplified in the chapter's closing vignette, *Looking at Teachers II*, and in Figure 2.2.[29] Remember that just

- Adult advocacy relationships for every student
- Teacher support for a student moving ahead one traditional grade, thereby accelerating the time a student passes through the grades
- Cooperative learning activities
- Curriculum comparing
- Extra efforts to provide academic and personal help
- High expectations for all students
- Individualized educational plans and instruction
- Integrating modern technologies into the curriculum
- Interdisciplinary learning and thematic instruction
- Looping
- Low (no higher than 17:1) teacher–student ratio
- Multiage grouping and midyear promotions
- Multidiscipline student-centered project-based learning
- Peer and cross-age teaching
- Problem-centered learning
- Second opportunity recovery strategies
- Service learning
- Specialized schools and nontraditional schedules

Figure 2.2

Multiple pathways to success: productive ways of attending to student differences, of providing a more challenging learning environment, and of stimulating the talents and motivation of each learner.

because a student has been identified as having one or more special needs does not preclude that person from being gifted or talented.

Congress stipulated in PL 94-142 that an Individualized Educational Program (IEP) be devised annually for each child with special needs. According to that law, an IEP is developed for each student each year by a team that includes special education teachers, the child's parents or guardians, and the regular education classroom teachers. The IEP contains a statement of the student's present educational levels, the educational goals for the year, specifications for the services to be provided, the extent to which the student should be expected to take part in the regular education program, and the evaluative criteria for the services to be provided. Consultation by special and skilled support personnel is essential in all IEP models. A consultant works directly with teachers or with students and parents or guardians. As a regular education teacher, you may play an active role in preparing the specifications for the students with special needs assigned to your classroom, as well as have a major responsibility for implementing the program.

Although the guidelines shown in Table 2.1 are important for teaching all students, they are especially important for working with students with special needs.

The trend today is to provide sufficient curriculum options, or multiple pathways, so each student can reach his or her potential. Because the advantage gained from using a combination of responsive practices concurrently is seemingly greater than is the gain from using any single practice by itself, in many instances in a given school, the practices overlap and are used simultaneously. These practices are shown in Figure 2.1 and are discussed in numerous places in this text. Please check the index for topic locations.

Table 2.1 Basic Guidelines for Students with Special Needs

Although guidelines represented by the information that follows are important for teaching all students, they are especially important for working with students with special needs.

1. Familiarize yourself with exactly what the special needs of each learner are. Privately ask the learner with special needs whether there is anything the student would like for you to know and what you can specifically do to facilitate the student's learning while in your classroom.

2. Adapt and modify materials and procedures to the special needs of each student. For example, a child who has extreme difficulty sitting still for more than a few minutes will need planned changes in learning activities. When establishing student-seating arrangements in the classroom, give consideration to students according to their special needs.

3. Try to incorporate into lessons activities that engage all learning modalities: visual, auditory, tactile, and kinesthetic. For the visual approach, a child can tell a story while the teacher writes down the words and says them (auditory), which later serve as the material the child learns to read. Next, the child repeats a word (auditory) and, finally, the child traces the word (kinesthetic and tactual). Also try simple and straightforward teaching techniques such as these: for prereading each paragraph, read aloud questions about the main ideas in the paragraph to the students; provide students with printed copies of the questions and the paragraph that the students are reading; discuss what the students can recall about the ideas.

4. Provide lesson structure and clear expectations by defining the learning objectives in behavioral terms. Teach children the correct procedures for everything. Break complex learning into simpler components (steps), moving from the most concrete (hands-on, role play) to the abstract, rather than the other way around. Check frequently for student understanding of instructions and procedures (more role play) and for skill development and the comprehension of content (observing and monitoring).

5. Use computers and other self-correcting materials for practice and for provision of immediate and private feedback to the student.

6. Develop your withitness, steadily monitoring children for signs of restlessness, frustration, anxiety, and off-task behaviors. Be ready to reassign individual learners to different activities as the situation warrants. Established classroom learning centers and learning activities at a designated table can be a big help.

7. Have all students maintain assignments for a week or some other period of time in an assignment book or in a folder that is kept in their notebooks. Post assignments in a special place in the classroom and frequently remind the students of assignments and deadlines. One assignment might be to have students ask themselves the prereading question "What am I reading and studying this paragraph for?" Then have the students find the main idea in the paragraph and underline it. Next, have each student think of a question about the main idea and write it. Individually, or as a group, look back at the questions and answers and talk about how this information provides the students with still more information.

8. Maintain consistency in your expectations and in your responses. Students with special needs, particularly, can become frustrated when they do not understand a teacher's expectations and when they cannot depend on a teacher's reactions.

(Continued)

Table 2.1 Basic Guidelines for Students with Special Needs (*Continued*)

9. Plan an interesting variety of activities to bridge learning, activities that help the children connect what is being learned with their world. Learning the connection of what is being learned with the real world helps motivate students and keeps them on task (e.g., for students' reading choices, display children's books showing workers in the community, and in lesson introductions, refer to the workers and the ways they use reading, writing, math, and so on).

10. Plan questions and questioning sequences and write them into your lesson plans. Plan questions that you will ask the students with special needs so that they are most likely to answer them with confidence. Use signals to let students know that you are likely to call on them in class (e.g., prolonged eye contact or mentioning your intention to the student before class begins). After asking a question, give the student adequate time to think and respond (wait time). Then, after the student responds, build upon the student's response to indicate that the child's contribution was accepted as being important.

11. Provide for and teach toward student success. Provide activities and experiences that ensure each student's success and mastery at some level. Reviewing student portfolios together can give evidence of progress and help build student confidence and self-esteem.

12. Provide time in class for children to work on assignments (perhaps called responsibility papers and responsibility projects). During this time, you can monitor the work of each child while looking for misconceptions and misunderstandings, thus ensuring that students get started on the right track.

13. Provide help in the organization of student learning. For example, give instruction in the organization of notes and notebooks. If using ring binders, have a three-hole punch available in the classroom so students can put papers into their binders immediately, thus avoiding disorganization and loss of papers. During class presentations, use a front-of-the-room board or an overhead projector with transparencies; students who need more time can then copy material from the board/transparencies. Ask students to read their notes aloud to each other in small groups, thereby aiding their recall and understanding and encouraging them to take notes for meaning rather than for rote learning. Encourage and provide for native-language peer support if needed, pair tutoring or coaching, or cross-age teaching. Ensure that the learner with special needs is included in all class activities to the fullest extent possible.[30]

14. Use collaborative and cooperative learning,[31] and select specially designed programs/instruction for English learners;[32] consider language and cultural differences,[33] use simplified vocabulary;[34] introduce response journals for students to record their responses to what they are reading and studying;[35] and work toward being parent friendly, that is, welcome parents and guardians in a variety of friendly ways.[36]

15. Communicate with all parents in a positive manner. For instance, terminology and information can be shared when appropriate: a child with exceptional ability in one or more of the visual or performing arts is termed *talented;*[37] *gifted* students are often unrecognized[38] and are sometimes at risk of dropping out of school;[39] it is estimated that between 10 and 20 percent of school dropouts are intelligent students who are in the range of being gifted;[40] and a list of indicators of superior intelligence ranges from (1) ability to extrapolate knowledge to (2) a different response to resiliency to (3) understanding one's cultural heritage.[41] Further, gifted students can have problems such as low self-esteem, indifference, hostility, and being critical of themselves.[42] When possible, provide multiple pathways (options such as children's books, educational games, or software as various approaches to curriculum) so achievement increases and students learn more because their individual learning capacities, styles, and modalities are identified and accommodated.[43,44]

16. You are legally mandated to report any suspicion of child abuse, a grave matter of pressing national concern. Some characteristics of children who are abused or neglected are sudden changes in behavior, crying, unclear, unexplained lacerations and bruises, and withdrawal from adult content and peer interaction.[45]

17. Consider character education as part of the district's developing curricula with the goal of developing "mature adults capable of responsible citizenship and moral actions."[46,47] A specific aspect of the curriculum might be having the students do research and present a particular stance on a controversial issue.[48]

LOOKING AT TEACHERS II

Integrated Technology, Multitasking

Given the diverse nature of elementary learners as seen in this chapter, teachers often ask, "What can be done to put the theory of multiple intelligences and multilevel instruction (a theory discussed earlier in this chapter), into practice?" Here is what one teacher did: In one fourth-grade classroom, during one week of a six-week thematic unit on weather, the students were concentrating on learning about the water cycle with computer searches and hands-on projects. As part of this study of the water cycle, the teacher asked, "What do you think makes clouds? What might happen when cool water vapor meets dust or smoke particles in the air?" To help the students demonstrate that the meeting of particles and cool water vapor in the air makes a cloud, the teacher had a student volunteer select a clear one-liter plastic bottle with a cap, put a drop of water from the water faucet into the bottle, and then the teacher lit a small match (with the principal's knowledge) and dropped it into the bottle. The teacher quickly put on the cap and the student started squeezing and releasing the sides of the plastic bottle. After a few squeezes and releases by the students, a white cloud started to appear in the clear plastic bottle and the group talked about what was going on. They observed that some of the water had evaporated and evidently had turned into water vapor that they could not see. When the students squeezed the plastic bottle, the vapor warmed up, and when the students released the bottle, the vapor cooled down. When the vapor cooled down enough, the vapor condensed into a cloud of visible drops that were caused from the particles of dust and smoke from the match.

With the students' further help, the teacher divided the class into several groups of three to five students per group to continue working on projects. The groups worked on six projects simultaneously to learn about the water cycle.

- One group of students designed, conducted, and repeated an experiment to discover the number of drops of water that can be held on one side of a new one-cent coin versus the number that can be held on the side of a worn one-cent coin.
- A second group worked, in part, with the first group and designed and prepared graphs to illustrate the results of the experiments of the first group.
- A third group of students created and composed the words and music of a song about the water cycle.
- A fourth group incorporated their combined interests in mathematics and art to design, collect the necessary materials for, and create a colorful and interactive bulletin board about the water cycle.
- A fifth group read about the water cycle in materials they researched from the Internet and various libraries. One source was *The Snowflake: A Water Cycle Story* (Millbrook, 2003) by N. Waldman.
- A sixth group created a puppet show about the water cycle.

At the end of the week, the groups shared their projects with the class. This chapter's content about the theory of multiple intelligences will help you put this theory into practice in your own classroom in the future.

SUMMARY

As a classroom teacher, you must acknowledge that the students in your classroom have different ways of receiving information and different ways of processing that information—different ways of knowing and of constructing their knowledge. These differences are unique and important, and, as you will learn in Part II of this text, are central considerations in curriculum development, instructional practice, and the assessment of learning.

You should try to learn as much as you can about how each student learns and processes information. But because you can never know everything about each student, the more you dialogue with members of the child's family and your colleagues, vary your teaching strategies, and assist students in integrating their learning, the most likely you are to reach more of the students more of the time.

You can extend your professional competency by interacting with one or more of the suggestions in the section that follows, Extending My Professional Competency. Perhaps you'll be interested in discussing class management, in observing the nature of elementary learners in a video on www.MyEducationLab.com, or in engaging in another interaction.

What's to Come. The chapters ahead will help you be an effective elementary school classroom teacher by encouraging you to (a) learn as much about your students and their preferred styles of learning as you can; (b) develop an eclectic style of teaching, one that is flexible and adaptable and (c) where possible, integrate the disciplines, thereby helping children make bridges or connections between their lives and all that is being learned.

Further, when you finish reading Chapter 3, you will want to work on extending your competencies in one of several ways. Examples: by planning your professional portfolio, by writing an answer to a response-type question similar to questions found on a teacher test for licensing and credentialing, or by responding to one of the other suggested interactions that follow at the end of that chapter.

EXTENDING MY PROFESSIONAL COMPETENCY

With Discussion

Classroom Management. How would I describe what a teacher should plan to do as a result of learning style information about his/her students? **To do:** Here is a class scenario to respond to: Brian, a social studies teacher, has a class of 33 sixth-graders who during his expository teaching (lecture, teacher-led discussion, and recitation lessons) are restless and inattentive, creating for Brian a problem in classroom management. At Brian's invitation, the school psychologist tests the students for learning modality and finds that of the 33 students, 29 are predominately kinesthetic learners. What guidance did this information give Brian? What should Brian plan to do as a result of this information?

With Video

Video Activity: Nature of Elementary Learners. How can I explain the nature of elementary learners to a colleague?

myeducationlab

> Go to the Video Examples section of Topic #13 Inclusion and Special Needs in the MyEducationLab for your course to view the video entitled "Lesson on Birds."

View the video with a colleague and take notes about the students and what they do and say. Discuss your notes about learning modalities, multiple intelligences, and the teacher's different methods for teaching the second-grade learners with learning disabilities. Your discussion will reflect your insight into the nature of the elementary learners that you see in the video, and that in turn will give you hints about the nature of the teaching that interacts with the learners. You'll remember that the nature of these learners affects teaching and encourages the teaching interactions you see. View the video again if needed.

With Portfolio

Portfolio Planning. How can I continue my professional portfolio and show my knowledge of elementary learners in connection with Principles 2 and 3 of INTASC and the Standards 1, 2, 3, 4, and 7 of NBPTS and the teacher test content (as seen on the inside of the front cover of this book)? **To do:** To continue your portfolio, you can develop and write a one- or two-page paper explaining your knowledge of elementary learners. Label your paper as Elementary Learners, and after reading and interacting with Chapter 2 in this text, state how you have developed your competency in one or two of this chapter's objectives:

- Explain one example of children's diversity, their learning styles, learning modalities, and learning capacities (multiple intelligences).
- Explain the importance of multicultural education and providing for student differences from your point of view.
- Return to the beginning of this chapter to select more of the objectives.

Place your paper in your portfolio folder or in your computer file. See additional help, if needed, from Portfolio Builders at MyEducationLab.com.

With Teacher Tests Study Guide

Teacher Tests for Future Licensing and Certification. If I wanted to prepare for taking a state teacher test to qualify for my teaching certificate/license and study the area of knowing the nature of elementary learners, how could I begin? **To do:** For this chapter, there is a constructed-response-type question similar to those found on state tests for teacher licensing and certification in Appendix A. The question, related to the nature of today's elementary learners, helps you take another look at the classroom vignette, *Looking at Teachers II*, at the end of this chapter. Write your response and, if you wish, discuss it with another teaching candidate. We suggest you review it as you prepare to take a state teacher test.

With Target Topics for Teacher Tests (TTTT)

If I wanted to start early to prepare for taking a state teacher test for licensing and certification and review subject matter content about teaching elementary learners, how could I begin? **To do:** Consider reviewing Target Topics for Teacher Tests (TTTT) in the subject index. To assist you as you prepare to take a teacher test, bullets (•) have been placed by selected word entries in the subject index and indicate Target Topics for Teacher Tests. The bullets highlight core subject matter—diversity, learning styles, student differences, special needs, and other areas for this chapter—that the authors suggest be reviewed in preparation for taking a teacher test similar to your state's test or to Praxis II Principles of Learning and Teaching exam.

WITH READING

Allington, R. L., and Johnson, P. H. (2002). *Reading to Learn: Lessons from Exemplary Fourth-Grade Classrooms.* New York: Guilford.

Armstrong, T. (2000). *Multiple Intelligences in the Classroom* (2nd ed.). Alexandria, VA: Association for Supervision and Curriculum Development.

Bennett, C. I. (2007). *Comprehensive Multicultural Education: Theory and Practice* (6th ed.). Boston: Pearson Education Inc.

Brisk, M. E., and Harrington, M. M. (2000). *Literacy and Bilingualism: A Handbook for All Teachers.* Mahwah, NJ: Erlbaum.

Buzzelli, C. A., and Johnston, B. (2002). *The Moral Dimensions of Teaching: Language, Power, and Culture in Classroom Interaction.* New York: RoutledgeFalmer.

Cavigliole, O., and Harris, I. (2003). *Thinking Visually: Step-by-Step Exercises That Promote Visual, Auditory, and Kinesthetic Learning.* New York: Pembrooke.

Cooper, J. (2003). *Classroom Teaching Skills* (7th ed.). Boston: Houghton Mifflin.

Council for Exceptional Children. (2000). *Bright Futures for Exceptional Learners: An Action Agenda to Achieve Quality Conditions for Teaching and Learning.* Reston, VA: Council for Exceptional Children.

Crane, B. (2000). *Teaching with the Internet: Strategies and Models for the K–12 Curricula.* New York: Neal-Schuman.

Diaz-Rico, L. T., and Weed, K. Z. (2010). *The Crosscultural, Language and Academic Development Handbook* (4th ed.). Boston: Pearson Education Inc.

Dickinson, T. S. (2001). *Reinventing the Middle School*. New York: RoutledgeFalmer.

Dougherty, E. (2001). *Shifting Gears: Standards, Assessment, Curriculum, and Instruction*. Golden, CO: Fulcrum Resources.

Echevarria, J., and Graves, A. (2007). *Sheltered Content Instruction*. Boston: Pearson Education Inc.

Franklin, J. (2001). Trying Too Hard? How Accountability and Testing Are Affecting Constructivist Teaching. *Education Update, 42*(3), 1–8.

Gibb, G. S., and Dyches, T. T. (2000). *Guide to Writing Quality Individualized Education Programs: What's Best for Students with Disabilities?* Needham Heights, MA: Allyn & Bacon.

Goldman, L. (2000). *Helping the Grieving Child in School*. Fastback 460. Bloomington, IN: Phi Delta Kappa Educational Foundation.

Good, T., and Brophy, J. (2003). *Looking in Classrooms* (9th ed.). New York: Longman.

Heacox, D. (2003). *Differentiating Instruction in the Regular Classroom*. Minneapolis, MN: Free Spirit.

Hoover, J. J. (2009). *Differentiating Learning Differences from Disabilities*. Upper Saddle River, NJ: Pearson Education Inc.

Huefner, D. S. (2006). *Getting Comfortable with Special Education Law: A Framework for Working with Children with Disabilities* (2nd ed.). Norwood, MA: Christopher-Gordon.

Irvine, J., and York, D. (2001). Learning Styles and Culturally Diverse Students: A Literature Review in J. Banks and C. Banks (Eds.), *Handbook of Research on Multicultural Education* (pp. 484–497). San Francisco: Jossey-Bass.

Kaye, C. B. (2003). *The Complete Guide to Service Learning*. Minneapolis, MN: Free Spirit.

Leiden University (2008). Learning from Mistakes Only Works After Age 12, Study Suggests. *Science Daily*. Retrieved from www.sciencedaily.com/releases/2008/09/080925104309.htm

Lucas, J. (2001). *Learning How to Learn*. Frisco, TX: Lucas Educational Systems.

Mercado, C. (2001). The Learner: "Race," "Ethnicity," and Linguistic Difference. In V. Richardson (Ed.), *Handbook of Research on Teaching* (pp. 668–694). Washington, DC: American Educational Research Association.

Miller, H. M. (2000). Teaching and Learning about Cultural Diversity: All of Us Together Have a Story to Tell. *The Reading Teacher, 54*(6), 666–667.

Murphy, F. V. (2002). *Making Inclusion Work: A Practical Guide for Teachers*. Norwood, MA: Christopher-Gordon.

Roberts, P. L. (2000). *Family Values Through Children's Literature, Grades K–3*. Lanham, MD: Scarecrow Press.

Roberts, P. L. (2004). *Family Values Through Children's Books and Activities, Grades 4–6*. Lanham, MD: Scarecrow Press.

Vaughn, S., and Bos, C. S. (2009). *Strategies for Teaching Students with Learning and Behavior Problems*. Upper Saddle River, NJ: Pearson Education Inc.

Vaughn, S., Bos, C. S., and Schumm, J. S. (2007). *Teaching Students Who Are Exceptional, Diverse, and at Risk*. Boston: Allyn & Bacon.

Wood, K., and Tinajero, J. (2002). Using Pictures to Teach Content to Second Language Learners. *Journal of Teacher Education, 19*, 23–42.

Yatvin, J. (2004). *A Room With a Differentiated View: How to Serve All Children as Individual Learners*. Portsmouth, ME: Heinemann.

WITH NOTES

1. As examples, a personal learning plan for each student is a feature of Celebration School (Celebration, FL)—see the website at www.cs.osceola.k12.fl.us; Also see Community Learning Center schools (Pre-K through adults) and contact Designs for Learning, 2233 University Ave. W, Suite 450, St. Paul, MN 55114, 651-645-0200; or see Community for Learning (K–12) and contact www.tcforlearning.edu.do.

2. J. D. Hill and K. M. Flynn, *Classroom Instruction That Works with English Language Learners* (Alexandria, VA: Association for Supervision and Curriculum Development, 2006), p. xii; See K. Hinton-Johnson, In the Process of Becoming Multicultural: Reflections of a First Year Teacher, *New Advocate, 15*, 309–13 (2002); See C. H. Rathbone, A Learner's Bill of Rights, *Phi Delta Kappan*, (Feb.), pp. 471–473, (2005); See J. Echevarria and A. Graves, *Sheltered Content Instruction: Teaching English Language Learners with Diverse Abilities*, 3rd ed. (Boston: Pearson/Allyn & Bacon, 2007).

3. R. Schroder-Arce, Walking on Ice: Facing Cultural and Lingual Challenges as an 'Other.' *Stage of the Act, 14*(3), 22–24 (2002).

4. T. L. Good and J. E. Brophy, *Looking in Classrooms*, 9th ed. (New York: Addison Wesley Longman, 2003), p. 127.

5. L. Burmark and L. Fournier. *Enlighten Up! An Educator's Guide to Stress-Free Living* (Alexandria, VA: Association for Supervision and Curriculum Development, 2003); See also Hill and Flynn, note 2.

6. E. W. Eisner, The Kind of Schools We Need, *Phi Delta Kappan, 84*, 579.

7. D. A. Kolb's earlier work, *Experiential Learning: Experience as the Source of Learning and Development* (Upper Saddle River, NJ: Prentice Hall, 1984).

8. M. Miller, What Do Students Think About Inclusion? *Phi Delta Kappan, 89*(5), 389–391; See W. Sailor and B. Roger, Rethinking Inclusion: Schoolwide Applications, *Phi Delta Kappan, 86*(7), 503–509; See also C. G. Jung's classic work *Psychological Types* (New York: Harcourt Brace, 1923).

9. B. McCarthy and D. McCarthy, *Teaching Around the 4MAT Cycle* (Thousand Oaks, Corwin Press, 2006).

10. A. S. Foster, Let the Dogs Out: Using Bobble Head Toys to Explore Force and Motion, *Science Scope, 26*(7), 16–9 (2003).

11. E. Eisner, see note 6.

12. The three phases of the learning cycle are comparable to the three levels of thinking, described variously by others and E. Eisner's earlier work, *The Educational Imagination* (New York: Macmillan, 1979); the levels are referred to as descriptive, interpretive, and evaluative.

13. For information about 4MAT, contact About Learning, Inc., 441 W. Bonner Road, Wauconda, IL 60084 or at www.aboutlearning.com/.

14. B. McCarthy and D. McCarthy, see note 9.

15. See articles in "Constructivist Suggestions," the Spring 2008 (Vol. 86, No. 3) theme issue of *Educational Horizons*. For discourse about the question "How does being a constructivist make your teaching different from someone who is not a constructivist?" see E. G. Rozycki, Preparing Teachers for Public Schools: Just More Cannon Fodder? *Educational Horizons, 81*(3), 2003.

16. For H. Gardner's distinction between *learning style* and *intelligences,* see Gardner's earlier work, Multiple Intelligences: Myths and Messages, *International Schools Journal, 15*(2), 8–22 (April 1996); See also E. Weber, *Multiple Intelligence Strategies in the Classroom and Beyond* (Boston: Pearson/Allyn & Bacon, 2005).

17. See Chapter 2 of L. Campbell and B. Campbell, *Multiple Intelligences and Student Achievement: Success Stories from Six Schools* (Alexandria, VA: Association for Supervision and Curriculum Development, 2000).

18. T. Armstrong, *The Multiple Intelligences of Reading and Writing: Making the Words Come Alive* (Alexandria, VA: Association of Supervision and Curriculum Development, 2003).

19. See T. Armstrong, note 18; Also see R. J. Sternberg's earlier work, Teaching and Assessing for Successful Intelligence, *School Administrator, 55*(1), 26–27, 30–31 (January 1998).

20. R. J. Marzano, 20th Century Advances in Instruction, Chapter 4 (pp. 67–95) of R. S. Brandt (Ed.), *Education in a New Era* (Alexandria, VA: ASCD Yearbook, Association for Supervision and Curriculum Development, 2000), p. 76.

21. R. Bromfield, *Handle with Care: Understanding Children and Teachers* (New York: Teachers College Press, 2003).

22. See Hill and Flynn, note 2.

23. L. Berk, *Child Development*, 6th ed. (Needham Heights, MA: Allyn & Bacon, 2003).

24. See note 23.

25. L. Berk, *Development Through the Lifespan*, 2nd ed. (Boston: Allyn & Bacon, 2001).

26. See *Education Week's* The Supreme Court and Special Education (November, 2006) p. 23; For more information, see *The Law and Special Education* by Mitchell L. Yell (Merrill/Prentice Hall) as found at www.ed.sc.edu/sped law/lawpage.htm.

27. J. Willis, *Brain-Friendly Strategies for the Inclusion Classroom* (Alexandria, VA: Association for Supervision and Curriculum Development, 2007).

28. For strategies for including English language learners, see J. Reiss, *ESOL Strategies for Teaching Content: Facilitating Instruction for English Language Learners*, (Upper Saddle River, NJ: Merrill Prentice Hall, 2001).

29. M. S. Carlo, D. August, B. McLaughlin, C. E. Snow, C. Dressler, D. N. Lippman, T. J. Lively, and C. E. White, Closing the Gap: Addressing the Vocabulary Needs of English-Language Learners in Bilingual and Mainstream Classrooms, *Reading Research Quarterly, 39*, 188–215 (2004).

30. See J. Willis, note 27.

31. F. Genesee, Teaching Linguistically Diverse Students, *Principal, 79*(5), 24–27 (May 2000).

32. S. Peregoy and O. Boyle, *Reading, Writing, and Learning in ESL*, 3rd ed. (New York: Longman, 2001).

33. L. Meyer, Barriers to Meaningful Instruction for English Learners, *Theory into Practice*, 228–236 (2000).

34. P. C. Miller and H. Endo, Understanding and Meeting the Needs of ESL Students, *Phi Delta Kappan, 85*, 786–791 (2004).

35. J. Echevarria, M. Vogt, and D. Short, *Making Content Comprehensible for English Language Learners: The SIOP Model* (Needham Heights, MA: Allyn & Bacon, 2000).

36. C. M. Brighton, Straddling the Fence: Implementing Best Practices in an Era of Accountability, *Gifted Child Today Magazine, 25*(3), 30–33 (2002).

37. J. Smutny, S. Walker, and E. Meckstroth, *Teaching Young Gifted Children in the Regular Classroom* (Minneapolis, MN: Free Spirit, 2005).

38. D. Slocumb and R. K. Payne, Identifying and Nurturing the Gifted Poor, *Principal, 79*(5), 28–32 (May 2000).

39. For more about gifted underachievers, see B. Louis, R. Subotnik, P. Breland, and M. Lewis, Establishing Criteria for High Ability versus Selective Admission to Gifted Programs: Implications for Policy and Practice, *Educational Psychology Review, 12*(3), 295–314 (2000).

40. C. R. Beck, Matching Strategies to Learning Style Preferences, *Teacher Educator, 37*(1), 1–15 (2001).

41. *Op. cit.,* Beck, note 40.

42. Update with information from Council for Exceptional Children, 1110 North Globe Road, Suite 300, Arlington, VA 22201.

43. *Ibid.*

44. J. S. Peterson and K. E. Ray, Bullying and the Gifted, *Gifted Child Quarterly, 50,* 148–168 (2006).

45. H. L. Hodgkinson, *Leaving Too Many Children Behind: A Demographer's View on the Neglect of America's Youngest Children* (Washington, DC: Institute for Educational Leadership, 2003).

46. S. Schwartz, Educating the Heart, *Educational Leadership*, April, 76–78 (2007).

47. *Ibid.*

48. K. S. Berger, Update on Bullying at School: Science Forgotten? *Developmental Review, 27*(1), 90–126 (2007).

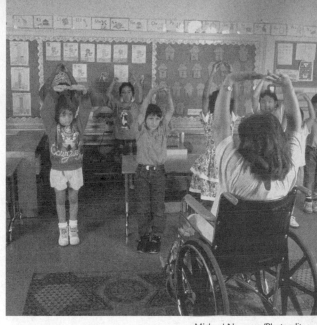

3

What Are the Expectations, Responsibilities, and Facilitating Behaviors of a Classroom Teacher?

Visual Chapter Organizer and Overview

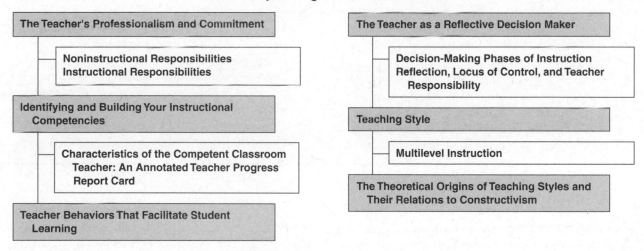

The Teacher's Professionalism and Commitment

> Noninstructional Responsibilities
> Instructional Responsibilities

Identifying and Building Your Instructional Competencies

> Characteristics of the Competent Classroom Teacher: An Annotated Teacher Progress Report Card

Teacher Behaviors That Facilitate Student Learning

The Teacher as a Reflective Decision Maker

> Decision-Making Phases of Instruction
> Reflection, Locus of Control, and Teacher Responsibility

Teaching Style

> Multilevel Instruction

The Theoretical Origins of Teaching Styles and Their Relations to Constructivism

---

LOOKING AT TEACHERS I

Integrated Technology, Podcasts

In a fourth-grade classroom, the students were beginning a unit on Midwest U.S. geography and they were to research the travels of Lewis and Clark as an opening activity. To help launch the unit, the school's instructional integration specialist worked with the teacher and scripted a podcast (a digital broadcast using a computer, a microphone, and audio editing software [GarageBand for Macintosh or Audacity for PC]). The specialist and the teacher recorded their scripts on the topic after school and posted the podcast on the class blog. In class the next day, they told the students what a podcast was, showed them their sample on the blog, and mentioned that others could listen to the podcast. To continue, the specialist developed a web page with links to resources about Lewis and Clark and their achievements. Each student was assigned to a podcast to listen to from this web page after the teacher demonstrated how to rewind, replay, pause, and take notes while listening to the podcast. After the listening activity, one group developed a question-and-answer podcast about Lewis and Clark and the rest of the class listened to it on the blog, submitted comments, and discussed it. After this introduction to podcasts, each student was assigned a state in the Midwest U.S. to start their research and to use what was found to write and script their own individual podcasts. The teacher suggested to them, "Create a podcast that will convince our U.S. president to select your state to live in. Imagine that the president will listen to each of your podcasts to make a decision about this." Then the school reading specialist was invited as a guest to the class to talk about ear-catching opening lines, descriptive language as a way to sell the features of a state to a listener, and interesting closings. The teacher also gave the students a rubric that showed how their work would be evaluated after their podcasts were on the blog. Evaluation included: Did they create a polished product for the web? Did they reach a diverse and real audience? Did they improve their writing? Did their listening skills improve? Did they get involved

with podcasts and blogs (two tools of the twenty-first century)? Did they get a positive response from parents, family, and friends?[1] To integrate technology further, students could access the application Map Machine, a way to print country, regional, and continent maps off the web along with geographic facts and photos, and develop a folder of material for the unit. See http://java.nationalgeographic.com/studentatlas/.

A Focus on English Language Learners

Ask some students each day to take turns sitting in the class Geography Chair (a class chair or perhaps a canvas-backed chair similar to a movie director's chair) before small groups or the whole class and describe what each would say to the U.S. president (1) if he or she were a person trying to convince the president to live in your state, (2) if he or she were talking to the president taking the persona of an object that was famous in your state, or (3) if he or she were the U.S. president and trying to choose a state to move to at a later date. Native-language peers can be partners to assist ELLs.

CHAPTER OBJECTIVES

Specifically, as you construct your understanding of the depth and breadth of the responsibilities of being an elementary school classroom teacher, upon the completion of this chapter, you should be able to:

1. Demonstrate your developing understanding of the concepts of professionalism/commitment and the basic areas of professional responsibilities of a beginning teacher.
2. Demonstrate your understanding of selected instructional competencies such as teacher use of

   praise, multilevel instruction, and hands-on and minds-on learning.
3. Demonstrate your understanding of the contrast between teacher facilitating behaviors and instructional strategies.
4. Describe the decision-making and thought-processing phases of instruction and one or more of the types of decisions you could make during each phase.
5. Develop a profile and a statement about your own emerging teaching style.

As shown in the teacher vignette, the primary expectation of any teacher is to facilitate student learning. As an elementary school classroom teacher, your professional responsibilities will extend well beyond the ability to work effectively with a group of children in a classroom attending school from approximately 8:30 a.m. until mid-afternoon. Attending school can be stressful for students—and teachers. Look at Mrs. Green, the new teacher, in *The Class from the Black Lagoon* (Scholastic, 2009) written by M. Thaler and illustrated by J. Lee. On the first day of school, Mrs. Green is anxious because of the things she has heard about her incoming class. Many worrisome thoughts turn into questions: How will she respond to the challenges as a new teacher? Are the students really as "weird" as she is led to believe? Did the last three

teachers retire because of the students' behavior? Will she be allowed to teach or be blocked by their actions? What can be in her survival kit for this class? The point is that teachers like Mrs. Green show they think ahead about their responsibilities and plan for their classes in many ways.

In this chapter, you will learn about the different responsibilities you will assume, as Mrs. Green did, and the competencies and behaviors necessary for fulfilling them. Four categories of responsibilities and important competencies are identified. The four categories are: (a) your commitment to children as learners and to the teaching profession; (b) your noninstructional responsibilities; (c) your instructional responsibilities and fundamental teaching behaviors; and (d) your responsibility as a reflective decision maker.

THE TEACHER'S PROFESSIONALISM AND COMMITMENT

The classroom teacher is expected to demonstrate commitment to the school's mission and to the personal as well as the intellectual development of the children. Not only do the most accomplished teachers expect, demand, and receive positive results in learning from their students while in the classroom, they are also interested and involved in the activities of the children outside the classroom, and willing to sacrifice personal time to give them attention and guidance.

Noninstructional Responsibilities

The daily behaviors of the teacher with professional commitments take on a very real dimension when you consider specific noninstruction-related and instruction-related responsibilities of the classroom teacher. Shown in Figure 3.1

Related to the Students

1. Be knowledgeable about activities of interest to the students.

2. Become familiar with the backgrounds of the students.

3. Get acquainted with your role in administering standardized assessments of student achievement.

4. Help children cope with frightening situations (post-9/11 aftermath) regarding their emotional safety by answering questions with simple, accurate information (no morbid details), by providing extra attention and comfort when needed, by modeling tolerance and understanding, and by allowing students to express their concerns (Merrow, 2004).

5. Help children value ideas and exploration regarding their intellectual safety and grow toward knowledge building as they make mistakes and raise questions so that learning happens (Merrow, 2004).

6. Help students see a physically safe school by keeping your presence where you can be seen. Be out in the halls where you can be talking with students as a responsible adult. Know most students by name, keep in contact with the students, and keep an eye on them because you have learned to like them. Always speak to strangers and find out what they are doing in the school.

Related to the School and Community

7. Become familiar with the school campus and community and be knowledgeable about a healthy school climate that contributes to a safe school. Teachers in a healthy school climate offer the following: They act as good models; send consistent, coherent messages about willingness to learn an appreciation for diverse points of view to students and their families; show depth of the school's mission statements through the use of books, songs, curriculum, and classroom practices; demonstrate democracy through shared decision making through class meetings and other practices; create opportunities for as many people in the community to become involved as possible; emphasize service to others that is valued through service learning; support strong relationships—student to student, teacher to student, teacher to family, administrator to teachers, and school to community (Noonan, 2004).

8. Get acquainted with members of the faculty and the support staff.

9. Be knowledgeable about school and district policies.

10. Become knowledgeable about procedures for such routine matters as arranging for and preparing displays for common areas of the school; class dismissal; collection of money for lunch; daily attendance records; distribution and collection of textbooks and other school materials; fire drills, emergency schedules, and severe weather schedules; planning and scheduling of before- and after-school activities; restroom regulations; school assemblies; and sharing of instructional space with other teachers.

11. Perform duties such as maintaining a cheerful, pleasant, productively efficient, and safe learning environment; obtaining materials/audio-visuals/technology needed for each lesson; keeping supplies orderly; supervising students who are helpers.

12. Attend the many conferences that are needed, such as those between teacher and teacher, teacher and resource specialist, teacher and student, and teacher parent/guardian, teacher, student, and parent/guardian, teacher and administrator, and teacher and a parent or community representative.

13. Attend professional meetings such as those of the faculty, the teaching team, other school and district committees, parent-teacher and community groups, and local, regional, state, and national professional organizations.

14. Become familiar with your role in the school's advisory or homeroom program.

15. Take time to relax and enjoy friends, family, and hobbies.

Figure 3.1
Noninstructional responsibilities of the elementary classroom teacher.

are categories of items that should alert you to the many noninstructional matters with which you should become familiar. Beginning teachers often underestimate their importance and the time they require.

Student Physical Safety: Rules and Guidelines

Teachers are responsible for preventing accidents and ensuring that the classroom is as safe as possible. Nevertheless, accidents and resulting injuries do occur to children at school. For instance, a student, during a language arts lesson, is injured by glass from a falling windowpane when the teacher attempts to open a stuck window. A student is injured when the child falls and lands on a lawn-sprinkler head on the playground during recess. While doing a science experiment, a student is burned by a candle flame. So, you need to understand what you can do as a classroom teacher to prevent accidents from happening. And, you need to know what you should and should not do when an accident does happen. One item on the list in Figure 3.1 (item 6) highlights your responsibility for providing a safe environment, both psychological and physical. Classroom safety rules and guidelines are described in Figure 3.2 (often an important basis for discussion with your colleagues). The school in which you ultimately teach will, of course, have its own

separate written rules and guidelines that may be more or less extensive than those found in this figure. Further, the physical safety aspect is highlighted here and the figure is basically a set of common-sense reminders that deserves to be mentioned, and the psychological aspect is discussed later in this chapter and in Chapter 4.

Instructional Responsibilities

The instructional responsibilities you will have as a classroom teacher are portrayed in Figure 3.3. These responsibilities in instruction (along with the areas of class management,[2] assessment, and professional development) are the primary focus of study during the remainder of the content of this resource guide. After reviewing the lists of instructional and noninstructional responsibilities of the classroom teacher, do Application Exercise 3.1.

IDENTIFYING AND BUILDING YOUR INSTRUCTIONAL COMPETENCIES

The overall purpose of this resource guide is to assist you in building your instructional competencies. To begin in

---

Accidents and First Aid

1. Maintain a well-supplied first aid kit in the classroom.

2. Know exactly what to do in case of emergencies, and have emergency procedures posted in the classroom.

3. Whenever an accident happens, notify the school office immediately by telephoning or sending a pair of students to the office.

4. You should give first aid only when necessary to save a child's life or limb. When that is not at risk, then you should follow school policy by referring the student immediately to professional care. When immediate professional care is unavailable and you believe that immediate first aid is necessary, then you can take prudent action, as if you were that child's parent or legal guardian. But you must always be cautious and knowledgeable about what you are doing, so to not cause further injury. To prepare for this, some teachers take beginning first aid courses offered in their local areas.

5. Unless you are a licensed medical professional, you should never give medication to a child, whether prescription or over-the-counter. See your school policy on this since some districts require written permission from the parent/guardian for any required medically approved medications to be taken by a child.

6. Avoid allowing children to overheat or to overexert themselves.

Place-Based Learning (field trip and virtual field trip)

7. When taking children on a field trip, solicit adult help, even when the destination is only a short distance from the school. A recommended guideline is one or more adults for every ten children. If you are interested in a virtual field trip (a webquest or a field trip on a site on the Internet), there is more about this topic in *Looking at Teachers I* in Chapter 4.

Figure 3.2
Safety rules and guidelines for the elementary school teacher and classroom.

1. Prepare the classroom; identify sources and resources.
2. Becoming familiar with relevant curriculum standards and assessment tools.
3. Reacquaint yourself with the developmental characteristics of children.
4. Learn the background of children with special problems who might cause concerns in the classroom.
5. Learn the interests of the children so the lessons and learning activities will reflect those interests.
6. Incorporate the individual learning modalities, learning styles, and capacities of the students into lesson plans.
7. Prepare activities, lessons, and units.
8. Develop techniques and plans for using cross-age tutoring, peer coaching, cooperative learning, project work, and other instructional strategies.
9. Develop an effective classroom management system.
10. Read student papers.
11. Assess and record student progress and achievements.
12. Reflect on and participate in professional growth and development, which may include attending university courses, workshops, and other presentations offered by the school district or professional organizations, and reading professional literature.
13. Devote time to team planning; student, parent conferences.

Figure 3.3
Instructional responsibilities of the classroom teacher.

this chapter, we want to introduce you to the identification and presentation of twenty-two specific competencies (such as slowing one's speech to ease a child's ability to listen). You will want to continue to reflect on and to build upon these competencies through your study of the remaining chapters of this book and, indeed, throughout your professional career—perhaps even investigating M. M. Kennedy's taxonomy of teacher qualities with dimensions of personal resources, performance, and effectiveness.[3]

CHARACTERISTICS OF THE COMPETENT CLASSROOM TEACHER: AN ANNOTATED TEACHER PROGRESS REPORT CARD

Before you read further, we want to caution you to please not feel overwhelmed by the following list on our Simulated Teacher Progress Report Card in Figure 3.4; helpful annotations are on the back of the simulated card; it may well be that no teacher expertly models all of the characteristics that are listed on the card. However, the characteristics on the Teacher Progress Card do represent an ideal model to strive for in four important professional education areas—management, instruction, assessment, and professional development.

If it would be helpful to your group, we suggest its members brainstorm characteristics of the competent

classroom teacher. Each member then lists on a piece of paper one characteristic about which he or she feels strongly. Members then spend two minutes writing examples or further explanations of the characteristic. The members stop, pass their papers clockwise, read what has already been written, and add a paragraph of new ideas. Continue until all members have commented on every characteristic and discussed the results. Then read the following discussion of the specific teacher behaviors that facilitate student learning to help in your development of these competencies that permeate this resource guide.

TEACHER BEHAVIORS THAT FACILITATE STUDENT LEARNING

Your ability to perform your instructional responsibilities effectively is directly dependent upon your knowledge of children and how they best learn and your knowledge of and the quality of your teaching skills. As we believe, development of your strategy repertoire along with your skills in using specific strategies should be ongoing throughout your teaching career. To be most effective, you need a large repertoire from which to select a specific strategy for a particular goal with a distinctive group of children. Related to specific strategies/behaviors, the top ten qualities of an outstanding educator have been

FOR YOUR NOTES

APPLICATION EXERCISE 3.1

*Reviewing the Professional Responsibilities
of a First-Year Teacher*

Instructions: The purpose of this exercise is to work cooperatively and collaboratively and review the responsibilities of a first-year teacher. With your teacher candidates, divide into six groups. Within each group, each member should play one of the following roles: (a) group facilitator, (b) recorder, (c) materials manager, or (d) reporter. The group is to choose one of these six categories of responsibilities.

1. Audiovisual/media
2. Classroom environment
3. Clerical
4. Instructional
5. Professional activities
6. Supervision

The group should then read the responsibilities for its selected category listed on the following cards and arrange them in prioritized order, beginning with the most important. The group facilitator will lead this discussion. Under the guidance of the materials manager, the group may cut the cards apart so that they can be physically manipulated as priorities are discussed. The recorder should take notes of the group's work, which can then be discussed to develop the report that will be made to the class.

After a prearranged discussion time, recall the entire class and ask each reporter to share the group's (a) prioritized order of responsibilities and (b) estimate of the amount of time that a beginning teacher might devote to these responsibilities each week.

As each group reports, all members of the class should enter its list of priorities and time estimate on the Recap Sheet.

After completion of this exercise, the class may wish to discuss the group dynamics of this model of cooperative learning (see Chapter 10). For discussion in either large or small groups, key questions might be:

1. Would you use this form of discussion in your own teaching?

2. How would you divide a class into groups of four?

Other questions may be generated by the group work. *Example:* Could a group member design a generic template for this activity? In what way would this be helpful?

☞

CARDS FOR EXERCISE 3.1
AUDIOVISUAL/MEDIA RESPONSIBILITIES

Selecting, ordering, and returning cassettes, films, videodisks, and other materials

Preparing and operating equipment	Reviewing selected materials
Planning class introduction to the audiovisual materials	Other responsibilities as determined

Estimated hours a beginning teacher will devote to audiovisual/media responsibilities each week = _____

CARDS FOR EXERCISE 3.1
CLASSROOM ENVIRONMENT RESPONSIBILITIES

Planning and constructing displays	Preparing bulletin boards
Reading, announcing, and posting class notices	Managing a classroom library
Opening and closing windows, arranging furniture, cleaning the writing board	Other responsibilities as determined

Estimated hours a beginning teacher will devote to classroom environment responsibilities each week = _____

CARDS FOR EXERCISE 3.1
CLERICAL RESPONSIBILITIES

Maintaining attendance and tardy records	Entering grades, scores, or marks into a record book or onto the computer
Preparing progress and grade reports	Typing, drawing, and duplicating instructional materials
Locating resource ideas and materials to support lessons	Other responsibilities as determined

Estimated hours a beginning teacher will devote to clerical responsibilities each week = _____

CARDS FOR EXERCISE 3.1
INSTRUCTIONAL RESPONSIBILITIES

Giving additional instruction (e.g., to students who need one-to-one attention, those who have been absent, or small review groups)	Correcting student work
Preparing special learning materials	Preparing, reading, and scoring tests; helping students self-evaluate
Writing information on the board	Preparing long-range and daily lesson plans
Grouping for instruction	Other responsibilities as determined

Estimated hours a beginning teacher will devote to instructional responsibilities each week = _____

CARDS FOR EXERCISE 3.1
PROFESSIONAL ACTIVITIES RESPONSIBILITIES

Researching and writing teacher reports	Attending teachers' and school district meetings
Planning and attending parent–teacher meetings	Attending local teachers' organization meetings
Attending state, regional, and national professional organizations; taking university classes	Other responsibilities as determined

Estimated hours a beginning teacher will devote to professional activities responsibilities each week = _____

CARDS FOR EXERCISE 3.1
SUPERVISION RESPONSIBILITIES

Supervising before- or after-school activities	Supervising hallways, lunchrooms, and bathrooms
Supervising student assemblies	Supervising field trips
Supervising laboratory activities	Helping students settle disputes
Other responsibilities as determined	

Estimated hours a beginning teacher will devote to supervision responsibilities each week = _____

APPLICATION EXERCISE 3.1 RECAP SHEET

Audiovisual/Media Responsibilities

1. _____
2. _____
3. _____
4. _____
5. _____

   Estimated hours = _____

Classroom Environment Responsibilities

1. _____
2. _____
3. _____
4. _____
5. _____
6. _____

   Estimated hours = _____

Clerical Responsibilities

1. _____
2. _____
3. _____
4. _____
5. _____
6. _____

   Estimated hours = _____

Instructional Responsibilities

1. _____
2. _____
3. _____
4. _____
5. _____
6. _____
7. _____
8. _____

   Estimated hours = _____

Professional Activities Responsibilities

1. _____
2. _____
3. _____
4. _____
5. _____
6. _____

  Estimated hours = _____

Supervision Responsibilities

1. _____
2. _____
3. _____
4. _____
5. _____
6. _____
7. _____

  Estimated hours = _____

TEACHER PROGRESS CARD

CHARACTERISTICS OF THE COMPETENT CLASSROOM TEACHER

NAME _____ SCHOOL YEAR _____

Symbols   S—Satisfactory   N—Needs improvement

MANAGEMENT

1. The teacher is quick to recognize a student who may be in need of special attention. _____
2. The teacher uses effective modeling behavior. _____
3. The teacher is nonprejudiced toward gender, sexual orientation, ethnicity, skin color, religion, special needs/disabilities, socioeconomic status, or national origin. _____
4. The teacher is open to change, willing to take risks, and to be held accountable. _____
5. The teacher is a capable communicator (e.g., speaks slowly to support a child's listening). _____
6. The teacher has a healthy sense of humor. _____

INSTRUCTION

7. The teacher understands the processes of learning. _____
8. The teacher is knowledgeable about the subject matter content expected to be taught. _____
9. The teacher is an educational broker and a technology partner. _____
10. The teacher makes specific and frequent efforts to demonstrate how the subject content may be related to the lives of the students. _____
11. The teacher organizes the classroom and plans lessons carefully. _____
12. The teacher demonstrates concern for the safety and health of the children. _____
13. The teacher can function effectively as a decision maker. _____

ASSESSMENT

14. The teacher demonstrates optimism for the learning of every student, while providing a constructive and positive environment for learning. _____
15. The teacher demonstrates confidence in every student's ability to learn. _____
16. The teacher is skillful and fair in the employment of strategies for the assessment of student learning. _____

PROFESSIONAL DEVELOPMENT

17. The teacher is in a perpetual learning mode, striving to further develop a repertoire of teaching strategies. _____
18. The teacher is reliable. _____
19. The teacher is skillful in working with parents and guardians, colleagues, administrators, and the school support staff, maintaining and nurturing friendly and ethical professional relationships. _____
20. The teacher is an active member of professional organizations, reads professional journals, dialogues with colleagues, and maintains currency both in methodology and about the students and the subject content the teacher is expected to teach. _____
21. The teacher demonstrates continuing interest in professional responsibilities and opportunities. _____
22. The teacher exhibits a wide range of interests. _____

Figure 3.4
Simulated teacher progress card: characteristics of the competent classroom teacher.

COMMENTS/ANNOTATIONS FOR
CHARACTERISTICS OF A COMPETENT CLASSROOM TEACHER

About Management: Progress Report Comments

Characteristic #1. A competent teacher, such as you, is alert to recognize any student who demonstrates behaviors indicating a need for special attention. You know how and where to refer the student, doing so with minimal class disruption and without embarrassment to the child. For example, a pattern of increasingly poor attendance or of steady negative-attention-seeking behaviors are two of the more obvious early signals of a troubled child, one who is potentially at risk of dropping out of school—and you recognize these patterns.

Characteristic #2. As part of your management system, your own behaviors are consistent with those expected of your students. When, for example, you want your students to demonstrate regular and punctual attendance, to have their work done on time, and to have their materials each day for learning, then you do likewise. You model similar behaviors and attitudes for children—cooperative behavior, respect for the rights and possessions of others, an open and inquisitive mind, critical thinking, and proper communication skills. As a teacher, you serve as an important role model for your students. Whether you realize it or not, your behavior sends important messages to students that complement curriculum content. By doing this, you serve the children well when you practice what you teach and when you model inclusive and collaborative approaches to learning.

Characteristic #3. You are cognizant of how teachers, male and female, knowingly or unknowingly, historically have mistreated female students and you avoid those same errors in your own teaching. Of course, this means no sexual innuendoes, religious or ethnic jokes, or racial slurs. It means that you learn about and attend to the needs of individual students in your classroom. It means having high expectations for every student.

Characteristic #4. You realize that if there were no difference between what is and what can be, than formal schooling would be of little value. As a competent teacher, you know about the historical and traditional values of knowledge, but also of the value of change, and you are willing to carefully plan and experiment, to move between that which is known and that which is not.[4]

Characteristic #5. As a competent teacher, you use thoughtfully selected words, carefully planned questions, expressive voice inflections, useful pauses, meaningful gestures, active listening, and productive and nonconfusing body language. Some of these are carefully and thoughtfully planned before or during instruction and others have, through your practice and reflection, become second-nature skills.

Characteristic #6. You realize that the positive effects of appropriate humor (that is, humor that is not self-deprecating or disrespectful of others) on learning are well established (Reid, 2002). You understand that humor has been known to have these effects: an increase in immune system activity; a decrease in stress-producing hormones; a drop in the pulse rate; a reduction in feelings of anxiety, tension, and stress; an activation in T-cells for the immune system; supports antibodies that fight against harmful microorganisms and gamma interferon; supports a hormone that fights viruses and regulates cell growth; and increases blood oxygen. Because of these effects, you consider that humor is a stimulant to not only healthy living, but to creativity and higher-level thinking. You realize that the students appreciate and learn more from a teacher who shares a healthy sense of humor and laughs with (not at) the children.[5, 6]

About Instruction: Progress Report Comments

Characteristic #7. You ensure that students understand the lesson objectives, your expectations, and the classroom procedures. You make them feel welcomed in your classroom, get them involved in the learning activities, and encourage them to have some control over the pacing of their own learning. Furthermore, when preparing lessons, you (a) consider the unique characteristics of each student; (b) see that content is presented in reasonably small doses—and in a logical and coherent sequence, (c) use learning activities that engage all learning modalities, with opportunities for guided practice and reinforcement; and (d) frequently check for student comprehension (we suggest one check every minute or so) to ensure that the students are learning. You accomplish checks for comprehension in different ways, such as by the questions you and the children ask during the lesson, by your awareness and understanding of student facial expressions and body language, and by the use of various kinds of checklists.[7]

Characteristic #8. You have both historical understanding and current knowledge of the structure of those subjects you are expected to teach, and you are aware of the facts, principles, concepts, and skills needed for those subjects.

Characteristic #9. You learn where and how to discover information about content you are expected to teach. You realize that you cannot know everything there is to know about each subject—indeed, you know that you will not always be able to predict all that will be learned—but you are knowledgeable about where and how to best research it and how to assist your students in developing those same skills. Among other things, this means that you are computer literate; that is, you have the ability to understand and use computers for research, writing, and communicating—as you do for reading and writing in verbal literacy.

Characteristic #10. You make a potentially dry and dull topic significant and bring it alive when you teach it. Regardless of the topic, one of the significant characteristics of your effectiveness is that you make the topic come alive and relevant to yourself and to your students, helping the students to make relevant connections. You realize that educational studies point out what should be obvious: Children don't learn much from dull, meaningless "drill and kill" exercises and assignments. Such unmotivated teaching may be one of the principal causes of student loss of interest and motivation and subsequent estrangement from school. Obtaining ideas from professional journals, attending workshops, and communicating with colleagues either personally or via electronic bulletin boards and websites, and using project-based and interdisciplinary thematic instruction, are ways you have of discovering how to make a potentially dry and boring topic interesting and alive for students (and for yourself).

Characteristic #11. Thoughtfully, you prepare and revise activities, lessons, and long-range plans or units reflectively, and implement them with creative, motivating, and effective strategies and skill.

(Continued)

Figure 3.4 *(Continued)*

Characteristic #12. As a competent teacher, you consistently model safety procedures (see for example, Figure 3.2), ensuring precautions necessary to protect the safety of children. You strive to maintain a comfortable room temperature with adequate ventilation and to prevent safety hazards in the classroom. You encourage students who are ill to recuperate at home and to get well. Rather than bringing germs to school, you model this same expectation. You are aware that the Centers for Disease Control has recommended that anyone with a cough or other respiratory symptoms immediately don a surgical mask (at a medical facility, this also means isolation from others) to minimize the threat of lung infections such as influenza, tuberculosis, and pneumonia. If you suspect that a student may be ill or may be suffering from neglect or abuse at home, you promptly act upon that concern.

Characteristic #13. You realize that the elementary school classroom is a complex place, busy with fast-paced activities. As a competent teacher, you are in control of classroom events rather than being controlled by them. You initiate, rather than merely react, are proactive, and in control of your interactions; you have learned how to manage time to analyze and develop effective interpersonal behaviors.

About Assessment: Progress Report Comments

Characteristic #14. As part of your assessment methods, both common sense and research tell you clearly that students enjoy and learn better from you when you are positive and optimistic, encouraging, nurturing, and happy, rather than from a teacher who is negative and pessimistic, discouraging, uninterested, and grumpy.

Characteristic #15. For a student, nothing is more satisfying than when you demonstrate confidence in that student's abilities. Unfortunately for some children, your show of confidence may be the only positive indicator that child ever receives. As a competent teacher, you demonstrate this confidence with each and every student. This doesn't mean that you must personally like every student with whom you will ever come into contact; it does mean that you accept each one as a person of dignity and who is worthy of receiving your respect and professional skills. You remember that each child is a work in progress.

Characteristic #16. As a competent teacher, you are knowledgeable about the importance of providing immediate intensive intervention when learning problems become apparent; you implement appropriate learning assessment tools and avoid the abuse of power you have through the assessment process.

About Professional Development: Progress Report Comments

Characteristic #17. As a competent teacher, you are a good student, and often continue your own learning by reflecting on and assessing your work, by attending workshops, by studying the work of others, and by talking with students, parents and guardians, and colleagues.

Characteristic #18. As a competent teacher, you can be relied on to fulfill professional responsibilities, promises, and commitments. You realize that a teacher who cannot be relied on is quick to lose credibility with colleagues and administrators (as well as with students, parents, guardians, and community members). You know that, regardless of the teacher's potential for effectiveness, an unreliable teacher is an incompetent teacher. And for whatever reason, a teacher who is chronically absent from his or her teaching duties is a teacher at risk.

Characteristic #19. You realize that teachers, parents, and guardians, administrators, cooks, bus drivers, custodians, secretaries, and other adults of the school community all share one common purpose, and that is to serve the education of the children. It is done best when they do it collaboratively. As an exemplary school and a skillful teacher, you work with others to ensure that parents or guardians are involved in their children's learning.

Characteristic #20. As a competent teacher, you are a learner among learners. This learning is supported through workshops, advanced university course work, and coaching and training; through the acquisition of further knowledge by reading and study; and through collaboration with colleagues and role modeling of other educators. Through your precredential work and beyond, you will be in a perpetual learning mode about teaching and learning.

Characteristic #21. Knowing that ultimately each and every school activity has an effect upon the classroom, you assume an active interest in the school community. You realize that the purpose of the school is to serve the education of the children, and the classroom is the primary, but not only, place where this occurs. You understand that every committee meeting, school event, team meeting, faculty meeting, school board meeting, office, program, and any other planned function that is related to school life shares in the ultimate purpose of better serving the education of the children who attend your school.

Characteristic #22. You realize that this includes professional interest in the activities of the students and the many aspects of the school and its surrounding community. As a competent teacher, you are interesting to others because of your interests; and when you have varied interests, you will more often motivate and capture the attention of more students. You realize that a teacher with no interests outside the classroom is likely, for the children, to be an exceedingly dull teacher.

Teacher Progress:

The basic characteristics of a competent classroom teacher have been satisfactorily met in:

Management _____   Instruction _____   Assessment _____   Professional Development _____

Assignment for next year: _____

Figure 3.4 Simulated teacher progress card: characteristics of the competent classroom teacher. (*Continued*)

identified by African American students and include the following: (a) explains things well; (b) makes work interesting; (c) gives extra help; (d) has patience; (e) is fair; (f) is friendly; (g) has a sense of humor; (h) challenges students academically; (i) is intelligent; and (j) makes the work relevant (Thompson, 2002). In addition, you need to develop skill in using the strategy that you choose for a particular goal. In support of this, this section is designed to help you begin building your specific strategies repertoire and to develop your skills in using these strategies.

The basic teacher behaviors create the conditions needed to enable students to think and to learn, whether the learning is a further understanding of concepts from the teacher's **prior knowledge,** the internalization of attitudes and values, the development of thinking processes, or the actuating of the most complex behaviors. The basic teacher behaviors are those that produce the following results: (a) the students are physically and mentally engaged in the learning activities; (b) instructional time is efficiently used; and (c) classroom distractions and interruptions are minimal. The effectiveness with which a teacher carries out the basic behaviors can be measured by how well the students learn.

THE TEACHER AS A REFLECTIVE DECISION MAKER

During any single school day, you will make hundreds of decisions. Some decisions will have been made prior to meeting your students for instruction, others will be made during the instructional activities, and yet still others are made later as you reflect on the school day. Now let's consider further the decision-making and thought-processing phases of instruction.

Decision-Making Phases of Instruction

Instruction can be divided into four decision-making and thought-processing phases: (a) the planning or preactive phase, (b) the teaching or interactive phase, (c) the analyzing and evaluating or reflective phase, and (d) the application or projective phase. Here are some clarifying explanations:

- The *preactive* phase consists of all those intellectual functions and decisions you will make prior to actual instruction. This includes decisions about the target goals and objectives, homework assignments, what children already know and can do, appropriate learning activities, questions to be asked (and possible answers), and the selection and preparation of instructional materials and the classroom.
- The *interactive* phase includes all the decisions made during the spontaneous teaching act. This includes

maintaining student attention, questions to be asked, types of feedback given to children, and ongoing adjustments to the lesson plan. Decisions made by you during this phase are likely to be more intuitive, unconscious, and routine than those made during the planning phase.

- The *reflective* phase is the time you will take to reflect on, analyze, and judge the decisions and behaviors that occurred during the interactive phase. It is during reflection that you make decisions about student learning, student grades, feedback given to parents and guardians, and adjustments on the content and instruction to follow.
- As a result of this reflection, decisions are made to use what was learned in subsequent teaching actions. At this point, you are in the projective phase, abstracting from your reflection and projecting your analysis into subsequent teaching behaviors.

Reflection, Locus of Control, and Teacher Responsibility

During the reflective phase, teachers have a choice of whether to assume full responsibility for the instructional outcomes or whether to assume responsibility for only the positive outcomes of the planned instruction while placing the blame for the negative outcomes on outside forces (e.g., parents and guardians, society in general, peers, other teachers, administrators, textbooks). Where the responsibility for outcomes is placed is referred to as **locus of control.**

Teachers who are intrinsically motivated and professionally accomplished tend to assume full responsibility for the instructional outcomes, regardless of whether or not the outcomes are as intended from the planning phase.[8] Of course, every teacher realizes that there are factors that the teacher cannot control, such as the negative effects on children from alcohol and drug abuse, gangs, and poverty, so they must do what they can within the confines of the classroom and their time with the children to reduce negative effects of such outside factors. History is full of examples of how a relatively few but positive moments with a truly caring and knowledgeable teacher can drastically change, for the better, the life of a child who, until then, had a history of mostly negative experiences. Now, further your understanding of reflective decision-making by doing Application Exercise 3.2.

TEACHING STYLE

Teaching style is the way teachers teach, which includes their distinctive mannerisms complemented by their choices of teaching behaviors and strategies. A teacher's style affects the way that the teacher presents

FOR YOUR NOTES

information and interacts with the students. It clearly is the manner and pattern of those interactions with students that determine a teacher's effectiveness in promoting student learning, positive attitudes about learning, and students' self-esteem.

A teacher's style is determined by the teacher's personal characteristics (especially the teacher's own learning style), experiences, and knowledge of research findings about how children learn. Teaching style can be altered, intentionally or unintentionally, as a result of changes in any of these three areas. While there are other ways to label and to describe teaching styles, we shall consider two contrasting styles—the traditional and the facilitating styles (see Table 3.1)—to emphasize that while today's teacher must use aspects from each (that is, be eclectic in style choice), there must be a strong inclination toward the facilitating style.

Multilevel Instruction

As emphasized in Chapter 2, children in your classroom have their own independent ways of knowing and learning. It is important to try to attend to how each student best learns and to where each student is developmentally, that is, to personalize both the content and the methods of learning. In essence, although perhaps not as detailed as are the IEPs prepared for special education students, at various times during the school year, you will be developing personalized educational plans for each student, perhaps in collaboration with members of your teaching team. To accomplish that, you can use multilevel instruction (known also as multitasking). Referring back to

Chapter 2 and the classroom vignette *Looking at Teachers II*, multilevel instruction is when individual students and groups of students are working at different tasks to accomplish the same or different objectives. For example, while some students may be working independently of the teacher—that is, within the facilitating mode of the teacher—others may be receiving explicit instruction—that is, more within the traditional mode.

When integrating student learning, as you will be reviewing in Part II of this resource guide, multitasking is an important and useful, perhaps even obligatory, strategy. Project-based learning is an instructional method that easily allows for the provision of multilevel instruction.

THE THEORETICAL ORIGINS OF TEACHING STYLES AND THEIR RELATIONS TO CONSTRUCTIVISM

Constructivism teaching and the integration of curriculum are not new to education. The importance of constructivism and curriculum integration approaches are found, for example, in the writings of John Dewey,[9] Arthur W. Combs,[10] Jean Piaget,[11] and Lev Vygotsky.[12]

Instructional styles are deeply rooted in certain theoretical assumptions about learners and their development, and while it is beyond the scope of this resource guide to explore deeply into these assumptions, there are, worth mentioning here, three major theoretical positions with research findings, each of which is based on certain philosophical and psychological assumptions

Table 3.1 A Contrast of Two Teaching Styles

Characteristic	Traditional Style	Facilitating Style
Teacher is:	Autocratic	Democratic
	Explicit	Implicit
	Dominative	Interactive
	Formal	Informal
	Informative	Inquiring
	Prescriptive	Reflective
	Curriculum-centered	Student-centered
Classroom is:	Linear	Grouped or circular
	Teacher-centered	Student-centered
Instructional modes are:	Abstract learning	Concrete learning
	Lectures	Peer, cross-age coaching
	Competitive	Cooperative
	Demonstrations	Inquiries by students
	Teacher-centered	Student-centered
	Transmission of information from teacher to students	Dialogue among all with reciprocal teaching, student discussions
	Some problem solving	Problem solving

that suggest different ways of working with children. The theoretical positions are described briefly in the next three paragraphs.

Central to the theoretical positions of **maturationism** (also **romanticism**) is the assumption that the learner's mind is neutral-passive to good-active, and the main focus in teaching should be the addition of new ideas to the subconscious store of old ones. Key persons include Jean J. Rousseau and Sigmund Freud; key instructional strategies include classic lecturing with rote memorization.

A major part of the theoretical position of **behaviorism** is the assumption that the learner's mind is neutral-passive with innate reflexes and needs, and the main focus in teaching should be on the successive, systematic changes in the learner's environment to increase the possibilities of desired behavior responses. Key persons include John Locke, B. F. Skinner, A. H. Thorndike, Robert Gagné, and John Watson; key instructional strategies include programmed instruction and practice and reinforcements as in workbook drill activities.

Linked to the theoretical position of **cognitive-experimentalism** (including **constructivism**) is the assumption that the learner is a neutral-interactive purposeful individual in simultaneous interaction with physical and biological environments. The main focus in teaching should be on facilitating the learner's gain and construction of new perceptions that lead to desired behavioral changes and ultimately to a more fully functioning individual. Key persons are John Dewey and others mentioned earlier; key instructional strategies include discovery, inquiry, project-centered teaching, cooperative and social-interactive learning, and integrated curriculum.

It is our opinion that with a diversity of students, to be most effective, an elementary schoolteacher must be eclectic, but with a strong emphasis toward cognitive-experimentalism-constructivism because of this theory's divergence in learning and the importance given to learning as a change in perception(s). An effective approach is to use, at appropriate times, the best of strategies and knowledgeable instructor behaviors, regardless of whether individually they can be classified within any style dichotomy, such as explicit vs. implicit, formal vs. informal, traditional vs. progressive, or didactic vs. facilitative. Now, to focus on your understanding of your emerging teaching style, do Application Exercise 3.3.

In this chapter, teaching style has been defined as the way teachers teach, their distinctive mannerisms complemented by their choices of teaching behaviors and strategies. Style develops from tradition, from experience, and from research findings. Many variables affect a teacher's style, some of which we know very little about, but what is believed about the reciprocal process of teaching and learning is that to effectively reach the highest percentage of students, the competent teacher must utilize a style that is eclectic. Chapter 4 further helps you identify your own teaching skills and weaknesses, an important next step in the development of a teaching style.

_____

_____

_____

_____

_____

At the completion of this book, you may want to revisit your philosophical statement and perhaps even revise it. It will be useful for you to have your educational philosophy in mind for your teaching interviews at a later date.

Sources: Earlier versions of this concept for developing a philosophical statement were from the early work of Richard D. Kellough and Patricia L. Roberts, _A Resource Guide for Elementary School Teaching: Planning for Competence_ (New York: Macmillan, 1985), pp. 83–85, and William H. Berquist and Steven R. Phillips, _A Handbook for Faculty Development_ (Washington, DC: The Council for Independent Colleges, June 1975), pp. 25–27.

LOOKING AT TEACHERS II
Integrated Technology, Electronic Handheld Devices

In her third-grade classroom, the teacher explained the concept of transplanting. One of her students with learning disabilities in the school's inclusion program got excited when he heard the teacher's explanation about transplanting, and he talked about his idea of transplanting flowers—an idea that led him to a service-learning project. The teacher encouraged the student to present his idea to the youth council at school—this was a group that provided students an opportunity to work through personal problems and make contributions to the school. With the teacher's support, the student and his classmates began planting and transplanting purple pansies to give to different teachers as gifts. The student continued with his interest in transplanting and said he thought the kids needed some shade and looked in a book about trees. He said that the book gave him the idea to plant small trees inside of peat pots first and then transplant them somewhere where people wouldn't step on them.

Eventually, all of the student's classmates were involved in working on a landscaping project for their school. The teacher saw the student's tree-planting idea as the springboard for the class to get involved in scientific research in an interdisciplinary way:

- The students investigated trees, soil conditions, and climate. (science)
- With more research, they learned where to get the seeds. (economics)
- They learned when to start the peat pots, when to set them out, and how to care for the saplings. (botany)

To integrate technology, students used a drawing program such as Sketchy loaded into electronic handheld devices (Palm Pilot) to create drawings of their project.

Working on activities related to content on this service-learning project improved the student's confidence and his grades; in addition, the skills and information that he and his classmates acquired surpassed the content of their third-grade science books.

Related to the value of service learning in a classroom project such as this one, a research agency evaluated the impact of service-learning as an instructional approach and compared classes in the same district and grade level in a western state where service learning *was* and *was not* provided. The results indicated the following:

- On their state (Colorado) standardized reading test, 79 percent of students who participated in service-learning scored ratings of *advanced* or *proficient* compared with 42 percent of nonparticipating students.
- On their state standardized math test, 53 percent of students who participated in service-learning scored *advanced* or *proficient* ratings compared with 38 percent of nonparticipating students.
- On their state standardized writing test, 49 percent of students who participated in service-learning scored ratings of *advanced* or *proficient* compared with 42 percent of nonparticipating students.
- Students who participated in service learning reported higher grade-point averages than comparison students. They also increased their GPAs over time while the comparison students' GPAs decreased over time. It appeared that service learning in this school district contributed to higher achievement.[13]

SUMMARY

You have reviewed the realities of the responsibilities of today's elementary school classroom teacher. Becoming a competent teacher takes time, commitment, concentrated effort, and just plain hard work—nobody truly knowledgeable about it ever said that competent teaching was easy.

You have learned that your professional responsibilities as a teacher will extend well beyond the four walls of the classroom, the six hours of the school day, the five days of the school week, and the many days of the school year. You learned of the many expectations (a) to be committed to young students, to the school's mission, and to

the profession; (b) to develop facilitating behaviors and to provide effective instruction; (c) to fulfill numerous noninstructional responsibilities; and (d) to demonstrate effective decision-making related to the many expectations. As you have read and discussed these responsibilities, you should have begun to fully comprehend the challenge and reality of becoming a competent classroom teacher.

Today, there seems to be much agreement that the essence of the learning process is a combination of self-awareness, self-monitoring, and active reflection. Children learn these skills best when exposed to teachers who themselves effectively model those same behaviors. The most effective teaching and learning is an interactive process and involves not only learning, but also thinking about learning and learning how to learn.

Related to the teaching-learning process, you reviewed that teaching style is the way teachers teach, their distinctive mannerisms complemented by their choices of teaching behaviors and strategies. Style develops from tradition, from one's beliefs and experiences, and from one's knowledge of the best of research findings. You began the development of your philosophy about teaching and learning, a philosophical statement that should be useful to you during later job interviews.

Exciting research findings continue to emerge from several related areas: learning, conceptual development and thinking, and neurophysiology. The findings continue to support the hypothesis that an elementary school classroom teacher's best teaching style choice is eclectic with an emphasis on a facilitating style, at least until the day arrives when students of certain styles of learning can be practically matched to teachers with particular teaching styles. The future may give us additional insight into the relationships among pedagogy, pedagogical styles, and student thinking and learning.

What's to Come. The next, and final, chapter of Part I in this resource guide presents ways of establishing an effective learning environment within which to carry out your professional responsibilities. After finishing Chapter 4, you'll be interested in extending your competencies with one or more of the interactions in the ending section, Extending My Professional Competency.

EXTENDING MY PROFESSIONAL COMPETENCY

With Discussion

Philosophy of Education. If a colleague asks me to articulate my philosophy of education, what will I say? **To do:** To prepare for your response, refer back to Application Exercise 3.3 in this chapter. Indicate your understanding of how children learn and your responsibility as a classroom teacher in one handwritten page. Give your written philosophy to someone in your group for feedback and discuss any parts that indicate professionalism and commitment. Discuss how your philosophy will affect your teaching style. You may rewrite your statement from time to time, but save it; you will be revisiting it in Chapter 11.

With Video

Video Activity: Educational Practice. In what way can I identify in the video, *Active Learning*, at least one specific example of educational practice? Perhaps it will be constructivist learning, teacher responsibility, decision-making, or multilevel instruction in the video that

supports an exemplary practice or theory as presented in this chapter. Do I see an example of any practice in the video that seems contradictory to what was discussed in this chapter?

myeducationlab

Go to the Video Examples section of Topic #3: Classroom Management in the MyEducationLab for your course to view the video entitled "Active Learning."

With Portfolio

Portfolio Planning. How can I continue my professional portfolio and show my knowledge of educational practice in connection with Principles 2, 3, and 5 of INTASC and Standards 2, 3, 5, and 7 of NBPTS as seen on the inside of the front cover of this book? **To do:** To continue your portfolio, you can develop and write a succinct one- to two-page paper explaining your knowledge of a few expectations, responsibilities, and facilitating behaviors of a classroom teacher. Label your paper as Behaviors of a Classroom Teacher, and after reading and interacting with Chapter 3 in this book, state how you have started developing your competency for one of the following objectives for this chapter:

- My developing understanding of professionalism/ commitment and the basic areas of responsibilities of a beginning teacher.
- My understanding of selected instructional competencies such as teacher use of praise, multilevel instruction, and hands-on and minds-on learning.
- Return to the beginning of this chapter for the remaining objectives.Place your paper in your portfolio folder or in your computer file. Note there are portfolio building suggestions on www.MyEducationLab.com.

With Teacher Tests Study Guide

Teacher Tests for Future Licensing and Certification. If I wanted to prepare for taking a state teacher test to qualify for my teaching certificate/license, how could I begin? **To do:** For this chapter, the constructed-response-type question similar to those found on state tests for teacher licensing and certification is found in Appendix A, *Teacher Tests Study Guide*. The question helps you take another look at the classroom vignette found in the *Looking at Teachers II* section at the end of this chapter. Write your response and, if you wish, discuss it with another teaching candidate. If appropriate, use one or two of your colleague's suggestions to help you change your response to the question. Place your response in a Teacher Test Study Guide folder or type/scan into a computer file. Plan to review and reread for study purposes before taking a scheduled teacher test.

With Target Topics for Teacher Tests (TTTT)

If I wanted to start now and prepare for taking a state teacher test for licensing and certification and review subject matter content about facilitating behaviors of an elementary classroom teacher, how could I begin? **To do:** Consider reviewing Target Topics for Teacher Tests (TTTT) in the subject index. To assist you as you prepare to take a teacher test, bullets (•) have been placed by selected word entries in the subject index and stand for Target Topics for Teacher Tests. The bullets highlight the core subject matter—instructional responsibilities, decision-making, multilevel instruction, teaching styles, and other areas—that the authors suggest can be reviewed in preparation for taking a teacher test similar to your state's test or the Praxis II Principles of Learning and Teaching exam.

WITH READING

Bondy, E. (2000). Warming Up to Classroom Research in a Professional Development School. *Contemporary Education, 72*(1), 8–13.

Good, T. L., and Brophy, J. E. (2003). *Looking in Classrooms.* (9th ed., Ch. 10). New York: Addison-Wesley Longman.

Gunzelmann, B. (2004, Fall). Hidden Dangers Within Our Schools: What Are These Safety Problems and How Can We Fix Them? *Educational Horizons, 83*(1), 66–76.

Kounin, J. (1970). *Discipline and Group Management in the Classroom.* (New York: Holt, Rinehart and Winston).

Marzano, R. J., Marzano, J. S., and Pickering, D. J. (2003). *Classroom Management That Works: Research-Based Strategies for Every Teacher.* Alexandria, VA: Association for Supervision and Curriculum Development.

Merrow, J. (2004, Fall). Safety and Excellence. *Educational Horizons, 83*(1), 19–32.

Noonan, J. (2004, Fall). School Climate and the Safe School: Seven Contributing Factors. *Educational Horizons, 83*(1), 61–65.

Reid, R. (2002). *Something Funny Happened at the Library: How to Create Humorous Programs for Children and Young Adults.* Chicago: American Library Association.

Thompson, G. L. (2002). Elementary Teachers In *African American Teens Discuss Their Schooling Experiences.* Needham Heights: Greenwood.

Thompson, G. L. (2003). *What African American Parents Want Educators to Know.* Needham Heights: Greenwood.

Thompson, G. L. (2003). *What Teachers Want to Know But Are Afraid to Ask about African American Students.* San Francisco: Jossey-Bass.

WITH NOTES

1. A. M. Dlott, A (Pod)cast of Thousands, *Educational Leadership*, pp. 80–82 (April 2007).
2. J. S. Kounin, *Discipline and Group Management in Classrooms* (New York: Holt, Rinehart, and Winston, 1970).
3. M. M. Kennedy, Sorting Out Teacher Quality, *Phi Delta Kappan, 90*(1), 59–63 (2008).
4. To see the value of change, you may be interested in learning more about Expeditionary Learning Outward Bound (ELOB) schools at www.elschools.org or visit several ELOB school sites such as Odyssey Elementary Charter School (Denver, CO) at www.odysseydenver.org/, Springdale Memphis Magnet School (Memphis, TN) at www.mcsk12.net/schools/springdalemagnet.es/site/index.shtml, or Alice B. Beal Elementary Magnet School (Springfield, MA) http:www.sps.springfield.ma.us/schoolsites/beal/default.asp
5. S. Feiman-Nemser, What New Teachers Need to Learn, *Educational Leadership, 60*(8), 25–29 (May 2003).
6. R. D. Kellough, *Your First Year of Teaching: Guidelines for Success*, 5th ed. (Boston: Pearson, 2009), p. 76.
7. S. M. Brookhart, *Grading* (Upper Saddle River, NJ: Merrill Prentice Hall, 2004); and T. L. Good and J. E. Brophy, *Looking in Classrooms*, 8th ed. (New York: Longman, 2000), p. 142.
8. M. Ness, Lessons of a First-Year Teacher, *Phi Delta Kappan, 82*, 700–701 (2001); S. Pope, Journal Reflections of a First-Year Teacher, *Learning Languages, 7*(2), 8–10 (2002 Winter).
9. J. Dewey's classic work, *How We Think* (Boston: Heath, 1933).
10. A. W. Combs (Ed.), *Perceiving, Behaving, and Becoming: A New Focus for Education* (Arlington, VA: 1962 ASCD Yearbook, Association for Supervision and Curriculum Development, 1962); You might be interested in the revisit to this 1962 yearbook with H. J. Freiberg's (Ed.), *Perceiving, Behaving, Becoming: Lessons Learned* (Alexandria, VA: Association for Supervision and Curriculum Development, 1999).
11. Read the original words of J. Piaget in *Science of Education and the Psychology of the Child* (New York: Orion, 1970).
12. See L., Vygotsky's early work, *Minds in Society: The Development of Higher Psychological Processes* (Cambridge, MA: Harvard University Press, 1978).
13. L. Turner, Service Learning and Student Achievement. *Educational Horizons, 81*(4), 188–189 (2003).

4

What Do I Need to Know to Manage an Effective, Safe, and Supportive Learning Environment?

Visual Chapter Organizer and Overview

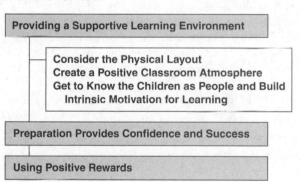

The Importance of Perceptions

Classroom Control: Its Meaning—Past and Present

Historical Meaning of Classroom Control
Today's Meaning of Classroom Control and the Concept of Classroom Management
Classroom Management: Contributions of Some Leading Authorities
Developing My Own Effective Approach to Classroom Management

Providing a Supportive Learning Environment

Consider the Physical Layout
Create a Positive Classroom Atmosphere
Get to Know the Children as People and Build Intrinsic Motivation for Learning

Preparation Provides Confidence and Success

Using Positive Rewards

LOOKING AT TEACHERS I

Integrated Technology, Virtual Field Trips

In a fifth-grade classroom with a goal of supporting the students as a community of learners, the teacher used videoconferencing technology (high-speed Internet connection, computer, camera for videoconferencing, large screen) to introduce her students to a virtual field trip to Crystal Cove State Park (California)—a place they might otherwise not see on a field trip because of several factors—the school's low budget, a need for years-ahead fundraising, and student safety concerns. Other obstacles were difficulty in getting required permission forms back on time from parents or guardians, the hassle of

scheduling a safe bus with a vetted driver, too much emphasis on test scores to ignore academics for a day, and the time constraints of returning by the close of the school day so students can return home via their usual arrangements. With the school's available integrated technology for a virtual field trip, a California park ranger, on camera on the large screen in the room, taught a lesson on tide-pool ecology. It seems that most students had never visited a real tide pool and some had never been to an ocean. However, a few brought shells from home and blew on them to make different sounds during the lesson. Additionally, the ranger showed the class hermit crabs, octopuses, and starfish while students heard and saw the crashing waves. Because there was a camera showing the students who were in the classroom, the ranger first asked individual students some questions about vertebrates, invertebrates, and bivalves and then answered such questions as, What happens if a poisonous jellyfish stings another one? (Most jellyfish are immune to the poisons of other jellyfish). Teachers like this one utilize some of the virtual field trips available from their state's Parks and Recreation Department. In California for example, the state Parks and Recreation Department's program is called Parks Online Resources for Teachers and Students (PORTS). The program includes virtual visits to state parks in various counties and helps students learn about elephant seals, paleontology, the Gold Rush, and other topics. Further, the rangers' lessons are linked to the science and social studies standards that teachers in public schools are expected to teach. At the closure of this video link to the field trip at Crystal Cove, the students' feedback was positive (e.g., "It was funner than a real field trip," "You got to see more things," "It was a dry-feet, clean-hands trip," "On a real field trip, you don't get to see sea stars and hermit crabs. You just go to the park or the pool."). For more about the use of this integrated technology, you might be interested in your state's Parks and Recreation website. Try GlobalLearn at www.globallearning.org/ (remote expedition teams), Global Schoolnet Foundation at www.gsn.org/ (resources and links) or www.ports.parks.ca.gov.[1]

Virtual Field Trips

Tour of Colonial Williamsburg through videos of historical events, people, and places: www.history.org/trips

Tours of destinations such as California coast for whale migration and Florida for Everglades environment: www.bsu.edu/eft/home2/31digest.php

Tour of NASA Jet Propulsion Lab: http://virtualfieldtrip.jpl.nasa.gov/smmk/top/gates

Tour of exhibits at Smithsonian: http://2k.si.edu/2k/node_rotunda/indexe.htm

A Focus on English Language Learners

Display pictures or outlined drawings of items shown on a virtual field trip. For this trip to Crystal Cove State Park about tide-pool ecology, show pictures/drawings of hermit crabs, octopuses, jellyfish, shells, and starfish. The teacher says he or she will select a picture in his or her mind and the students can guess what it is after the teacher tells something about its looks by playing the familiar visual game, "I Spy." For instance, the teacher might say, "I spy something that is colored yellow" (first clue and the students guess), and then, "I spy something

that reminds me of a star" (second clue and the students guess). Of course, the first student to guess the item becomes the next one to select a picture and give the "I Spy" clues.

To become and remain an effective teacher, as the fifth-grade teacher was in the preceding classroom vignette, you should (a) apply your knowledge of the characteristics and developmental needs of children with whom you work, (b) practice the behaviors that facilitate student learning, and (c) do so in an environment conducive to learning—that includes inviting a park ranger to a video teleconference in your classroom. The first two requirements have been the foci of the first three chapters and the third requirement is the main focus of this final chapter of Part I in this resource guide. The establishment and maintenance of a learning environment derive from one's knowledge about children and how they learn and from careful thought and planning. These responsibilities should not be left for the new teacher to learn on the job in a sink-or-swim situation.

Teachers know that classroom management is vital for instruction to occur effectively. Students who appreciate and value each other are more likely to work well in academic settings. Cooperation is a key element in making this happen. Reading aloud a story about cooperating, such as *Zinnia and Dot* by Lisa Campbell Ernst (Viking, 1992) demonstrates to students that cooperation has lasting rewards. In the case of the two highly-competitive chickens, Zinnia and Dot, who lost all but one egg to a weasel, decide they must band together to protect their offspring. But working together had its problems. Who would sit on the egg? Whose chick would it be once it was hatched? Only by working together do the hens save the baby chick, who grows up with its two loving mothers. Putting aside individual differences and working as a team are two factors that help Zinnia and Dot succeed. Transferring this message to students can help promote a workable classroom environment, and this chapter will provide you with several ways to establish an effective teaching situation in your classroom.

A conducive learning environment in the classroom is one that is psychologically safe, that helps the children to perceive the importance of what is being taught, that helps them realize they can achieve, and that is instructive and supportive in the procedures for learning. While it is important that they learn to control impulses and delay their need for gratification, children are more willing to spend time on a learning task when they perceive value or reward in doing so, when they possess some ownership in planning and carrying out the task, and when they feel they can indeed accomplish the task. Thoughtful and thorough planning of your procedures for classroom management, even the careful placement of the desks/furniture, is as important a part of your proactive (planning) phase of instruction as is the preparation of units and lessons, discussed in Part II. Indeed, classroom management is perhaps the single most important factor that influences student learning.

Thus, this chapter presents guidelines and resources that will help you to establish and manage a classroom environment that is safe for children and favorable to their learning.

CHAPTER OBJECTIVES

Specifically, upon completion of this chapter, you should be able to:

1. Explain, as a teacher, what helpful information about managing a safe and effective classroom you have received.
2. Describe the steps you should take in preparing for a classroom management system that would be implemented the first few days of school and emphasize at least three guidelines for acceptable student behavior.
3. Use knowledge about how other teachers manage their classrooms and begin preparation of the management system (including rewards if you decide to use them) that you will want to explain to your students the first day or first week of school.
4. Describe the value of class meetings and ways some experienced teachers open their meetings.
5. Develop an awareness of at least three common teaching mistakes to avoid and determine the first action you would take in determining measure of control in a selected situation of your choice.

THE IMPORTANCE OF PERCEPTIONS

Unless you believe your students can learn, they will not. Unless your students believe they can learn and until they want to learn, they will not. We all know of, or have heard of, teachers who get the very best from their students, even from those students that many teachers find to be the most challenging to teach. Regardless of individual circumstances, those teachers (a) *know* that, when given adequate support and reinforcement, all children can learn, (b) *expect* the best from each student, (c) *establish* a classroom environment that motivates students to do their best, and (d) *manage* their classrooms to see that class time is efficiently used, that is, with the least amount of distraction to the learning process.

Regardless of how well you have planned for the day's instruction, certain perceptions by students must be in place to support the successful implementation of those plans. Students must perceive that (a) the classroom environment is supportive of their efforts, (b) you care about their learning and they are welcome in your classroom, and (c) the expected learning is challenging, but not impossible, and (d) the anticipated learning outcomes are worthy of their time and effort to try to achieve.

CLASSROOM CONTROL: ITS MEANING—PAST AND PRESENT

Classroom control frequently is of the greatest concern to beginning teachers—and they have good cause to be concerned. Even experienced teachers sometimes find control difficult, particularly with children who come to school with so much psychological baggage that they have already become alienated due to negative experiences in their lives.

In one respect, being a classroom teacher is much like being a medical response ambulance driver/technician (who's always concerned about the patient), and who must remain alert in different driving conditions—especially difficult ones such as going down a steep and winding grade; otherwise the ambulance most assuredly will get out of control, veer off the highway, and crash. This chapter has been thoughtfully designed to help you with your concerns about control—and to help you avoid a crash.

Historical Meaning of Classroom Control

To set the stage, for your comprehension, consider what the term **classroom control** has meant historically and what it means today. In the 1800s, instead of classroom control, educators spoke of classroom **discipline,** and that meant punishment. Such an interpretation was consistent with the then-popular learning theory that assumed children were innately naughty and that inappropriate behavior could be prevented by strictness or treated with punishment. Schools of the mid-1800s have been described as "wild and unruly places" and full of "idleness and disorder."[2]

By the early 1900s, educators were asking, "Why are the children still misbehaving?" The accepted answer was that the children were misbehaving because of the rigid punitive system. On this point, the era of progressive education began, providing students more freedom to decide what they would learn. The teacher's job, then, became one of providing a rich classroom of resources and materials to stimulate the student's natural curiosity. And since the system no longer would be causing misbehavior, punishment would no longer be necessary. Classes of the 1930s that were highly permissive, however, turned out to cause more anxiety than did the restrictive classes of the 1800s.

Today's Meaning of Classroom Control and the Concept of Classroom Management

Today, rather than classroom discipline, educators talk of classroom control, the process of influencing student behavior in the classroom. Classroom control is an important aspect of the broader concept of **classroom management.** Classroom control is part of a management plan designed to (a) prevent inappropriate student behaviors, (b) help children develop self-control, and (c) suggest procedures for dealing with inappropriate student behaviors.

Effective teaching requires a well-organized and businesslike classroom in which motivated students work diligently at their learning tasks, free from distractions and interruptions. Providing such a setting for learning requires careful thought and preparation and is called effective classroom management. Effective classroom management is the process of organizing and conducting a classroom so that it maximizes student learning.

A teacher's procedures for classroom control reflect that teacher's philosophy about how children learn and the teacher's interpretation and commitment to the school's stated mission. In sum, those procedures represent the teacher's concept of classroom management. Although often eclectic in their approaches, today's teachers share a concern for selecting management techniques that enhance student self-esteem and that empower the students; that is, the students learn how to assume control of their behavior and ownership of their learning.

While some schools subscribe heavily to one approach or another, such as Gay's culturally responsive classroom/teaching or Gordon's Teacher Effectiveness Training (TET) model, still other schools are more eclectic, with approaches having evolved from the historical works of leading authorities. Let's consider what some authorities have said. To assist your understanding, refer to Table 4.1, which illustrates the main ideas of each authority and provides a comparison of their recommended approaches. As mentioned previously the guidelines and suggestions that are presented throughout this chapter represent an eclectic approach, borrowing from many of these authorities.

Classroom Management: Contributions of Some Leading Authorities

B. F. Skinner (1904–1990)

You are probably familiar with the term *behavior modification,* which describes several high-control techniques for changing behavior in an observable and predictable way. You may also know B. F. Skinner's ideas about how students learn and how behavior can be modified by using reinforcers (rewards) and how his principles of behavior shaping have been extended by others.[3]

Behavior modification begins with four steps: (a) identify the behavior to be modified; (b) record how often and under what conditions that behavior occurs; (c) cause a change by reinforcing a desired behavior with a positive reinforcer (a reward); and (d) choose the type of positive reinforcers to award, such as the following:

- *Activity or privilege reinforcers,* such as choice of playing a game, running the projection equipment for the group, caring for a class animal, free reading, decorating the classroom, free art time, activity choice at a learning center, freed without penalty from doing an assignment or a test, or taking responsibility for an errand for the teacher.
- *Graphic reinforcers,* such as numerals and symbols made by rubber stamps.
- *Social reinforcers,* such as verbal attention or praise, and nonverbal such as proximity of teacher to students, and facial (a smile) or bodily expressions (a handshake or pat on the arm) of approval.
- *Tangible reinforcers,* such as badges, books, certificates, stickers, or popcorn and other edibles to which students are not allergic.
- *Token reinforcers,* such as points, stars, script, or tickets that can be accumulated and cashed in later for a tangible reinforcer, such as a trip to the local pizza place with parents or lining up to visit the traveling ice cream delivery truck with the teacher during a scheduled front-of-the-school appointment (with permission of school authority and parent). See Figure 4.1.

Lee Canter, Marlene Canter

Lee Canter, a child guidance specialist, and Marlene Canter, a specialist in teaching people with learning disabilities, developed their *assertive discipline model.* Using an approach that emphasizes both reinforcement for appropriate behavior and consequences or punishment for inappropriate behaviors, their model emphasizes four major points. First, as a teacher, you have professional rights in your classroom and should expect appropriate student behavior. Second, your students have rights to choose how to behave in your classroom, and you should plan limits for inappropriate behavior. Third, an assertive discipline approach means you clearly state your expectations in a firm voice and explain the

Figure 4.1
Token reinforcers.

- Some teachers give points, stars, script, or tickets to students who are exhibiting target behavior, e.g., working steadily and quietly. The students exchange the reinforcers for an activity time in class to engage in educational games and work independently at learning centers.

- Other teachers give a certain number of points to the students each Monday morning. If a student infringes on a procedure/rule, he or she loses a point. On Friday, a student may trade his or her remaining points for a ticket that can be used to acquire something special for the day or following week, e.g., receiving something from a special box, being in charge of the kick ball, being first in line to leave or enter the classroom, selecting a seat in class, moving desk to a special place in the classroom, and participating in an activity center in the room.

- Still other teachers give points as a bonus for a student's improvement in his or her academic work (calculated in points) in the upper elementary grades/middle school grades. As an example of this, the teacher can average each student's grades for the weekly spelling tests, and then suggest that the students earn bonus points by scoring higher than their average.

- Some teachers give tokens that can be accumulated over time by the students. Tokens of a certain color (A) are given to students who work quietly; five tokens of color A can be turned in for one token of color B; five tokens of color B can be turned in for one token of color C, which can be turned in for a tangible reinforcer.

- Token reinforcers (points, bonus points, stars, script, tickets) can be turned in later for a tangible reinforcer such as a certificate for edibles at a nearby fast-food place or a trip to a pizza restaurant or ice cream store with the teacher. Arrangements with the school/district administration might be made for a local ice cream vendor/truck to drive to the school on Friday afternoon or for a pizza delivery to be made to the school on a certain day so the students' tokens can be turned in for a treat. Other tangible reinforcers can include candy, favorite edibles, badges, certificates, stickers, and books.

- Cash incentives in return for good grades and better scores on tests are part of the Earning By Learning (EBL, Dallas, Texas) Program and are offered to students to motivate them and encourage reading. Note that critics point out that such incentives may change behavior only short-term, that students need to be naturally motivated to succeed, and that only parents or guardians should decide if students should be paid for good grades and better scores. See www.ascd.org/publications/newsletters/education_update/mar09/vol51/num03/toc.aspx.

boundaries for behavior. And fourth, you should plan a system of positive consequences (e.g., awards and rewards, special privileges, and sending positive messages home [see Application Exercise 4.1]) for appropriate behavior and establish consequences (e.g., time out, withdrawal of privileges, parent/guardian conference) for inappropriate student misbehavior. Consistent follow-though is necessary.[4] Today, primarily because of its heavy reliance on the external control of student behavior with the use of threat and punishment, the assertive discipline model is considered to be "less helpful than more eclectically derived programs" that emphasize rational explanations, logical or natural consequences, and the development of student self-control.[5]

Rudolf Dreikurs (1897–1972)

Advocating a *logical* or *natural consequences approach*, Rudolf Dreikurs, a psychiatrist specializing in child and family counseling, emphasized six points:

1. Be fair, firm, and friendly, and involve your students in developing and implementing class rules.

Table 4.1 Comparing Approaches to Classroom Management

Authority	To Know What Is Going On	To Provide Smooth Transitions
Canter/Jones/Gay	Realize that the student has the right to choose how to behave in your class with the understanding of the consequences that will follow his or her choice. Cultural heritage affects dispositions, attitudes, and approaches to learning.	Insist on decent, responsible behavior.
Dreikurs/Albert/Nelsen	Realize that the student wants status, recognition, and a feeling of belonging. Misbehavior is associated with mistaken goals of getting attention, seeking power, getting revenge, and wanting to be left alone.	Identify a mistaken student goal; act in ways that do not reinforce these goals.
Ginott	Communicate with the student to find out his or her feelings about a situation and about him/herself.	Invite student cooperation.
Glasser/Rogers/Freiberg/Gordon	Realize that the student is a rational being; he or she can control his or her own behavior.	Help the student make good choices; good choices produce good behavior and bad choices produce bad behavior.
Kounin	Develop *withitness,* a skill enabling you to see what is happening in all parts of the classroom at all times.	Avoid jerkiness, which consists of thrusts (giving directions before your group is ready), dangles (leaving one activity dangling in the verbal air, starting another one, and then returning to the first activity), and flip-flops (terminating one activity, beginning another one, and then returning to the first activity you terminated).
Skinner	Realize value of nonverbal interaction (i.e., smiles, pats, and handshakes) to communicate to students that you know what is going on.	Realize that smooth transition may be part of your procedures for awarding reinforcers (i.e., points and tokens) to reward appropriate behavior.

2. Students need to clearly understand the standards of expected behavior and the logical consequences for misbehavior. For example, a logical consequence for a student who has painted graffiti on a school wall would be to clean the wall or pay for a school custodian to do it.
3. Allow the students to be responsible not only for their own actions, but also for influencing others to maintain appropriate behavior in your classroom.
4. Encourage students to show respect for themselves and for others, and provide each student with a sense of belonging to the class.

5. Recognize and encourage student goals of belonging, gaining status, and gaining recognition.
6. Recognize but do not reinforce correlated student goals of getting attention, seeking power, and taking revenge.[6]

Linda Albert

Continuing the work of Dreikurs, Linda Albert, a former student of Dreikurs, has developed *cooperative discipline*, a detailed discipline system that is being used in many schools. The cooperative discipline model makes use of Dreikurs' fundamental concepts, with emphasis

To Maintain Group Alertness	To Involve Students	To Attend to Misbehavior
Set clear limits and consequences; follow through consistently; state what you expect, state the consequences and why the limits are needed; be part of a collective effort; use cooperative learning.	Use firm tone of voice; keep eye contact; use nonverbal gestures and verbal statements; use hints, questions, and direct messages in requesting student behavior; give and praise one another's positive attributes and cultural heritage.	Follow through with your promises and the reasonable, previously stated consequences that have been established in your class; use instructional strategies connected to learning styles.
Provide firm guidance and leadership.	Allow students to have a say in establishing rules and consequences in your class.	Make it clear that unpleasant consequences will follow inappropriate behavior.
Model the behavior you expect to see in your students.	Build student's self-esteem.	Give a message that addresses the situation and does not attack the student's character.
Understand that class rules are essential.	Realize that classroom meetings are effective means for attending to rules, behavior, and discipline.	Accept no excuses for inappropriate behavior; see that reasonable consequences always follow.
Avoid slowdowns (delays and time wasting) that can be caused by overdwelling (too much time spent on explanations) and by fragmentation (breaking down an activity into several unnecessary steps). Develop a group focus (active participation by all students in the group) through accountability (holding all students accountable for the concept of the lesson) and by attention (seeing all the students and using unison and individual responses).	Avoid boredom by providing a feeling of progress for the students, by offering challenges, by varying class activities, by changing the level of intellectual challenge, by varying lesson presentations, and by using many different learning materials and aids.	Understand that teacher correction influences behavior of other nearby students (the ripple effect).
Set rules, rewards, and consequences; emphasize that responsibility for good behavior rests with each student.	Involve students in "token economies," in contracts, and in charting behavior performance.	Provide tangibles to students who follow the class rules; represent tangibles as "points" for the whole class to use to "purchase" a special activity.

added on three C's: capability (encouragement), connectedness (student ownership of goals), and contributions (class meetings).[7]

Jane Nelsen

Also building upon the work of Dreikurs, psychotherapist Jane Nelsen provides guidelines for helping children develop *positive feelings* of self. Key points made by Nelsen and that are reflected throughout this resource guide are (a) use natural and logical consequences as a means to inspire a positive classroom atmosphere, (b) understand that children have goals that drive them toward misbehavior (assumed adequacy, attention, power, and revenge), (c) use kindness (student retains dignity) and firmness when administering consequences for a student's misbehavior, (d) establish a climate of mutual respect, (e) use class meetings to give students ownership in problem solving and goal setting, and (f) offer encouragement as a means of inspiring self-evaluation and focusing on the students' behaviors.[8]

William Glasser

Psychiatrist William Glasser developed his concept of *reality therapy* (i.e., the condition of the present rather than that of the past contributes to inappropriate behavior) for the classroom. Glasser emphasizes that students have a responsibility to learn at school and to maintain appropriate behavior while there. He stresses that with the teacher's help, students can make appropriate choices about their behavior in school—that they can, in fact, learn self-control.[9] Glasser suggests holding class meetings that are devoted to establishing class rules, identifying standards for student behavior, matters of misbehavior, and the consequences of misbehavior. Since the publication of his first book in 1965, Glasser has expanded his message to include more student needs of belonging and love, control, freedom, and fun, asserting that if these needs are ignored and unattended at school, children are bound to become unmotivated and fail.[10]

Carl Rogers, H. Jerome Freiberg

Today's commitment to quality education is not only largely derived from the recent work of Glasser, but also the corresponding concept of the *person-centered* classroom as advanced by Carl Rogers and H. Jerome Freiberg in their 1994 book *Freedom to Learn* (Columbus, OH: Merrill). In schools committed to quality education and the person-centered classroom, students feel a sense of belonging, enjoy some degree of power of self-discipline, have fun learning, and experience a sense of freedom in the process.[11]

G. Gay

In her book *Culturally Responsive Teaching: Theory, Research & Practice* (New York: Teachers College Press, 2000), educator Gay emphasizes that *culturally responsive teaching* (CTR) teaches to and through the strengths of diverse students. CTR uses the cultural knowledge, prior experiences, and performance styles of students to make learning more appropriate and effective for them. She advises teachers that cultural legacies affect students' dispositions, attitudes, and approaches to learning, and that instructional strategies may be connected to the students' different learning styles (see Chapter 2). The activities should include auditory, tactile, and visual opportunities. Additionally, J. J. Hoover has contributed to culturally responsive assessment practices (*avoid misdiagnosing* learning differences as disabilities) and culturally responsive collaboration in *tiered instruction* (this means instructional intervention in levels for students—i.e., level 1 is evidence-based teacher interventions for student progress in a general class core curriculum; level 2 is supplemental interventions for struggling learners not meeting general education core curriculum benchmarks; and level 3 is intensive interventions for students who fail to make progress toward benchmarks in level 2 instruction).[12]

Haim G. Ginott (1922–1973)

Psychologist Haim G. Ginott emphasized ways for teacher and student to communicate in his *communication model*. He advised teachers to send a clear message (or messages) about situations rather than about the children. He stressed that teachers must model the behavior they expect from students.[13] Ginott's suggested messages are those that express feelings appropriately, acknowledge students' feelings, give appropriate direction, and invite cooperation.

Thomas Gordon

In his book *Discipline That Works: Promoting Self-Discipline in Children* (New York: Penguin, 1989), clinical psychologist Thomas Gordon emphasizes influence over control and decries use of reinforcement (i.e., rewards and punishment) as ineffective tools for achieving a positive influence over a child's behavior.[14] Rather than using reinforcements for appropriate behavior and punishment for inappropriate behaviors, Gordon *advocates encouragement and development of student self-control and self-regulated behavior*. To have a positive influence and to encourage self-control, the teacher (and school) should provide a rich and positive learning environment, with rich and stimulating learning activities. Specific teacher behaviors include active listening, sending I-messages (rather than you-messages) shifting from I-messages to listening when there is student resistance to an I-message, clearly identifying ownership of problems to the student when such is the case (i.e., teacher not assuming ownership if it is a student's problem), and encouraging collaborative problem solving.

Frederic Jones

Psychologist Frederic Jones promotes the idea of *helping students support their own self-control* by way of a negative reinforcement method in which rewards follow good behavior.[15] Preferred activity time (PAT), for example, is an invention derived from the Jones Model. The Jones Model makes four recommendations. First, you should properly structure your classroom so students understand the **rules** (the expectation standards for classroom behavior) and **procedures** (the means for accomplishing routine tasks). Second, you maintain control by selecting appropriate instructional *strategies.* Third, you build patterns of cooperative work. Finally, you develop appropriate *backup methods* for dealing with inappropriate student behavior.

Jacob Kounin

Well known for his identification of the *ripple effect* (i.e., the effect of a teacher's response to one student's misbehavior on students whose behavior was appropriate), Jacob Kounin also emphasizes the teacher's withitness (i.e., the teacher's ability to remain alert in the classroom, to spot quickly and redirect potential student misbehavior, which is analogous to having "eyes in the back of your head").[16]

Developing My Own Effective Approach to Classroom Management

To develop your own approach to class management, you may want to begin by reviewing the tenets of culturally responsive teaching (CRT). These are ideas that can support you in the classroom: (a) concentrating your attention to cultural heritage and legacies that affect students' dispositions, attitudes, and learning (see Chapter 2), (b) attending to instructional strategies that are connected to students' different learning styles (Chapter 2), (c) maintaining alertness to multicultural information, resources, and materials in all subjects (Chapter 5), (d) acknowledging cultural heritage as worthy content to be taught in the curriculum (Chapter 5), and (e) involving students in knowing and praising one another's cultural heritage, connecting home and school experiences, and incorporating everyday-life concepts such as consumer habits, jobs and employment, and the economy.

Using the criteria of your own philosophy, feelings, values, knowledge, and perceptions, you are encouraged to construct a classroom environment and management system that is positive and effective for you and your students, and then to consistently apply it. Use the guidelines shown in Figure 4.2 to begin the thinking process for developing your personal plan for classroom management—this process begins now and continues in Application Exercise 4.1 and throughout your professional career.

PROVIDING A SUPPORTIVE LEARNING ENVIRONMENT

For you it is probably no surprise to hear that teachers whose classrooms are pleasant, positive, and challenging but supportive places to be, find that their students learn and behave better than do the students of teachers whose classroom atmospheres are harsh, negative, repressive, and unchallenging. What follows now are specific suggestions for making your classroom a pleasant, positive, and challenging place, that is, an environment that is conducive to the development of meaningful understandings.

Consider the Physical Layout

There is much in the arrangement of the classrooms that can either contribute to or help prevent classroom management problems. There is no one best way to arrange desks or learning stations in a classroom. Some teachers suggest that you sketch the possible traffic patterns in your room on paper before school begins for the year so you don't place students' desks in the traffic path to the pencil sharpener or water fountain. The arrangement should be kept flexible so children may be deployed in the ways most suitable for accomplishing specific tasks.

The guideline is simple. Just as it is true with adults, when children are seated side by side, it is perfectly natural for them to talk to each other. Therefore, if your purpose is to encourage social interaction, as when using cooperative learning and small-group project work, seat children close together; if you would rather they work independently such as when taking independent achievement tests, separate them. It is unreasonable to place children in situations that encourage maximum interaction and then to admonish or berate them for whispering and talking. Sometimes, so to not disturb the learning going on in neighboring classrooms, you may need to remind the children to whisper, talk softly, or "use their 6-inch voices."

You will not (or should not) be seated in your desk chair much of the time during the school day; but consider that your teacher's desk is located out of the main traffic pattern—perhaps away from traffic near the water fountain or pencil sharpener. One teacher we know liked her desk near the classroom entry door facing the students' desks, but with the back of the desk chair toward the class wall/display board. Thus, the teacher was there standing at her desk to say something pleasant to each student as he or she entered the room, to observe behavior and interactions, to get the materials on the desk needed for the next lesson, to mention it's time to get started, and to turn to the display board to discuss the objectives/standards of the next lesson. When the students left for the next recess, the teacher was by the class door and the desk to make individual comments of encouragement, praise, and support, and to observe students interactions. At times, the teacher asked each student to briefly mention one thing learned during the previous lesson as each one left the classroom.

Create a Positive Classroom Atmosphere

You have heard it before and now we say it again: All children should feel welcome in your classroom and accepted by you as individuals of dignity. Though these feelings and behaviors should be reciprocal, that is, expected of the children as well, they may have to begin with your frequent modeling of the behaviors expected of the students. You must help students know that any denial by you of a child's specific behavior is not a denial of that individual child as a worthwhile person who is still welcomed to come to your class to learn as long as the student agrees to follow expected procedures. Specific things you can do to create a positive classroom environment, some of which are repeated from preceding chapters and others that are addressed in later chapters, are the following:

For the Classroom

- Attend to the classroom's physical appearance and comfort—it is your place (and the students' place) of work; show pride in that fact.

DEVELOPING THE PERSONAL CLASSROOM MANAGEMENT SYSTEM

MY EMERGING PLAN FOR CLASSROOM MANAGEMENT: A CHECKLIST

Grade level _____   Name _____

Plans Before the First Day

1. I can describe my classroom with respect to the physical room arrangement and organization, and the positive and caring classroom community that I aim to create.
   yes _____   no _____   somewhat _____

2. I can describe communication I will initiate with my students and their families prior to the first day of school.
   yes _____   no _____   somewhat _____

3. I can describe characteristics of my classroom that will signal to the children that it is a friendly and safe place to be.
   yes _____   no _____   somewhat _____

4. I can describe how I will get to know the children and what I will do to help the children get to know me and each other.
   yes _____   no _____   somewhat _____

The First Day

5. I can describe how I will greet the children when they arrive for the first day.
   yes _____   no _____   somewhat _____

6. I can describe the rules or procedural expectations that I will have already in place and how they will be presented to the children. I have made a sketch of a visual aid I could make with a poster board and markers to create a set of procedures/rules to display in the classroom.
   yes _____   no _____   somewhat _____

7. I can describe how I will have children contribute to these rules/procedures and expectations.
   yes _____   no _____   somewhat _____

8. I can describe my classroom procedures for
   - absences
   - making up missed work and instruction
   - assigning helpers for class responsibilities such as taking care of pets, plants, the calendar, and so forth
   - bringing toys, plants, and pets into the classroom
   - collecting notes, money, and forms
   - distributing and collecting papers and materials
   - eating and drinking in the classroom
   - going to the bathroom
   - late arrival and early dismissal
   - movement in the halls

   - storing personal belongings
   - taking attendance
   - using the class sink
   - using the pencil sharpener
   - using the teacher's desk
   - using the water fountain
   - using other materials and equipment
   - wearing hats and other articles of clothing in the classroom
   - what to do in an emergency situation
   - when a visitor comes into the classroom

   yes _____   no _____   somewhat _____

9. I can describe the morning opening and afternoon closure; I can tell about a teaching activity (20 minutes) I would use for the class in case of an early release procedure for students, bell changes, or other interruptions. I can tell one or two short activities I would use (such as lessons in an e-teaching kit, Chapter 11) during brief periods of time when needed during the first two to three weeks.
   yes _____   no _____   somewhat _____

Figure 4.2
Developing the personal classroom management system.

Managing the Curriculum

10. I can describe how I will help the children with their organization and assignments.
    yes _____ no _____ somewhat _____

11. I can describe my homework (responsibility papers) expectations. I've answered these questions: Will there be homework? How much and how often? Will parents and guardians be informed? If so, how? What is their involvement to be? Is there a school homework hotline?
    yes _____ no _____ somewhat _____

12. I can describe my procedure for incomplete, unacceptable, or incorrect student work (and for a recovery option).
    yes _____ no _____ somewhat _____

13. I can describe ways I'll provide comments, feedback, or corrections in student work.
    yes _____ no _____ somewhat _____

14. I can describe ways I'll use marks of some sort—grades, value words, figures, and so forth—for assesment.
    yes _____ no _____ somewhat _____

15. I can describe ways students will be rewarded for their group work, how I'll assess group learning, and how I'll assess individual learning from group work.
    yes _____ no _____ somewhat _____

16. I can describe the student portfolio expectation and indicate where the portfolios will be stored and when the students will work on them.
    yes _____ no _____ somewhat _____

17. I can describe my plan for communication with parents/guardians.
    yes _____ no _____ somewhat _____

Maintaining Classroom Relations and Personal Behavior

18. I can describe how I will bring an off-task child back on task.
    yes _____ no _____ somewhat _____

19. I can describe to students what is and what is not an appropriate level of classroom noise.
    yes _____ no _____ somewhat _____

20. I can describe to students when I signal a need for hands, and when, if ever, it is okay to call out without raising hands.
    yes _____ no _____ somewhat _____

21. I can describe how I will indicate my support for appropriate student behavior.
    yes _____ no _____ somewhat _____

22. I can describe how I will discourage inappropriate student behavior.
    yes _____ no _____ somewhat _____

23. I can describe my order of explicit and implicit behavior intervention strategies.
    yes _____ no _____ somewhat _____

24. I can describe how I will signal my need for attention from the class.
    yes _____ no _____ somewhat _____

25. I can describe how I will respond when two errant behaviors are happening simultaneously at opposing locations in the classroom.
    yes _____ no _____ somewhat _____

26. I can describe how I will position the desks/furniture to maintain positive classroom relations.
    yes _____ no _____ somewhat _____

When the Going Gets Tough

27. I can describe my pattern of escalating consequences.
    yes _____ no _____ somewhat _____

28. I can describe how I will deal with disrespectful, inappropriate comments from students.
    yes _____ no _____ somewhat _____

29. I can describe how I will respond to remarks that are sexist or racist or that stereotype people in inappropriate and cruel ways.
    yes _____ no _____ somewhat _____

30. I can describe how I will respond to serious and dangerous student behaviors.
    yes _____ no _____ somewhat _____

31. I can identify one person I can go to for support.
    yes _____ no _____ somewhat _____

Figure 4.2 (*Continued*)

For Students

- Admonish behavior, not the person.
- Encourage students to set high yet realistic goals for themselves, and then show them how to work in increments toward meting their goal—letting each child know that you are confident in that child's ability to achieve.
- Ensure that no prejudice is ever displayed against any person.
- Help students develop their skills in interactive and cooperative learning.
- Involve students in every aspect of their learning, including the planning of classroom expectations, procedures, and learning activities, thereby empowering them—giving them part ownership and responsibility—in their learning.
- Make the learning enjoyable, at least to the extent possible and reasonable.

For Self Reflection

- Be an interesting person and an optimistic and enthusiastic teacher.
- Model the very expectations that you have for the children.
- Recognize and reward truly positive behaviors and individual successes, no matter how meager they might seem to you to be.
- Use interesting and motivating learning activities.
- Send positive messages (sometimes called Happygrams) home to parents or guardians, even if you have to get help and write the message in the language used in the student's home.

Behaviors to Avoid

Two items in the preceding list are statements about giving encouragement. When using encouragement to motivate student learning, there are certain behaviors that you should avoid because they inhibit learning.

- Avoid encouraging competition and comparing one child with another, or one group of children with another.
- Avoid giving up or appearing to give up on any child.
- Avoid telling a child how much better she or he could be.
- Avoid using names of individuals during class meetings that are called for discussing issues where the individuals were involved.
- Avoid using qualifying statements, such as "It's about time."

Get to Know the Children as People and Build Intrinsic Motivation for Learning

For classes to move forward smoothly and efficiently, they should fit the learners' learning styles, learning capacities, developmental needs, and interests. To make the learning meaningful and longest lasting, build curriculum around student interests, capacities, perceptions, and perspectives (as you will learn to do in Part II that follows). Therefore, you need to know your students well enough to be able to provide learning experiences that they will find interesting, valuable, intrinsically motivating, challenging, and rewarding. Knowing your students is as important as knowing the content of the subjects you are expected to teach. The following paragraphs describe a number of actions you can take to get to know your students as people.

Quickly Learn and Use Student Names

Like everyone else, children appreciate being recognized and addressed by name. Quickly learning and using their names is an important motivating strategy. To learn students' names quickly, one teacher, with parental permission, takes snapshot photographs of each child on the first day of school. Later, the children use the photographs as a portion of the covers of their portfolios. Another technique for learning names quickly is to use a seating chart. Laminate the seating chart onto an attractive (perhaps neon-colored) clipboard that you can carry in class. Another teacher we know uses an alliteration name game to learn students' names. For the game, each student introduces his or her name with a term related to the content being studied. For science, Lisa might introduce herself as Lithosphere Lisa. Going clockwise in a circle, each student introduces himself or herself, and then the student to the left repeats that alliterative name and then adds his or her own. The third student would repeat the first name, the second, and then his or her own name. The teacher can be last and repeat all of the alliterative names in order.

Some teachers prefer to assign "homebase" seating (an assigned seat for each child to be in at the start and end of each school day) and then make seating charts from which they can unobtrusively check the roll while the students are doing assignment work. It is usually best to get your students into the lesson before taking roll and before doing other housekeeping chores.

Addressing students by name every time you speak to them helps you to quickly learn and remember their names. (Be sure to learn to pronounce their names correctly: that helps in making a good impression.) Another helpful way to learn student names is to have elementary students make individual name cards (tented poster board 6 × 12 in.) for their desks, or have primary-grade students wear name tags on the first day/days of school, or return papers yourself by calling student names and then handing the papers to them, paying careful attention to look at each student and make mental notes that may help you to associate names with faces.

Let Students Share During the First Week of School

During the first week of school, some teachers take time each day to have students present information about themselves and/or about the day's lessons or an assignment. For instance, perhaps five or six students each day are selected to answer questions such as "What name would you like to be called by?" "Where did you attend school last year?" "Tell us about your interests or hobbies." "What interested you about yesterday's lesson on _____?" You might have your students share information of this sort with each other in dyads or small groups while you visit each group in turn.

Me in a Bag Activity. Another approach is the "Me in a Bag" activity, where each student brings to school a paper bag (one large grocery bag) that contains inexpensive items (or sketches of items) brought from home that represent that student. The student is given time in class to share the items brought. (Note: Be sure that parents/guardians are aware of the home assignment so nothing of value from home gets lost in the process.)

Sketches. As an option instead of a home assignment, the students can sketch the items on small squares of art paper in class and place the squares in the bag for the Me in a Bag activity at school.

Answering Questions. How each student answers questions or participates in beginning activities can be as revealing about the student as the information (or the lack thereof) that the student shares. From what is revealed during sharing activities, you sometimes get clues about additional information you would like to obtain about the student.

Observe Students in the Classroom: Develop and Practice Your Withitness

During learning activities, the effective teacher is constantly moving around the classroom and is alert to the individual behavior (nonverbal as well as verbal) of each child in the class, whether the student is on task or gazing off and perhaps thinking about other things (i.e., the teacher is exhibiting **withitness**). Be cautious, however—just because a child is gazing out the window does not mean that the child is not thinking about the learning task. During group work is a particularly good time to observe children and get to know more about each child's skills and interests. For these observations, a behavior checklist is sometimes useful (see Chapter 11). You'll be interested to know that some adults seeking careers in teaching, early-childhood education, and child development, enrolled in community college courses, and successfully passing background checks, can observe elementary students and their teachers through one-way viewing windows at the Innovative Learning Center at Phil Stokoe Elementary School (K–5, Riverside, California). Cameras and ceiling microphones let the adults listen to elementary student discussions without disrupting the groups and observation corridors allow teacher candidates to observe more than one classroom. For more about this, see www.pe.com/localnews/highereducation/stories/PE_News_Local_S_center15.1299715.html.

Observe Students Outside the Classroom

Another way to learn more about students is by observing them outside class, for example, at recess, during lunch, on the playground, and at other school events. Observations outside the classroom can give information about student friendships, interests, personalities, and potentialities. For instance, you may find that a student who seems phlegmatic, lackadaisical, or uninterested in your classroom is a real fireball on the soccer field.

Have Conferences and Interviews with Students

Conferences with students, and sometimes with family members, afford yet another opportunity to show that you are genuinely interested in each child as a person and as a student. Some teachers and teaching teams plan a series of conferences during the first few weeks in which, individually or in small groups, students are interviewed by the teacher or by the teaching team. Such conferences and interviews are managed by using open-ended questions. The teacher indicates by the questions, by listening, and by nonjudgmental and empathic responses (i.e., being able to "step into the shoes" of the students, thereby understanding from where the student is coming) a genuine interest in the students. Keep in mind, however, that children who feel they have been betrayed by prior adult associations may at first be distrustful of your sincerity. In such instances, don't force it. Be patient, but do not hesitate to take advantage of the opportunity afforded by talking with individual students outside of the regular classroom. Investing a few minutes of time in a positive conversation with a student, during which you indicate a genuine interest in that child, can pay real dividends when it comes to that child's learning in your classroom.

When using interviews with children, consider having the children individually write one or two questions that they would like to ask you in the interview. This ensures that the child is an active participant.

Plan Student Writing and Questionnaires

Student Writing. Much can be learned about children by what they write or draw. It is important to encourage writing in your classroom, and (with varying degrees of intensity) to read everything that students write and to ask for clarification when needed. Journals and portfolios are valuable for this approach since writing can especially help children feel more secure during the first days of school. Here are two writing suggestions:

- *Imaginary classmates for grades K–3.* Invite the children to imagine two imaginary classmates and suggest their physical characteristics, clothing, personalities, and fears. Encourage them to share their thoughts about the imaginary classmates to the whole group. Suggest that when any student has a problem, the student can write anonymously to one of the imaginary classmates and "mail" it in a mailbag (a brown paper bag affixed to a bulletin board). If appropriate, distribute the mail to the students and ask them to take the role of the imaginary classmates by writing the advice they would give the sender. The advice letters can be displayed beneath the writing board, and the students can be invited to browse and read during independent reading time.

- *An invisible student for grades 4–6.* Invite the students to imagine an invisible classmate in the room and distribute to the class a list of fifteen questions about problems that they would ask the invisible student. Ask the students to copy the list and take a week to answer the questions as if they were the invisible student. At the end of the week, invite the students to read one of the questions and answers aloud to the class. If appropriate, they can suggest additional problems and concerns they are facing at school. Have each student select one problematic situation or concern and write a brief scenario in which the invisible student handles it in the best way possible. Ask for volunteers to read their short stories aloud to a small group.

Questionnaires. Some teachers use open-ended interest-discovering and autobiographical questionnaires to learn more about the students. Student responses to questionnaires can provide ideas about how to tailor assignments and learning activities for individual students. However, you must assure students that their answers are optional, that you are not invading their privacy.

- *In an interest-discovering questionnaire,* students are asked to answer questions such as: "When you read for fun or pleasure, what do you usually read?" "What are your favorite movies, videos, games, or TV shows?" "Who are your favorite music video performers? Athletes?" "How would you describe your favorite hobby or other nonschool-related activity?" "What are your favorite sport activities to participate in and watch as a spectator?" "What would you like to become?" and "How do you like to spend your leisure time?"

- *In an autobiographical questionnaire,* the student is asked to answer such questions as "How many siblings do you have?" "Where have you lived?" "Do you have any pets?" "Do you have a favorite hobby or

interest? What is it?" You might want to model the process and begin it by reading the children your own autobiographical answers.

Rely on Cumulative Records, Discussions with Colleagues, and Experiential Backgrounds

Held in the school office is the cumulative record for each student, containing information recorded from year to year by teachers and other school professionals—information about the student's academic background and standardized test scores. However, the Family Educational Rights and Privacy Act (FERPA) of 1974, and its subsequent amendments and local policies, may forbid you from reviewing the record, except perhaps in collaboration with an administrator or counselor and when you have a legitimate educational purpose for doing so. While you must use discretion before arriving at any conclusion about information contained in the cumulative record, the record may afford information for getting to know a particular student better. Remember though, a student's past is history and should not be held against that child, but instead used as a means for understanding a child's past experiences as part of the student's present learning experience. One of the advantages of schools that use looping (where the teacher and students stay together more than one year) or using small cohorts (families, pods) of students is that teachers and students get to know each other better.

Another way of getting to know your students is to spend time in the neighborhoods in which they live. Observe and listen, finding and noting things that you can use as examples or as learning activities. Some school districts encourage home visits by teachers and even provide financial incentives to teachers who visit the homes of their students. Of course, teachers must exercise safety precautions when making home visits, perhaps traveling in teams rather than alone.

PREPARATION PROVIDES CONFIDENCE AND SUCCESS

For successful classroom management, beginning the school term well may make all the difference in the world. Remember that you have only one opportunity to make a first and lasting impression. Therefore, you should appear at the first class meeting as well-prepared and confident as possible.

In schools, genuinely respond to students, and demonstrate that the teachers and administrators hold high expectations for themselves and for one another.

Perhaps in the beginning, you will feel nervous and apprehensive, but being ready and well prepared will help you at least appear to be confident. It is likely that every beginning teacher is to some degree nervous and apprehensive; the secret is not to appear so. Being well-prepared provides the confidence necessary to cloud feelings of apprehension. A good antiperspirant and a slow under-the-breath counting to 10 at the start can help, too. Then, if you proceed in a businesslike, matter-of-fact way, you won't have much time to be nervous, because the impetus of your well-prepared beginning will most likely cause the day, week, and year to proceed as you desired. Consider preparing a long-term plan or outline too, because a student might ask, "What are we learning this year?" or "What will we be doing?" Be assured that your anxieties will lessen with each new school year. And now, to further your understanding of classroom management and to begin the development of your own management system, do Application Exercise 4.1.

USING POSITIVE REWARDS

Reinforcement theory contends that a person's gratification derived from receiving a reward strengthens the tendency for that person to continue to act in a certain way, while the lack of a reward (or the promise of a reward) weakens the tendency to act that way. For example, according to the theory, if students are promised a reward of preferred activity time (PAT) on Friday if they work well all week long, then the students are likely to work toward that reward, thus improving their standards of learning. Some educators argue that (a) once the extrinsic reinforcement (i.e., the reward from outside the learner) has been removed, the desired behavior tends to diminish; and that (b) rather than extrinsic sources of reinforcement, focus should be on increasing the student's internal sense of accomplishment, an intrinsic reward. Further, rewarding children for complying with expected/standard behavior sends the wrong message. It reinforces the mentality of "What do I get for doing what I am supposed to do?" If common as a school practice, it carries over into home situations and eventually to adulthood. A principal does not reward a teacher for showing up on time, attending a faculty meeting, or having report cards prepared on time. Those are expected standard behaviors. Perhaps, for the daily work of a teacher in a classroom of many diverse individuals, the practical reality is somewhere between. After all, the reality of classroom teaching is less than ideal, and all activities cannot be intrinsically rewarding. Further, for many children, intrinsic rewards are often too remote to be effective. The promise of extrinsic rewards is not always necessary or beneficial. Students generally will work harder to learn something because they want to learn it (i.e., it is intrinsically motivating) than they will merely to earn PAT, points, grades, candy, or some other form of reward (called an extrinsic motivator). In addition, regarding the promise of PAT on Friday, so many children are so preoccupied with the "here and now" that, for them, the promise on Monday of preferred activity time on Friday will probably have little desired effect on their behavior on Monday. To them on Monday, Friday seems a long way off.

Activities that are interesting and intrinsically rewarding are not further served by the addition of extrinsic rewards. This is especially true when working with students who are already highly motivated to learn. Adding extrinsic incentives to learning activities that are already highly motivating tends to reduce student motivation. For most students, the use of extrinsic motivators should be minimal and is probably most useful in skills learning, where there is a lot of repetition and the potential for boredom. While we are fully aware of the resentment students might feel if other teachers give out candy, stickers, and so on, and theirs did not, when students are working diligently on a highly motivating student-initiated project of study, extrinsic rewards are probably not necessary and could even have negative effects.[17] To minimize problems, a teacher can discourage time wasting, avoid some common mistakes, and use interventions such as class meetings, conflict resolution, and judicious consequences.[18–21] Further, the teacher can use nonverbal cues, and be aware of students' impulse control.[22–24]

LOOKING AT TEACHERS II

Integrated Technology, Software

After reading this chapter about the teacher's need to establish an effective and safe environment, what is the role of procedures and rules in the classroom from your point of view? It seems that rules must be designed to equally support and value all members of a community of learners in the classroom. With this in mind, what procedures/rules might be needed for some of the following classroom activities in this following vignette? In what way could the students, rather than the teacher, accept the rules you suggest and assume responsibility for their actions and make their classroom a community of learners? Here's the vignette to consider:

In one second-grade classroom, the teacher guided her students in a thematic unit centered on extinct animals—the dinosaurs. The learning activities integrated math and science, drawing and crafts, music and reading, and publishing original books to support the study. Connecting reading to music, the students listened to a song about each dinosaur being studied. Students read sentence strips with the words of the songs. They added sound effects, sang each song several times, and added a rhythmic beat with their fingers and hands. Additionally, the students prepared their own dinosaur-shaped books, wrote original pages, and created illustrations. To survey favorite dinosaurs, graphing was introduced. The students built their own line graph in the classroom and each drew a favorite dinosaur on a small square of paper and placed it on a line that was labeled with the dinosaur's name on a large graph. Students made individual copies of the graph and recorded what was added to the large graph. They marked Xs with their pencils in appropriate places. When the class graph was finished, the students read information from it (guided by the teacher) and talked about the information they had gathered. The unit encompassed a number of multidisciplinary activities related to the topic. For example,

- *History.* Students developed a graphic time line showing the long period of time that the dinosaurs were dominant on Earth; they visited a museum that featured dinosaur exhibits.
- *Mathematics.* Students categorized the types of dinosaurs and created graphs that illustrated the variety and proportional sizes of dinosaurs.
- *Reading, Writing, and Art.* Students created and wrote illustrated stories about a favorite dinosaur.
- *Science.* Students speculated about why the dinosaurs were so successful and about the events that led to their rather quick disappearance from Earth.
- *Integrated Technology.* To prepare for an upcoming Open House, the teacher used a color printer and Adobe Acrobat Reader software to download files in the PDF format from the Gale Group website. This site offered free images on bookmarks, reading certificates, flyers/posters and thank-you cards—useful items for students to give to their parents/guardians at Open House night.

The culminating event took place at the school's spring Open House. Each student's assignment for Open House was to bring an adult and to explain to that person what he or she had been learning at school. Confidently, the students told their visitors about dinosaurs and proudly displayed their dinosaur books, dinosaur mobile, dinosaur body shapes from felt, and dinosaur clay models. Information about other animals for similar projects are available online.[25]

SUMMARY

In this chapter, you learned ways to cope with the daily challenges of classroom teaching and guidelines for effectively managing children in the classroom. Within that framework, your attention was then focused on specific approaches and additional guidelines for effective classroom management and control of the learning environment. You were offered advice for setting up and maintaining a classroom environment that is favorable to student learning and for establishing procedures for positively influencing student behavior and encouraging student learning. To become an accomplished classroom manager takes thoughtful and thorough planning, consistent and confident application, and reflective experience. Be patient with yourself as you accumulate the prerequisite knowledge and practice and hone the necessary skills. To accumulate practice and hone your skills, select one interaction in the following section, Extending My Professional Competency.

What's to Come. This is the end of the overview about teaching, learning, and class management. You are now ready for Part II, Planning for Curriculum and Instruction.

EXTENDING MY PROFESSIONAL COMPETENCY

With Discussion

Inappropriate Behavior. What would I say to give my opinion about responding to inappropriate behavior at a selected grade level? **To do:** To offer your view, organize a group discussion or debate on this issue after reviewing the following information: Some educators are concerned about the increased violence in schools, weapons, harassment, bullying, intimidation, gangs, cult activity, and arson. They argue that schools are responsible for turning a child's behavior into an opportunity to teach character and self-control. When self-disciplined adults create a problem, they apologize, accept the consequences, make restitution, and learn from their mistakes. The same educators also argue that we have a responsibility for teaching children to do the same. Further, an important characteristic of exemplary schooling is that of maintaining respect for a child's dignity even when responding to the child's inappropriate behavior. (Take notes about your view.)

With Video

Video Activity: Supportive Learning Environment. What would I say about one or two of my own school experiences and the contrast of those experiences with those recently observed in the following two videos?

myeducationlab

> Go to the Video Examples section of Topic #3: Classroom Management in the MyEducationLab for your course to view the videos entitled "Conflict Resolution" and "Student Conflict Managers."

View each video, take notes, and in a small group, discuss at least one situation from your experience and compare it with what you saw in the video. Can you reach a conclusion about past vs. present school experiences? Are they similar? Different? In what way? Share your group's conclusion with those of the other groups in the class.

With Portfolio

Portfolio Planning. In my portfolio, what would I say about how I would develop and manage an effective, safe, and supportive learning environment? How could I show my knowledge of a supportive learning environment related to Principles 2 and 5 of INTASC and the Standards 1 and 3 of NBPTS and the Praxis II teacher test content (as seen on the inside of the front cover of this book)? **To do:** Review Chapter 4, the chapter about a supportive learning environment. To continue, write a one- to two-page paper explaining your knowledge of an effective, safe, and supportive learning environment. Label your paper as Supportive Learning Environment, and after reading and interacting with this chapter, state how you have developed your competency for one of the following objectives for this chapter:

- Gaining, as a beginning teacher, helpful information about managing a safe and effective classroom and recognizing what you value the most.

- Describing the steps I could take in preparing for a classroom management system that would be implemented the first few days of school and emphasize at least three guidelines for acceptable student behavior from my point of view.
- Return to the beginning of this chapter to review the other objectives.
- Place your paper in your portfolio folder or in your computer file. If needed, refer to Portfolio Builders on www.MyEducationLab.com.

With Teacher Tests Study Guide

Teacher Tests for Future Licensing and Certification. If I wanted to prepare for taking a state teacher test to qualify for my teaching certificate/license and review my knowledge about managing a supportive learning environment, how could I begin? **To do:** To support you as you prepare for teaching, you will find constructed-response-type questions similar to those found on state tests for teacher licensing and certification in Appendix A of this book, the Teacher Tests Study Guide. The question related to this chapter and a supportive learning environment helps you take another look at the classroom vignette found in *Looking at Teachers II*, Chapter 4. Write your response and, if you wish, discuss it with another teaching candidate. If appropriate, use one or two of your colleague's suggestions to help you change your response to the question. Place your response in a Teacher Test Study Guide folder or type/scan into a computer file. Plan to review and reread for study purposes before taking a scheduled teacher test.

With Target Topics for Teacher Tests (TTTT)

If I wanted to start early and prepare for taking a state teacher test for licensing and certification and review subject matter content about managing a supportive learning environment, how could I begin? **To do:** Consider reviewing Target Topics for Teacher Tests (TTTT) in the subject index. To assist you as you prepare to take a teacher test, bullets (•) have been placed by selected word entries in the subject index and indicate Target Topics for Teacher Tests. The bullets highlight the core subject matter—class management, positive classroom atmosphere, preparation, and other areas—that the authors suggest can be reviewed in preparation for taking a teacher test similar to your state's test or the Praxis II Principles of Learning and Teaching exam.

WITH READING

Bicard, D. F. (2000). Using Classroom Rules to Construct Behavior. *Middle School Journal, 31*(5), 37–45.

Cole, R. W. (ed.) (2008). *Educating Everybody's Children: Diverse Teaching Strategies for Diverse Learners* (rev.).

Baltimore: Association for Supervision and Curriculum Development.

Cummings, C. (2000). *Winning Strategies for Classroom Management.* Alexandria, VA: Association for Supervision and Curriculum Development.

DiGiulio, R. (2000). *Positive Classroom Management: A Step by Step Guide to Successfully Running the Show Without Destroying Student Dignity* (2nd ed.). Thousand Oaks, CA: Corwin.

Gibbs, J. L. (2000). Value-Based Discipline in a Fifth Grade Classroom. *Middle School Journal, 31*(5), 46–50.

Good, T. L., and Brophy, J. E. (2003). *Looking in Classrooms* (9th ed., Chps. 4 and 5). New York: Addison Wesley Longman.

Hardin, C. J., and Harris, E. A. (2000). *Managing Classroom Crises* (Fastback 465). Bloomington, IN: Phi Delta Kappa Educational Foundation.

Harmin, M., and Toth, M. (2006). *Inspiring Active Learning: A Complete ASCD Handbook for Today's Teachers* (expanded 2nd ed.). Baltimore: Association for Supervision and Curriculum Development, 2006.

Hill, J. D., and Flynn, K. M. (2006). *Classroom Instruction That Works with English Language Learners.* Baltimore: Association for Supervision and Curriculum Development.

Iverson, A. M. (2003). *Building Competence in Classroom Management and Discipline* (4th ed.). Upper Saddle River, NJ: Prentice-Hall.

Kira, N. (2002). Developing the New Basic Skills. *Society for the Studies of Cross-Cultural Communication and Business and Cultural Studies, 6*(2), 17–34.

Landau, B. M., and Gathercoal, F. (2000). Creating Peaceful Classrooms: Judicious Discipline and Class Meetings. *Phi Delta Kappan, 81*(6), 450–452, 454.

Manning. M. L., and Bucher, K. T. (2003). *Classroom Management: Models, Applications, and Cases.* Upper Saddle River, NJ: Prentice-Hall.

McEwan, B. (2000). *The Art of Classroom Management: Effective Practices for Building Equitable Learning Communities.* Upper Saddle River, NJ: Merrill/Prentice Hall.

Morgan, R. R., Ponticell, J. A., and Gordon, E. E. (2000). *Rethinking Creativity* (Fastback 458). Bloomington, IN: Phi Delta Kappa Educational Foundation.

Nissman, B. S. (2000). *Teacher-Tested Classroom Management Strategies.* Upper Saddle River, NJ: Merrill/Prentice Hall.

Wong, H. (2001). *The First Days of School.* Mountain View, CA: Harry K. Wong.

WITH NOTES

1. See more about videoconferencing technology at www.ports.parks.ca.gov.

2. J. G. Thompson, *The First Year Teacher's Survival Kit* (Bloomington, IL: Delta Kappa International, 2003).

3. See B. F. Skinner's early work, *Beyond Freedom and Dignity* (New York: Knopf, 1971).

4. See L. Canter and M. Canter's management approach in *Assertive Discipline: Positive Behavior Management for Today's Schools,* rev. ed. (Santa Monica, CA: Lee Canter & Associates, 1992).

5. T. L. Good and J. E. Brophy, *Looking in Classrooms,* 9th ed. (New York: Addison Wesley Longman, 2003), p. 201.

6. See R. Dreikurs, B. B. Grunwald, and F. C. Pepper's early work, *Maintaining Sanity in the Classroom: Classroom Management Techniques,* 2nd ed. (New York: Harper & Row, 1982).

7. See P. Angiano, A First-Year Teacher's Plan to Reduce Misbehavior in the Classroom, *Teaching Exceptional Children, 33*(3), 52–55 (2001); Also L. Albert's later revision, *A Teacher's Guide to Cooperative Discipline: How to Manage Your Classroom and Promote Self-Esteem* (Circle Pines, MN: American Guidance Service, 1989, revised 1996).

8. For class meetings, see B. M. Landau and P. Gathercoal, Creating Peaceful Classrooms: Judicious Discipline and Class Meetings, *Phi Delta Kappan, 81*(6), 450–452, 454 (February, 2000). Also see J. Nelsen, L. Lott, and H. S. Glenn's early book *Positive Discipline in the Classroom: How to Effectively Use Class Meetings and Other Positive Discipline Strategies* (Rocklin, CA: Prima Publishing, 1993) or Nelsen's *Positive Discipline,* 2nd ed. (New York: Ballatine Books, 1987).

9. See R. J. Marzano, *Classroom Management That Works: Research-Based Strategies for Every Teacher* (Alexandria, VA: Association for Supervision and Curriculum Development, 2003); Also see W. Glasser's earlier article, A New Look at School Failure and School Success, *Phi Delta Kappan, 78*(8), 597–602 (April 1997).

10. See G. Colvin, *7 Steps for Developing a Proactive Schoolwide Discipline Plan: A Guide for Principals and Leadership Teams* (Thousand Oaks, CA: Corwin, 2007); Also see W. Glasser's early work, *Schools Without Failure* (New York: Harper & Row, 1969) and *Control Theory in the Classroom* (New York: Harper & Row, 1986), or his later writings *The Quality School* (New York: Harper & Row, 1990), and *The Quality School Teacher* (New York: Harper-Perennial, 1993).

11. C. Rogers and H. J. Freiberg's early book, *Freedom to Learn* (Columbus, OH: Merrill/Prentice Hall, 1994); See also H. J. Freiberg (Ed.), *Beyond Behaviorism: Changing the Classroom Management Paradigm* (Boston: Allyn & Bacon, 1997). and *Perceiving, Behaving, Becoming: Lessons Learned* (Alexandria, VA: Association for Supervision and Curriculum Development, 1999).

12. G. Gay, *Culturally Responsive Teaching: Theory, Research & Practice* (New York: Teachers College Press, 2000); See more about culturally responsive assessment and culturally responsive collaboration in tiered instruction by J. J. Hoover, in *Differentiating Learning Differences from Disabilities: Meeting Diverse Needs through Multi-tiered Response to Intervention* (Upper Saddle River, NJ: Pearson, 2009).

13. See H. G. Ginott's early work, *Teacher and Child* (New York: Macmillan, 1971).

14. See T. Gordon's early discussion of *Discipline That Works: Promoting Self-Discipline in Children* (New York: Penguin, 1989).

15. See F. Jones' early work, *Positive Classroom Discipline* (New York: McGraw-Hill, 1987).

16. See J. S. Kounin's early work, *Discipline and Group Management in Classrooms* (New York: Holt, Rinehart and Winston, 1977). Building on Kounin's concept of

withitness, Wong and Wong give ideas for preparing traffic patterns in the classroom in *The First Days of School* (Mountain View, CA: Wong, 2001). Also, research evidence from these authorities reminds you of the importance of the following: (a) concentrating your attention on desirable student behaviors, (b) attending to inappropriate behavior, (c) maintaining alertness to all that is happening, (d) providing smooth transitions, keeping the class on task, preventing dead time, (e) involving students by providing challenges, class meetings, ways to establish rules and consequences, opportunities to receive and return compliments, and chances to build self-control and self-esteem.

17. See R. R. Morgan, J. A. Ponticell, and E. E. Gordon, *Rethinking Creativity* (Fastback 458) (Bloomington, IN: Phi Delta Kappa Educational Foundation, 2000).

18. At the beginning of student teaching, you may need to follow the opening procedures already established by your host teacher. If those procedures are largely ineffective, then without hesitation you should talk with your university supervisor about being reassigned to a different placement.

19. K. S. Berger, Update on Bullying at School: Science Forgotten? *Developmental Review, 27*(1), 90–126 (2007); L. M., Crothers, J. B. Kolbert, and W. F. Barker, Middle School Students' Preferences for Anti-Bullying Interventions, *School Psychology International, 27*, 475–487 (2006); M. Franek, Foiling Cyberbullies in the New Wild West, *Educational Leadership, 53*(4), 39–43 (2006); L. Lumsden, *Preventing Bullying.* ERIC Clearinghouse on Educational Management Document No. ED 463563; J. S. Peterson and K. E. Ray, Bullying and the Gifted, *Gifted Child Quarterly, 50*, 148–168 (2006).

20. Landau and Gathercoal, *op. cit.*, pp. 450–452, 454. See R. T. Scarpaci, Bullying: Effective Strategies for Its Prevention, *Kappa Delta Pi Record, 42*(4), 170–174 (2005); See also B. McEwan, P. Gathercoal, V. Nimmo, Applications of Judicious Discipline: A Common Language for Classroom Management, in H. J. Freiberg's (Ed.) earlier book, *Beyond Behaviorism: Changing the Classroom Management Paradigm* (Boston: Allyn & Bacon, 1999).

21. See Committee for Children on the Internet at www.cfchildren.org/programs/.

22. N. Willard, Flame Retardant: Cyberbullies Torment Their Victims 24/7: Here's How to Stop the Abuse, *School Library Journal, 52*(4), 54 (2006).

23. S. Schwartz, Educating the Heart, *Educational Leadership,* 76–78 (April, 2007); N. Protheroe, Emotional Support and Student Learning, *Principal, 86*(4), 50–54; Find more about the relation between impulse control and intelligence in two earlier writings, D. Goleman, *Emotional Intelligence: Why It Can Matter More Than IQ* (New York: Bantam Books, 1995), and D. Harrington-Lueker, Emotional Intelligence, *High Strides, 9*(4), 1,4–5 (March/April 1997).

24. For facilitative procedures/rules to establish a community of learners, i.e., problem solving sessions, see B. McEwan, *The Art of Classroom Managements: Effective Practices for Building Equitable Learning Communities* (Upper Saddle River, NJ: Merrill/Prentice Hall, 2000); See also S. Vaughn and C. S. Bos, *Teaching Students with Learning and Behavior Problems,* 7th ed. (Upper Saddle River, NJ: Pearson, 2009).

25. See Grzimek's Animal Life at www.gale.com/animallife.

PART 2

Planning for Curriculum and Instruction

Mary Kate Denny/Photoedit

Chapter 5   How Do I Plan and Select Content?

Chapter 6   How Do I Assess, Use, and Report Student Achievement?

Chapter 7   How Do I Prepare Activities, Lessons, and Units?

Shutterstock

5

How Do I Plan and Select Content?

Visual Chapter Organizer and Overview

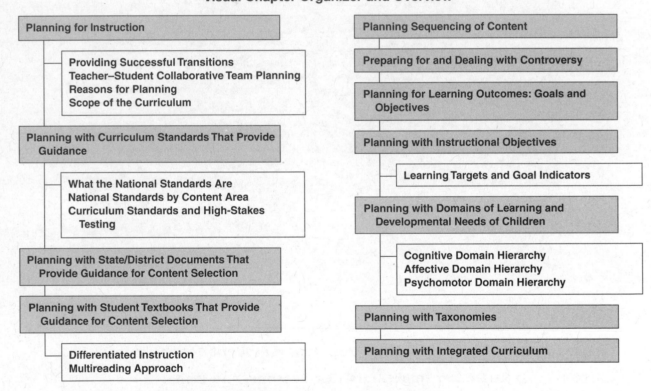

Planning for Instruction

- Providing Successful Transitions
  Teacher–Student Collaborative Team Planning
  Reasons for Planning
  Scope of the Curriculum

Planning with Curriculum Standards That Provide Guidance

- What the National Standards Are
  National Standards by Content Area
  Curriculum Standards and High-Stakes Testing

Planning with State/District Documents That Provide Guidance for Content Selection

Planning with Student Textbooks That Provide Guidance for Content Selection

- Differentiated Instruction
  Multireading Approach

Planning Sequencing of Content

Preparing for and Dealing with Controversy

Planning for Learning Outcomes: Goals and Objectives

Planning with Instructional Objectives

- Learning Targets and Goal Indicators

Planning with Domains of Learning and Developmental Needs of Children

- Cognitive Domain Hierarchy
  Affective Domain Hierarchy
  Psychomotor Domain Hierarchy

Planning with Taxonomies

Planning with Integrated Curriculum

LOOKING AT TEACHERS I

Integrated Technology, Energy

At the foot of Diamond Head Volcanic Crater, a sixth-grade teacher at Waikiki Elementary School observes the students in a science class demonstrate basic environmentally friendly energy techniques to students from other classrooms. The school has *integrated the technology of energy* as part of the *content* in its classrooms. Another sixth-grade teacher works with students as they show their use of technology and push their class-made battery-operated car during a show-and-tell display of their green science projects. A fourth-grade teacher supervises as students work in a seeding garden. Still another teacher meets parents who turn out to tend a school orchard of newly planted fruit trees and some parents stay to run an after-school technology enrichment class to teach children about solar power. A kindergarten teacher mentions that the students under age five seem to be more mellow working at school in natural light than in lightbulb light, and at Kahuku Intermediate School and High School, teachers and students research technology to find ways to cool portable classrooms.

Some students have suggested installing sun-powered vents and using energy neutral rooms (without electricity), and this has caused concerns among some community members. They are supporters of using electricity for after-school care, increased technology, and for computer use, and they are not in favor of having classrooms without electricity.

However, supporters of energy conservation in the schools focus on decreasing the number of mini-refrigerators, microwave ovens, coffeemakers, even class aquariums, and suggest using laptops that require less energy. The laptops can be charged at home rather than using energy in class for desk computers. In all of the schools, the teachers model conservation behavior and keep all lights off as much as possible to keep the classrooms cooler, save electricity, and reduce their schools' cost of energy. They also open the louvered blinds on windows and let cross breezes blow into classrooms and school balconies. This allows the teachers to turn off ceiling fans and air conditioning by 4:30 p.m. Additionally, the schools use minimum security lights at night and install photovoltaic systems on school roofs when the roofs need to be replaced. Even the assistant state superintendent rides his bike, rain or shine, to work each day to encourage environmental awareness and conservation of energy use.

So why are Hawaiian educators and students so interested in energy use and costs and why have they integrated the technology of energy as part of the content in their classrooms? Right now, there are rising energy costs in Hawaii. As an example, just one kilowatt hour of power recently increased greatly in cost in Hawaii. To address this, conservation efforts are now the top priority in all government agencies. Hawaii's energy director announced the state's goal is to use less oil by installing a network of thousands of auto charging stations throughout the state to prepare for large-scale electric car use in the upcoming years (as is being done in Portland, Oregon, San Francisco, California, and other cities). To do its part in conservation, the Hawaii Department of Education has started a program of integrating energy/technology conservation in which schools can earn back half the amount they save in electric costs over the semester. They can use the money saved for any purpose the school chooses.[1]

A Focus on English Language Learners

When two students in the classroom share a common first language, pair the more proficient English language learners with less-proficient students and encourage the students to be partners and discuss what they are doing.

Thus, the teacher can ask a question about the technology used in the class-made car or the energy conservation in the green science projects and the paired students think of a response and interview one another to share their answers. They can discuss questions about what they did when they worked in a garden or tended an orchard or attended an after-school class to learn about the power of the sun. When any of these lessons are over, the teacher reviews (What did we learn in our lesson about energy conservation?) to briefly emphasize the main objectives, selected vocabulary, and concepts, and to link the lesson to standards to highlight the value of the lesson's information.

As the previous vignette about the teachers employed by the Hawaii Department of Education points out, your effective teaching does not just happen; it is produced through your thoughtful planning of each phase of the learning process. And indeed, one part of the process can include incorporating children's literature linked to content—just as the content of going green in Hawaii could be linked to the Green Belt Movement in Africa through the picture biography of environmentalist Kenyan Wangari Maathai. In *Wangari's Trees of Peace: A True Story from Africa* (Harcourt, 2008) by J. Winter, Maathai returns to Africa after studying on a scholarship in America and finds the tree-covered land she knew as a child has turned barren. To change this, Maathai plants trees in her own yard at her home and encourages other women to do the same. Today, more than 30 million trees have been planted by members of Maathai's Green Belt Movement, and to recognize her work, she was awarded the Nobel Prize in 2004. In addition to selecting children's literature, such as this book, to link to content prior to teaching the content, some teachers begin their planning months before meeting students for the first time. They realize that daily activities become parts of daily lessons that in turn, form parts of a larger planning scheme. This planning scheme is designed to accomplish the teacher's long-range goals for the semester or year and to correlate with the school's mission statement and the expectation standards related to district and state documents.

Like the construction of a very large bridge, learning what is the most meaningful is a gradual and sometimes painstakingly slow process. When compared with traditional instruction, teaching in a constructivist mode is slower; it involves more discussion, more debate, and time for the re-creation of ideas. Rather than always following defined and previously established steps, the curriculum evolves. Such a curriculum depends heavily on materials, and to a great extent, it is the students' interests and questions that determine it. Less content is covered, fewer facts are memorized and tested for, and progress is sometimes tediously slow.[2] The rationale for careful planning for instruction, the components of that planning, and the selection of content are the main topics of this chapter.

CHAPTER OBJECTIVES

Specifically, upon completion of this chapter, you should be able to:

1. Explain your familiarity with the national curriculum standards for various subjects of the K–6 curriculum that can be resources for planning and selecting content.
2. Explain your familiarity with curriculum documents published by your state department of education as well as local curriculum documents.
3. Explain the value of diagnostic and formative assessment of student learning as related to curriculum and instruction.
4. Demonstrate how you would organize your ideas about subject content and the sequencing of content as well as explain your understanding of controversial topics and issues that may arise while teaching and what you might do if and when they do arise.
5. Demonstrate that you can recognize verbs that are acceptable for overt objectives, that you can recognize parts of criterion-referenced instructional objectives, that you can recognize objectives that are measurable, and that you can prepare instructional objectives for each of the three domains of learning and at various levels of the taxonomies within each domain.

PLANNING FOR INSTRUCTION

As a classroom teacher, planning for instruction is a major part of your job, even if you are using an externally developed and highly scripted program. At some level of complexity, you will be responsible for planning at several levels the activities, the lessons, the units, and the school year.

You need not do all your instructional planning from scratch, and you need not do all your planning alone. As a matter of fact, in many elementary schools today, especially for mathematics and reading, the curricula are purchased by the district and handed to the teachers. The program may be highly scripted and the teacher may be expected to follow the script closely or even exactly. However, it is our opinion that because writers of these programs do not know your students as well as you, to be most effective with a particular group of children, any scripted program will need tweaking by the teacher who is using it.

In many schools, curricula are developed or, in the case of scripted programs, are enhanced by a team of teachers. Teams of teachers collectively plan the curricula for their specific cohorts of students. Team members either plan together or divide the responsibilities and then share their individual plans. A final plan is then developed collaboratively.

The heart of good planning is good decision making and at the heart of good decision making is, as mentioned in Chapter 4, knowledge of the children for whom the instruction is planned. For every plan and at each of the levels, you and your team of colleagues must make decisions about the goals and objectives to be set, the subject to be introduced, the materials and equipment to be used, the methods to be adopted, and the assessments to be made. This decision-making process is complicated because so many options are available at each level. Decisions made at all levels result in a total plan.

Although the planning process continues year after year, the task becomes somewhat easier after the first year as you learn to adapt your plans. The process is also made easier via research and communication by reviewing documents and sharing ideas and plans with other teachers.

Providing Successful Transitions

Within the framework of exemplary school organization lie several components that form a comprehensive albeit ever-changing program. Central to the school's purpose and its organizational structure is the concerted effort to see that all children make successful **transitions** from one level to the next, from home to school, from one grade to the next, from elementary to middle school, from middle school to high school, and from high school to postsecondary education or work. Every aspect of the elementary school program is, in some way, designed to help children to make those transitions. Combining to form the program that students experience are two terms you will frequently encounter, **curriculum** (we define as all experiences students encounter) and **instruction** (we define as experiences associated with methods facilitating student learning).

Teacher–Student Collaborative Team Planning

Many teachers and teaching teams encourage their students to participate in the planning of some phase of their learning, anywhere from planning complete interdisciplinary thematic units to specific activities within a unit. Such collaborative planning tends to give students a proprietary interest in the activities, thereby increasing their motivation for learning. What students have contributed to the plan often seems more meaningful to them than what others have planned for them. Children like to see their own plans succeed. Thus, teacher–student collaboration in planning is usually an effective motivational tool.

Classrooms today tend to be more project-oriented and student- and group-centered than the traditional teacher-centered classroom of the past, in which the teacher served as the primary provider of information. Today's students more actively participate in their learning, in collaboration with the teacher. The teacher provides some structure and assistance, but the collaborative approach requires that students inquire and interact, generate ideas, seriously listen, and talk with one another, and recognize that their thoughts and experiences are valuable and essential to meaningful learning. In such a collaborative atmosphere, children not only learn the subject matter content of the curriculum, but develop important and valuable social skills.

Reasons for Planning

Planning is done for a number of reasons, perhaps foremost of which is to ensure curriculum coherence. Periodic activities and lesson plans are an integral part of a larger plan, represented by grade-level goals and objectives and by the school- and district-wide mission and district/state outcome standards. Students' learning experiences are thoughtfully planned in sequence and then orchestrated by teachers who understand the rationale for their respective positions in the curriculum. Of course, such plans do not preclude an occasional diversion from predetermined activities.

Another reason for planning is, as discussed in Chapter 2, to give considerations to students' experiential and cultural backgrounds, learning capacities and styles, reading levels, and special needs.

Planning is necessary to ensure efficient and effective teaching with a minimum of classroom management problems. After deciding what to teach, you have the important task of deciding how to teach it. To use precious instructional time efficiently, planning should be accomplished with three goals in mind: (a) show that you value everyone's time during instruction, (b) select strategies that most effectively promote the anticipated student learning, that is, that target learning outcomes, and (c) adapt instruction for ELLs and English-speaking students with learning problems.

Planning also helps ensure program continuation. The program must continue even if you are absent and a substitute teacher is needed. Planning provides a criterion for reflective practice and self-assessment. After a learning activity and at the end of a school term, you can reflect on and assess what was done and how it affected student learning. Planning provides a means to evaluate your teaching. Your plans represent a criterion recognized and evaluated by administrators. With those experienced in such matters, it is clear that inadequate planning is usually a precursor to incompetent teaching. Put simply, failing to plan is planning to fail. See Figure 5.1.

Scope of the Curriculum

When planning the scope of the curriculum, you must decide what it is to be accomplished in that period of time, such as for a semester or for a school year. To help in setting your goals, you should (a) examine school and other resource documents for mandates and guidelines, (b) communicate with colleagues to learn of common expectations (e.g., special education teacher for assistance with ELLs), and (c) probe, analyze, and translate your own convictions, knowledge, and skills into behaviors that foster the intellectual and psychological development of your students.

PLANNING WITH CURRICULUM STANDARDS THAT PROVIDE GUIDANCE

Curriculum Standards

Curriculum standards are defined as what students should know (content) and be able to do (process and performance). At the national level, curriculum standards did not exist in the United States until the standards that were developed and released for mathematics education in 1989. Shortly after the release of the mathematics standards, support for national goals in education was endorsed by the National Governors Association. The National Council on Education Standards and Testing recommended that in addition to those for mathematics, national standards for subject matter content in K–12 education be developed for the arts, civics/social studies, English/language-arts/reading, geography, history, and science. As part of this historical sequence, the U.S. Department of Education provided initial funding for the development of national standards. In 1994, the U.S. Congress passed the Goals 2000: Educate America Act, amended in 1996 with an Appropriations Act, encouraging states to set standards. Long before this, however, national organizations devoted to various disciplines were already defining standards as was done earlier for mathematics by the National Council for Teachers of Mathematics.

What the National Standards Are

The national standards represent the best thinking by expert panels about what are the essential elements of a basic core of subject knowledge that all students should

Arts, visual and performing. Developed jointly by the American Alliance for Theater and Education, the National Art Education Association, the National Dance Association, and the Music Educators National Conference, The National Standards for Arts Education were completed and released in 1994. (http://artsedge.kennedy-center.org/teach/standards.cfm)

Economics. Developed by the Council for Economic Education, standards for the study of economics were published in 1997. (www.councilforeconed.org/ea/standards)

Literacy/English/language arts/reading. Developed jointly by the International Reading Association, the National Council of Teachers of English, and the University of Illinois Center for the Study of Reading, standards for literacy/English education, including ELLs using their first language and reading about cultures, were completed and released in 1996. (www.ncte.org/standards)

National and State Curriculum Standards and Frameworks

Foreign languages. *Standards for Foreign Language Learning: Preparing for the 21st Century* was completed and released by the American Council on the Teaching of Foreign Languages (ACTFL) in 1996.[3] (www.actfl.org/i4a/pages/index.cfm?pageid=3392)

Geography. Developed jointly by the Association of American Geographers, the National Council for Geographic Education, and the National Geographic Society, standards for geography education were completed and released in 1994.[4] (http://www.nationalgeographic.com/xpeditions/standards)

State standards. (www.statestandards.com)
General and multiple disciplines(math/science). (www.goenc.com)

History/civics/social studies. The Center for Civic Education and the National Center for Social Studies developed standards for civics and government, and the National Center for History in the Schools developed the standards for history, all of which were completed and released in 1994. (www.socialstudies.org/standards)

Health. Developed by the Joint Committee for National School Health Education Standards, *National Health Education Standards: Achieving Health Literacy* was published in 1995.[5] (www.aahperd.org)

Information literacy:standards-based guidelines for school library media programs. Examples posted on the Ohio Department of Education website and on North Dakota Department of Public Instruction. (www.dpi.state.nd.us/standard/content/tech.pdf)

Mathematics. The National Council of Teachers of Mathematics (NCTM) published Curriculum and Evaluation Standards for School Mathematics (in 1989 with revised editions released in 2000 and 2006). Recent guidelines are in *Curriculum Focal Points for Pre-Kindergarten through Grade 8 Mathematics*. (www.nctm.org)

Native American Indian supplements. Supplements to national standards are available from the Bureau of Indian Affairs for civics and government, geography, health, language arts, mathematics, science, social studies, and the visual and the performing arts and are useful to districts serving American Indian children in adapting state standards to be more culturally relevant to their communities. They may also be used by Indian nations as guides in their preparation of tribally specific standards.[6] (www.bia.gov)

Family–School Partnerships: National Standards. For a copy, of the national standards (formerly from Parent-Teacher Association), contact the National PTA, 541 N. Fairbanks Court, Suite 1300, Chicago, IL 60611-3396. (www.pta.org/1216.htm)

Physical education. The National Association of Sport and Physical Education (NAASPE) published National Standards and Guidelines for Physical Education (2009). Teacher Education (3rd Ed.) (http://iweb.aahperd.org/iweb/purchase/productdetail.aspx?product_code=304-10460)

Science. With input from the American Association for the Advancement of Science and the National Science Teachers Association, the National Research Council's National Committee on Science Education Standards and Assessment developed and published standards for science education (1996). (www.nap.edu/openbook.php?record_id=4962)

Technology. Prepared by the International Technology Education Association, technology literacy standards were released in 2000. (www.iste.org/NETS, www.aect.org, or http://cnets.iste.org)

Teachers of English to Speakers of Other Languages. Prepared by TESOL, language competencies that English learners need in revised standards, 2006. (www.tesol.org)

Figure 5.1
Internet resources on national and state curriculum standards and frameworks.

acquire. They serve not as national mandates but rather as voluntary guidelines to encourage curriculum development to promote higher student achievement. It is the discretion of state and local curriculum developers in deciding the extent to which the standards are used. Strongly influenced by these national standards, nearly all fifty states have completed or are presently developing state standards for the various disciplines.

National Standards by Content Area

The following paragraphs describe national standards development for content areas in the K–12 curriculum. The standards are available on the Internet (Figure 5.1), and to help you become familiar with the national curriculum standards for various subjects of the K–6 grades, you are asked to do Application Exercise 5.1.

FOR YOUR NOTES

APPLICATION EXERCISE 5.1

Examining National Curriculum Standards

Instructions: The purpose of this exercise is to work cooperatively and collaboratively with others in your group and to become familiar with the national curriculum standards for various subjects of the K–6 curriculum. Using the addresses of sources provided in Figure 5.1, National Curriculum Standards, and other sources, such as professional journals, review the standards for your subject or subjects. Remove the perforated pages of this exercise from the book to use in small- or large-group discussions. Select any of the following questions as guidelines for the discussions. As an option, have subject-area group discussions (e.g., everyone interested in math in one group, interested in literacy in another group, then share the developments in each field with the rest of the class).

Subject area _____

1. Name of the standards document reviewed*

2. Year of document publication

3. Developed by

4. Specific K–6 goals specified by the new standards

5. Are the standards specific as to subject matter content for each grade level? Explain.

6. Do the standards offer specific strategies for instruction? Describe.

☞

7. Do the standards offer suggestions for teaching children with special needs? Describe.

8. Do the standards offer suggestions or guidelines for dealing with controversial topics?

9. Do the standards offer suggestions for specific resources? Describe.

10. Do the standards refer to assessment? Describe.

11. In summary, compared with what has been taught and how it has been taught in this field, what is new with the standards?*

12. Is there anything else about the standards you would like to discuss in your group? From these standards, what are the general purposes that you can determine for students' learning in the subject area you reviewed?

*As a reference, also look at your State Department of Education website for your state's standards for the subject/grade level you are interested in teaching.

Curriculum Standards and High-Stakes Testing

As mentioned previously, curriculum standards define what students should know and be able to do. The adoption of tougher K–12 standards throughout the United States along with an increased emphasis on high-stakes testing to assess how schools and teachers are helping their students meet those standards has provoked considerable debate. Educators, parents and guardians, politicians, and business people, have acted and reacted to the adoption of standards and high-stakes testing. Some argue that this renewed emphasis on testing means too much teaching to the test at the expense of more meaningful learning, and that it also means that the influence of the home, community, and other factors in society is being ignored. Some argue that educators need to find ways to identify what others in the business world are doing to promote education, because schools cannot do all the work alone. Nevertheless, here is what some teachers do to prepare for high-stakes testing:

- Responding to the call for increased accountability, some teachers in some schools put aside the regular curriculum for several weeks before the testing date and concentrate on the direct preparation of their students for the test, including teaching thinking skills that are often required. ELLs and others practice reading questions carefully, discuss the question, read all the choices for answers, and talk about the best answer from their point of view.

- Preparing for the tests, other teachers address the regular curriculum two days a week and prepare for tests three days a week during a pretest period. Analyzing questions is part of the preparation, especially for ELLs. Students learn to reread a given selection over and over when considering an answer to a comprehension question. They learn to answer the questions they know first and then go back and remember to mark an answer for each question on the test.

- Still other teachers use selected materials that are available to help prepare students for state-mandated tests, such as the TAKS (Texas Assessment of Knowledge and Skills) practice books with standards-based material. Other helpful resources are TestSmart Digital Lessons on CD based on the International Reading Association and National Council of Teachers of English standards (both are from ECS Learning Systems, Inc., P.O. Box 440, Bulverde, TX 78163).[7] The Texas Assessment of Knowledge and Skills practice books address the objectives for given subject areas, represent instructional targets, focus on content, familiarize students with the test question format, and contain authentic reading passages. The CD digital lessons relate to areas of reading/language arts standards such as genres, language expressions, mechanics, listening, reading operations, speaking, spelling, study skills, and writing.

- As another example, one publisher (The Critical Thinking Co., P.O. Box 1610, Seaside, CA 93955, phone 800-458-4849) offers materials for students preparing for assessments. For instance, the series *Math Detective*, grades 3–8, focuses on reading comprehension, reasoning, and writing in math, to prepare for California Achievement Tests (CAT/5), Iowa Tests of Basic Skills (ITBS), Stanford Achievement Test (SAT/10), Otis-Lennon School Ability Test (OLSAT-8), and the Metropolitan Achievement Test (MAT 7 and MAT 8). Another series, *Editor-in-Chief*, grades 3–12, is a standards-based thinking approach (grammar, spelling, details) to prepare for such assessments as Indiana Statewide Test for Ed. Progress (ISTEP), Arizona Instrument to Measure Standards (AIMS), and New York State English Language Arts Test (ELA).

- Another teacher resource focuses on the standards of reading, language arts, and writing. It is *Greening the Reading and Writing Standards: Integrating Environmental Education with Middle School Language Arts* (master's thesis, University of Arizona) by L. A. Packard. Packard's resource lists Arizona's state literacy standards and offers suggested activities and related children's literature to address each standard.

- Some teachers put aside true-false items and other test situations and only turn to multiple-choice tests with fill-in-the-bubble answer sheets to help students get acquainted with the answer-response "bubble" format.

- Using such pretest materials, teachers are well aware of the possibility (although certainly not an all-inclusive situation) that state and federal funding may be withheld from schools and/or jobs may be on the line for teachers and administrators when students do not score well.

Although the interest in student practice for pretesting has been rekindled in recent years, this often-called "drill and kill" approach is certainly not new. When comparing standardized testing of today with that of the past half-century, it is probably reasonable to conclude the following:

- The purpose of statewide standardized testing remains unchanged: it is to determine how well students are learning, at least to the extent determined by the particular test instrument.

- The test design is accomplished today with much greater precision and accuracy.

- The focus of today's testing is taking precious time away from the most creative aspects of teaching and learning.

- The manner in which test results are being used today and the long-term results of that use may have ramifications considerably more serious than at any time before.

To keep up-to-date with information about this issue of high-stakes testing and others, use your national professional associations as sources. For these Internet addresses, see Chapter 1, Figure 1.4. For more about ELLs in a culturally responsive classroom, see the National Center for Culturally Responsive Educational Systems (NCCRESt) at www.nccrest.org/index.html.

PLANNING WITH STATE/DISTRICT DOCUMENTS THAT PROVIDE GUIDANCE FOR CONTENT SELECTION

In addition to relying on national and state standards for planning and selecting curriculum content, you can rely on state and district documents. With the guidance of this chapter's Application Exercise 5.1, you can now examine major types of documents that help guide you in selecting the content of your curriculum. These can consist of national standards, state department of education standards, curriculum documents, school or district curriculum frameworks, courses of study, school-adopted printed or nonprinted materials, and related websites. Sources for your examination of these documents include sites on the Internet as listed in Figure 5.1, your college or university library, and collaborating teachers or administrative personnel at local schools or the district office. Related websites include National Research Center on Learning Disabilities at www.nrcld.org/, Success for All Foundation (learners-at-risk) at www.successforall.net/about/, and The Access Center (special education) at www.k8accesscenter.org/index.php.

PLANNING WITH STUDENT TEXTBOOKS THAT PROVIDE GUIDANCE FOR CONTENT SELECTION

In addition to relying on national and state standards, and state and district documents, you will rely on student textbooks for planning and selecting curriculum content. For several reasons—the recognition of the diversity of learning styles, learning capacities, and learning modalities of students, the cost of textbooks, and the availability of nonprint materials—textbook appearance, content, and use has changed considerably in recent years, and with advancing computer technology and e-books (and increasing Internet/energy costs), is likely to continue changing.

School districts periodically adopt new textbooks (usually every five to eight years). If you are a student teacher or a first-year teacher, this will most likely mean that someone will tell you, "Here are the student books you will be using."

Differentiated Instruction

Personalize the learning (*provide tiered instruction or differentiated instruction*) for students of various reading abilities. Consider the differentiated reading and workbook assignments in the textbook and several supplementary sources such as the multireading approach discussed in the next section. Except to make life simpler for the teacher, there is no advantage in all students working out of the same book and doing the same exercises. Some students benefit from the drill, practice, and reinforcement afforded by workbooks and computer programs that accompany textbooks, but this is not true for all students, nor do all benefit from the same activity. You should consider demonstrations, cooperative learning, guided oral and silent work, journals, graphic organizers, and the inquiry method. In addition, adjust instruction to meet the students' needs with corrective and developmental instruction, reteaching, follow-up lessons, and enrichment learning activities. In fact, the traditional workbook may eventually become extinct and be replaced by computer technology and e-books unless energy and product costs dictate otherwise.

Computers and other interactive media provide students with a psychologically safer learning environment in which they have greater control over the pace of the instruction, can repeat instruction if necessary, and can ask for clarification without the fear of having to do so publicly. Several methods have been used by teachers to help their students develop their higher-level thinking skills and better comprehend expository materials. Some of these are shown in Figure 5.2 and in Figure 5.3.

Just because something is in print or on the Internet does not mean it is necessarily accurate or even true. Whatever amount of time we spend teaching students how to find items on the Internet, we need to expend even more effort teaching them how to *interpret* what they have found. To do this, encourage students to be alert for errors in the text, both in content and printing. You might even give them some sort of credit reward, such as points, when they bring an error to your attention. This helps students develop the skills of critical reading, critical thinking, and healthy skepticism. As an example, an information book about the Pilgrims is reported to have stated that King Henry VIII ruled England in the 1600s. He died, with witnesses, in 1547. For another example, a history book is reported to have stated that the first person to lead a group through the length of the Grand Canyon was John Wesley Powell. Critically thinking students quickly made the point that perhaps Powell was the first person with European heritage to do this, but that Native Americans (the first people in the land now America) had traveled the length of the Grand Canyon for centuries.[8]

Figure 5.2
Methods* for identifying and building on students' prior knowledge and helping students develop their higher-order thinking skills and their comprehension of expository material.[9,10]

*These methods, along with KWL (beneficial for English language learners and English-speaking students with learning problems), KWLQ, TPS, and TWPS in Figure 6.1, are also suitable for preassessment.

- **PQRST:** Students preview (P) material, ask questions (Q), read (R), and state (S) the main idea; they test (T) themselves by answering the questions asked earlier.
- **RR,** reciprocal reading: Students take turns asking questions, summarizing, making predictions, and clarifying a story.
- **SQ3R:** Students survey (S) the material, ask questions (Q) about what was surveyed, read (R) the material, recite information (R), and review what was read (R). Supports English language learners and monolingual students with learning problems when instruction is adjusted into sequential steps/mini-lessons with graphic organizer of S column, Q column, etc.
- **SQ4R:** Students survey the material (S), ask questions about what was surveyed (Q), read to answer the questions (R), recite the answers (R), record important items from the materials into their journals/notebooks (R), then review what was read and done (R).
- **SRQ2R:** Students survey material (S), read it (R), ask questions about what was read (Q), recite the answers (R), and review what was read (R).

Multireading Approach

Rather than a single textbook approach, some teachers use a strategy that incorporates multiple readings that vary in detail and vocabulary but that have a common focus.[11] This strategy gives children a choice in what they read. The multiple readings allow for differences in reading ability and interest level, and stimulate a sharing of what is read and being learned. The use of multiple sources can be helpful in encouraging children to evaluate written communications and to think critically. By using a teacher's guide such as the sample in Figure 5.3, all the children can be directed toward specific information and concepts, but they do not have to all read the same selections.

PLANNING SEQUENCING OF CONTENT

As you have reviewed the rationale and components of instructional planning, and examined state and local curriculum documents, national standards, and student reading materials, you have undoubtedly reflected on your own opinion regarding content that should be included in a subject at a particular grade level. Now it is time to obtain some practical experience in long-range planning. While some authors believe that the first step in planning to teach is to write the learning objectives, others believe that a more logical starting point is to prepare a sequential topic outline from which you can then prepare the major learning objectives.

The topic outlines and learning objectives and even scripted lessons may be presented to most beginning teachers with the expectation that they will teach from them. For you this may be the case, but someone had to have written those curriculum materials and that someone was a classroom teacher. Further, some teachers organize

their long-term planning by setting up a large sheet of butcher paper (or charts/plain newsprint paper) on a table or wall. They divide it into time segments (six weeks, semester, year) and fill it in with adhesive notes marked with topics, activities, and lesson ideas. They use this visual planner throughout the instructional block being considered and move, add, remove, and rewrite the adhesive notes. The planning paper is placed where it can be referred to again and again. This approach to the stretches of time involved in long-term planning makes a teacher's planning immediate, tactile, tangible, and less abstract.

PREPARING FOR AND DEALING WITH CONTROVERSY

Controversial content and issues abound in teaching, for example, in English/language arts, over certain books; in mathematics, over the extent of the use of calculators in the classroom; in science, over biological evolution; and in social studies, over values and moral issues. As a general rule, trust your intuition: If you have concern that a particular topic or activity might create controversy, it probably will. During your teaching career, you undoubtedly will have to make decisions about how you will handle such matters. Some teachers stage several debates at the beginning of the school year so that the students begin to develop the skills to debate and to approach later unanticipated debates during the year, or "teachable moments." When selecting content or methods that might be controversial, consider as guidelines the information in the paragraphs that follow.

Maintain a perspective with respect to your own goal, that is, at the moment, to obtain your teaching credential, and then a teaching job, and then perhaps tenure.

**Multiple Readings Guide: Children's Bibliography
to Promote Global Awareness/Understanding***

- *Purpose*

  To engage students in multiple readings on the selected topic of global awareness and understanding, and to engage students in their own learning by motivating them to explore ideas further for enrichment; to foster continued interest through discussions about what the students liked/disliked about a selected story; and, to engage in role playing, critical thinking, and problem solving related to the topic.

- *Bibliography*

  Choi, Y. (2001). *The Name Jar*. New York: Knopf Books for Young Readers.

  Copsey, S. E. (1995). *Children Just Like Me*. Illustrated by B. Kindersley. New York: DK Children.

  D'Aluisio, F. (2008). *What the World Eats*. Illustrated by P. Menzel. New York: Tricycle.

  DK Publishing (2007). *A School Like Mine*. New York: DK Publishing.

  Dooley, N. (1992). *Everybody Cooks Rice*. Illustrated by P. J. Thornton. Minneapolis: Carolrhoda Books.

  Dooley, N. (2005). *Everybody Brings Noodles*. Illustrated by P. J. Thornton. Minneapolis: Carolrhoda Books.

  Fox, M. (2007). *Whoever You Are*. Illustrated by L. Staub. Orlando, FL: Red Wagon Books.

  Hollyer, B. (2004). *Let's Eat: What Children Eat around the World*. New York: Henry Holt and Co.

  Kissinger, K. (2002). *All the Colors We Are: Todos los colores de nuestra piel/The Story of How We Get Our Skin Color*. Illustrated by W. Krutein. St. Paul, MN: Redleaf Press.

  Lester, J. (2005). *Let's Talk about Race*. Illustrated by K. Barbour. New York: HarperCollins/Amisted.

  Lin, G. (1999). *The Ugly Vegetables*. Watertown, MA: Charlesbridge.

  Montanari, D. (2008) *Children around the World*. Toronto: Kids Can Press.

  Morris, A. (1993). *Bread, Bread, Bread*. Illustrated by K. Hayman. New York: HarperTrophy.

  Morris, A. (2000). *Families*. New York: HarperCollins.

  Morris, A. (1995). *Houses and Homes*. Illustrated by K. Heyman. New York: HarperTrophy.

  Priceman, M. (1996). *How to Make an Apple Pie and See the World*. Albuquerque, NM: Dragonfly Books.

  Shulevitz, U. (2008). *How I Learned Geography*. New York: Farrar.

  Simon, N. (1999). *All Kinds of Children*. Illustrated by D. Paterson. Walnut Creek, CA: Shen's Books.

  Smith, D. (2002). *If the World Were a Village: A Book about the World's People*. Illustrated by S. Armstrong. Toronto: Kids Can Press.

  Spier, P. (1988). *People*. New York: Doubleday Books for Young Readers.

  Swett, S. (2005). *Kids Weaving*. Illustrated by C. Hartlove and L. Corwin. San Francisco: Stewart, Tabori, and Chang.

Figure 5.3

Sample multiple readings guide and children's bibliography to promote global awareness/understanding.

*Reading aloud to English language learners and students with learning problems can introduce them to texts too difficult to read individually, lead them to discussions of content in relevant stories, and increase vocabulary, sentence-structure skills, grammar skills, and information retention. Additionally, the teacher can identify a selected number of foods and each day, a different book about foods is read aloud. The students divide into groups of five or six and receive a copy of one of the books read aloud. Each group prepares a chart of the features of a food shown in the book they have and records what they have learned about the food—ingredients, process of making, looks of the product, and use by the people in a culture. The teacher records features of the foods on a large food chart. Discussion leads to generalization about the foods—that not all are grown in the same way, look the same, or are made the same. Thus, there is variability in food in the cultures—in how it is planted, grown, harvested, transported, and valued by the people in a particular culture.

Our point is that student teaching is not a good time to become involved in controversy. If you communicate closely with your host teacher and your college or university supervisor, you should be able to prevent most major problems dealing with controversial issues. Sometimes, during normal discussion in the classroom, a controversial topic will emerge spontaneously, catching the teacher off guard. *If this happens, think before saying anything.* Consider suspending further discussion on the topic until you have had an opportunity to review the issues with colleagues or your supervisors. Controversial topics can seem to rise from nowhere for any teacher, and this is perfectly normal. Children are works in progress! They need to be allowed to develop their skills in flexible thinking (one of the characteristics of intelligent behavior discussed later in Chapter 9), which they can only do as they learn to consider alternative points of view and to deal with several sources of information simultaneously. They are in the process of developing their moral and value systems, and they need and want to know how adults feel about issues that are important to them, particularly those adults they hold in esteem—their teachers. For some children, unfortunately, their classroom teacher may be the only adult they can hold in esteem. Students need to discuss issues that are important to society, and there is absolutely nothing wrong with dealing with those issues as long as certain guidelines are observed.

First, students should learn about all sides of an issue. Controversial issues are open-ended and should be treated as such. They do not have "right" answers or "correct" answers. If they did, there would be no controversy. (As used in this book, an issue differs from a problem in that a problem generally has a solution, whereas an issue has many opinions and several alternative solutions.) Therefore, the focus should be on process as well as on content. A major goal is to help children learn how to deal with controversy and to mediate wise decisions on the basis of carefully considered information. Another goal is to help children learn how to disagree without being disagreeable—how to resolve conflict. To that end, children need to learn the difference between conflicts that are destructive and those that can be constructive; in other words, to see that conflict (disagreement) can be healthy, that it can have value. A third goal, of course, is to help students learn about the content of an issue so, when necessary, they can make decisions based on knowledge, not on ignorance.

Second, as with all lesson plans, one dealing with a topic that could lead to controversy should be well thought out ahead of time—that is, during the preactive/ planning phase of instruction. Potential problem areas and resources must be carefully considered and prepared in advance. You might want to send home a letter to parents outlining what you plan to teach and the resources you will use. Be sure they sign and return the letter. Consider inviting the parents to a preview night where they hear about how you will approach the topic and see the materials you will incorporate. Write a rationale for your plans that includes your goals and objectives, the materials you reviewed, and why you decided to use the books, videos, and so on, that you plan to share, and your lesson plans. Be sure to include the process that the materials went through according to the district Material Selection Policy (if the materials did). Sign and date the rationale. This verifies your careful planning, should the need arise.

It is a good idea to consult with your site administrator about your rationale. If parents or guardians or paraprofessionals work in your classroom, be sure they understand the curriculum. Often these people are your best community liaisons. As we have said before (see Chapter 3, for example), problems for the teacher are most likely to occur when insufficient attention is given to the preactive phase of instruction and decision making.

Third, no matter how carefully you plan, a challenge may arise to something you plan to teach or have taught. This may come from students, parents and guardians, community representatives, or other faculty. Parents or guardians have the right *sans penalty* to ask that their child receive an alternate activity or be excused from the lesson. However, they do not have the right to censor content for all children. Most school districts have written policies that deal with challenges to instructional content or materials. As a beginning teacher, you should become aware of the policies of your school district (often called the Materials Reconsideration Policy). In addition, professional associations such as NCTE, IRA, NCSS, NBTA, and NSTA have published guidelines for dealing with controversial content or materials. NCTE offers an online resource about censorship at www.ncte.org/action/ anti-censorship. Here's an "APPLE" to help you remember how to deal with censorship:

A = Awareness/Acceptance
To see that the potential for a challenge does exist for any educator.

P = Prepare
To prepare as mentioned previously.

P = Practice
To promote calm, objective responses to a challenge, reflect about how you would handle different types of challenges (e.g., sexism, violence, racism, profanity, etc.). Role play your response to a challenge with your peers.

L = Locate
To know where you can get support. Some national organizations are listed in this chapter.

E = Evaluate
To be aware of any changes occurring in the selection and reconsideration policies of the school district.

Fourth, there is nothing wrong with children knowing a teacher's opinion about an issue as long as it is clear that the students may disagree sans reprisal or academic penalty. However, it is probably best to give your opinion only after the children have had full opportunity to study and report on facts and opinions from other sources. Sometimes it is helpful to assist students in separating facts

Figure 5.4
Fact-opinion table.

The issue:	
Statements of fact:	Statements of opinion:

from opinions on a particular issue being studied by setting up a fact-opinion table on the overhead or on the writing board, with the issue stated at the top followed by two parallel columns, one for facts and one for related opinions (see Figure 5.4).

A characteristic that has made the United States such a great nation is the freedom for its entire people to speak out on issues. This freedom should not be excluded from public school classrooms. Teachers and students should be encouraged to express their opinions about the great issues of today, to study the issues, to suspend judgment while collecting data, and then form and accept each other's reasoned opinions. As educators, we must understand the difference between teaching truth, values, and morals, and teaching *about* truth, values, and morals.

As a public school teacher, there are limits to your academic freedom, much greater than are the limits on a university professor. You must understand this fact. The primary difference is that the students with whom you will be working are not yet adults. As children, they must be protected from dogma and allowed the freedom to learn and to develop their values and opinions, free from coercion from those who have power and control over their learning.

PLANNING FOR LEARNING OUTCOMES: AIMS, GOALS, AND OBJECTIVES

Now that you have examined content typical of the curriculum (even controversial issues) and, perhaps have exercised the option of preparing a content outline for a subject at a grade level at which you intend to teach, you are ready to write instructional objectives for content learning. **Instructional objectives** (also called **learning objectives**) are statements describing what the student will be able to do upon completion of the instructional experience. Whereas some authors distinguish between instructional objectives (objectives that are behavior specific), the terms are used here as if they are synonymous to emphasize the importance of writing instructional objectives in terms that are measurable. *Terminal objective* is sometimes used to distinguish between instructional objectives that are intermediate and those that are final, or terminal, to an area of learning.

PLANNING WITH INSTRUCTIONAL OBJECTIVES

As implied in the preceding paragraphs, goals guide the instructional methods; objectives drive student performance. Assessment of student achievement in learning should be an assessment of that performance. When the assessment procedure does match the instructional objectives, that is sometimes referred to as assessment that is *aligned* or *authentic*. If the term **authentic assessment** sounds rather silly to you, we agree. After all, if the objectives and assessment don't match, then that particular assessment should be discarded or modified until it does match. In other words, assessment that is not authentic is "poor assessment" and should not be used. When objectives, instruction, and assessment match the stated goals, we have what is referred to as an **aligned curriculum.** Again, a curriculum that does not align is nonsensical and should be corrected or discarded.[12]

While instructional goals may not always be quantifiable, that is, readily measurable, instructional objectives should be measurable. Furthermore, those objectives then become the essence of what is measured for in instruments designed to assess student learning—they are the learning targets. Consider the examples shown in Figure 5.5.

Figure 5.5
Examples of goals and objectives.

Goals

1. To acquire knowledge about the physical geography of North America.
2. To develop an appreciation for music.
3. To develop enjoyment for reading.

Objectives

1. On a map, the student will identify at least three specific mountain ranges of North America.
2. The student will identify five out of ten different musical instruments by listening to a tape recording of the Boston Pops Symphony Orchestra and identify which instrument is being played at specified times as determined by the teacher.
3. The student will read two books, three short stories, and five newspaper articles at home, within a two-month period and will maintain a daily written log of these activities.

Learning Targets and Goal Indicators

One purpose for writing objectives in performance terms is to be able to assess with precision whether the instruction has resulted in the desired behavior. In many schools, the educational goals are established as **learning targets,** competencies that the students are expected to achieve. These goals are then divided into performance objectives, sometimes referred to as **goal indicators.** Instruction is designed to teach toward those objectives. When students perform the competencies called for by these objectives, their education is considered successful. Over recent years, this has become known variously as **criterion-referenced, competency-based, performance-based, results-driven,** or **outcome-based education.** Expecting students to achieve one set of competencies before moving on to the next set is called mastery learning (see Chapter 10). The success of the student achievement, teacher performance, and the school may each be assessed according to these criteria.

PLANNING WITH DOMAINS OF LEARNING AND DEVELOPMENTAL NEEDS OF CHILDREN

Educators attempt to design learning experiences to meet the five areas of developmental needs of the total child: intellectual, physical, emotional/psychological, social, and moral/ethical.[13] As a teacher, you must include objectives that address learning within each of these categories of needs. While the intellectual needs are primarily within the cognitive domain and the physical are within the psychomotor, the other needs are mostly within the affective domain.

Too frequently, teachers focus on the cognitive domain while only assuming that the psychomotor and affective will take care of themselves. Many experts argue that teachers should do just the opposite; that when the affective is directly attended to, the psychomotor and cognitive naturally develop. In any case, you should plan your teaching so your students are guided from the lowest to the highest levels of operation within each of the domains separately or simultaneously.

The three developmental hierarchies are discussed next to guide your understanding of each of the five areas of needs. Notice the illustrative verbs within each hierarchy. These verbs help you fashion objectives when you are developing activities, lesson plans, and unit plans. (To see how goals and objectives fit into a selected lesson plan, turn ahead to Figure 7.7 in Chapter 7 to see a Multiple-Day, Project-Centered, Interdisciplinary and Transcultural Lesson Using World Wide Communication via the Internet). Caution, however, must be urged, for there can be considerable overlap among the levels at which some action verbs may appropriately be used. For example, the verb phrase *will identify* is appropriate in each of the following objectives at different levels (identified in parentheses) within the cognitive domain:

The student will identify the correct definition of the term *magnetism.* (remembering knowledge)

The student will identify examples of the principle of magnetic attraction. (understanding/comprehending)

The student will identify the magnetic effect when two materials, one magnetic and one nonmagnetic, are brought together. (applying)

The student will identify the effect when iron filings are brought into a magnetic field. (analyzing)

The student will identify a new format (creating an Internet ad, writing a news advertisement, a TV song, or rap) to convey the effect of iron filings brought into a magnetic field/kept out of a magnetic field. (creating)

Cognitive Domain Hierarchy

In a widely accepted taxonomy of objectives, Bloom and his associates arranged cognitive objectives into classifications according to the complexity of the skills and abilities they embodied.[14] The result was a multitiered arrangement ranging from the simplest to the most complex intellectual processes. Within each domain, prerequisite to a student's ability to function at one particular level of the hierarchy is the ability to function at the preceding level or levels. In other words, when a student is functioning at the third level of the cognitive domain, that student is automatically also functioning at the first and second levels. Note that rather than an orderly progression from simple to complex mental operations as illustrated by Bloom's newly revised taxonomy, other researchers prefer a contrastive organization of cognitive abilities that ranges from simple information storage and retrieval, through a higher level of discrimination and concept attainment, to the highest cognitive ability to recognize and solve problems.[15]

The six major categories (or levels) in Bloom's revised taxonomy of cognitive objectives are (a) **remembering knowledge**—recognizing and recalling information; (b) **understanding/comprehension**—getting the meaning of information; (c) **applying**—using the informational fact; (d) **analyzing**—distinguishing/dissecting information into its component parts to comprehend their relationships; (e) **evaluating**—justifying and judging the worth of an idea, notion, theory, thesis, proposition, information, or opinion; and (f) **creating/synthesizing**—putting components together to generate new ideas. In this taxonomy, the top four categories of levels—applying, analyzing, evaluating, and creating/synthesizing—represent higher-order thinking skills.[16]

Affective Domain Hierarchy

Kratwohl, Bloom, and Masia developed a taxonomy of the affective domain.[17] The following are their major levels (or categories) from least internalized to most internalized: (a) **receiving**—being aware of the affective stimulus and beginning to have favorable feelings toward it; (b) **responding**—taking an interest in the stimulus and viewing it favorably; (c) **valuing**—showing a tentative belief in the value of the effective stimulus and becoming committed to it; (d) **organizing**—placing values into a system of dominant and supporting values; and (e) **internalizing**—demonstrating consistent beliefs and behavior that have become a way of life. While there is considerable overlap from one category to another within the affective domain, these categories do give a basis by which to judge the quality of objectives and the nature of learning within this area.

Psychomotor Domain Hierarchy

Whereas identification and classification within the cognitive and affective domains are generally agreed upon, there is less agreement in the classification within the psychomotor domain. Originally, the goal of this domain was simply to develop and categorize proficiency in skills, particularly those dealing with gross and fine motor control. The classification of the domain presented here follows this lead, but includes at its highest level the most creative and inventive behaviors, thus coordinating skills and knowledge from all three domains. Consequently, the objectives are in a hierarchy ranging from simple gross locomotor control to the most creative and complex, requiring originality and fine locomotor control—for example, from simply turning on a computer to designing a software program. From Harrow, we offer the following taxonomy of the psychomotor domain: (a) **moving,** (b) **manipulating,** (c) **communicating,** and (d) **creating.**[18]

While space does not allow elaboration here, the different taxonomies include various subcategories within each of the major categories. It is probably less important that an objective be absolutely classified than it is to be cognizant of the hierarchies and to understand the importance of attending to student behavior from lower to higher levels of operation in all three domains. For a further discussion of each of these taxonomies and some action verbs and objectives for each category, turn to selected readings at the end of this chapter.

Now, use this chapter's Application Exercise 5.2 to begin writing your own objectives in a selected domain for use in your teaching. You may want to turn ahead to Chapter 7 and correlate writing your own objectives with some of the Application Exercises there. If time permits, discuss one or two of your objectives with one of your classmates or your instructor.

APPLICATION EXERCISE 5.2

Preparing My Own Instructional Objectives

Instructions: The purpose of this application exercise is to work cooperatively and collaboratively with a peer and begin writing your own behavioral objectives. Remove the perforated pages for this exercise and for a subject and a grade level of your choice, write 10 specific instructional objectives or a number indicated by your instructor. It is not necessary to include audience, conditions, and performance level unless requested by your course instructor.* If you wish, you can refer to other Application Exercises in this resource guide for help, namely, Application Exercise 7.1 Putting Objectives, Resources, and Learning Activities Together for a Teaching Plan, and Application Exercise 7.2 Preparing a Lesson Plan. Exchange this completed exercise with a classmate. Then discuss the objectives and make changes where necessary.

Subject _____

Grade level: _____

1. Affective (low level) _____

   _____

2. Affective (highest level) _____

   _____

3. Cognitive knowledge _____

   _____

4. Cognitive comprehension _____

   _____

5. Cognitive application _____

   _____

6. Cognitive analysis _____

   _____

7. Cognitive synthesis _____

   _____

8. Cognitive evaluation _____

   _____

9. Psychomotor (low level) _____

   _____

10. Psychomotor (high level) _____

    _____

*If needed, review the levels of the affective domain, cognitive domain, and psychomotor domain in this chapter and selected references at the end of this chapter.

PLANNING WITH TAXONOMIES

Theoretically, the taxonomies are so constructed that students achieve each lower level before being ready to move to the higher levels. But, because categories and behaviors overlap, as they should, this theory does not always hold in practice. Furthermore, as explained by others, feelings and thoughts are inextricably interconnected—they cannot be neatly separated as the taxonomies would imply.[19]

The taxonomies are important in that they emphasize the various levels to which instruction must aspire. For learning to be worthwhile, you must formulate and teach to objectives from the higher levels of the taxonomies as well as from the lower ones.

Student thinking and behaving must be moved from the lowest to the highest levels of thinking and doing. When all is said and done, it is, perhaps, the highest level of the psychomotor domain (creating) to which we aspire.

In using the taxonomies, remember that the point is to formulate the best objectives for the job to be done. In schools that use results-driven education models, those models describe levels of mastery standards (rubrics) for each target outcome. The taxonomies provide the mechanism for ensuring that you do not spend a disproportionate amount of time on facts and other low-level learning and can be of tremendous help where teachers are expected to correlate learning activities to one of the school's or district's outcome standards.

Preparing objectives is essential to the preparation of good items for the assessment of student learning. Clearly communicating your performance expectations to students and then specifically assessing student learning against those expectations makes the teaching most efficient and effective, and it makes the assessment of the learning closer to being authentic. This does not mean to imply that you will always write performance objectives for everything taught, nor will you always be able to accurately measure what students have learned. As said earlier, learning that is meaningful to students is not as easily compartmentalized as the taxonomies of educational objectives would imply.

PLANNING WITH INTEGRATED CURRICULUM

When learning about **integrated curriculum** (IC), it is easy to be confused by the plethora of terms that are used. Other terms for IC are **interdisciplinary curriculum,** *integrated studies, thematic instruction, multidisciplinary teaching, integrated curriculum,* and *interdisciplinary thematic instruction.* In essence, regardless of which of these terms is being used, the reference is to the same approach to teaching.

Because it is not always easy to tell where the term *curriculum* leaves off and the term *instruction* begins,

let's assume for now that for the sake of better understanding the meaning of integrated curriculum, there is no difference between the two terms. In other words, for the intent of this discussion, whether we use the term *integrated curriculum* or the term *integrated instruction*, we will be referring to the same thing.

Let's now look at reinforcing the "how" of planning and selecting content. If learning is defined only as the accumulation of bits and pieces of information, then we already know everything about how to teach and how children learn. But the accumulation of pieces of information is at the lowest end of a spectrum of types of learning. Discoveries are still being made about the processes involved in higher forms of learning—that is, for meaningful understanding and the reflective application of that understanding. The results of recent research support the use of instructional strategies that help children make connections as they learn. These strategies include the literature-based approach to reading, discovery learning, inquiry learning, cooperative learning, and interdisciplinary thematic instruction, with a total curriculum that is integrated and connected to students' life experiences.

This methodology uses what is referred to as **hands-on** and **minds-on learning.** The learner is learning by doing and is thinking about what she or he is doing and learning. When thoughtfully coupled, these approaches help construct, and often reconstruct, the learner's perceptions. Hands-on learning engages the learner's mind, causing questioning. Then, with the teacher's competent guidance, the children devise ways of investigating satisfactory, though sometimes only tentative, answers to their questions.

As a classroom teacher, your instructional task then is twofold: (a) to plan hands-on experiences, providing the materials and the supportive environment necessary for students' meaningful exploration and discovery learning, and (b) to know how to facilitate the most meaningful and longest-lasting learning possible once the learner's mind has been engaged by the hands-on learning. To accomplish this requires your knowledge about, and competence in the use of, varied and developmentally appropriate methods of instruction. Assisting you in the acquisition of that knowledge and competence is the primary purpose of this resource guide. The chapters of this part of the resource guide address the planning aspect. As you proceed through these chapters and begin the development of your instructional plans, from time to time, you will want to refer to the topic of assessment of student learning in Chapter 6 and to particular topics of interest to you in the chapters of Part III. Instruction and assessment go hand in hand and cannot be as easily separated as might be implied from their placement in the organization of this resource guide. Their separation here is done not for your implementation of them, but as explained in the Preface of this guide, for your understanding of them.

LOOKING AT TEACHERS II

Integrated Technology, Interactive Whiteboard

During a sixth-grade brainstorming session with features of listening as the language arts content, a teacher, as part of her planning, records student contributions on a large sheet of butcher paper that has been taped to the classroom wall. She solicits student responses about the content being studied. Some of the responses are deciding to listen, reading all stimuli, investing time wisely, verifying what was heard, and expending energy to listen. She acknowledges those responses, holds and manipulates the writing pen, walks to the wall, and writes on the paper. Each of these actions requires decisions and movements that consume precious instructional time and that can distract her from her students. An effective alternative would be to have a reliable student helper (or classroom aide/parent volunteer) do the writing while the teacher handles the solicitation and acknowledgment of

student contributions. With that approach, she has fewer decisions and fewer actions to distract her and does not have to turn her back to the students to write their responses on the paper. She does not lose eye contact and proximity with the classroom of students.

As another alternative, one that integrates technology (but uses electricity and may increase the school's energy costs), the teacher can give the students a hands-on experience with an interactive whiteboard connected to the class computer. A projector shows an image of the students' contributions after brainstorming features of listening. The contributions are typed into a computer and shown on a screen or board. Using an electronic pen or pointer, the teacher (or student) then writes the students' responses during the class discussion. If needed, graphics, sounds, or a video of the students can be incorporated.

SUMMARY

In this chapter, you learned of the differences between the terms *goals* and *objectives*. Regardless of how these terms are defined, the important point is this: *Teachers must be clear about what it is they want their students to learn, must be clear about the kind of evidence needed to verify their learning, and must communicate those things to the students so they are clearly understood.*

You'll recall that many teachers do not bother to write specific objectives for all the learning activities in their teaching plans. However, when teachers do prepare specific objectives (by writing them themselves or by borrowing them from textbooks and other curriculum documents), teach toward them, and assess students' progress against them, student learning is enhanced; this is called *performance-based teaching* and *criterion-referenced measurement*. It is also known as an *aligned curriculum*. In schools using results-driven education mastery learning models, those models describe levels of mastery standards or rubrics for each outcome or learning target. The taxonomies are of tremendous help in schools where teachers are expected to correlate learning activities to the school's outcome standards.

As a teacher, you will be expected to (a) plan your lessons well, (b) convey specific expectations to your students, and (c) assess their learning against that specificity. However, because it tends toward high objectivity, there is the danger that such performance-based teaching could become too objective, which can have negative consequences. If students are treated as objects, then

the relationship between teacher and student becomes impersonal and counterproductive to real learning. Highly specific and impersonal teaching can be discouraging to serendipity, creativity, and the excitement of discovery, to say nothing of its possibly negative impact on the development of students' self-esteem.

To be a most effective teacher, your challenge is to use performance-based criteria together with a teaching style that encourages the development of intrinsic sources of student motivation and that allows for, provides for, and encourages coincidental learning—learning that goes beyond what might be considered as predictable, immediately measurable, and representative of minimal expectations. Your final decisions about what content to teach are guided by (a) discussions with other teachers; (b) review of national, state, and local standards and documents, and articles from the professional journals/websites; (c) your personal convictions, knowledge, and skills; and (d) the unique characteristics of your students.

What's to Come. With knowledge of the content of school curriculum and the value of instructional objectives, you are now ready to consider student assessment and then detailed instructional plans with sequenced lessons as the subjects of the next two chapters. When you finish reading the next chapter (Chapter 6), you'll be ready to complete a Midpoint Self-Check Reflection Guide (in Appendix B) to assess your competencies up to this point. You'll note that reflecting about your self-check responses means you'll spend some time in careful thought about the items on the self-check. It means you'll give some attention and consideration to the items and then you'll reconsider any previous actions, events, or decisions you've made related to the items.

Also, you can interact in various ways to extend your competencies in the next chapter's section, Extending My Professional Competency. Now, please turn your attention to the following section closing this chapter.

EXTENDING MY PROFESSIONAL COMPETENCY

With Discussion

Documents. If a teaching colleague believes—and fears—that national curriculum standards are a first step forward toward national assessment of student learning (and thus national assessment of a teacher's instruction), what would be your response to your colleague's statement? **To do:** Consider the information you have read about planning and selecting content and the national curriculum standards and explain your point of view about the effects of national assessment on your classroom.

With Video

Video Activity: Planning and Selecting Content. Can critical-thinking skills be taught while teaching literacy?

myeducationlab

> Go to the Video Examples section of Topic #12: Diversity: Cultural and Linguistic in the MyEducationLab for your course to view the video entitled "An ESL Vocabulary Lesson."

Watch a teacher demonstrate ESL strategies for teaching vocabulary and word identification to first-graders. Think of a way that at least one critical thinking skill can be taught in the video's lesson. Be able to describe at least one observable behavior that would enable you to tell if a child is learning to think critically and point it out to a colleague. Refer back to this chapter as needed.

With Portfolio

Portfolio Planning. In my portfolio, what would I say about how I would select content? How could I show my knowledge of curriculum reflecting Principles 1, 4, and 7 of INTASC, and Standards 2 and 6 of NBPTS as seen on the inside of the front cover of this book? **To do:** Review Chapter 5 and then write a one- to two-page paper explaining your view of planning and selecting content for a grade of your choice. Label your paper as Selecting Content, and after returning to sections of interest to you in this chapter, state how you have developed your competency so far for one of the following objectives:

- Becoming familiar with the national curriculum standards for various subjects of the K–6 curriculum that can be resources for planning and selecting content.

- Becoming familiar with curriculum documents published by my state's department of education as well as local curriculum documents.
- To review the rest, turn to the section on Chapter Objectives at the beginning of this chapter. Place your paper in your portfolio folder or in your computer file.

With Teacher Tests Study Guide

Teacher Tests for Future Licensing and Certification. If I wanted to prepare for taking a state teacher test to qualify for my teaching certificate/license and review my knowledge about planning and selecting content, how could I begin? **To do:** To support you as you prepare for teaching, you will find constructed response-type questions similar to those found on state tests for teacher licensing and certification in Appendix A of this book. The question related to this chapter helps you take another look at the classroom vignette found in *Looking at Teachers II*. Write your response to this chapter's question and, if you wish, discuss it with another teaching candidate. If appropriate, use one or two of your colleague's suggestions to help you change your response to the question. Place your response in a Teacher Test Study Guide folder or type/scan into a computer file. Plan to review and reread for study purposes before taking a scheduled teacher test.

With Target Topics for Teacher Tests (TTTT)

If I wanted to start early and prepare for taking a state teacher test for licensing and certification and review subject matter about planning and selecting content, how could I begin? **To do:** Consider reviewing Target Topics for Teacher Tests (TTTT) in the subject index. To assist you as you prepare to take a teacher test, bullets (•) have been placed by selected word entries in the subject index and indicate Target Topics for Teacher Tests. The bullets highlight selected core subject matter for this chapter (and other chapters)—sequencing, instructional objectives, learning domains, taxonomies—that the authors suggest be reviewed in preparation for taking a teacher test similar to your state's test.

WITH READING

Barton, K. C., and Smith, L. A. (2000). Themes or Motifs? Aiming for Coherence through Interdisciplinary Outlines. *The Reading Teacher, 54*(1), 54–63.

Cooper, J. (2003). *Classroom Teaching Skills* (7th ed.). Boston: Houghton Mifflin.

Davidson, M., and Myhre, O. (2000). Measuring Reading at Grade Level. *Educational Leadership, 57*(5), 25–28.

Duffy, G. G., and Hoffman, J. V. (1999). In Pursuit of an Illusion: The Flawed Search for a Perfect Method. *The Reading Teacher, 53*(1), 10–16.

Glickman, C. (2002–2001). Holding Sacred Ground: The Impact of Standardization. *Educational Leadership, 58*(4), 46–51.

Good, T. L., and Brophy, J. E. (2003). *Looking in Classrooms* (9th ed., Ch. 10). New York: Addison Wesley Longman.

Lambert, L. T. (2000). The New Physical Education. *Educational Leadership, 57*(6), 34–38.

Rubin, D. (2000). *Teaching Elementary Language Arts: A Balanced Approach* (6th ed.). Needham Heights, MA: Allyn & Bacon.

Teachers of English to Speakers of Other Languages (2006). *PreK–12 English Language Proficiency Standards in the Core Content Areas.* Alexandria, VA: TESOL.

TenBrink, T. D. (2003). Instructional Objectives, in J. Cooper (Ed.), *Classroom Teaching Skills* (7th ed.). Boston: Houghton Mifflin.

Tomlinson, C.A. (2008). Making a Difference. *Teacher Magazine,* September 10, 1–6. Go to www.teachermagazine.org/tsb/articles/2008/09/10/01tomlinson.h02.html.

WITH NOTES

1. L. Jacobson, Hawaii Schools See Green, *Education Week,* pp. 21–23 (October 28, 2008).

2. R. J. Stiggins, *Student-Centered Classroom Assessment,* 3rd ed. (Upper Saddle River, NJ: Merrill/Prentice Hall, 2001).

3. Contact American Council on the Teaching of Foreign Languages (ACTFL), 1001 N. Fairfax St., Suite 200, Alexandria, VA, 22314.

4. Contact National Geographic Society, P.O. Box 98199, Washington, DC 20090-8199.

5. Contact the American Alliance for Health, Physical Education, Recreation and Dance (AAHPRD), 1900 Association Drive, Reston, VA 20191-1598.

6. Bureau of Indian Affairs, 1849 C St., NW, Washington, DC 20240.

7. Standards for English literacy education at www.ncte.org/standards. Some states use statewide textbook adoption committees to review books and to then provide local districts with lists of recommended titles from which to choose.

8. R. Reinhold, Class Struggle, *The New York Times Magazine,* p. 46 (September 29, 1991).

9. Source of PQRST: E. B. Kelly, *Memory Enhancement for Educators,* Fastback 365 (Bloomington, IN: Phi Delta Kappa Educational Foundation, 1994), p. 18; source of SQ3R: The original source of SQ3R is unknown, but see the early work of F. P. Robinson, *Effective Study,* rev. ed. (New York: Harper & Brothers, 1961); for source of SRQ2R, see M. L. Walker, Help for the "Fourth-Grade Slump"—SRQ2R Plus Instruction in Text Structure or Main Idea, *Reading Horizons, 36*(1), 38–58 (1995).

10. See also Figure 6.1 in Chapter 6 for use of KWL methods as preassessment with these sources: early source for KWL: J. Bryan, K–W–L: Questioning the Known. *A Journal of the International Reading Association: Teaching Reading, 51*(7), 618–620 (1998); early source of KWLQ: P. R. Schmidt, KWLQ: Inquiry and Literacy Learning in Science, *Reading Teacher, 52*(7), 789–792 (April 1999).

11. See, for example, H. M. Miller, Teaching and Learning about Cultural Diversity: All of Us Together Have a Story to Tell, *The Reading Teacher, 53*(8), 666–667 (May, 2000); D. Camp, It Takes Two: Teaching with Twin Texts of Fact and Fiction, *The Reading Teacher, 53*(5), 400–408 (February, 2000); The Book Review: Grade 5 and up, *School Library Journal, 49*(7), 136 (July 2003).

12. T. L. Good and J. E. Brophy, *Looking in Classrooms,* 9th ed. (New York: Addison-Wesley-Longman, 2003), pp. 252–253.

13. See B. Cambourne, Holistic, Integrated Approaches to Reading and Language Arts Instruction: The Constructionist Framework on an Instructional Theory. In A. Farstrup and J. Samuels (Eds.), *What Research Has to Say About Reading Instruction* (Newark, DE: International Reading Association, 2002). Also read articles in The Constructivist Classroom theme issue of *Educational Leadership, 57*(3).

14. B. S. Bloom (Ed.), *Taxonomy of Educational Objectives, Book 1, Cognitive Domain* (White Plains, NY: Longman, 1984).

15. See early writing of R. M. Gagné, L. J. Briggs, and W. W. Wager, *Principles of Instructional Design,* 4th ed. (New York: Holt, Rinehart and Winston, 1994).

16. L. W. Anderson and D. R. Krathwohl (Eds.). (2001), *A Taxonomy for Learning, Teaching, and Assessing: A Revision of Bloom's Taxonomy of Educational Objectives: Complete Edition* (New York: Longman), pp. 67–68. You can compare Bloom's early writing about higher-order cognitive thinking skills with R. H. Ennis's *A Taxonomy of Critical Thinking Dispositions and Abilities,* in J. B. Barron and R. J. Sternberg (Eds.), *Teaching Thinking Skills: Theory and Practice* (New York: W. H. Freeman, 1987), and with Marzano's *A Different Kind of Classroom: Teaching with Dimensions of Learning* (Alexandria, VA: Association for Supervision and Curriculum Development, 1992).

17. See original work of D. R. Krathwohl, B. S. Bloom, and B. B. Masia, *Taxonomy of Educational Goals, Book 2, Affective Domain* (New York: Longman, 1984).

18. See early taxonomy of A. J. Harrow, *Taxonomy of the Psychomotor Domain* (New York: Longman, 1977). A similar taxonomy for this domain is that of E. J. Simpson, The Classification of Educational Objectives in the Psychomotor Domain, in *The Psychomotor Domain, Volume 3* (Washington, DC: Gryphon House, 1972).

19. Krathwohl, Bloom, and Masia, see note 17.

Michael Newman/Photoedit

How Do I Assess, Use, and Report Student Achievement?

6

Visual Chapter Organizer and Overview

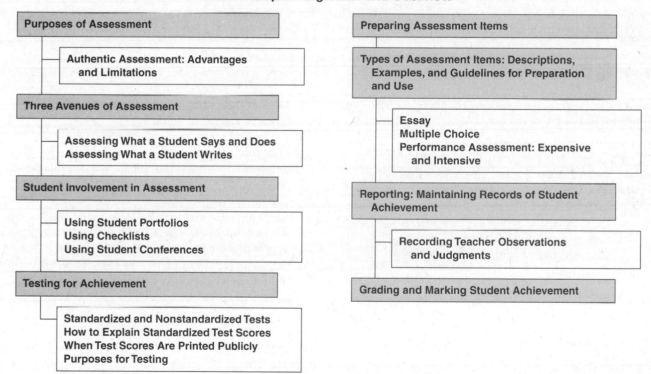

Purposes of Assessment
Authentic Assessment: Advantages and Limitations

Three Avenues of Assessment
Assessing What a Student Says and Does
Assessing What a Student Writes

Student Involvement in Assessment
Using Student Portfolios
Using Checklists
Using Student Conferences

Testing for Achievement
Standardized and Nonstandardized Tests
How to Explain Standardized Test Scores
When Test Scores Are Printed Publicly
Purposes for Testing

Preparing Assessment Items
Types of Assessment Items: Descriptions, Examples, and Guidelines for Preparation and Use

| Essay
Multiple Choice
Performance Assessment: Expensive and Intensive |

Reporting: Maintaining Records of Student Achievement
Recording Teacher Observations and Judgments

| Grading and Marking Student Achievement |

LOOKING AT TEACHERS I

Integrated Technology, MP3 Players

In an elementary school in a western state, an educator developed an International Reading Association award-winning program, Reading Buddies. Beginning readers in the Reading Buddies program used MP3 players to increase their literacy skills. Here's what was done:

- *Here's how the Reading Buddies program was initiated and assessed:* The young students were first tested on the Dynamic Indicators of Basic Early Literacy Skills and then every two weeks on prereading and early reading skills during a ten-week pilot program. Indicators consisted of naming letters, phonemic awareness, and ease of decoding nonsense words accurately.

- *Here's how it was implemented:* In this take-home program, each child took home an MP3 player overnight four days a week to listen to podcasts of the educator reading a twenty-five-minute story. Each beginning reader received a packet that supported the school's goal of using multiple modalities when teaching the whole child—the school's stated interest and approach. To encompass multiple modalities, the packet contained the book from which the educator was reading in the podcast, questions to think about, and scripts and songs that helped the reader to sound out and trace target letters and then match letters with pictures (B is for boy, and so on), and a requirement that the material be discussed with an adult in the home. The next morning, the students returned their packets and a parental/guardian/adult checklist or comments. After a brief conference with students, the Reading Buddies work was connected to the day's reading lesson.
- *Here's what the assessment indicated:* After six weeks, some of the beginning readers who had been at the 10th and 20th percentiles had moved up to the 40th and

50th percentiles. At the end of ten weeks, students were at or above the test's goal for student improvement. According to the educator, the students had not only higher test scores, but also had increased comprehension and confidence. As the beginning readers continued to progress even further at school, instruction was differentiated after assessment on their comprehension and written work with reading assignments given on individual ability levels by using the software KidBiz 3000 and Achieve 3000. The results were used to help select, plan, and differentiate instruction for the students beyond beginning reading in second grade through fifth grade.[1]

A Focus on English Language Learners

You can invite students to participate in a variety of activities related to a book that you are reading aloud. You can ask questions to think about, play parts in short scripts, sing songs that help repeat words, trace letters, and match letters to pictures (A is for apple, and so on). Students can clap the number of syllables in a word, rhyme words with a key word, blend sounds of a word together, and repeat/create short sentences that are alliterative (e.g., The boy's big brown bucket blew backwards).

CHAPTER OBJECTIVES

Specifically, upon completion of this chapter, you should be able to:

1. Explain the meaning of assessment as a continuous process, what you do with the assessment (information) results, and ways you interpret data to tell to others.
2. Compare and contrast three avenues for assessing student learning as well as when and how to use such assessment as observations, oral reports, records, informal reading inventories, portfolios, and performance samples.

3. Demonstrate your skill in preparing different types of assessment items.
4. Explain why criterion-referenced grading is preferred over norm-referenced grading and the difference among standardized tests, publisher-produced tests, and screening tests.
5. Differentiate among diagnostic assessment, summative assessment, and formative assessment, with examples of when and how each can be used at a particular grade level.
6. Self-assess and evaluate your competencies with the midpoint checklist in Appendix B.

Today's interest is (or should be) more on what the student can do (performance testing) as a result of learning than merely on what the student can recall (memory testing) from the experience. As a result of these and other concerns, a variety of systems of assessment and reporting have evolved, are still evolving, and will likely continue to evolve throughout your professional career.[2]

When teachers are aware of alternative systems, they may be able to develop assessment and reporting processes that are fair and effective for particular situations. So, after beginning with assessment, the final focus in this

chapter considers today's principles and practices in grading and reporting student achievement.

PURPOSES OF ASSESSMENT

Assessing student progress is an important part of a teacher's responsibility, and as was mentioned in Chapter 1, standardized testing is gaining importance as a measure of educational achievement. However, standardized tests are only one form of measurement and one may argue about their usefulness for the individual child. Looking at tests in a humorous way, Miss Malarkey and her colleagues prepare their students for the Instructional Performance Through Understanding (IPTU) test in the picture book *Testing Miss Malarkey* by J. Finchler and illustrated by K. O'Malley (Walker & Company, 2003). She assures her class that "THE TEST" will not affect their grades or being promoted to the next grade. But the students play Multiplication Mambo and Funny Phonics at recess, eat fish for lunch because it is considered "brain food," and practice filling in circles as part of art. The principal even sharpens pencils for everyone. One PTA meeting features Dr. Scorewell, "the Svengali of tests," and soon after that, parents abandon bedtime stories for textbook drills. Later, after the school is named #1 IPTU County Champion because of the high test scores, the test quickly fades in importance as the school gets back to its normal routines. While this story is meant to be humorous and is often read by teachers to students to alleviate the stress of formal testing, it does highlight how high-stakes testing can affect a child's daily education and progress. This is why standardized tests should be viewed as just one way of assessment. Multiple measures, as described in this chapter, are necessary to accurately determine a child's skills and knowledge. **Assessment** of achievement in student learning is designed to serve several purposes:

1. **To assist in student learning.** This is the purpose usually first thought of when speaking of assessment, and it is the principal topic of this chapter. For the classroom teacher, it is (or should be) the most important purpose.

2. **To identify students' strengths and weaknesses.** Identification and assessment of children's strengths and weaknesses are necessary for two reasons: to structure and restructure the learning activities and to restructure the curriculum. Concerning the first, for example, data on student strengths and weaknesses in content and process skills are important in planning activities appropriate for both skill development and intellectual development. This is diagnostic assessment (known also as preassessment or assessment of student readiness). For the second, data on student strengths and weaknesses in content and skills are useful for making appropriate modifications to the curriculum. Some teachers use their methods of preassessment as ways to build on students' prior knowledge and to help their students develop their comprehension of expository materials and their higher-order thinking skills. As resources, see Figure 6.1, and refer back to Chapter 5 and Figure 5.2.

3. **To assess the effectiveness of a particular instructional strategy.** It is important for you to know how well a particular strategy helped accomplish a particular goal or achieve a specific objective. Skilled teachers continually reflect on and evaluate their strategy choices, using a number of sources: student achievement as measured by assessment instruments such as student oral reports, records, portfolios, and performance samples, their own intuition and observations, and informal feedback given by colleagues, such as members of a teaching team or mentor teachers. (The topic of mentor teachers is further presented in Chapter 11).

4. **To assess and improve the effectiveness of curriculum programs.** Components of the curriculum are assessed continually by committees composed of teachers and administrators and sometimes receive feedback from parents, guardians, students, and other members of the school and community. The assessment is usually done both while students are learning (i.e., **formative assessment,** which can lead to re-teaching parts not mastered) and after the instruction (**summative assessment,** which can lead to grouping students for subsequent teaching).

5. **To assess and improve teaching effectiveness.** To improve learning, teachers are evaluated on the basis of (a) their commitment to working with students at a particular level, (b) their ability to cope with students at a particular age, developmental level, or grade, or (c) their ability to show mastery of appropriate instructional techniques—techniques that are articulated throughout this resource guide. For instance, working with ELLs may include allowing more time for English language learners to take a test or taking the test in parts or providing word support for difficult language.

6. **To provide data that assist in decision making about a student's future.** Assessment of student achievement is important in guiding decision making about grade-level and program placement, promotion, school transfer, and eligibility for special recognition and perhaps career planning.

7. **To provide data to communicate with and involve parents and guardians in their children's learning.** Parents and guardians, communities, and school boards all share accountability for the effectiveness of students' learning. Today's schools are reaching out more than ever before and engaging parents, guardians, and the community in their children's education. All teachers play an important role in the process of communicating with, reaching out to, and involving parents, guardians, and the community. As an example of preparing for a parent conference, some teachers keep self-adhesive notes nearby, observe students' learning behavior, and write information

- **TPS:** Think–pair–share is a strategy where students, in pairs, examine a new topic about to be studied. The topic/question/issue/problem can be written on the board and the students are asked in pairs to think about the topic, discuss it between themselves, and then the pairs share with the whole class what they know or think they already know about it while the teacher or student volunteer writes the major thoughts on the board, perhaps in the form of a graphic concept web. As an option, after the students in each dyad discuss the topic, they can record what they already know as a preassessment, then they can present their perceptions to the whole group. At this time, some of the students' perceptions may be revealed as misconceptions (something that the students *think* they know). This is an excellent technique for preassessment and for this type of discovery learning about a topic.

- **TWPS:** The think–pair–share strategy can be extended to include a writing step and is referred to as think–write–pair–share. This extended strategy of TWPS is where students, in pairs, examine a new topic to be studied; they discuss and write down what they know (as a preassessment tool), but they also go on and refer to what they have written to write conclusions about what they know before sharing their information with the larger group. Remind the students that to write a conclusion means to write about their reasoning about the topic; it can be a judgment based on their reasons and experience and should be a brief summing up of all of their words.

- **KWL:** In the KWL strategy, the students record what they already know to participate in a preassessment (*K* for *know*) about a topic being studied. With the teacher leading an ensuing discussion, three columns are formed on a chart, on the board, or on a transparency on the stage of an overhead projector. The students can take notes or take the dictation of their peers to make their own three-column facsimiles. In the left-hand column, the teacher, classroom aide, or a volunteer writes what students say they already KNOW or think they know about the topic. Then they generate questions about what they want to learn about the topic (*W* for *want to know*) and in the middle column, the writer makes a list of what the students WANT to learn about the topic. The right-hand column is left blank. Next they participate in the study and then they answer their questions to record what they learned. They fill in the right-hand column at the end of the lesson or study with what has been LEARNED about the topic. They then self-assess (formative assessment) their answers (*L* is for what they *learned*).

- **KWLQ:** Students record what they already *know* for preassessment (K) about a topic, formulate questions about what they *want* to learn about the topic (W), assess their answers to their questions to see what they have *learned* (L), and then ask more *questions* for further study (Q).

- **CT:** For this *correction type* (CT) preassessment, students receive word patterns, sentences, or paragraphs with underlined or italicized words and change the words to make the underlined/italicized material correct.

- **TF MODIFICATIONS:** For this *true-false* modification (TF) preassessment, students read a statement and circle true or false as a response. After discussion/evaluation, if a student has circled false as an answer, then the student writes a sentence on a line underneath to make the statement correct.

Figure 6.1
Methods of preassessment.[*3]
*These methods are avenues to build on students' prior knowledge and also help students assess their comprehension of expository materials and higher-order thinking skills. Also consider Figure 5.2 in Chapter 5.

on the notes. The notes go in the students' files and are shared at a parent conference to show an observational record (valuable for ELLs and English-speaking students with learning problems).

Authentic Assessment: Advantages and Limitations

When assessing for student achievement, it is important that you use procedures that are compatible with the instructional objectives. This is referred to as **authentic assessment.** Other terms used for authentic assessment are *accurate, active, aligned, alternative,* and *direct.*

Although it is sometimes used, performance assessment refers to the types of student response that are being assessed, whereas authentic assessment refers to the assessment situation. Although not all performance assessments are authentic, assessments that are authentic are most assuredly performance assessments. This assessment type asks students to do real tasks rather than repeat their knowledge.

Advantages

Advantages claimed for the use of authentic assessment include (a) the explicit (also known as performance-based, criterion-referenced, outcome-based, or direct) measurement of what students should know and can do, and (b) and emphasis on higher-order thinking.

You'll realize that some tests are limited in measuring language use. In language arts, for example, although it may seem fairly easy to develop a criterion-referenced test, administer it, and grade it, tests often measure language skills rather than language use. It is extremely difficult to measure students' communicative competence with a test. For example, tests do not measure listening and talking very well, and a test on punctuation marks does not indicate the students' ability to add punctuation marks to a set of sentences created by someone else or to proofread and spot punctuation errors in someone else's writing.[4] An alternative and far better approach is to examine how students use punctuation marks in their own writing. This permits you to authentically assess the students' understanding of that which the student has been learning—a performance-based assessment procedure.

Consider another example. "If students have been actively involved in classifying objects using multiple characteristics, it sends them a confusing message if they are then required to take a paper-and-pencil test that asks them to 'define classification' or recite a memorized list of characteristics of good classification schemes."[5] An authentic assessment technique would be to use a performance item that actually involves the students in classifying objects. In other words, to obtain an accurate assessment of a student's learning, the teacher uses a performance-based assessment procedure, that is, a procedure that requires students to produce rather than to select a response.

Limitations

Some limitations of authentic assessment include (a) a higher cost, (b) difficulty in making results consistent and usable, and (c) problems with validity (Does the measuring instrument actually measure that which it is intended to measure?), reliability (Does the assessment technique consistently measure that which it does measure? In other words, does it give similar scores when it is taken again?), and comparability (How would you compare it with direct measurement and show its value for giving consistent and usable results?). In addition, a teacher, unfortunately, may never see a particular student again after a given school semester or year is over, and thus the teacher may never observe the effects he or she has had on a student's values and attitudes. In schools where groups or teams of teachers remain with the same cohort of students for longer than the traditional time—as in looping programs where students and teachers remain together for several years—those teachers often do have better opportunity to observe the positive changes in their students' values and attitudes.

THREE AVENUES OF ASSESSMENT

There are three general avenues open to you for assessing a student's achievement in learning. You can assess:

1. What the student *says*—for example, the quantity and quality of a student's contributions to class discussions
2. What the student *does*—for example, a student's performance (e.g., the amount and quality of a student's participation in the learning activities and performance tests)
3. What the student *writes*—for example, as shown by items in the student's portfolio (e.g., homework assignments [also called responsibility papers], checklists, project work, and written tests)

While your own situations and personal philosophy will dictate the levels of importance and weight you give to each avenue of assessment, you should have a strong rationale if you value and weigh the three avenues for assessment differently than one-third each.

Assessing What a Student Says and Does

When evaluating what a student says, you should (a) listen to the student's oral reports, questions, responses, and interactions with others and (b) observe the student's attentiveness, involvement in class activities, creativeness, and responses to challenges including the challenges afforded by performance testing. Notice that we say you should *listen* and *observe*. While listening to what the student is saying, you should also be observing the student's nonverbal behaviors. For this, you can use narrative observation forms (see Figure 6.2) and you can use observations with behavioral **checklists** and **scoring guides** or **rubrics** as well as periodic conferences with the student. There are sample checklists in Figures 6.3, 6.4, and 6.5 and also sample scoring guides/rubrics in Figures 6.6 and 6.7.

With each technique used, you must proceed from your awareness of anticipated learning outcomes (the learning target or instructional objectives), and you must assess a student's progress toward meeting those objectives. That is referred to as explicit/direct or **criterion-referenced assessment.**

Observation Form

Figure 6.2, mentioned earlier, illustrates a sample generic form for recording and evaluating teacher observations of a student's verbal and nonverbal behaviors. With modern technology, such as that provided by the software program Learner Profile, a teacher can record observations electronically anywhere at any time.[6]

Student _____	Grade/Subject _____	School _____
Observer _____	Date _____	Period/Time _____

Objective	Desired behavior	What the student did, said, or wrote

Figure 6.2

Sample form for evaluating and recording a student's verbal and nonverbal behaviors.

Sample scoring guide/rubric for assessing a student's skill in listening

Score Point 3—Strong listener:
   Responds immediately to oral directions
   Focuses on speaker
   Maintains appropriate attention span
   Listens to what others are saying
   Is interactive

Score Point 2—Capable listener:
   Follows oral directions
   Usually attentive to speaker and to discussions
   Listens to others without interrupting

Score Point 1—Developing listener:
   Has difficulty following directions
   Relies on repetition
   Is often inattentive
   Has short attention span
   Often interrupts the speaker

Sample checklist for assessing a student's skill in map work:

Check each item if the map comes up to standard in this particular category
   _____ 1. Accuracy
   _____ 2. Neatness
   _____ 3. Attention to details

Figure 6.3

Checklist and scoring guide/rubric compared.*

*The difference between a checklist and a rubric is minimal. The difference is that a rubric shows the *degrees* for the desired characteristics while a checklist usually shows only the desired *characteristics*. A checklist can be made into a rubric by adding degrees (maximum success, minimum success) for characteristics. A rubric can be called a scoring guide when there are point values (1 point, 2 points). A rubric can easily be made into a checklist by listing only characteristics and deleting degrees or points.

Scoring Guide/Rubric: Assessing Student Writing

Student _____ Date _____

Teacher _____ Time _____

Here is an example of data you can get from a student's writing sample.

Did the student	Yes	No	Comment
—have an understanding of the specific assignment	_____	_____	_____
—stay focused on the task	_____	_____	_____
—stay within the time period	_____	_____	_____
—use his or her time well	_____	_____	_____
—show an ability to use syntax (word order)	_____	_____	_____
—use verbs that agree in subject and tense	_____	_____	_____
—use subjective pronouns (he, she, I)	_____	_____	_____
—use objective pronouns (her, him, me)	_____	_____	_____
—rely on invented spelling	_____	_____	_____
—show a positive attitude toward writing	_____	_____	_____
—demonstrate the level of writing skills for the student's age/grade level and level of development	_____	_____	_____
—show organizational skills in thinking and writing	_____	_____	_____

Assessing student writing*   **Scores**

If the student demonstrates
—correct purpose, mode, audience
—effective elaboration
—consistent organization
—clear sense of order and completeness
—fluent language   Score 4

If the student demonstrates
—correct purpose, mode, audience
—moderate elaboration
—organized but possible brief digressions
—clear, effective language   Score 3

If the student demonstrates
—correct purpose, mode, audience
—some elaboration
—some specific details
—gaps in organization
—limited language control   Score 2

If the student demonstrates
—an attempt to address audience
—being brief, vague, unelaborated
—wandering off topic
—lack of language control
—little or no organization
—wrong purpose and mode   Score 1

Figure 6.4
Sample scoring guide/rubric for assessing student writing.
*Note: In a student's writing, a teacher will notice error patterns (spelling, use of verbs, word order, etc.) and assist the student. To help individually or in small groups, a teacher can review the errors and the use of language related to the errors. For example, if there is a pronoun error pattern, the teacher can review the use of each type of pronoun and word order placement in sentences through examples, activities, and educational games. This technique is beneficial for ELLs and English-speaking students with learning problems.

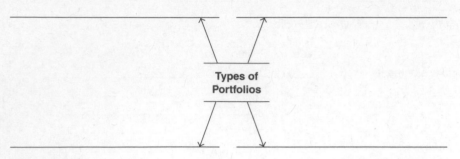

Selected Works Portfolio

Holds samples of work prompted by teacher

Showcase Portfolio

Holds selections by students to show best work

Figure 6.5
Student portfolio categories.

Types of Portfolios

Growth Portfolio

Holds student work to show achievement toward goals from beginning to end of the study, semester, or year

Passport Portfolio

Holds work that will enable student to transition from one grade to the next

Assessing What a Student Writes

When assessing what a student writes, you can use worksheets, written homework, assignment papers, student journal writing, student writing projects, student portfolios, and tests (all discussed later in this chapter). In many schools, portfolios, worksheets, and homework assignments are the tools usually used for the formative evaluation of each student's achievement. See Figure 6.4. Tests, too, should be a part of this evaluation, but tests are also used for summative evaluation at the end of a unit and for diagnostic purposes. Your summative evaluation of a student's achievement and any other final judgment made by you about a student can have impact upon the emotional and intellectual development of that child. Special attention is given to this later in the section *Recording Teacher Observations and Judgments.*

STUDENT INVOLVEMENT IN ASSESSMENT

Students' continuous self-assessment should be planned as an important component of the assessment program. If elementary students are to progress in their intellectual development, then they must receive instruction and guidance in how to become more responsible for their own learning. During that empowerment process, they learn to think in positive ways about themselves and about their individual capabilities. To achieve this self-understanding and improved self-esteem requires the experiences afforded by successes, along with guidance in self-understanding and self-assessment.

To meet these goals, teachers provide opportunities for elementary students to think about what they are learning,

about how they are learning it, and about how far they have progressed. One procedure is to ask the students to maintain portfolios of their work, using rating scales or checklists periodically to self-assess their progress.

Using Student Portfolios

Portfolios are used by teachers as a means of instruction and by teachers and students as one means of self-reflection and of assessing student learning. You get, as an initial assessment value, a picture of general development of skills and abilities over time. Though there is little research to support or refute the claim, educators believe that the instructional value comes from the process of the student's assembling and maintaining a personal portfolio. During that creative process, the student is expected to self-reflect and to think critically about what has and is being learned, and the student is assuming some degree of responsibility for her or his own learning. Indeed, federal officials now allow states to assess English-learning students through portfolios of their work over the school year instead of through a state's reading test.[7] With the help of the special resource teacher, contents for ELLs often include list of goals accomplished, a progress summary, list of books read, writing samples, and anecdotal records.

Student portfolios can be grouped into four general categories shown in Figure 6.5. In a given situation, the purpose of portfolios can transcend any combination of the four.

Student portfolios should be organized and, depending on the category (which reflects the portfolio's purpose), should contain assignment sheets, worksheets, the results of homework, project binders, forms for student self-assessment and reflection on their work, and other class materials thought important by the students and teacher. Computer software programs are available for assisting students in electronic portfolio development and management.[8] As a model of a real-life portfolio, you can show the students your own career portfolio (see Chapter 11).

Portfolio Assessment: Dealing with Its Limitations

Although portfolio assessment as an alternative to traditional methods of evaluating student progress has gained momentum in recent years, establishing standards has been difficult. Research on the use of portfolios for assessment indicates that validity and reliability of teacher evaluation are often quite low.[9] It seems portfolio assessment is not always practical for use by every teacher. For example, if you are the sole art teacher for a school and are responsible for teaching art to all of the 375 children in the school, you are unlikely to have the time or storage capacity for 375 portfolios. For assessment of student learning, the use of checklists, scoring guides/rubrics, and student self-assessment may be more practical.[10]

Before using portfolios as an alternative to traditional testing, you are advised to consider carefully and understand clearly the reasons for doing it and its practicality in your situation. Then decide carefully portfolio content, establish scoring guides/rubrics or expectation standards, anticipate grading problems, and consider and prepare for parent and guardian reactions.

Using Checklists

One of the items that can be maintained by students in their portfolios is a series of checklists. A checklist and the included items can be used easily by a student to compare the items with a previous self-assessment. Items on the checklist will vary depending on your purpose and grade level. (See sample forms in Figure 6.6 and Figure 6.7.) For example, open-ended questions can be included to allow the student to provide additional information as well as to do some expressive writing. After a student has demonstrated each of the skills satisfactorily, each student receives a check next to the student's name, made either by the teacher alone or in conference with the student.

Using Student Conferences

While emphasizing the criteria for assessment, rating scales and checklists provide children with means of expressing their feelings and give the teacher still another source of input data for use in assessment. To provide students with reinforcement and guidance to improve their learning and development, teachers can meet with individual students to discuss a self-assessment. Such conferences should provide students with understandable and achievable short-term goals as well as help them develop and maintain an adequate self-esteem.[11]

Although almost any instrument a teacher uses for assessing can be used for student self-assessment, in some cases, it might be better to construct specific instruments with the student's understanding of the instrument in mind. Student self assessment and self reflection should be done on a regular and continuing basis so students can make comparisons periodically. You will want to discuss how to analyze these comparisons with students. Comparisons should provide a student with information previously not recognized about his or her own progress and growth.

TESTING FOR ACHIEVEMENT

One source of information used for determining grades is data obtained from testing for student achievement. There are two kinds of tests, those that are standardized and those that are not.

Standardized and Nonstandardized Tests

Standardized tests are those published by testing bureaus and used by states/districts to determine student achievement, principally in reading, mathematics, and science. Usually based on a state or national level, norms for particular age groups of children are established for a test based on its administration to large groups of children. Norms are standardized test scores from a representative group of students that are used to construct national norms. **Norms** can also be the median achievement or middle score of a large group; thus, the **median** identifies the middle score in a distribution of scores achieved by test takers. The **mode** is the most frequent score in a distribution of scores taken by test takers. Standardized **norm-referenced** tests are best for diagnostic purposes and should not be used by a classroom teacher for determining the grades of students.

As mentioned in Chapter 1, the administration of standardized achievement tests and the use of their results have become major concerns to classroom teachers and school principals. In some locales, for example, their salaries and indeed their jobs are contingent on the results of student scores on standardized achievement tests. Now, for the purposes of this resource guide, we will briefly consider standardized achievement testing by explaining test scores and discussing scores related to the Academic Performance Index (API).

How to Explain Standardized Test Scores

When explaining standardized tests scores to a parent or guardian, point out that all test scores begin by being raw scores (the number of items that the child answered

Checklist: Oral Report Assessment

Student _____   Date _____

Teacher _____   Time _____

Did the student:

1. Speak so that everyone could hear?   Yes   No   Comments

2. Finish sentences?   Yes   No   Comments

3. Seem comfortable in front of group?   Yes   No   Comments

4. Give a good introduction?   Yes   No   Comments

5. Seem well-informed about the topic?   Yes   No   Comments

6. Explain ideas clearly?   Yes   No   Comments

7. Stay on the topic?   Yes   No   Comments

8. Give a good conclusion?   Yes   No   Comments

9. Use effective visuals to make the presentation interesting?   Yes   No   Comments

10. Give good answers to questions from the audience?   Yes   No   Comments

Figure 6.6
Sample checklist: Assessing a student's oral report.

Checklist: Interdisciplinary Thematic Unit Learning

Student _____   Date _____

Teacher _____   Time _____

Did the student:	Yes	No	Comment
1. Identify theme, topic, main idea of the unit	____	____	_____
2. Identify contributions of others to the theme	____	____	_____
3. Identify problems related to the unit study	____	____	_____
4. Develop skills in the following areas	____	____	_____
Applying knowledge	____	____	_____
Assuming responsibility	____	____	_____
Classifying	____	____	_____
Categorizing	____	____	_____
Decision making	____	____	_____
Discussing	____	____	_____
Gathering resources	____	____	_____
Impulse control	____	____	_____
Inquiry learning	____	____	_____
Justifying choices	____	____	_____
Listening to others	____	____	_____
Locating information	____	____	_____
Metacognition	____	____	_____
Ordering	____	____	_____
Organizing information	____	____	_____
Problem recognition/identification	____	____	_____
Problem solving	____	____	_____
Reading text	____	____	_____
Reading maps and globes	____	____	_____
Reasoning	____	____	_____
Reflecting	____	____	_____
Reporting to others	____	____	_____
Self-assessing	____	____	_____
Sharing	____	____	_____
Studying	____	____	_____
Summarizing	____	____	_____
Thinking	____	____	_____
Using resources	____	____	_____
Working with others	____	____	_____
Working independently	____	____	_____
(Other unique to the unit)	____	____	_____

Additional teacher and student comments: _____

_____

Figure 6.7
Sample checklist: Student learning assessment for use with interdisciplinary thematic instruction.

Name of Standardized Test

Teacher _____   Year _____   Grade _____   Student Skills _____

School _____   Semester _____   Form _____   Analysis for Student _____

District _____   Test Date _____   Level _____

Tests	No. of items	Raw score	Natl. % rank/stanine	Local % rank/stanine	Grade equivalent
Total Reading	93	48	40–4*	41–4	4.1

Figure 6.8

Test scores a teacher can explain.

* According to some test publishers and their way of sending test information, **stanines** (students' standardized test performance as shown on a normal curve) can be indicated to educators by putting stanines after dashes behind a student's percentile rank. It is often published as follows: 40-4. The first numeral tells you the national (or local) percentile rank of the student and the numeral after the dash tells you the stanine the student is in for this particular test.

correctly on a standardized test that had X number of items). See Figure 6.8 as an example of what scores can be explained. Point out that we can compare the child's raw score to other scores of other children. To do this, we can use percentile or a percentile rank (PR or % rank), that is, a ranking that compares a child's score with the scores of all the other children who have taken the test. For example, looking at Figure 6.8, the child's raw score of 48 in reading placed her in the 40th percentile nationally and the 41th percentile locally. This means that her score was as high (or higher) than 40 percent of the children who took the test across the nation and 41 percent of the many children who took the test in her district locally.

Academic Performance Index (API) Scores

At times, you need to not only explain the test scores, but also explain something about the tests themselves. Get acquainted with the tests that your students will encounter during the school year so you can describe how test scores are reported and so you can give an overview of what tests are coming toward your students. For instance, in many states, the Academic Performance Index (API) scores are based on the tests students take annually and are used by state education officials to measure how individual schools are doing on statewide tests. Sometimes, the core of a school's API score is based on the results of a norm-referenced test, similar to the SAT-9 (Stanford Achievement) test, which measures the students' performance with their peers across the country. At other times, the core of the API is measured by the results of a state's Standards Tests, which were designed to match up with the state's mandated curriculum and educational standards. Usually, the Index scores (results) can range from 200 to 1,000 and schools that score below 800

must improve each year, with their improvement target set by the state. For example, one school may have a 6-point improvement target while another school may have a different target. When the index scores improve, teachers and principals usually attribute the improvement to such educational practices as working hard to improve instruction, reading and math intervention programs, structured language arts programs, programs for students testing below grade level, before- and after-school tutoring, and a definite focus on teaching state standards. In some states, the API has caused controversy because state education officials have used the rankings to award money to schools and teachers. Recently, one western state awarded cash bonuses to teachers. But later, the bonuses were suspended when the state experienced budget cuts.

When Test Scores Are Printed Publicly

How do you think that you'll react when the test scores are printed in the newspaper or put on the Internet? When you and other teachers are pressured to improve students' scores? When this happens, it's possible that you and your school faculty or grade-level teaching team may meet and, together, go over the test scores to identify areas in the curriculum that need greater attention. Your team can organize information about the test scores into a package of assessment information for the students and the parents/guardians. You may want to communicate test results clearly to both the students and their parents/guardians through a handout, newsletter, or a packet of information. When you meet with a student and the parent/guardian during a conference, you can use the assessment information to identify overall areas of strength and areas that need improvement for the school or grade level as well as to serve as a reference for specific information about each individual student's scores. If a parent/guardian is concerned about test bias, point out that you and your colleagues can use some strategies to eliminate or minimize test bias. First, there are other information sources, such as performance assessments, on which parents/guardians can rely. You can assure the parents/guardians that standardized test results are just one source of information for the child. Second, pre- and post-test examinations can be conducted. You can examine the test content before testing and then analyze the test results after testing to help minimize content bias. Third, there are adaptations that could be initiated. Perhaps you can adapt testing procedures to specific student needs (perhaps English language learners need more time) and before the test, teach students to adapt to testing procedures when you give them opportunities to practice. At this point in this resource guide, our focus will turn to nonstandardized criterion-referenced tests, ones that you design (or collaboratively design) for your own unique group of students for determination of their level of learning on particular instructional objectives. In no way do we intend to devalue the concern that you will have for more information about standardized norm-referenced achievement testing as a classroom teacher. It simply means that purpose and space in this guide does not allow for more in-depth attention to that topic and we encourage you to read more about this form of testing by seeing the recommended readings at the end of this chapter.

Purposes for Testing

Tests can be designed for several purposes, and a variety of kinds of tests and alternate test items will keep your testing program interesting, useful, and reliable. As a college student, you are probably the most experienced with testing for measuring achievement, but you will use tests for other reasons as well. Tests are also used to assess and aid in curriculum development; help determine teaching effectiveness; help students develop positive attitudes, appreciations, and values; help students increase their understanding and retention of facts, principles, skills, and concepts; motivate children; provide diagnostic information for planning for personalization of the instruction; provide review and drill to enhance teaching and learning; and serve as informational data for children and their parents or guardians.

PREPARING ASSESSMENT ITEMS

Writing good assessment items is yet another professional skill, and to become proficient at it takes study, time, practice, and reflection. Because of the importance of an assessment program, please assume this professional charge seriously and responsibly. Although poorly prepared items take no time at all to construct, they will cause you more trouble than you can ever imagine.

As a professional, you should study different types of assessment items that can be used and how best to write them, and then practice writing them. Remember, when preparing items, ensure that they match and sufficiently cover the instructional objectives. You should prepare each item carefully enough to be reasonably confident that each item can be understood by the student in the manner that you anticipate the item being understood. With the diversity of children in today's public school classroom, especially with respect to their proficiency in oral and written English language, and for students with disabilities, this is an especially important point. To see how ELL teachers integrate assessment with instruction in the classroom, we suggest looking at *Scenarios for ESL Standards-Based Assessment* by Teachers of English to Speakers of Other Languages (TESOL, 2006). Finally, after administering a test, you should take time to analyze the results and reflect on the value of each item before ever using that item again.

TYPES OF ASSESSMENT ITEMS: DESCRIPTIONS, EXAMPLES, AND GUIDELINES FOR PREPARATION AND USE

This section presents descriptions, advantages and disadvantages, and guidelines for preparing and using different types of assessment items. When reading about each type, you will notice that some types are appropriate for use in performance assessment, while others are not.

Essay

Description: A question or problem is presented, and the student is to compose a response in the form of sustained prose, using the student's own words, phrases, and ideas, within the limits of the question or problem. The essay item can also be considered a performance test item, perhaps the most familiar example of performance assessment.

Example 1: In the story just read, does the author elaborate the setting in great detail or barely sketch it? Explain your response.

Example 2: A healthy green plant sitting in front of you has been placed in fertile soil and sealed with paraffin in a glass jar. If we place the jar on the windowsill where it will receive strong sunlight and the temperature inside the jar is maintained between 60 and 80 degrees Fahrenheit, how long do you predict the plant will live? Justify your prediction.

Advantages: This type measures conceptual knowledge and higher mental processes, such as the ability to synthesize material and to express ideas in clear and precise written language. It is especially useful in integrated thematic teaching. It provides practice in written expression and can be used in performance assessment, as is the case for Example 2.

Limitations: Essay items require a good deal of time to read and to score. They tend to provide an unreliable sampling of achievement and are vulnerable to teacher subjectivity and unreliable scoring. They tend to punish the student who writes slowly or who has limited proficiency in the written language though the student may have achieved as well as another student who writes faster and is more proficient in the language. They tend to favor students who have fluency with words but whose achievement may not necessarily be better. In addition, unless the students have been given instruction in the meaning of key directive verbs and in how to respond to them, the teacher should not assume that all students understand such verbs (such as *explain* in the first example and *predict* and *justify* in the second).

Guidelines for Using an Essay Item

1. When preparing an essay-only test, many questions, each requiring a relatively short prose response (see the short explanation type later in this discussion), are preferable to a smaller number of questions requiring long prose responses. Briefer answers tend to be more precise, and the use of many items provides a more reliable sampling of student achievement. When preparing short prose responses, be sure to avoid using words verbatim from the student textbook.

2. Allow students adequate test time for a full response.

3. Different qualities of achievement are more likely comparable when all students must answer the same questions, as opposed to providing a list of essay items from which students may select a certain number they wish to answer.

4. After preparing essay items, make a tentative scoring guide or key, deciding the key ideas you expect the students to identify and how many points will be allotted to each.

5. Students should be informed about the relative test value for each item. Point values, if different for each item, can be listed in the margin of the test next to each item.

6. Inform students of the role/importance of spelling, grammar, and sentence structure in your scoring of their essay items.

7. When reading responses, read all student papers for one item at a time in one sitting, and, while doing that, make notes to yourself, then repeat, and while reading that item again, score each student's paper for that item. Repeat the process for the next item but alternate the order of the stack of papers so you are not reading them in the same order by student. While scoring essay responses, keep in mind the nature of the objective being measured, which may or may not include the qualities of handwriting, grammar, spelling, punctuation, and neatness.

8. To nullify the halo effect, an effect that can occur when you know whose paper you are reading, have the students put their name on the back of the paper and use a number code rather than having students put their names on the front of the essay papers, so that while reading the papers, you are unaware of whose paper is being read.

9. While having some understanding of a concept, many children are not yet facile with written expression, so you must remember to be patient, tolerant, positive, and prescriptive. Mark papers with positive and constructive comments, showing students how they could have explained or responded more clearly.

10. Prior to this type of test item, instruct students in the meaning of selected key directive verbs and help them practice responding to the verbs, such as *compare-contrast, explain-identify,* and *evaluate-summarize.*

Multiple Choice

Description: This type is similar to the completion item in that statements are presented (the stem), sometimes in incomplete form, but with several options or alternatives requiring recognition or even higher cognitive processes rather than mere recall.

Example 1: Of four cylinders with the following dimensions, the one that would cause the highest-pitched sound would be

(a) 4 inches long and 3 inches in diameter

(b) 4 inches long and 1 inch in diameter

(c) 8 inches long and 3 inches in diameter

(d) 8 inches long and 1 inch in diameter

Example 2: Which of the following words is spelled correctly?

(a) truly

(b) forty

(c) argument

(d) all of the above

Advantages: Items can be answered and scored quickly. A wide range of content and higher levels of cognition can be tested in a relatively short time. This type is excellent for all testing purposes—motivation, review, and assessment of learning.

Limitations: Unfortunately, because multiple-choice items are relatively easy to write, there is a tendency to write items measuring only for low levels of cognition. Multiple-choice items are excellent for major testing, but it takes care and time to write quality questions that measure higher levels of thinking and learning.

Guidelines for Using Multiple-Choice Items

1. If the item is in the form of an incomplete statement, it should be meaningful in itself and imply a direct question rather than merely lead into a collection of unrelated true and false statements.

2. Use a level of language that is easy enough for even the poorest readers and those with limited proficiency in English to understand; avoid unnecessary wordiness.

3. If there is variation in the length of alternatives, arrange the alternatives in order from shortest to longest (i.e., first alternative is the shortest, last alternative is the longest). For single-word alternatives, consistent use of arrangement of alternatives is recommended, such as by length of answer or alphabetically.

4. Arrangement of alternatives should be uniform throughout the test and listed in vertical (column) form rather than in horizontal (paragraph) form.

5. Incorrect responses (distracters) should be plausible and related to the same concept as the correct alternative. Although an occasional humorous or absurd distracter may help relieve text anxiety, they should generally be avoided. They offer no measuring value, increase the likelihood of the student guessing the correct response, and increase the time it takes for the student to take the test.

6. It is not necessary to maintain a fixed number of alternatives for every item, but the use of fewer than three is not recommended. While it is not always possible to come up with four or five plausible responses, the use of four or five reduces chance responses and guessing, thereby increasing reliability for the item. (Three-choice items may be preferable for use with young children and other slower readers.) If you cannot think of enough plausible distracters, include the item on a test the first time as a completion item. As students respond, wrong answers will provide you with a number of plausible distracters that you can use the next time to make the item a multiple-choice-type item.

7. Some students with special needs may work better when allowed to circle their selected response rather than writing its letters or number in a blank space.

8. Responses such as "all of the above" or "none of the above" should be used only when they will contribute more than another plausible distracter. Care must be taken that such responses answer or complete the item. "All of the above" is a poorer alternative than "none of the above" because items that use it as a correct response need to have four or five correct answers; also, if it is the right answer, knowledge of any two of the distracters will cue it.

9. Every item should be grammatically consistent. For example, if the stem is in the form of an incomplete sentence, it should be possible to complete the sentence by attaching any of the alternatives to it.

10. The stem should state a single and specific point.

Performance Assessment: Expensive and Intensive

Description: Provided with certain conditions or materials, the student solves a problem or accomplishes some other action. For instance, a student is asked to write a retelling of a favorite fable and then create a diorama to go along with the retelling. A performance assessment can also include arrangement and essay types of assessment.

Example 1: A student is given a microscope and asked to carry it properly from one location to another in the room or to hold a jumping rope in place (gross motor skill) or to focus a microscope or to jump rope (fine motor skill).

Example 2: A student or a group of students are given the problem of creating from discarded materials a habitat for an imaginary animal and then instructed to display the habitat, write about it, and orally present their product to the rest of the class.

Advantages: A good program of assessment will use performance testing and other alternate forms of assessment and not rely solely on one form, such as written assessment, or rely on one type of written assessment, such as multiple choice. This type of assessment is a flexible one, because the type of test and items that you use depend upon your purpose and objectives. For instance, as a culminating project for a unit on sound, groups of students may be challenged to design and make their own musical instruments. A student's performance assessment can include:

1. Playing the instrument for the group.
2. Showing others the part of the instrument that makes the sound.
3. Describing the function of the other parts of the instrument.

4. Demonstrating how the student can change the pitch of the sound.
5. Sharing with others how the student made the instrument.

Performance test item types come closer to direct measurement (authentic assessment) of certain expected outcomes than do most other types. Other types of assessment can actually be prepared as performance-type items, that is, where the student actually *does* what he or she is being tested for during the performance.

Limitations: Performance testing is usually more expensive and time consuming than is verbal testing, which in turn is more time demanding and expensive than is written testing. You need to take the time to perform content validity checks and to account for the individual differences in students, so your performance testing program should include assessment items of different types. This is what writers of articles in professional journals are referring to when they talk about alternative assessment. They are encouraging the use of multiple assessment items (though time consuming), as opposed to the traditional heavy reliance on objective items such as multiple-choice questions. This performance type of assessing can be difficult to administer to a group of students. Adequate supply of materials could be a problem. As said in our discussion of the essay type, scoring of performance items may tend to be subjective. Especially when materials are involved, it could be difficult to give makeup tests to students who were absent.

Guidelines for Using Performance Assessment

Use your creativity to design and use performance tests, since they tend to measure well the important objectives. To reduce subjectivity in scoring, prepare for distinct scoring guidelines (rubrics), as was discussed in scoring essay-type items.

Now do Application Exercise 6.1 to start the development of your skill in writing assessment items. As you work on Application Exercise 6.1, you may want to review writing assessment items by locating discussions in this book's index.

APPLICATION EXERCISE 6.1
Preparing Assessment Items

Instructions: The purpose of this application exercise is to work cooperatively and collaboratively with your colleagues after you practice your skill in preparing the different types of assessment items discussed in this chapter. For use in your own teaching, select one specific instructional objective and write one assessment item for it. When completed, share this exercise with your colleagues for their feedback.

Objective

_____

Grade and Subject

_____

From this chapter

 1. Essay item _____

_____

_____

_____

_____

_____

_____

 2. Multiple-choice item _____

_____

_____

_____

_____

_____

_____

 3. Performance item _____

_____

_____

_____

_____

_____

_____

REPORTING: MAINTAINING RECORDS OF STUDENT ACHIEVEMENT

You must maintain well-organized and complete records of student achievement. You may do this in a written record book or on an electronic record, whichever will be furnished by the school. At the very least, the record book should include attendance records and all records of scores on tests, homework, projects, and other assignments. The record book is a legal document that (at the end of the school year), *may* have to be turned in to the school office unless there is a duplicate file of the information in the office computer system.

Daily interactions and events occur in the classroom that may provide informative data about a student's intellectual, emotional, and physical development. Maintaining a dated log of your observations of these interactions and events can provide important information that might otherwise be forgotten. At the end of a unit of study and again at the conclusion of a grading period, you will want to review your records. During the course of the school year, your anecdotal records (and those of other members of your teaching team) will provide important information about the intellectual, psychological, and physical development of each student and ideas for attention to be given to individual students.

Recording Teacher Observations and Judgments

You must think carefully about any written comments that you intend to make about a child. Children can be quite sensitive to what others say about them, and most particularly to comments about them made by their teachers.

Additionally, we have seen anecdotal comments in students' permanent records that said more about their teachers who made the comments than about the recipient students. Comments that have been carelessly, hurriedly, and thoughtlessly made can be detrimental to a child's welfare and progress in school. Teacher comments must be professional; that is, they must be diagnostically useful to the continued intellectual and psychological development of the child. This is true for any comment you make or write, whether on a student's paper, on the child's permanent school record, or on a message sent to the student's home.

For students' continued intellectual and psychological development, your comments should be useful, productive, analytical, diagnostic, and prescriptive. The professional teacher makes diagnoses and prepares descriptions; a professional teacher does *not* label students with terms such as *lazy, vulgar, slow, stupid, difficult,* or *dumb.* The professional teacher sees the behavior of a child as being goal-directed. The primary professional task of any teacher is not to punish, but to facilitate the learner's understanding (perception) of a goal and help the learner identify acceptable behaviors positively designed to teach that goal.

That which separates the professional teacher from "anyone off the street" is the teacher's ability to go beyond mere description of behavior. Keep that in mind always when you write comments that will be read by the students, by their parents or guardians, and by other teachers.[12]

The term *achievement* is used frequently throughout this resource guide. If conditions were ideal (which they are not), and if teachers did their job perfectly well (which many of us do not), then all students would receive top marks (the ultimate in mastery or quality learning) and there would be less of a need here to talk about grading and marking. Believing that letter grades do not reflect the nature of the developmental progress of young children, many school districts hold off using letter grades until children are in at least the third grade or even the sixth grade, and instead, favor checklists and narratives.[13] See an example of a progress report for students in Figure 6.9 or Application Exercise 6.2. Mastery learning implies that some end point of learning is attainable (but there probably isn't an end point). In any case, because conditions for teaching are never ideal and we teachers are mere humans, this topic of grading and marking will undoubtedly continue to be of interest to you, your students, their parents or guardians, school counselors, administrators, members of the school board, and to many others, such as potential employers, providers of scholarships, and college admissions officers.

PROGRESS REPORT: Arlington Heights School

Student: _Anthony von Hauser_   Course: _Introduction to Algebra grade 6_   Date: _September 14, 2009_

This progress report form incorporates evaluation by student, teacher, and parent. The form will be completed by the student on Wednesday and by the teacher on Thursday and reviewed by the office and returned to the student on Friday. The student will take the form home for parental review, comments, and signature.

Section I: Self-Assessment: The student is asked to evaluate progress in the course in terms of goals and how closely these goals are being achieved. Do you feel you have made progress since the last progress report?

   By taking this algebra class I achieved a greater understanding of it. I feel I have made a lot of progress since I took the class in 6th grade. It is also taught much better which makes it easier.

Section II: Teacher Assessment: The teacher is asked to assess the student's entry, competency, and achievement to date and make recommendations.

   Anthony is doing quite well. He has had to make some adjustments from previous work habits (e.g., showing work), but he has made an excellent transition. Anthony has great skills and strong understanding of concepts.

PRESENT STATUS (Rated A–F)

_B+_	Class work/participation	A = Excellent
_C+_	Homework	B = Above Average
_A_	Portfolio	C = Average
_A_	Quizzes	D = Below Average
_A−_	Tests	F = Failing
_A−_	Overall	

WHAT IS NEEDED

_✓_	Emphasis on homework
_____	Improve class participation
_____	More careful preparation for tests
_✓_	Keep up the good work
_____	Contact teacher
_____	Improve portfolio
_____	Other _____

Office Initial _CM_

Section III: Parent Evaluation and Comments: Parents are asked to respond and sign this progress report.
I thank you for this timely report. I am delighted that Anthony has started off well and is liking the class. He talks at home a lot about the class and the interesting activities; a tribute to good teaching. I can tell from our conversations at home that he is feeling much better about his math capability. I thank you.

Eric von Hauser

Figure 6.9
Progress report: subject-specific with student and parent/guardian input.

APPLICATION EXERCISE 6.2

Preparing a Rubric*

Instructions: The purpose of this application exercise is to work cooperatively and collaboratively with others after you practice your skill in preparing a rubric for a skill or lesson of your choice. To prepare a rubric, you will show the *degrees* (aware, somewhat aware, not aware) of a student's satisfactory completion for desired characteristics (or behavior or performance). Remember that you can easily turn a checklist into a rubric by *assigning degrees*. If you want a checklist to work from, you can turn to Figure 6.6, Sample Checklist: Assessing a Student's Oral Report, or Figure 6.7, Sample Checklist: Student Learning Assessment for Use with Interdisciplinary Thematic Instruction. Remove the perforated pages of this exercise from this book, write your first draft on the pages, and then show your work to a colleague to get feedback about making changes.

Design your rubric for a skill or lesson of your choice. When finished, share your rubric with another in your class. Provide feedback for one another. Make changes. If you wish, provide copies to all in the group so you each will have a collection of sample rubrics for various skills or lessons. Now to begin, check (✓) the information that you want to include in the rubric you are designing:

Step 1. *I can determine the characteristics of performance by the students.* I have studied student work related to this rubric to determine realistic characteristics of various performances at different levels of proficiency for my students. _____

   Example: Some characteristics of an oral report performance by students can include speaking so that everyone can hear, finishing sentences, seeming comfortable in front of the group, and so on.

Step 2. *I can determine the important step-by-step elements of the task.* I can include the most important elements (some teachers consider this criteria) of the assigned task. _____ I can explain clearly what a student knows and can do on the rubric. _____

   Example: Writing step-by-step elements begins with the first thing the student should do (in giving an oral report, a student should give a good introduction and speak so that everyone can hear) and ends with the last thing (a student should give a good conclusion and give good answers to questions from the audience). See Figure 6.6 or 6.7 again.

Step 3. *I can transform characteristics of the task into degrees (or levels of proficiency).* I can transform the characteristics of this rubric into words that describe the degrees (or levels of proficiency). This means I have written clear sentences about the activity step-by-step so I can ascribe levels of proficiency step-by-step._____

   Example: Characteristic I selected: Did the student speak so that everyone could hear? (This is one characteristic of the task of giving an oral report). *Degrees/levels of proficiency I selected:*

   maximum success   average success   minimal success

Step 4. *I can transform characteristics into criteria and degrees of success.* I have listed the criteria most characteristic of the task along with the degrees of success for each criteria.

   Example: Criteria I selected: Did the student . . .

☞

A. Speak so that everyone could hear? (This is one characteristic of the task of giving an oral report). *Degrees/levels of proficiency I selected:*

maximum success   average success   minimal success

B. Finish sentences? (This is one characteristic of the task of giving an oral report). *Degrees/levels of proficiency I selected:*

maximum success   average success   minimal success

Step 5. *I can transform degrees/levels of proficiency into easy-to-use numerical values for a rating scale if the school requires numerical values.* I can use a rating scale to evaluate student performance and provide easy-to-use values for each answer to make the results clear. The rating scale will differentiate among the degrees/levels of proficiency.

Example: Numerical values I selected for degrees/levels of proficiency: Maximum success (5); average success (4); minimal success (3)

Step 6. *I can double-check my preparation of a rubric to ensure I have shown a range of competence in the abilities of students.* I want to show a range of competence among students.

_____

Example: Criteria I selected: Did the student:

Speak so that everyone could hear? *Range of competence in abilities I determined:*
Speak so that all could hear? Maximum success
Speak so that most could hear? Average success
Speak so that few could hear? Minimal success

Step 7. *I can present and discuss the rubric with students.*

Example:

A. I have included a space for comments about thinking about one's own thinking (metacognitive knowledge) to encourage self-assessment by the student. _____

B. I can encourage a student's recognition about prior knowledge, about criteria, and about what represents quality work on this task. To do this, I will show and discuss this rubric with the students before they begin the task. _____

C. I can encourage my students to be creative (original, artistic), flexible (adaptable), and use individual initiative (plan, propose, invent, have an idea or project, present to authentic audience, conduct/discuss an experiment, discuss a real-life problem) _____

D. I can schedule students, especially ELLs and English-speaking students with learning problems, to have a teacher conference and revise their final drafts if appropriate.

_____

E. I can encourage student to self-evaluate. This means my sentences will begin with words such as *I can explain why I think I was creative (flexible, used individual initiative),* and students will receive the rubric again after completing the task so they can self-evaluate their work _____

---

* You'll recall that a rubric shows the *degrees* for the desired characteristics (maximum/minimum success), that a scoring guide assigns *point values* (point value = 1 for minimum success), and that a checklist usually shows only the desired *characteristics* (also called criteria or range of abilities, such as "the student will speak so that most could hear"). A checklist with characteristics can be changed into a scoring guide by assigning point values to the characteristics or into a rubric by assigning degrees for the characteristics. A rubric or scoring guide can be transformed into a checklist by showing only characteristics (other terms for characteristics are *criteria, range of abilities, behaviors,* or *performance*).

LOOKING AT TEACHERS II

Integrated Technology, Videos

In a middle school in a southern state, one teacher covered the outside of the classroom door with paper painted to look like stone blocks (student-made) inscribed with hieroglyphs (patterned paper that looks like rocks, cobblestones, or flagstones is available from www.ShindigZ.com). Inside, the room was changed to reflect the time of Hammurabi, a ruler during the golden age of Babylon around 2000 B.C.E. The classroom walls were covered with pictures of ancient sites that were located east of the Mediterranean Sea. Illustrations of artifacts were placed at strategic locations in the classroom. There was a copy of Hammurabi's code of laws, with examples of some of its 200+ legal provisions, to reflect his interest in the welfare of his people. The code set up a social order built on the rights of the individual, protected by the authority of law. The code's essence was the idea that the strong should not injure the weak. The code also included laws concerning accusations that were false, debts, family rights, land and business law, loans, military service, tariffs, trades, and wages. In addition to Hammurabi's administrative code, he built irrigation canals to improve agriculture, set up maximum prices and minimum wages, and reorganized taxation on a fair and efficient basis.

To help enrich the environment and extend the study beyond Babylon, a picture of a large Egyptian obelisk stood in one corner. Beside the obelisk was a poster of the Washington Monument. To further develop each student's understanding of the multiple connections among world history, social change, and American laws, the teacher asked the students to take on the personas of famous world leaders across history and societies. Some of the roles chosen were Lincoln, Mandela, and Mother Theresa. A conceptual statement, also used as a debate statement in the classroom, was one that brought together some connections among world history, social change, and American laws—this statement was "All men/women are created equal." Questions such as these were asked: How was this statement brought to life for the people who lived with Hammurabi? For the people who lived under the shadow of the Egyptian obelisk each day? For the people who see the Washington Monument each morning? How did Hammurabi's code of laws portray that all men/women were created equal? How does today's code in our town/city/state portray equality? What social changes related to "All men/women are created equal" have happened since the time of the building of the obelisk up to the building of the Washington Monument? What social changes have happened since the time of Hammurabi that you think are the most significant to you?

In their roles related to world history, the students campaigned for or against the statement. As part of their campaigns as famous world leaders, they prepared their remarks for a videotaped press conference, a campaign commercial, and a classroom discussion/debate. For a final authentic assessment (sometimes called the right evaluation at the right time for the right purpose), the final product was a portfolio of each student's understanding of these connections. The portfolios included a wide variety of materials: essays, videos, short multiple-choice tests, and final reflections on the project. The multiple-choice exams were coordinated with the state's learning objectives. A colleague who taught English helped with the writing assignments and the school technologist used the students in her classes to help edit the videotapes and computer searches about famous world leaders. Students could search for ancient civilizations at the Institute of Museum and Library Services at the University of Chicago and begin with http://mesopotamia.lib.uchicago.edu. With integrated technology, this project incorporated multiples of many important features of teaching—multiple learning styles, intelligences, contents, and multiple teaching styles.[14]

SUMMARY

Whereas the first four chapters of this resource guide addressed the *why* component of teaching and the fifth chapter addressed the *what* component, this chapter has focused your attention on the aspects of assessment and reporting student achievement. Assessment is an integral and ongoing factor in the *what* component as part of the teaching-learning process; consequently, this chapter has emphasized the importance of including the following in your teaching performance:

- Consider your assessment and grading procedures carefully, plan them, and explain your policies to the students and their parents and guardians.
- Involve students in the assessment process; keep students informed of their progress. Return papers

promptly, review answers to all questions, and respond to inquiries about marks given.

- Maintain accurate and clear records of assessment results so that you will have an adequate supply of data on which to base your judgmental decisions about achievement.
- Make sure to explain any ambiguities that result from the terminology used, and base your assessments on the material that has been taught.
- Strive for objective and impartial assessment as you put your assessment plan into operation.
- Try to minimize arguments about grades, cheating, and teacher subjectivity by involving students in the planning, reinforcing individual student development, and providing an accepting, stimulating learning environment.
- Use a variety of instruments to collect a body of evidence to most reliably assess the learning of students that focus on their individual development.

Because teaching and learning work hand in hand and because they are reciprocal processes where one depends on and affects the other, the focus of this chapter has considered the assessment of the learning of the students as a basis for the *what* component of planning for instruction.

What's to Come. The next chapter (Chapter 7) of this guide will consider how to prepare for activities, lessons, and units. After reading the material in the next chapter, you will want to extend your competencies further by selecting one of the suggested interactions in the section Extending My Professional Competency (just as we encourage you to do for this chapter). Now please turn your attention to the following section. Your choices for this chapter begin with participating in a discussion about student-led parent-teacher conferences and observing a video about standardized tests.

EXTENDING MY PROFESSIONAL COMPETENCY

With Discussion
Student-Led Parent-Teacher-Student Conferences. If a principal interviewed me for a teaching job, what would be my response if I were asked, "Do you support student-led parent-teacher-student conferences? Why or why not?" **To do:** Research the topic and report to your class about the practice. Discuss this and your thoughts about it with your classmates.

With Video
Video Activity: Assessment. If a colleague asked me to tell some of the ways tests are used currently, what would I say?

After seeing the video, determine the difference between norm-referenced and criterion-reference tests. Give one example of a test preparation method that interests you and talk about your example with a classmate. Discuss any agreement you have about test preparation methods seen in the video and ask your colleague for any disagreements about a method.

With Portfolio
Portfolio Planning. How can I continue developing my professional portfolio and show my knowledge of assessing and reporting student achievement in connection with assessment as shown on teacher tests and in Principle 8 of INTASC and Standards 3, 6, and 8 of NBPTS? **To do:** To add to your portfolio, you can write a one- to two-page paper for this chapter explaining how you intend to assess and report student achievement in a grade of your choice. You might also consider briefly mentioning your understanding of this chapter's objectives in your response. This can include one or more of the following:

- Your succinct explanation of the meaning of assessment as a continuous progress, an example of what you will do with an example of assessment (information) results, and two ways you can interpret data to tell to others.
- Your brief statement about comparing and contrasting three avenues for assessing student learning as well as when and how to use such assessment as observations, oral reports, records, portfolios, and performance samples.
- Your statement about preparing at least two different types of assessment items.
- Please turn back to the beginning of this chapter for the rest of the objectives. Label your portfolio paper Assessing and Reporting Student Achievement, and place your paper in your portfolio. If needed, refer to Portfolio Builders in this book's accompanying website at www.MyEducationLab.com.

With Teacher Tests Study Guide
Teacher Tests for Future Licensing and Certification. If I wanted to prepare for taking a state teacher test to qualify for my teaching certificate/license and review my knowledge about assessing and reporting student achieement, how could I begin? **To do:** To support you as you prepare for teaching, you will find constructed response-type questions similar to those found on state tests for

teacher licensing and certification in Appendix A of this book, Teacher Tests Study Guide. The question related to this chapter helps you take another look at the classroom vignette found in *Looking at Teachers II*. Write your response and, if you wish, discuss it with another teaching candidate. If appropriate, use one or two of your colleague's suggestions to help you change your response to the question. Place your response in a Teacher Test Study Guide folder or type/scan into a computer file. Plan to review your response and reread it for study purposes before taking a teacher test.

With Target Topics for Teacher Tests (TTTT)

If I wanted a source to prepare for taking a state teacher test to qualify for licensing and certification, what could I use? **To do:** You'll recall that if you are preparing to take a teacher test, you can review subject matter, such as content related to this chapter, by locating Target Topics for Teacher Tests in the subject index at the end of this book. The topics are called out with bullets (•) that are placed by selected word entries. The selected word entries identify selected core subject matter—assessment, student achievement, and other terms—that the authors suggest reviewing to prepare for taking a teacher test exam for licensing and certification similar to your state's test.

With Midpoint Self-Check Reflection Guide

Midpoint Self-Check Reflection Guide. If I wanted to self-assess and evaluate my competencies as guided by the first six chapters in this resource guide, how could I begin? **To do:** You can begin with a midpoint self-check reflection of what you know about today's elementary schools, the learners, teacher responsibilities, safe learning environment, selecting content, and assessing student achievement. For this self-check, go to Appendix B to find the Midpoint Self-Check Reflection Guide for this book. Complete the Reflection Guide for this midpoint self-check and think about the knowledge that you show on the self-check. If you wish, discuss any items that concern you with a colleague. Use these items to guide you in increasing your awareness of today's elementary schools, the learners, your responsibilities as a teacher, supporting a safe learning environment, content selection, and assessing achievement. What are one or two steps you plan to take to do this? If required for an assessment review for an instructional course, give this self-check material to the instructor.

WITH READING

Airasian, P. W. (2001). *Classroom Assessment: Concepts and Applications* (4th ed.). Boston: McGraw-Hill.

Andrade, H. G. (2000, February). Using Rubrics to Promote Thinking and Learning. *Educational Leadership, 57*(5), 13–18.

Arter, J., and McTighe, J. (2001). *Scoring Rubrics in the Classroom: Using Performance Criteria for Assessing and Improving Student Performances*. Thousand Oaks, CA: Corwin.

Asp, E. (2000). Assessment in Education: Where Have We Been? Where Are We Headed? In R. S. Brandt (Ed.), *Education in a New Era* (pp. 123–157). Alexandria, VA: ASCD Yearbook, Association for Supervision and Curriculum Development.

Bracey, G. W. (2000). *A Short Guide to Standardized Testing* (Fastback 459). Bloomington, IN: Phi Delta Kappa Educational Foundation.

Brookhart, S. M. (2004). *Grading*. Upper Saddle River, NJ: Merrill/Prentice Hall.

Carr, J. F., and Harris, D. E. (2001). *Succeeding with Standards: Linking Curriculum, Assessment, and Action Planning*. Alexandria, VA: Association of Supervision and Curriculum Development.

Chandler, M. A., and Glod, M. (2008, Summer). *Testing Change Raises Scores: Va. Assesses Those Learning English on Class Work*. Accessed at www.washingtonpost.com/wp-dyn/content/article/2008/08/27/AR2008082701813.html.

Chen, Y., and Martin, M. A. (2000, Spring). Using Performance Assessment and Portfolio Assessment Together in the Elementary Classroom. *Reading Improvement, 37*(1), 32–38.

Cullotta, K. A. (2008). The Parent-Teacher Talk Gains a New Participant. *New York Times*. Available at www.nytimes.com/2008/12/28/education/28conferences.html.

Danna, Stephen. (2003, February-March). Pursuing National Board Certification. *Educational Horizons*, p. 5.

Demers, C. (2000, October). Beyond Paper-and-Pencil Assessment. *Science and Children, 36*(2), 24–29, 60.

Ellis, A. K. (2001). *Teaching, Learning, and Assessment Together: The Reflective Classroom*. Larchmont, NY: Eye on Education.

Flatt, J. M. S. The Scholarship of Teaching and Learning. (2005, Fall). *Phi Kappa Phi Forum, 85*(3), 3, 5.

Gareis, C. R., and Grant, L. W. (2008). *Teacher-Made Assessments: How to Connect Curriculum, Instruction, and Student Learning*. Larchmont, NY: Eye on Education.

Georgiady, N. P., and Romano, L. G. (2002). *Positive Parent-Teacher Conferences* (Fastback 491). Bloomington, IN: Phi Delta Kappa Educational Foundation.

Kober, N. (2002, June). Teaching to the Test: The Good, the Bad, and Who's Responsible. *Testtalk, 1,* 1–12.

Marzano, R. J. (2000). *Transforming Classroom Grading*. Alexandria, VA: Association for Supervision and Curriculum Development.

Montgomery, K. (2000, July/August). Classroom Rubrics: Systematizing What Teachers Do Naturally. *Clearing House, 73*(6), 324–328.

Moskal, B. M. (2000). *Scoring Rubrics Part I: What and When*. Washington, DC: Assessment and Evaluation. (ED446110).

Ronis, D. (2000). *Brain Compatible Assessments*. Arlington Heights, IL: Skyline.

Skillings, M. J., and Ferrell, R. (2000, March). Student-Generated Rubrics: Bring Students Into the Assessment Process. *Reading Teacher, 53*(6), 452–455.

Smith, J. K., Smith, L. F., and De Lisi, R. (2001). *Natural Classroom Assessment: Designing Seamless Instruction & Assessment*. Thousand Oaks, CA: Corwin Press.

Southwest Educational Development Laboratory. (2003). *SEDL Helps Parents Prepare for Parent-Teacher Conferences*. Austin, TX: Author.

Teachers of English to Speakers of Other Languages. (2006). *Scenarios for ESL Standards-based Assessment*. Alexandria, VA: TESOL.

Tuttle, H. G. (2008). *Formative Assessment: Responding to Your Students*. Larchmont, NY: Eye on Education.

WITH NOTES

1. Association of Supervision and Curriculum Development, Leveraging Technology to Improve Literacy, *Education Update, 50*(10), 1,5, 6 (October 2008).

2. Southwest Educational Development Laboratory. *SEDL Helps Parents Prepare for Parent-Teacher Conferences* (Austin, TX: Author, 2003) Available at www.sedl.org/new/pressrelease/20031001_16.html.

3. See R. Marzano, J. Pickering, and J. E. Pollock, *Classroom Instruction That Works*. (Alexandria, VA: Association for Supervision and /Curriculum Development, 2001); J. Bryan, K-W-L: Questioning the Known, *A Journal of the International Reading Association: Reading Teacher, 51*(7), 618–620 (1998).

4. C. Temple, D. Ogle, A. Crawford, and P. Freppan, *All Children Read: Teaching for Literacy in Today's Diverse Classroom* (Boston: Allyn & Bacon, 2005).

5. See special section on testing in *Phi Delta Kappan, 85*(5), 352–387 (January 2004); and special section on testing/school improvement in *Phi Delta Kappan, 85*(10), 735–761 (June 2004).

6. Learner Profile is available from Sunburst Technology, 1550 Executive Dr., Elgin, IL 60123, 1-800-321-7511.

7. See C. Diehm, From Worn-Out to Web-Based: Better Student Portfolios, *Phi Delta Kappan, 85*(10), 792–795 (June, 2004); M. A. Chandler and M. Glod, Testing Change Raises Scores, *Washington Post,* p. B01, (Thursday, August 28, 2008), at www.washingtonpost.com/wp-dyn/content/article/2008/08/27/AR2008082701813.html.

8. Software packages for the development of student electronic portfolios are available, such as Classroom Manager from CTB Macmillan/McGraw-Hill (Monterey, CA), Electronic Portfolio from Learning Quest (Corvallis, OR), and Grady Profile from Auerbach and Associates (St. Louis, MO).

9. V. Klenowski, *Portfolio Use and Assessment* (New York: Taylor & Francis, 2002).

10. T. Kubiszyn and G. Borick, *Educational Testing Measurement: Classroom Applications and Practice,* 6th ed. (New York: Wiley, 2003); D. Barone and J. Taylor, *The Practical Guide to Classroom Literacy Assessment* (Thousand Oaks, CA: Corwin, 2006).

11. C. Diehm, see note 7.

12. A. Costa and B. Kalliek (Eds.), *Assessing and Reporting on Habits of Mind* (Arlington, VA: Association for Supervision and Curriculum Development, 2000); B. J. Ricci, How about Parent-Teacher Student Conferences? *Principal, 79*(5), 53–43 (May 2000).

13. H. G. Andrade, Using Rubrics to Promote Thinking and Learning, *Educational Leadership, 57*(5), 13–18 (February 2000).

14. H. Burley and M. Price, What Works with Authentic Assessment, *Educational Horizons, 81*(4), 193–196, 2003.

How Do I Prepare Activities, Lessons, and Units?

7

LOOKING AT TEACHERS I

Integrated Technology, Podcasts

At Spring Street School in Shrewsbury, Massachusetts, a third-grade teacher knew that the curriculum required that the students learn about the history of their town. In past years, third-graders had toured the historic landmarks of their area and had written reports about the sites (place-based education). To change from requiring written reports to using technology integration, the teacher asked the students to do digital reporting. The students were asked to create a podcast (a digital broadcast using computer, microphone, and audio editing software) of an audio walking tour of the historic part of Shrewsbury. Having models of other city tours, the teacher showed the students an example of a city audio tour that she found on www.audisseyguides.com. After seeing the model, the class was divided into groups and each group was assigned one of the historic landmarks in the city—for instance, one group was assigned to study the city's one-room schoolhouse built in 1830. The teacher's brief interest-generating talks about each of the groups' landmarks served as springboards to launch additional student interest. Then, the whole group participated in making a walking tour map to show the location of the groups' landmarks and developed a key to the location of each landmark on the tour. Each group made a list of questions about their landmark and then conducted their research to find the answers and to write a script. The criteria for this included (1) describing the landmark's physical features, (2) discussing its history, and (3) writing at least one sentence to link or connect the listener from their landmark to the next group's landmark/location on the tour. As part of the history description, two students wrote short stories. One student wrote about a town doctor who practiced in the nineteenth century (the same time period when the historic schoolhouse was built) and another wrote a description of what the common area in the center of town would have looked like in the 1700s (more than 100 years before the historic schoolhouse was built). When the audio walking tour was completed, it was posted on the class blog. Students, parents, and others were able to download the podcast to their MP3 players and, if they wished, take the walking tour to see historic landmarks in Shewsbury. See http://spsaudiotours.blogspot.com/2006/06/history-of-shrewsbury-center.html.[1]

To further integrate technology related to a walking tour in your class, you could include the following:

- Arrange a historical landmark tour with a digital camera on hand. With the needed permissions to take pictures of the students on file at the school, you could keep all the pictures wanted and delete the ones not wanted. Back in the classroom, you could plug the digital camera into the classroom TV and instantly show a recap of the tour along with "good manners on the tour" as well as a review of the historical landmarks. If a photo printer is connected to the class TV, the transfer device can be taken out of the camera and placed into the printer and then photos of the students on the tour can be printed (perhaps to accompany a positive note [a Happygram] home to the parents). Further, the students can watch the photos on TV and have a class meeting about what is seen and to discuss the information they gained during the historical landmark tour.
- Arrange to use a wireless digital camera phone on any place-based education tour. A camera phone, available with different features, permits you as the teacher/adult volunteer to make immediate emergency calls, to call the principal/school or parents, to access news and weather, to take photos of any expected or unexpected events, and to surf the web for backup information needed.

- Arrange to use a set of two-way radios while you or adult volunteers and students are on a walking tour. This communication arrangement allows the teacher to talk to the adult volunteer who is with the students at the back of the tour group or who is with the line of students going on a restroom break or who is with the last group of students crossing in a safety crosswalk on a busy street.

A Focus on English Language Learners

Give every student a copy of a labeled map showing the school and the historic part of Shrewsbury (or a larger area) so that the names of places can be read. Put the names of places on small cards and have the students select them during an educational activity called "Who Knows the Road to Old Shrewsbury?" The student who has the first turn is given a copy of the labeled map and draws a card that gives the name of the place that the student is to locate. To locate it, the student traces the route from the school to the place on his or her map and gives directions about how to get there. As the student describes how to get from the school to the place named on the card drawn, the other students look at their maps to follow the directions and see if they can determine how to get to the named place. Each student can ask a certain number of questions (two, three, etc.), determined by the teacher, if they want to get additional information. When the places are identified, the activity is over and if time permits, the group can give feedback and talk about what they heard that was helpful in identifying the route.

In this chapter, you will learn how the theoretical considerations filter your choices of instructional strategies for activities, lessons, and units. You have learned, in past chapters, about children in the elementary school, their needs, and the importance of providing an accepting and supportive learning environment, as well as about teacher behaviors that are necessary to facilitate the most meaningful student learning. You also realize that learning modalities, instructional modes, and cultural/linguistic diversity can affect a student's learning.

So in this chapter, we point out that the theoretical considerations affect the continued building you will do to increase your knowledge base about why planning is important. We give you an opportunity to find ways that you can sequence activities into lessons, about ways that you can sequence lessons into units, and how all three—activities, lessons, and units—are useful pedagogical tools. You'll realize that developing activities, lessons, and units of instruction that integrate student learning and provide a sense of meaning for the students requires coordination throughout the curriculum. Hence, for students, learning is a process of discovering how information, knowledge, and ideas are interrelated so they can make sense out of self, school, and life. For example, to relate the concept of historical landmarks in one's town to the concept that life around the landmarks moves forward from the past and has a cycle, your favorite children's book about one of nature's cycles can be introduced. Another choice, one best for individual viewing with parental permission because of a farmer's use of a gun, might be *The Story Goes On* (New York: Roaring Brook/Neal Porter Books, 2005) by A. Fisher. The book shows the circular journey of the growth of a seed in the soil (perhaps similar to the soil around one of the town's landmarks) and then shows the

contribution to life the seed makes to the food chain—a bug, frog, snake, hawk, coyote, and finally, back to the enrichment of the soil. Preparing chunks of information like this into activities and activities into lessons and lessons into units is one way to help students process and understand knowledge. Thus, in this chapter, we help you consider activities and lessons and then develop your first unit of instruction to assist you in becoming a competent planner of instruction.

CHAPTER OBJECTIVES

Specifically, upon completion of this chapter you should be able to:

1. For a specified grade level, give examples of learning experiences/activities from each of these categories: verbal, visual, vicarious, simulated, and direct/explicit.
2. Use a lesson format that is approved by your instructor and prepare a lesson plan for a grade/course of your choice; be able to evaluate your own lesson plan and the plan of one of your peers.

3. Write a specific teaching plan with goals, objectives, resources, and learning activities.
4. Prepare a regular instructional unit or an interdisciplinary thematic unit with sequential lesson plans and a closure, one that you can use in your teaching; if you prepare an interdisciplinary unit, you will demonstrate your knowledge about including activities and lessons that focus on interdisciplinary content.

UNDERSTANDING THEORETICAL CONSIDERATIONS FOR THE SELECTION OF INSTRUCTIONAL STRATEGIES

As you prepare to detail your instructional plan, you will be narrowing in on selecting and planning the instructional activities. In Chapter 2, you learned about how children differ in learning styles and learning capacities and of the importance of varying the instructional strategies and of using multilevel instruction. In Chapter 3, you learned about specific teacher behaviors that must be in place for students to learn—structuring the learning environment; accepting and sharing instructional accountability; demonstrating withitness and overlapping; providing a variety of motivating and challenging activities; modeling appropriate behaviors; facilitating students' acquisition of data; creating a psychologically safe environment; clarifying whenever necessary; using periods of silence and teacher talk; and questioning thoughtfully. In the paragraphs that follow, you will learn not only about how to implement some of those fundamental behaviors, but also about the large repertoire of other strategies, aids, media, and resources available to you (see Figure 7.1). You will learn how to select and implement from this repertoire.

Decision Making and Strategy Selection

You must make a myriad of decisions to select and implement a particular teaching strategy effectively. The selection of a strategy depends in part upon your decision whether to deliver information directly (explicit,

expository, or didactic teaching) or to provide students with access to information (implicit or facilitative teaching). Explicit teaching can be seen as teacher-centered, while implicit teaching can be seen as more student-centered. To assist in your selection of strategies, it is important that you understand the basic principles of learning summarized in the following paragraphs.

Explicit and Implicit Instruction: A Clarification of Terms

You are probably well aware that professional education is rampant with its own special jargon, which can be confusing to the neophyte. Indeed, rest assured, it can be overwhelming even to those of us who are well-seasoned. The use of the term **explicit teaching** (or its synonyms, *explicit instruction*, **direct instruction,** or *teacher-centered instruction*), and one of its antonyms, **implicit experiences,** provides examples of how confusing the jargon can be. The term *explicit instruction* can also have a variety of definitions, depending on who is doing the defining. (*Note:* In addition to the generic term *explicit* or *direct instruction*, there is a *Direct Instruction Model* that has evolved from an original curriculum program for beginning reading, language arts, and mathematics developed in 1968 and published by the Science Research Associates [SRA] under the name DISTAR, Direct Instruction System for Teaching and Remediation. This program for grades K–6 is comprised of highly scripted lessons that are designed around a very specific knowledge base and a well-defined set of skills.)[2] For

Assignment	Group work	Panel discussion
Autotutorial	Guest speaker	Problem solving
Brainstorming	Homework	Project
Coaching	Individualized instruction	Questioning
Collaborative learning	Inquiry learning	Review/practice
Cooperative learning	Interactive media	Role play
Debate	Journal writing	Self-instructional module
Demonstration	Laboratory investigation	Script writing
Diorama	Laser videodisc	Simulation
Discovery learning	Learning center	Study guide
Drama	Lecture	Symposium
Drill center	Library/resource	Telecommunication
Expository learning	Metacognition	Term paper
Field trip/virtual	Mock-up model	Textbook
Game	Multimedia	Think–pair–share

Figure 7.1
Selected instructional strategies.

now, you should keep this distinction in mind—do not confuse the term *explicit/direct instruction* with the term *explicit* or *direct experiences*. The two terms indicate two separate, though not incompatible, instructional modes. The dichotomy of pedagogical opposites shown in Figure 7.2 provides a useful visual distinction of the opposites. Although terms in one column are similar if not synonymous, they are near or exact opposites (antonyms) of those across from them in the other column.

Degrees of Directness

Rather than having your teaching characterized by thinking and behaving in terms of opposites, as may be suggested by Figure 7.2, it is more likely that "degrees of directness (being explicit)," or "degrees of indirectness (being implicit)" will characterize your teaching. For example, for a unit of instruction, the teacher may give directions for a culminating project in an explicit/direct mini-lesson, followed then by student-designed inquiry learning that leads to the final project.

Rather than focus your attention on the selection of a particular mode of teaching, we emphasize the importance of an eclectic model—selecting the best from various models or approaches. As indicated by the example of the preceding paragraph, there will be times when you want to use an explicit, teacher-centered approach, perhaps by a mini-lecture or a demonstration, or both. And then there will be many more times when you will want to use an implicit, student-centered or social-interactive approach, such as the use of cooperative learning and investigative projects. And perhaps there will be even more times when you will be doing both at the same time, for example, working with a teacher-centered approach with one small group of students, perhaps giving them explicit instruction, while another group or several groups of children, in various areas of the classroom, are working on their project studies (a student-centered approach) or at learning stations. The information that follows and specific descriptions in Part III will help you make decisions about when each approach is most appropriate and will provide guidelines for their use.

Principles of Classroom Instruction and Learning: A Synopsis

A child does not learn to write by learning to recognize grammatical constructions of sentences. Neither does a person learn to play soccer solely by listening to a lecture on soccer. Learning is superficial unless the learning activities and instructional methods are developmentally and

Delivery mode of instruction	versus	Access mode
Didactic instruction	versus	Facilitative teaching
Explicit instruction	versus	Implicit instruction
Expository teaching	versus	Discovery learning
Teacher-centered instruction	versus	Student-centered instruction
Direct/explicit teaching	versus	Direct/explicit experiences

Figure 7.2
Pedagogical opposites.

intellectually appropriate—that is, unless they are (a) developmentally appropriate for the learners and (b) intellectually appropriate for the learners' understanding, skills, and attitudes desired. Memorizing, for instance, is not the same as understanding. Yet far too often, memorization seems all that is expected of students in many classrooms. The result is low-level learning, a mere verbalism or mouthing of poorly understood words and sentences. That is not intellectually appropriate and it is not teaching, but just the orchestration of short-term memory exercises. An old-fashioned mental model of learning that assumes that a human brain is capable of doing only one thing at a time is invidiously erroneous. When selecting the mode of instruction, bear in mind the following basic principles of classroom instruction and learning shown in Figure 7.3.

Procedural and Conceptual Knowledge

Whereas procedural knowledge entails the recording in memory of the meanings of symbols and rules and procedures needed to accomplish tasks, conceptual knowledge refers to the understanding of relationships. Unless it is connected in meaningful ways for the formation of conceptual knowledge, the accumulation of memorized procedural knowledge is fragmented and will be maintained in the brain for only a brief time.

To help elementary students establish conceptual knowledge, the learning for them must be meaningful. To help make learning meaningful for your students, you should use explicit (direct) and real experiences as often as practical and possible. Vicarious experiences are sometimes necessary to provide students with otherwise unattainable knowledge; however, explicit experiences that engage all the student's senses and all their learning modalities are more powerful. Students learn to write by writing and by receiving coaching and feedback about their progress in writing. They learn to play soccer by experiencing playing soccer and by receiving coaching and feedback about their developing skills and knowledge in playing the game. They learn these things best when they are actively (hands-on) and mentally (minds-on) engaged in doing them. This is real learning, learning that is meaningful; it is **authentic learning.**

Explicit versus Implicit Instructional Modes: Strengths and Limitations of Each

Selecting an instructional strategy entails two distinct choices (modes) from which you must make a decision: Should you deliver information to students directly or should you provide students with access to information?

Figure 7.3
Basic principles of classroom instruction.

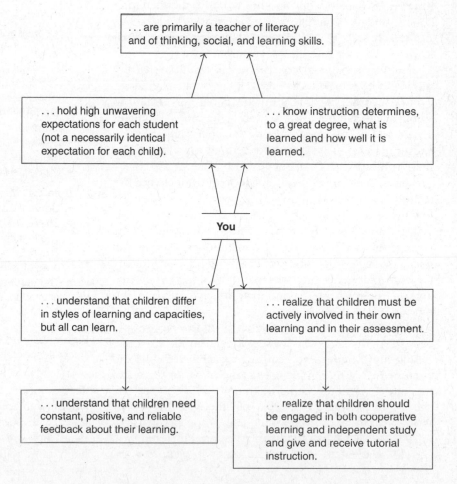

(Refer to the comparison of pedagogical opposites in Figure 7.2.)

The **delivery mode** (known as the **didactic, expository,** or **traditional instructional** style) is to deliver information. Knowledge is passed on from those who know (the teachers, with the aid of textbooks or other media) to those who do not (the students). Within the delivery mode, traditional and time-honored strategies are textbook reading, the lecture, questioning, and teacher-centered or teacher-planned discussions. See Figure 7.4.

With the **access mode,** instead of direct delivery of information and direct control over what is learned, the teacher provides students with access to information by working *with* the students. In collaboration with the students, experiences are designed that facilitate the building of their existing schemata and their obtaining new knowledge and skills. Within the access mode, important instructional strategies include cooperative learning, inquiry learning, and student-centered project-based learning, each of which most certainly will use teacher talk and questioning, though the questions more often will come from the students than from you or the textbook or some other source extrinsic to the student. Discussions and lectures on particular topics also may be involved. But when used in the access mode, discussions and lectures occur during or after (rather than before) explicit, hands-on learning by the students. In other words, rather than preceding student inquiry learning, discussions and lectures *result from* student inquiry learning, and then may be followed by further student investigation.

You are probably more experienced with the delivery mode. To be most effective as a classroom teacher, however, you must become knowledgeable and skillful in using access strategies. For young learners, strategies within the access mode clearly facilitate their positive learning and acquisition of conceptual knowledge and help build their self-esteem.

You should appropriately select and effectively use strategies from both modes, but with a strong leaning toward access strategies. Thus, from your study of this chapter and the chapters that follow, you will become knowledgeable about specific techniques so you can make intelligent decisions for choosing the best strategy for particular goals and objectives for subjects you teach and the interests, needs, and maturity level of your own unique group of students.

Figures 7.4 and 7.5 provide an overview of the specific strengths and weaknesses of each mode. By comparing those figures, you can see that the strengths and weaknesses of one mode are nearly mirror opposites of the other. As noted earlier, although as a teacher you should be skillful in the use of strategies from both modes, for the most developmentally appropriate teaching for most groups of elementary school children, you should concentrate more on using strategies from the

---

Delivery Mode

Strengths
- Much content can be covered within a short span of time, usually by formal teacher talk, which then may be followed by an experiential activity.
- The teacher is in control of what content is covered.
- The teacher is in control of time allotted to specific content coverage.
- Strategies within the delivery mode are consistent with competency-based instruction.
- Student achievement of specific content is predictable and manageable.

Potential Weaknesses
- The sources of student motivation are mostly extrinsic.
- Students have little control over the pacing of their learning.
- Students make few important decisions about their learning.
- There may be little opportunity for divergent or creative thinking.
- Student self-esteem may be inadequately served.

Figure 7.4
Delivery mode: its strengths and weaknesses.

Access Mode

Strengths
- Students learn content in more depth.
- The sources of student motivation are more likely intrinsic.
- Students make important decisions about their own learning.
- Students have more control over the pacing of their learning.
- Students develop a sense of personal self-worth.

Potential Weaknesses
- Content coverage may be more limited.
- Strategies are time consuming.
- The teacher has less control over content and time.
- The specific results of student learning are less predictable.
- The teacher may have less control over class procedures.

Figure 7.5
Access mode: its strengths and weaknesses.

---

access mode. Strategies within that mode are more student-centered, hands-on, and concrete; students interact with one another and are actually closer to doing what they are learning to do—that is, the learning is likely more authentic. Learning that occurs from the use of that mode is longer lasting (fixes into long-term memory). And, as the children interact with one another and with their learning, they develop a sense of "can do," which enhances their self-esteem.

SELECTING LEARNING ACTIVITIES THAT ARE DEVELOPMENTALLY APPROPRIATE

Returning to our soccer example, can you imagine a soccer coach teaching students the skills and knowledge needed to play soccer without ever letting them experience playing the game? Can you imagine a geography teacher teaching students how to read a map without ever letting them put their eyes and hands on a real map? Can you imagine teaching children the letters of the alphabet without ever letting them put the letters together to form words? Can you imagine teaching a child to play a piano without ever allowing the child to touch a real keyboard? Unfortunately, still today, too many teachers do almost those exact things—they try to teach students to do something without letting the students practice doing it.

In planning and selecting developmentally appropriate learning activities, an important rule to remember is to select activities that are as close to the real thing as possible and sensible. That is learning through direct experiencing. When students are involved in direct experiences, they are using more of their sensory input channels, their learning modalities (see Chapter 2). And when all the senses are engaged, learning is more integrated, and is most effective, meaningful, and longest-lasting. This "learning by doing" is authentic learning—or, as referred to earlier, hands-on and minds-on learning.

The Learning Experiences Ladder

The learning experiences ladder, a visual depiction of a range of learning experiences from which a teacher may select, is shown in Figure 7.6. Hands-on, minds-on learning is at the bottom of the ladder. At the top are

Figure 7.6
The learning experiences ladder.
Source: If interested in the development of this experiences ladder, earlier versions of this concept are found in C. F. Hoban, Sr., et al., *Visualizing the Curriculum* (New York: Dryden, 1937), p. 39; J. S. Bruner, *Toward a Theory of Instruction* (Cambridge, MA: Harvard University Press, 1966), p. 49; E. Dale, *Audio-Visual Methods in Teaching* (New York: Holt, Rinehart & Winston, 1969). p. 108; and first appeared in E. C. Kim and R. D. Kellough, *A Resource Guide for Secondary School Teaching*, 2nd ed. (Englewood Cliffs, NJ: Merrill/Prentice Hall, 1978), p. 136.

Verbal Experiences Teacher talk, written words; engaging only one sense; using the most abstract symbolization; students physically inactive. *Examples*: (a) Listening to the teacher talk about tide pools. (b) Listening to a student report about the Grand Canyon. (c) Listening to a guest speaker talk about how the state legislature functions.

Visual Experiences Still pictures, diagrams, charts; engaging only one sense; typically symbolic; students physically inactive. *Examples*: (a) Viewing slide photographs of tide pools. (b) Viewing drawings and photographs of the Grand Canyon. (c) Listening to a guest speaker talk about the state legislature and viewing slides of it in action.

Vicarious Experiences Laser videodisc programs, computer programs, video programs; engaging more than one sense; learner indirectly "doing"; may be some limited physical activity. *Examples*: (a) Interacting with a computer program about wave action and life in tide pools. (b) Viewing and listening to a video program about the Grand Canyon. (c) Taking a field trip to observe the state legislature in action.

Simulated Experiences Role playing, experimenting, simulations, mock-ups, working models; all or nearly all senses engaged; activity often integrating disciplines; closest to the real thing. *Examples*: (a) Building a classroom working model of a tide pool. (b) Building a classroom working model of the Grand Canyon. (c) Designing a classroom role-play simulation patterned after the operating procedures of the state legislature.

Direct Experiences Learner actually doing what is being learned; true inquiry; all senses engaged; usually integrates disciplines; the real thing. *Examples*: (a) Visiting and experiencing a tide pool. (b) Visiting and experiencing the Grand Canyon. (c) Designing an elected representative body to oversee the operation of the school-within-the-school program, and patterned after the state legislative assembly.

ABSTRACT ↑

↓ CONCRETE

abstract experiences, where the learner is exposed only to symbolization (i.e., letters and numbers) and uses only one or two senses (auditory or visual). The teacher lectures while the students sit and watch and hear. Visual and verbal symbolic experiences, while impossible to avoid when teaching, are less effective in ensuring that planned and meaningful learning occurs. This is especially so with young children, learners who have special needs, learners with ethnic and cultural differences, and students who are English learners. Thus, when planning learning experiences and selecting instructional materials, you are advised to select activities that engage the learners in the most explicit/direct experiences possible and that are developmentally and intellectually appropriate for your specific group of students.

As can be inferred from the learning experiences ladder, when teaching about tide pools (the first example for each step), the most effective mode is to take the students to a tide pool (explicit/direct experience), where students can see, hear, touch, smell, and perhaps even taste (if not polluted with toxins) the water from the tip of a finger dipped in the tide pool. The least effective mode is for the teacher to merely talk about the tide pool (verbal experience, the most abstract and symbolic experience), engaging only one sense—auditory.

Of course, for various reasons—such as time, matters of safety, lack of resources, and geographic location of your school—you may not be able to take your students to a tide pool. You cannot always use the most explicit/direct experience, so sometimes you must select an experience higher on the ladder. Self-discovery teaching is not always appropriate. Sometimes, it is more appropriate to build upon what others have discovered and learned. While learners do not need to "reinvent the wheel," the most effective and longest-lasting learning is that which engages most or all of their senses. On the learning experiences ladder, those are the experiences that fall within the bottom three categories—direct/explicit, simulated, and vicarious. This is as true of adult learners as it is with kindergarten children or students of any age group in between.

Direct, Simulated, and Vicarious Experiences Help Connect Student Learning

Another value of explicit, simulated, and vicarious experiences is that they tend to be interdisciplinary; that is, they blur or bridge subject-content boundaries. That

makes those experiences especially useful for teachers who want to help students connect the learning of one discipline with that of others and to bridge what is being learned with their own life experiences. Explicit, simulated, and vicarious experiences are more like real life. That means that the learning resulting from those experiences is authentic.

Developing the Learning Activities: The Heart and Spirit of Lessons

Activities that engage the students in meaningful learning constitute the heart and spirit of the lessons (and thus, the instructional unit). The activities that start with a beginning lesson (or start a unit into motion) are called **initiating activities** or *"launching" activities*; those that comprise the heart of the lessons and the unit are the ongoing **developmental activities;** and those that bring the study to a natural close are **culminating activities** found in the final lessons/end of the unit.

Although the possibilities are nearly limitless, refer back to the list in Figure 7.1 since it gives you an idea of the many options from which you can choose activities for any of these three categories, some of which, of course, may overlap in one regard or another and some of which might naturally fit one category better than another.

Initiating Activities

A unit of study can be initiated by a limitless variety of activities and lessons. You must decide which ways are appropriate to incorporate into your lessons for your educational goals and objectives, for your intended time duration, and for your own unique group of students, considering their level of maturity, interests, abilities, and skills. You might start with a current event, a community problem or concern, a student experience, an outdoor adventure, an artifact, a book, or something found on the Internet.

Ongoing Developmental Activities

Once the initiating activities and lessons have started the study (unit), students become occupied with a variety of ongoing activities such as those listed in Figure 7.1. In working with students in selecting and planning the ongoing learning activities, you will want to keep in mind the concept represented by the learning experiences ladder (Figure 7.6) as well as predetermined goals and target objectives (refer to Chapter 5). Now begin Application Exercise 7.1.

APPLICATION EXERCISE 7.1

*Putting Objectives, Resources, and Learning Activities
Together for a Teaching Plan*

Instructions: The purpose of this application exercise is to write a specific teaching plan for a minimum of one day that incorporates what you have done so far: preparing goals, writing objectives, selecting resources, and selecting and planning learning activities. You may want to reference the learning activities to state frameworks, district documents, and local school curriculum. Work cooperatively and collaboratively with a colleague by removing the perforated pages for this application exercise and hand it to your peer to read and react to your teaching plan. Does your plan convey what you intended to say? What new questions came to mind as you wrote the plan and then had it reviewed?

Teaching Plan

Standard/interdisciplinary unit theme:

Main focus question:

Related subquestions:

Objectives

(What will the students learn?)

(What thinking skills, such as observing, communicating, comparing, contrasting, categorizing, inferring, and applying will the students develop?)

(What attitudes will be fostered?)

Resources

(Information supporting ELLs, media, display visuals, artifacts, computer, and software)

Specifics of Learning Activities

Preassessment of Student Learning

(How will you determine what students know or think they know about the subject at the start of the unit?)

Example 1: Use a think–pair–share activity where the topic/question is written on the board and the students are asked in pairs to think about the topic, discuss it between themselves, and then the pairs share with the whole class what they know or think they already know about it while the teacher or a selected student writes the major thoughts on the board, perhaps in the form of a visual concept web.

Example 2: Use a KWL reading comprehension (or preassessment) activity where three columns are formed on the board, computer projection, or overhead projector and the students are asked to make their own three-column format on paper. They write down what they already *KNOW* or think they know about the topic/question in the first left-hand column; they write a list of what they *WANT* to learn about the topic/question in the middle column; they fill in the blank right-hand column at the end or during the study with what is being learned or what has been *LEARNED* about the topic/question.)

Formative Assessment

(Techniques used to assess student learning in progress to ensure they are on the right track.)
Check discipline areas drawn upon and give a brief description of one technique you will use to assess student learning in the area.

_____   1. Mathematics
           Description:

_____   2. Music and dance
           Description:

_____   3. Painting and sculpture
           Description:

_____   4. Poetry and prose
           Description:

_____   5. Physical education/health
           Description:

_____   6. Reading and language
           Description:

_____   7. Sciences
           Description:

_____ 8. Social sciences/history/geography

Description:

_____ 9. Other

Description:

Feedback:

1. In your opinion, does your plan effectively convey what you originally envisioned?

2. Does your plan need more detail or revision?

3. Do your selected learning activities appropriately address the varied learning styles of your students? Have you considered assistance from a web source such as www.usd.edu/trio/tut/ts/style.html?

4. What was the reaction of your peer to your teaching plan?

5. What new questions came to mind as you wrote the plan and as it was reviewed?

Culminating Activity

A culminating activity within a lesson brings a study/unit to a close. Such an activity often includes an exhibition or sharing of the product of the students' study. You could accept the students' suggestions for a culminating activity if it engages them in summarizing and sharing what they have learned with others. A culminating activity that brings closure to the study can give the children an opportunity for synthesis (by assembling, constructing, creating, inventing, producing, or incorporating something) and even an opportunity to present that synthesis to an audience, such as by sharing with parents and guardians at a classroom, school, or community event, or by sharing their project on the school's website.

With a culminating activity, you can facilitate the students to move from recording information to reporting on their learning. For example, one activity might be for the students to get involved in place-based learning, that is, to take field trips to study something related to a unit and then synthesize their learning after the trip in a way that culminates the study. During place-based learning, students can carry student-prepared notepads similar to the ones reporters use, take notes, and make sketches of what they see and learn. They can review what questions they have on the ride to the site. Students can discuss what they liked and did not like on the ride back to school. After the trip, each student can choose something that he or she saw and then build it (or draw it) to scale, so the students can have a scale model of something they saw on the trip that caught their interest. Teacher and students might devote one full afternoon, or more, to working with rulers, yardsticks, cardboard, clay, and other materials. If drawing something to scale, the teacher might cut up a picture (of something taken with the camera on the trip) into one-inch squares that have been numbered in sequence on the back, one square per student. Giving one square to each student, the teacher asks all to enlarge what they see in their squares in a ratio of 1 to 10 to make a larger picture of their trip. The numbers on the back of the squares help the students keep the sequence of the large mural drawing on the classroom wall. The students can present a narration to tell others what the drawing represents and its importance to their study. The students might also present an art show of drawings about the study with a narration that informs others about their study. You might also schedule a culminating activity that asks students to report on individual projects—the aspect of the study each student formerly reserved for individual study.

Examples of actual culminating activities and products for lessons and units are endless. Culminating activities are opportunities for students to proudly demonstrate and share their learning in different, creative, and individual ways.

PREPARING LESSON PLANS: RATIONALE AND ASSUMPTIONS

As described at the beginning of this chapter, one step of the several steps of instructional planning is the preparation of lessons for class meetings. The process of designing a lesson is important in learning to provide the most efficient use of valuable and limited instructional time and the most effective learning for the students to meet the anticipated learning outcomes.

Notice that the title of this section does not refer to *daily* lesson plans, but rather simply to lesson plans. The focus is on how to prepare a lesson plan, and that plan may, in fact, be a daily plan or it may not. In some instances, a lesson plan may extend for more than one period or block of time or day, perhaps two or three. In other instances, the lesson plan is in fact a daily plan and may run for an entire class period or block of time.

Accomplished elementary school teachers are always planning for their teaching. For the long-range plan, they plan the scope and sequence and develop content. Within this long-range planning, they develop units and lessons, and within lessons, they design the activities to be used and the assessments of learning to be done. They familiarize themselves with books, materials, media, and innovations in their special fields of interest such as literacy, mathematics, science, or social studies. Some teachers prefer to plan first with activities that fit into lessons that then support a plan for a unit of study. Yet, despite all this planning activity, the lesson plan remains pivotal to the planning process. Regardless of where you begin, consider now the rationale, description, and guidelines for writing detailed lesson plans.

Rationale for Preparing Written Lesson Plans

First, carefully prepared and written lesson plans show everyone—first and foremost your students, then your colleagues, your administrator, and, if you are a student teacher, your host teacher and your college or university supervisor—that you are a committed professional. Sometimes, beginning teachers are concerned with being seen by their students using a written plan in class, thinking it may suggest that the teacher has not mastered the material. On the contrary, a lesson plan is tangible evidence that you are working at your job, it demonstrates respect for the students, yourself, and for the profession. A written lesson plan shows that thinking/planning have taken place. There is absolutely no excuse for appearing before a classroom of children without evidence of being prepared.

Written and detailed lesson plans provide an important sense of security, which is especially useful to a beginning teacher. Like a rudder of a ship, a plan helps keep you on course. Without it, you are likely to drift aimlessly. Sometimes a disturbance in the classroom can distract from the lesson, causing the teacher to go off track or to forget an important part of the lesson. Another way to look at its value is that a written and detailed lesson plan provides a road map to guide you and help keep you on the road to your educational destination.

Written lesson plans help you to be or become a reflective decision maker. Without a written plan, it is difficult or impossible to analyze how something might have been planned or implemented differently after the lesson has been taught. Written lesson plans serve as resources for the next time you teach the same or a similar lesson and are useful for teacher self-assessment and for the assessment of student learning and the curriculum.

Written lesson plans help you organize material and search for loopholes, loose ends, or incomplete content. Careful and thorough planning during the preactive phase of instruction includes anticipation of how the lesson activities will develop as the lesson is being taught. During this anticipation you will actually visualize yourself in the classroom teaching the children, using that visualization to anticipate possible problems.

Written plans help other members of the teaching team understand what you are doing and how you are doing it.

Written lesson plans also provide substitute teachers with a guide to follow in your absence from teaching.

Those reasons clearly express the need to write detailed lesson plans. The list is not exhaustive, however, and you may discover additional reasons why written lesson plans are crucial to effective teaching. In summary, two points are: (a) lesson planning is an important and ongoing process; and (b) teachers must take time to plan, reflect, write, test, evaluate, and rewrite their plans to reach optimal performance. In short, preparing written lesson plans is important professional work.

Assumptions about Lesson Planning

Not all teachers need elaborate written plans for every lesson. Sometimes, accomplished veteran teachers need only a sketchy outline. Other times, they may not need written plans at all. Still other times, accomplished teachers who have taught the topic many times in the past may need only the presence of a classroom of students to stimulate a pattern of presentation that has often been successful (though frequent use of old patterns may lead one into the boring rut of unimaginative and uninspiring teaching). Your skill in being calm and following a train of thought in the presence of distraction will influence the amount of detail necessary when planning activities and writing the lesson plan.

Considering the diversity among elementary schoolteachers, their instructional styles, their students, and what research has shown, certain assumptions can be made about lesson planning, as is done in Figure 7.7.

In summary, well-written lesson plans provide many advantages. They give a teacher an agenda or outline to follow in teaching a lesson; they give a substitute teacher a basis for presenting appropriate lessons to a class,

thereby retaining lesson continuity in the regular teacher's absence; they are certainly very useful when a teacher is planning to use the same lesson again in the future; they provide the teacher with something to fall back on in case of a memory lapse, an interruption, or some distraction such as a call from the office or a fire drill; using a written plan demonstrates to students that you care and are working for them; and, above all, they provide beginners security because, with a carefully prepared plan, a beginning teacher can walk into a classroom with confidence and professional pride gained from having developed a sensible framework for that day's instruction.

Thus, as a beginning teacher, you should make considerably detailed lesson plans. Naturally, this will require a great deal of work for at least the first year or two, but the reward of knowing that you have prepared and presented effective lessons will compensate for that effort.

CONSTRUCTING A LESSON PLAN: FORMAT, COMPONENTS, AND SAMPLES

While it is true that each teacher develops a personal system of lesson planning—the system that works best for that teacher in that teacher's unique situation—a beginning teacher needs a more substantial framework from which to work. For that, this section provides a preferred lesson plan format, (see Figure 7.8). Nothing is hallowed about this format, however. Review the preferred format and samples, and unless your program of teacher preparation insists otherwise, use it until you find or develop a better model.

Basic Elements of a Lesson Plan

The well-written lesson plan should contain the following basic elements: (a) descriptive data, (b) goals and objectives, (c) rationale, (d) procedure, (e) assignments and assignment reminders, (f) materials and equipment, and (g) a section for assessment of student learning, reflection on the lesson, and ideas for lesson revision.

Note that not all seven elements (as seen in Figure 7.8) and their subsections need be present in every written lesson plan, nor must they be presented in any particular order. Nor are they inclusive or exclusive. You might choose to include additional components or subsections. Figure 7.9 displays a completed multiple-day lesson plan that incorporates many of the developmentally appropriate learning activities discussed in this resource guide. Following are descriptions of the seven elements of the preferred format, with examples and explanations of why each is important.

Descriptive Data

A lesson plan's descriptive data are demographic and logistical information that identify details about the group of children. Anyone reading this information should be able to identify when and where the group meets, who is teaching it, and what is being taught. Although as the

Figure 7.7
Assumptions about lesson planning.

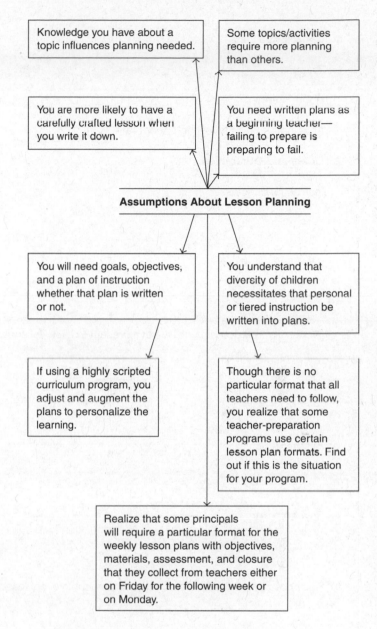

teacher you know this information, someone else may not. Members of the teaching team, administrators, mentors, and substitute teachers (and, if you are the student teacher, your university supervisor and host teacher) appreciate this information, especially when asked to fill in for you, even if only for a few minutes during a class session. Most teachers discover which items of descriptive data are most beneficial in their situation and then develop their own identifiers. Remember this: The mark of a well-prepared, clearly written lesson plan is the ease with which someone else (such as another member of your teaching team or a substitute teacher) could implement it.

As shown in the sample plan of Figure 7.9, the descriptive data include the following:

1. **Name of course or class.** These serve as headings for the plan and facilitate orderly filing of plans.

Language Arts/Science (integrated block course)

2. **Name of the unit** for which the lessons are prepared. Inclusion of this facilitates the orderly control of the hundreds of lesson plans a teacher constructs. For example:

Unit: Investigative Research and Generative Writing

3. **Topic to be considered within the unit.** This is also useful for control and identification. For example:

Writing Response and Peer Assessment via the Internet

Anticipated Noise Level

Although not included in the sample lesson plan, you might include in the descriptive data the category of "anticipated classroom noise level" such as "high," "moderate," or "silent or low." Its inclusion, or at least considering the idea, is useful during the planning phase of instruction in that it prompts you to think about how active and noisy

1. **Descriptive Data**

   Teacher _____ Class _____ Date _____ Grade level _____

   Room number _____ Period _____ Unit _____ Lesson number _____ Topic _____

   Anticipated noise level (high, moderate, low)

2. **Goals and Objectives**

   Instructional goals:

   Specific objectives:

   [*Note:* All three domains not always present in every lesson]

   Cognitive:

   Affective:

   Psychomotor:

3. **Rationale** [*Note:* Rationale not always present in every lesson]

4. **Procedure** [Procedure with modeling examples, planned transitions, and so on; should usually take up most of the space of lesson plan, often a full page]

   _____ minutes. Activity 1: Set (introduction)

   _____ minutes. Activity 2:

Figure 7.8
Preferred lesson plan format with seven components.

_____ minutes. Activity 3: (the exact number of activities in the procedures will vary)

_____ minutes. Final Activity (Lesson Conclusion or Closure):

If time remains:

5. Assignments and Reminders of Assignments

Special notes and reminders to myself:

6. Materials and Equipment Needed

Audiovisual:

Other:

7. Assessment, Reflection, and Revision

Assessment of student learning, how it will be done:

Reflective thoughts about lesson after taught:

Suggestions for revision if used again:

Figure 7.8 (*Continued*)

1. **Descriptive Data**

   Teacher _____ Class/disciplines English/Language Arts/Science _____

   Date _____ Grade level __5–6__

   Unit __Investigative Research and Generative Writing__ _____

   Lesson Topic __Writing Response and Peer Assessment via the Internet_____ Time Duration: __several days__

2. **Goals and Objectives of Unit**

   Instructional Goals:

   2.1 One goal for this lesson is for students to collaborate with and prepare response papers to peers from around the world who have shared the results of their own experimental research findings and research papers about ozone concentrations in the atmosphere.

   2.2 The ultimate goal of this unit is for students around the world to prepare and publish for worldwide dissemination a final paper about global ozone levels in the atmosphere.

   Objectives:

   Not all three domains (cognitive, affective, and psychomotor) are necessarily represented in every lesson, but here are examples, if needed.

   Cognitive

   a. Through cooperative group action, students will conduct experimental research to collect data from at least three different sources about the ozone level of air in their environment. (application)

   b. In cooperative groups, students will analyze the results of their experiments. (analyze)

   c. Students will compile data from at least three sources as well as their experimental data and make at least two inferences from their sources and experimental data. (synthesis and evaluation)

   d. Through collaborative writing groups, the students will prepare at least one final paper that summarizes their research study of local atmospheric ozone levels. (evaluation)

   e. Through sharing via the Internet, students will write and share at least three response papers to their peers from other locations in the world. (evaluation)

   f. From their own collaborative research and worldwide communications with their peers, the students will draw their conclusions about global atmospheric ozone levels and write at least one conclusion paper. (evaluation)

   Affective

   a. Students will respond attentively to the response papers of their peers by reading at least one paper and making a comment about the content. (attending)

   b. Students will willingly cooperate with others during 9 out of 10 of the group activities. (responding)

   c. The students will offer at least one opinion each in writing about the atmospheric levels of ozone. (valuing)

   d. The students will form at least one judgment each about the different ozone levels related to local, regional, and world ozone levels. (organizing)

   e. The students will communicate accurately their findings in an oral presentation to the group and electronically respond at least once to the work of their worldwide peers. (internalizing)

   Psychomotor

   a. The students will manipulate the computer so that their e-mail communications are transmitted accurately. (manipulating)

   b. In a final summary to the study, students, reading their summaries orally, will describe their thoughts about atmospheric ozone concentrations. (communicating)

   c. The students will ultimately create at least one proposal for worldwide dissemination. (creating)

3. **Rationale**

   3.1 Important to improvement in one's writing and communication skills are the processes of selecting a topic, making decisions, arranging, drafting, proofing, reviewing with peers, commenting, revising, editing, rewriting, and publishing the results—processes that are focused on in the writing aspect of this unit.

   3.2 Student writers need many readers to respond to their work. Through worldwide communication with peers and dissemination of their final product, this need can be satisfied.

   3.3 Students learn best when they are actively pursuing a topic of interest and meaning to them. Resulting from brainstorming potential problems and arriving at their own topic, this unit provides that interest.

   3.4 Real-world problems are interdisciplinary and transcultural; involving writing, data collecting, graphing (through English, science, mathematics) and intercultural communication, this unit is an interdisciplinary transcultural unit.

Figure 7.9
Lesson plan sample: multiple-day, project-centered, interdisciplinary, and transcultural lesson using worldwide communication via the Internet.

4. **Procedure**

   Content:

   At the start of this unit, collaborative groups were established via ePals Global Community at http://www.epals.com/ with other classes from schools around the world. These groups of students conducted several scientific research experiments on the ozone levels of their local atmospheric air. To obtain relative measurements of ozone concentrations in the air, students set up experiments that involved stretching rubber bands on a board (no one was allergic to latex to his/her knowledge), then observing the number of days until the bands broke. Students maintained daily journal logs of the temperature, barometric pressure, and the wind speed/direction, and of the number of days that it took for bands to break. After compiling their data and preparing single-page summaries of their results, then the students exchanged data with other groups on the Internet. From data collected worldwide, students wrote a one-page summary as to what conditions may account for the difference in levels of ozone. Following the exchange of students' written responses and their subsequent revisions based on feedback from the worldwide peers, students are now preparing a final summary report about the world's atmospheric ozone level. The intention is to disseminate worldwide (to newspaper and contacts via the Internet) this final report.

   Activity 1: Introduction (10 minutes)
   (The teacher refers to this activity as think–share–new pairs [instead of the more common term of think–pair–share] because the teacher wants the students to first think about the topic independently and write notes, then share thoughts and discuss it with a student nearby, and last, pair up with still another student to get further input or a different point of view before revising the thoughts and presenting them to the group). The teacher says: Today, in this think–share–new pairs activity, you will think about the topic, discuss it between yourselves, and then write your notes about what you know or think you know about the world's ozone level (preassessment, use of prior knowledge). Next, you'll share your notes with the group. We'll write the major thoughts on the board. To begin, consider what you know about the world's ozone level and talk about it with your partner. (Students send e-mail to groups worldwide.)

   Activity 2: Continuation (30 minutes)
   Today, again in think–share pairs, you will prepare initial responses to the e-mail responses we have received from other groups around the world. (Teacher shares the list of places from which e-mail has been received.) Any questions before we get started? As we discussed earlier, here are the instructions: In your think–share pairs (each pair is given one response received via e-mail), prepare written responses according to the following outline: (a) Note points or information you would like to incorporate in the final paper to be forwarded via the Internet; (b) comment on one aspect of the written response you like best; and (c) provide questions to the sender to seek clarification or elaboration. I think you should be able to finish this in about 30 minutes, so let's try for that.

   Activity 3: (open time)
   Preparation of dyad responses.

   Activity 4: (open time)
   "Let's now hear from each response pair." Dyad responses are shared with the whole group for discussion of inclusion in the response paper to be sent via the Internet.

   Activity 5: (open time)
   Discussion, conclusion, and preparation of final drafts to be sent to each e-mail corresponder to be done by co-operative groups. (The number of groups needed is decided by the number of e-mail corresponders at this time.) Later, as students receive e-mail responses from the groups, the responses will be printed and reviewed. The class then responds to each using the same criteria as before and returns this response to the e-mail sender.

   Closure:
   The process continues until all groups (from around the world) have agreed on and prepared the final report to disseminate.

5. **Assignments and Reminders**

   Remind students of important dates and decisions to be made.

6. **Materials and Equipment Needed**

   School computers with Internet access; printers; copies of e-mail responses.

7. **Assessment, Reflection, and Revision**

   Assessment of student learning for this lesson is preassessment and then formative: journals, daily checklist of student participation in groups, and writing drafts.

   Reflective thoughts about the lesson and suggestions for revision.

Figure 7.9 (*Continued*)

the children might become during the lesson, what reminders to give the class before the lesson, how you might prepare for an anticipated noise level, through a class meeting perhaps, and whether you should advise an administrator or the teachers in the neighboring classrooms of the anticipated noise level.

Goals and Objectives

The instructional goals are general statements of intended accomplishments from that lesson. Teachers and students need to know what the lesson is designed to accomplish. In clear, understandable language, the general goal statement provides that information. From the sample, the goals are as follows:

- To collaborate and prepare response papers to peers from around the world who have shared the results of their own experimental research findings and research papers about ozone concentrations in the atmosphere.
- For students worldwide to prepare and publish for worldwide dissemination a final paper about worldwide ozone levels in the atmosphere.

Because the goals are also included in the unit plan, sometimes a teacher may include only the objectives in the daily lesson plan, but not the goals. As a beginning teacher, it usually is a good idea to include both.

A crucial step in the development of any lesson plan is that of setting the objectives. It is at this point that many lessons go wrong and where many beginning teachers have problems.

Learning Activity versus Learning Objective

Sometimes, teachers confuse **learning activity** (how the students will learn it) with the **learning objective** (what the students will learn as a result of the learning activity). For example, teachers sometimes mistakenly list what they intend to do—such as "lead a discussion about the Earth's continents"—and fail to focus on just what the learning objectives in these activities truly are—that is, what the students will be able to do (performance) as a result of the instructional activity. Or, rather than specifying what the student will be able to do as a result of the learning activities, the teacher mistakenly writes what the students will do in the class (the learning activity)—such as, "in pairs the students will answer the 10 questions on page 72"—as if that were the learning objective.

When you approach this step in your lesson planning, to avoid error, ask yourself, "What should students learn *as a result* of the activities of this lesson?" Your answer to that question is your objective! Objectives of the lesson are included then as specific statements of performance expectations, detailing precisely what students will be able to do as a result of the instructional activities.

No Need to Include All Domain and Hierarchies in Every Lesson

Not all three domains (cognitive, affective, and psychomotor) are necessarily represented in every lesson. As a matter of fact, any given lesson plan may be directed to only one or two, or a few, specific objectives. Over the course of a unit of instruction, however, all domains, and most, if not all, levels within each should be addressed.

From the sample lesson shown in Figure 7.9, here are some sample objectives with the domain and the level within that domain shown in parentheses:

- Through cooperative group action, students will conduct experimental research to collect data from at least three different sources about the ozone level of air in their environment. (cognitive, application)
- Through sharing via the Internet, students will write and share at least three response papers to their peers from other locations in the world. (cognitive, evaluation)
- The students will form at least one judgment each about the different ozone levels related to local, regional, and world ozone levels. (affective, organizing)
- The students will ultimately create at least one proposal for worldwide dissemination. (psychomotor, creating)

Rationale

The rationale is an explanation of why the lesson is important and why the instructional methods chosen will achieve the objectives. Parents and guardians, students, teachers, administrators, and others have the right to know why specific content is being taught and why the methods employed are being used. Prepare yourself well by always being prepared with intelligent answers to those two questions.

Teachers become reflective decision makers when they challenge themselves to think about *what* (the content) they are teaching, *how* (the learning activities) they are teaching it, and *why* (the rationale) it must be taught. Sometimes, the rationale is included within the unit introduction and goals, but not in every lesson plan of the unit. Some lessons are carryovers or continuations of a lesson; we see no reason to repeat the rationale for a continuing lesson.

Procedure

The procedure consists of the instructional activities for a scheduled period of time. The substance of the lesson—the information to be presented, obtained, and learned—is the content. Appropriate information is selected to meet the learning objectives, the level of competence of the students, and the grade level of course requirements. To be sure your lesson actually covers what it should, you should write down exactly what minimum content you intend to cover. This material may be placed in a separate section or combined with the procedure section. It is most important to be sure that your information is written down so you can refer to it quickly and easily when you need to.

If, for instance, you intend to conduct the lesson using discussion, you should write out the key discussion questions. Or, if you are going to introduce new material using a 10-minute lecture, then you need to outline the content of that lecture. The word *outline* is not used casually—you don't need pages of notes to sift through; nor should you ever read declarative statements to your students. You should be familiar enough with the content so that an outline (in as much detail as you believe necessary) will be sufficient to carry on the lesson.

The procedures to be used, sometimes referred to as the **instructional components,** comprise the **procedure** component of the lesson plan. It is the section that outlines what you and your students will do during the lesson. Appropriate instructional activities are chosen to meet the objectives, to match the students' learning styles and individual needs, and to ensure that all students have an equal opportunity to learn. Ordinarily, you should plan this section of your lesson as an organized entity having a beginning (an introduction or set), a middle, and an end (called the **closure**) to be completed during the lesson. This structure is not always needed, because some lessons are simply parts of units or long-term plans and merely carry on activities spelled out in those long-term plans. Still, most lessons need to include the following in the procedure: (a) an *introduction*, the process used to prepare the students mentally for the lesson, sometimes referred to as the *set*, or *initiating activity*; (b) *lesson development*, the detailing of *activities* that occur between the beginning and the end of the lesson, including the transitions that connect activities (see the discussion regarding transitions in Chapter 4); (c) plans for *practice* or sometimes referred to as the follow-up—that is, ways that you intend to have students interact in the classroom, such as individual practice, in dyads, or small groups, or receive guidance or coaching from each other and from you; (d) the *lesson conclusion* (or closure), the planned process of bringing the lesson to an end, thereby providing students with a sense of completeness and, with effective teaching, accomplishment and comprehension by helping students to synthesize the information learned from the lesson; (e) a *timetable* that serves simply as a planning and implementation guide; (f) *a plan* for what to do if you finish the lesson and time remains; and (g) *assignments*, that is, what students are instructed to do as follow-up to the lesson, either as homework (responsibility papers) or as in-class work, providing students an opportunity to practice and enhance what is being learned. Let's now consider some of those components in detail.

Introduction to the Lesson

Like any good performance, a lesson needs an effective beginning. In many respects, the introduction sets the tone for the rest of the lesson by alerting the students that the business of learning is to begin. The introduction should be an attention-getter. If it is exciting, interesting, or innovative, it can create a favorable mood for the lesson. One teacher we know follows a planned way of introducing the lesson that varies with the subject/discipline being taught. For example, to introduce a science lesson, the teacher sets up specific items for an experiment in the front of a class. As the students walk into the room, they see the items for the lesson and the teacher asks them to write a question/hypothesis that could be reflected in an experiment they can think of by using those items. Then they read their questions and hypotheses about their experiment ideas in think–share–new pairs groups. After that, the teacher presents the experiment that involves the items for the lesson. For a language lesson, a teacher can begin a lesson with a sentence on the board with a blank or with a scrambled sentence from the previous lesson that leads into this new lesson.

In any case, a thoughtful introduction serves as a solid indicator that you are well prepared. While it is difficult to develop an exciting introduction to every lesson, there are always many options available by which to spice up the launching of a lesson. You might, for instance, begin the lessons by briefly reviewing the previous lesson, thereby helping students connect the learning. Another possibility is to review vocabulary words from previous lessons and to introduce new ones. Still another possibility is to use the key point of the day's lesson as an introduction and then again as the conclusion. Sometimes, teachers begin a lesson by presenting a strange but true scenario or by demonstrating a discrepant event (i.e., an event that is contrary to what one might expect—see Figure 8.7 in Chapter 8) or, as it is sometimes referred to, "a teaser, an interest-maker, a hook."[3] Yet, another possibility is to begin the lesson with a writing activity on some controversial aspect of the ensuing lesson,

- A sample introduction for history and the study of westward expansion that could lead to writing: The teacher asks, "Who has lived somewhere else other than (*name of your state*)? After students raise hands and answer, the teacher asks individuals why they moved to (*name of your state*). After discussion, the teacher then asks students to recall why the first European settlers came to the United States; then the teacher moves on to ask students to write their thoughts about reasons why settlers came to the United States.
- Another sample introduction for science and the study of the science process skill of predicting: The teacher takes a glass filled to the brim with colored water (colored so it is more visible) and asks students to discuss and predict (in dyads) how many pennies can be added to the glass before any water spills over the rim of the glass. The teacher records their predictions on the writing board, then moves on to ask the students to record their thoughts in their learning journals about what they learned.

In short, you can use the introduction of the lesson in different ways: to review past learning with the KWL approach; to bridge the new lesson to the previous lesson; to introduce new material; to point out the objectives of the new lesson; to help students connect their learning with other disciplines or with real life; to induce in students some motivation and a mind-set favorable to the new lesson; and to show what will be learned and why the learning is important—perhaps through a brief discussion of a few community workers (seen in children's literature in the class/school library) who use the reading (the math, the science, the writing) that is being learned in the lesson and deem it important. For example, consider *Our Corner Grocery Store* (Montreal: Tundra, 2009, grades K–3) by J. F. Schwartz. Through this story of an Italian neighborhood market, students, especially ELLs and English-speaking students with learning problems, can discuss the importance of reading grocery signs, writing signs to display among produce, writing an order for a bakery delivery, understanding science/technology that keeps some items frozen, and understanding math to use money, make change, and sell products. Another example is *A Walk in New York* (Somerville, MA: Candlewick Press, 2009, grades 2–5) by S. Rubbino, where a boy and his father go on a one-day outing to see some of the sights—Grand Central Terminal (often erroneously called a station), the New York Public Library, Empire State Building, and of course, the myriad of taxicabs on the streets. For the students, the city's workers at these sites can exemplify all who use reading (math, science, and writing) that are the skills being learned in a particular lesson and become the focus of a brief lesson introduction.

Lesson Development

The developmental activities comprise the bulk of the plan and are the specifics by which you intend to achieve your lesson objectives. They include activities that present information, demonstrate skills, provide reinforcement of previously learned material, and furnish other opportunities to develop understanding and skill. Furthermore, by actions and words, during lesson development the teacher models the behaviors expected of the children. Children need such modeling. By effective modeling, the teacher can exemplify the anticipated learning outcomes. Activities of this section of the lesson plan should be described in some detail (a) so you will know exactly what it is you plan to do and (b) so during the interactions of the class meeting, you do not forget important details and content. It is for this reason you should consider, for example, noting answers (if known) to questions you intend to ask and solutions (if known) to problems you intend to have the students solve.

Lesson Conclusion

Having a concise closure to the lesson is as important as having a strong introduction. The concluding activity should summarize and secure what has ensued in the developmental stage and should reinforce the principal points of the lesson. As an example, in summarizing a discovery learning activity, the conclusion can reveal the major point of the lesson for the first time. Also, one way to accomplish these ends is to restate the key points of the lesson. Another is to briefly outline the major points. Still another is to review the major concept. Sometimes the closure is not only a review of what was learned but also the summarizing of a question left unanswered, signaling a change in your plan of activities for the next day. In other words, it becomes a transitional closure.

Assessment, Reflection, and Revision

Details of how you will assess students' *prior knowledge* (preassessment), of how well students *are* learning (formative assessment), and how well they *have* learned (summative assessment) should be included in your lesson plan. This does not mean to imply that these types of assessment will be in *every* daily plan, although formative assessment can occur on a daily basis.

Formative assessment of student learning that is taking place should be frequent, perhaps including teacher observations and questions as often as on the average of once every few minutes during direct instruction and during individual or small-group coaching. Checks for comprehension can be in the form of the questions that you ask and that the children ask during the lesson (in the procedural section), as well as in the form of various kinds of checklists. Teachers of ELLs often observe, circulate, and monitor during a lesson; they can measure students' work against a checklist or rubric, give feedback, and reteach individually or in small groups.

For summative assessment, teachers typically use review questions at the end of a lesson (as a closure) or at the beginning of the next lesson (as a review or a transfer introduction). They also use student independent practice, summary activities, quizzes, and tests such as fill-in-the-blanks, short-answer, and multiple-choice tests at the completion of a lesson or unit of study. For a final grade at the end of a lesson, or on a final test, or for homework or classwork, teachers of ELLs often use scoring guides with points assigned to items and grades linked to total points.

In most lesson plan formats, there is a section reserved for the teacher to write reflective comments about the lesson. Some teachers begin their reflective comments with positive comments: they list individual student achievements, the time when they felt the most positive during the lesson, how smooth a transition went between activities, and they write about how well-prepared and organized they thought they were even if part of the lesson was a failure experience. Many student teachers seem to prefer to write their reflections at the end or on the reverse page of their lesson plans (these comments are easily transferred to your lesson plans on your computer if you are using www.taskstream.com or a similar lesson plan software program; ask your colleagues for their suggestions about additional web-based instructional design/lesson plan material). One teacher we know has designed a lesson plan template that includes the following: "What went well: _____," followed by "How students responded: _____," and "How the lesson could have been better. _____." To feel optimistic and enthusiastic, the teacher reflects on what is *positive* about the lesson *first*.

As well as being useful for yourself, reflections about the lesson are useful for those who are supervising or mentoring you (see more in the professional development chapter, Chapter 11).

Writing and later reading your reflections can provide not only ideas that may be helpful if you plan to use the lesson again at some later date, but offer catharsis, easing any tension caused from teaching. To continue working effectively at a challenging task (that is, to prevent intellectual downshifting, which is reverting to earlier-learned, lower-cognitive-level behaviors) requires significant amounts of reflection.

PREPARING INSTRUCTIONAL UNITS

The instructional unit is a major subdivision of a course of study (for one course or a self-contained classroom, there are several to many units of instruction) and is comprised of learning activities that are planned around a central theme, topic, issue, or problem. Organizing the content of the semester or year into units makes the teaching process more manageable than when no plans or only random choices are made by a teacher.

The instructional unit is not unlike a chapter in a book, an act or scene in a play, or a phase of work when undertaking a project such as building a house. Breaking down information or actions into component parts and then grouping the related parts makes sense out of learning and doing. The unit brings a sense of cohesiveness and structure to student learning and avoids the piecemeal approach that might otherwise unfold. You can learn to articulate lessons within, between, and among unit plans and focus on important elements while not ignoring tangential information of importance. Students remember "chunks" of information, especially when those chunks are related to specific units.

While the steps for developing any type of instructional unit are basically the same, units can be organized in a number of ways. For the purpose of this resource guide, we consider two basic types of units—the standard unit and the integrated thematic unit.

A **standard unit** (known also as a conventional, regular, or traditional unit) consists of a series of activities built into lessons centered on a topic, major concept, or block of subject matter. Each lesson builds on the previous lesson by contributing additional subject matter, providing further illustrations, and supplying more practice or other added instruction—all of which are aimed at bringing about mastery of the knowledge and skills on which the unit is centered.

When a standard unit is centered on a central theme (as was discussed in Chapter 5), the unit may be referred to as a **thematic unit.** When, by design, the thematic unit integrates disciplines, such as combining the learning of science and mathematics, or combining social studies and English/language arts, or combining all four core (or any other) disciplines, then it is called an **integrated** or **interdisciplinary thematic unit** (ITU) or, simply, an integrated unit.

Planning and Developing Any Unit of Instruction

Whether for a standard unit or an integrated thematic unit, the steps in planning and developing the unit are the same and are described in the following paragraphs:

1. **Select a suitable theme, topic, issue, or problem.** These may be already identified in your course of study or textbook or have been agreed on by members of your teaching team. Many schools change their themes or add new ones from year to year. As an example, your school recently may have included the theme of understanding the water cycle.

2. **Select the goals of the unit and prepare the overview.** The goals are written as an overview or rationale, covering what the unit is about and what the students are to learn. In selecting the goals, you should (a) become as familiar as possible with the topic and materials used; (b) consult curriculum documents, such as courses of study, state and local frameworks and standards, and resource units for ideas; (c) decide the content and procedures (i.e., what the students should learn about the topic and how; (d) write the rationale or overview, where you summarize what you expect the students will learn about the topic; and (e) be sure your goals are congruent with those of the course or grade level program. For instance, referring back to your school choosing the theme of understanding the water cycle, a teaching team may have suggested what ELLs should learn about the topic and how they can present their knowledge, that is, through drawing, labeling diagrams, preparing an oral report, and giving a summary about some of the latest research on the topic. You'll consider those suggestions along with your goals.

3. **Select suitable instructional objectives.** In doing this, you should (a) include understandings, skills, attitudes, and appreciations; (b) be specific, avoiding vagueness and generalizations; (c) write the objectives in performance terms; and (d) be as certain as possible that the objectives will

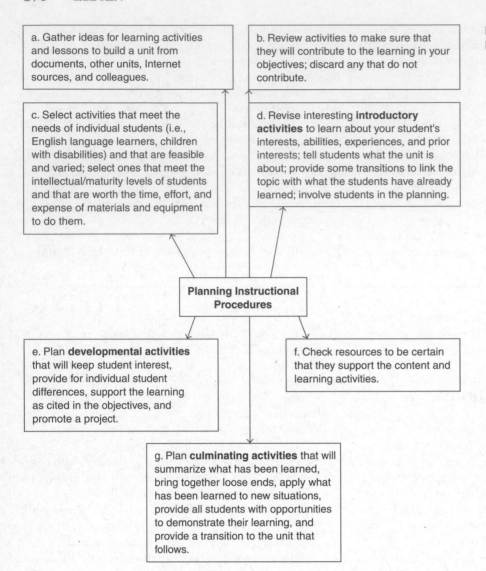

a. Gather ideas for learning activities and lessons to build a unit from documents, other units, Internet sources, and colleagues.

b. Review activities to make sure that they will contribute to the learning in your objectives; discard any that do not contribute.

c. Select activities that meet the needs of individual students (i.e., English language learners, children with disabilities) and that are feasible and varied; select ones that meet the intellectual/maturity levels of students and that are worth the time, effort, and expense of materials and equipment to do them.

d. Revise interesting **introductory activities** to learn about your student's interests, abilities, experiences, and prior interests; tell students what the unit is about; provide some transitions to link the topic with what the students have already learned; involve students in the planning.

Planning Instructional Procedures

e. Plan **developmental activities** that will keep student interest, provide for individual student differences, support the learning as cited in the objectives, and promote a project.

f. Check resources to be certain that they support the content and learning activities.

g. Plan **culminating activities** that will summarize what has been learned, bring together loose ends, apply what has been learned to new situations, provide all students with opportunities to demonstrate their learning, and provide a transition to the unit that follows.

Figure 7.10
Planning instructional procedures.

contribute to the major learning and target goals as presented in the overview.

4. **Detail the instructional procedures.** These procedures include the subject content and the learning activities, established as a series of lessons. Proceed with the steps shown in Figure 7.10 in your initial planning of the instructional procedures.

5. **Plan for preassessment and assessment of student learning.** Preassess what students already know or think they know. Assessment of student progress in achievement of the learning objectives (formative evaluation) should permeate the entire unit (that is, as often as possible, assessment should be a daily component of lessons). Plan to gather information in several ways, including informal observations, checklist observations of student performance and their portfolios, and paper-and-pencil tests. As discussed in Chapters 5

and 6, assessment, to be meaningful, must be congruent with the instructional objectives.

6. **Provide for the materials and tools of instruction.** The unit cannot function without materials. Therefore, you must plan long before the unit begins for media equipment and materials, references, reading materials, reproduced materials, and community resources. Librarians and media center personnel are usually quite willing to assist in finding appropriate materials to support a unit of instruction.

Unit Format, Inclusive Elements, and Time Duration

Follow the previous six steps to develop any type of unit. In addition, two general points should be made. First, while there is no single best format for a teaching unit, there are minimum inclusions. Particular formats may be best for

Figure 7.11
Elements in a unit plan.

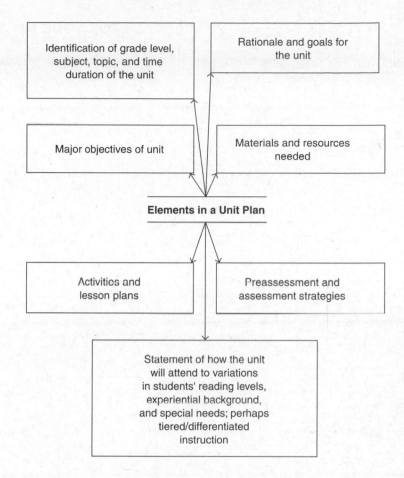

the interdisciplinary thematic unit (ITU), which may consist of smaller subject-specific conventional units developed according to the immediately foregoing guidelines. Because developing interdisciplinary thematic units is an essential task for many of today's teachers, you should learn this process now.

The primary responsibility for the development of interdisciplinary thematic units can depend on a single teacher or upon the cooperation of several teachers. A teaching team may develop from one to several interdisciplinary thematic units a year. Over time, then, a team will have several units that are available for implementation. However, the most effective units are often those that are the most current or the most meaningful to students. This means that ever-changing global, national, and local topics provide a virtual smorgasbord from which to choose, and teachers and teaching teams must constantly update old units and develop new and exciting ones. Open lines of communication within, between, and among teams and schools within a school district are critical to the success of interdisciplinary thematic teaching.[4]

Now to get started, refer to Application Exercise 7.1, then begin Application Exercise 7.2, and finally, do Application Exercise 7.3.

specific disciplines or grade levels, topics, and types of activities. During your student teaching, your college or university program for teacher preparation and/or your host teacher may have a format that you will be expected to follow. Regardless of the format, Figure 7.11 shows the elements that should be evident in any unit plan.

Second, there is no set time duration for a unit plan, although for specific units, curriculum guides will recommend certain time spans. Units may extend for a minimum of several days, or, as in the case of some interdisciplinary thematic units, for several weeks to an entire school year. However, be aware that when standard units last more than two or three weeks, they tend to lose the character of clearly identifiable units. For the unit of instruction, the exact time duration will be dictated by several factors, including the topic, problem, or theme; the age, interests, and maturity of the students; and the scope of the learning activities.

PLANNING AND DEVELOPING AN INTERDISCIPLINARY THEMATIC UNIT

The six steps mentioned earlier in this chapter are essential for planning any type of teaching unit, including

FOR YOUR NOTES

APPLICATION EXERCISE 7.2

Preparing a Lesson Plan

Instructions: Use the model lesson format in this resource guide or an alternative format that is approved by your instructor to prepare a _____ -minute lesson (length to be decide in your class) for a grade and subject of your choice. After completing your lesson plan, remove your work on the perforated pages so you can work cooperatively and collaboratively with a peer. Hand your pages to a peer to get feedback about your plan before turning it in for your instructor's evaluation. You may use this lesson as one of your lessons for Application Exercise 7.3.

Your notes from your peer's evaluation:

APPLICATION EXERCISE 7.3

Preparing an Instructional Unit: Bringing It All Together

Instructions: The purpose of this exercise is threefold: (a) to give you an experience in preparing an instructional unit and realize that activities sequence lessons and lessons sequence a unit, (b) to assist you in preparing an instructional unit that you can use in your teaching, and (c) to start your collection of instructional units that you may be able to use later in your teaching. This is an assignment that will take several hours to complete, and you may need to remove the perforated pages for this application exercise and read ahead in this resource guide (Chapters 8–10). Our advice, therefore, is that the assignment be started early, with a due date much later in the course. Your course instructor may have specific guidelines for your completion of this Application Exercise. What follows reviews the essence of what you are to do.

First, divide your class into two teams, each with a different assignment pertaining to this exercise. The units completed by these teams are to be shared with all members of the class for cooperative and collaborative feedback and for possible use later.

Team 1

Members of this team, individually or in dyads, will develop standard teaching units, perhaps with different grade levels in mind. (You will need to review the content of Chapters 8–10). Using a format that is practical, *each member* or *pair* of this team will develop a minimum 2-week (10-day) unit for a particular grade level, subject, and topic. Regardless of the format chosen, each unit plan should include the following elements:

1. Identification of (a) grade level, (b) subject, (c) topic, and (d) time duration.

2. Statement of rationale and general goals.

3. Separate listing of instructional objectives for each daily lesson. Wherever possible, the unit should include objectives from all three domains—cognitive, affective, and psychomotor.

4. List of the materials and resources needed and where they can be obtained (if you have that information). These should be listed for each daily lesson.

5. Ten consecutive daily lesson plans (see Application Exercise 7.2).

6. List all items, including preassessment/determining students' prior knowledge, that will be used to assess student learning *during* and *at completion* of the unit of study.

7. Statement of how the unit will attend to variations in students' reading levels, socioethnic backgrounds, and special needs.

Team 2

With collaboration and also following the criteria in the list above, members of this team will develop interdisciplinary thematic units. Depending upon the number of students in your class, Team 2 may actually comprise several teams with each team developing an ITU. Each team should be comprised of no less than two members (e.g., a math specialist and a science specialist) and no more than four (e.g., social studies, language arts/reading, mathematics, and science).

LOOKING AT TEACHERS II

Integrated Technology, Moodling

Casey was teaching a sixth-grade humanities block, a two-hour block course that integrates student learning in social studies, reading, and language arts. On this particular day, while Casey and her students were discussing the topic of Manifest Destiny, one of the students raised his hand and when acknowledged by Casey, asked the question, "Why aren't we (referring to the United States) still adding states?" (which meant adding territory to the United States). Casey immediately replied with "There aren't any more states to add." By responding too quickly, Casey missed one of those "teachable moments," a time when the teacher has the students' attention right where she or he wants them, that is, where the students are thinking and asking questions. What could Casey have done? When was Hawaii added as a state? Why hasn't the District of Columbia become a state? Guam? Puerto Rico? Aren't those possibilities? Why *aren't* more states or territories being added? What are the political and social ramifications today of adding states and how do they differ from those of the 1800s? Is there a language ramification?

- To integrate technology about countries and trends in a situation such as this, Casey and the students could begin by researching curriculum units and projects and databases about the United Nations' member countries and global trends at *United Nations CyberSchool Bus* at www.un.org/CyberSchoolBus/.

- Another possibility is to employ Moodling (http://moodle.org). This is a free, password-protected, teacher-supervised online system that allows universities, colleges, and now K–12 schools, to create environments to share files, notes, wikis, podcasts, and more. By integrating Moodling, students can practice social networking (ELLs are encouraged to use language they are learning in school) while internalizing content. To begin with students, discuss examples of classes involved in Moodling. For example, students in two elementary schools (Florida) and their teachers meet other educators and students in cities (such as Bangkok) and interact with them online. They type, enter time lines, communicate, correspond, teleconference, and chat with one another about their lives, cultures, and societies. Further, students focus on their daily school schedules and ask each other questions about life in a different part of our planet Earth. See www.tampabay.com/news/education/k12/article964604.ece.

SUMMARY

So far, in this resource guide, you have learned of the importance of learning modalities and instructional modes. You have reviewed information about children, their needs, and the importance of providing an accepting and supportive learning environment, as well as about teacher behaviors that are necessary to facilitate the most meaningful student learning and the value of assessment.

With this chapter in particular, you continued building your knowledge base about why planning is important and developed your understanding of theoretical considerations for the selection of instructional strategies such as explicit and implicit instruction; for the selection of learning activities (initiating, ongoing, culminating) that are developmentally appropriate; and for the preparation of lesson plans with rationale, procedures, introduction, lesson development, and conclusion. You have considered the importance of assessment, reflection, and revision in planning. Further, you have planned and started to develop your first lesson plan and first unit of instruction and have put objectives, resources, and learning activities together for a teaching plan.

In this chapter, you continued building your knowledge about why planning is important and how planning activities in lessons and lessons in units are useful pedagogical tools. You found that developing activities, lessons, and units of instruction that integrate student learning and provide a sense of meaning for the students requires coordination throughout the curriculum. Hence, for your students, you realized that learning is a process of discovering how information, knowledge, and ideas are interrelated so they can make sense out of self, school, and life. Indeed, when you turn chunks of information into activities, and activities into lessons, and lessons into units, you help your students process and understand knowledge. Doing this, you are well on your way to becoming a competent planner of instruction.

What's to Come. To prepare for Part III, you have been guided in Part II (Chapters 5 through 7) through the processes necessary to prepare yourself to teach in a classroom. In Part III (Chapters 8–11), your attention will be directed to still more strategies, more effective teaching, and your further professional development. You will find out about the selection and implementation of additional specific strategies, aids, and resources from which you may select to facilitate student learning of particular skills and content, beginning with teacher talk and the use of questioning. Later, after you have studied Part III, you may choose to revisit this chapter and make revisions to your ideas for activities, lessons, and your completed unit.

EXTENDING MY PROFESSIONAL COMPETENCY

With Discussion

Lesson Plans. What would I say if a colleague asked me about the reasons why a student teacher and a first-year teacher need to prepare detailed lesson plans? **To do:** Discuss this question in the whole group and describe, when, if ever, the teacher can or should divert from the written lesson plan.

With Video

Video Activity: Explicit and Implicit Curriculum. How would I explain implicit/indirect instruction to another educator or parent?

PEARSON
myeducationlab

> Go to the Video Examples section of Topic #9: Group Interaction Models in the MyEducationLab for your course to view the video entitled "Indirect Instruction."

In this video, identify one activity in this graphing lesson that you would use in your own teaching. Give your example and talk about your understanding of explicit and implicit teaching with a classmate. Would you be able to explain implicit/indirect instruction in a job interview or in a parent conference?

With Portfolio

Planning a Portfolio. How can I continue my professional portfolio and show my knowledge of instructional planning for activities, lessons, and units in connection with Principles 2, 4, 5 and 7 of INTASC and the Standards 1, 2, 3, 4, 5 and 6 of NBPTS (as seen on the inside of the front cover of this book)? **To do:** To continue your portfolio, you can develop and write a one- to two-page paper explaining your competency in developing activities, lessons, and units. Label your paper Activities, Lessons, and Units. After reading and interacting with Chapter 7 in this text, you can summarize your competency development about one or two of this chapter's objectives in your paper. Describe how you can do one or more of the following:

- Give one example of learning experiences/activities for a specified grade level from each of these categories: verbal, visual, vicarious, simulated, and direct.
- Give a brief summary of a lesson plan that you have prepared for a grade/course of your choice and your self-evaluation of the plan.
- For the rest of the objectives, please return to the beginning of this chapter. Place your paper in your portfolio folder or in your computer file.

With Teacher Tests Study Guide

Teacher Tests for Future Licensing and Certification. If I wanted to prepare for taking a state teacher test to qualify for my teaching certificate/license and review my knowledge about preparing activities, lessons, and units, how could I begin? **To do:** To support you as you prepare for teaching, you will find constructed-response-type questions similar to those found on state tests for teacher licensing and certification in Appendix A. The question related to this chapter and activities, lessons, and units, helps you take another look at the classroom vignette found in *Looking at Teachers II.* Write your response and, if you wish, discuss it with another teaching candidate. If appropriate, use one or two of your colleague's suggestions to help you change your response to the question. Place your response in a Teacher Test Study Guide folder or type/scan into a computer file. Plan to review and reread for study purposes before taking a scheduled teacher test.

With Target Topics for Teacher Tests (TTTT)

If I wanted to start early and get ready to take a state teacher test for licensing and certification and review subject matter content about preparing activities, lessons, and units, how could I begin? **To do:** Consider reviewing key words, also known as Target Topics for Teacher Tests (TTTT), in the subject index. Find key words that interest you in the visual organizer and overview at the beginning of this chapter, or in bold in this chapter's narrative, or in the chapter headings. To assist you, bullets (•) have been placed by selected word entries in the subject index. These bullets highlight core subject matter in this chapter—such as learning activities, lesson plan format, an instructional unit, and an interdisciplinary thematic unit—content that the authors suggest can be reviewed in preparation for taking a teacher test similar to your state's test.

WITH READING

Borich, G. D. (2004). *Effective Teaching Methods* (5th ed.). Upper Saddle River, NJ: Merrill/Prentice Hall.

Costa, A., and Kallick, B. (2000). *Discovering and Exploring Habits of Mind.* Alexandria, VA: Association for Supervision and Curriculum Development.

Danna, S. (2003, February/March). Pursuing National Board Certification. *Pi Lambda Theta Educational Horizons,* 5 (Bloomington, IN).

Fuchs, L. (2000). *Asia and Australia: Language Arts around the World, Volume III. Cross Curricular Activities for Grades 4–6.* Bloomington, IN: Family Learning Association.

Fuchs, L. (2000). *Europe: Language Arts around the World, Volume I. Cross Curricular Activities for Grades 4–6.* Bloomington, IN: Family Learning Association.

Kellough, R. D. (2007). *A Resource Guide for Teaching K–12* (5th ed.). Upper Saddle River, NJ: Merrill/Prentice Hall.

Kellough R. D., and Jarolimek, J. (2008). *Teaching and Learning K–8: A Guide to Methods and Resources* (9th ed.). Upper Saddle River, NJ: Merrill/Prentice Hall.

McAllister, E. A., Hildebrand, J. M., and Ericson, J. H. (2000). *Our Environment. Language Arts Theme Units, Volume I. Cross Curricular Activities for Primary Grades.* Bloomington, IN: Family Learning Association.

McAllister, E. A., Hildebrand, J. M., and Ericson, J. H. (2000). *People around Us. Language Arts Theme Units, Volume V. Cross Curricular Activities for Primary Grades.* Bloomington, IN: Family Learning Association.

Morine-Dershimer, G. (2003). Instructional Planning. In J. Cooper (Ed.), *Classroom Teaching Skills* (7th ed.). Boston: Houghton Mifflin.

Roberts, P. L., and Kellough, R. D. (2008). *A Guide for Developing an Interdisciplinary Thematic Unit* (4th ed.). Upper Saddle River, NJ: Merrill/Prentice Hall.

WITH NOTES

1. Dlott, A. M. (Pod) cast of Thousands. *Educational Leadership,* pp. 80–82 (April 2007).

2. For additional information, see www.adihome.org or phone 541-485-1293.

3. J. Bromann. *Storytime Action!: 2,000+ Ideas for Making 500 Picture Books Interactive* (New York: Neal-Schuman, 2003); J. Dreher, *Easy Steps to Writing Fantastic Research Reports* (Chicago: Scholastic, 2000).

4. R.C. Barton and L.A. Smith, Themes or Motifs? Aiming for Coherence through Interdisciplinary Outlines, *Reading Teacher,* 54(1), 54–63 (2000); S. Wineburg and P. Grossman (Eds.), *Interdisciplinary Curriculum: Challenges to Implementation* (New York: Teachers College Press, 2000).

PART 3

Effective Instruction, Teacher Assessment, and Professional Development

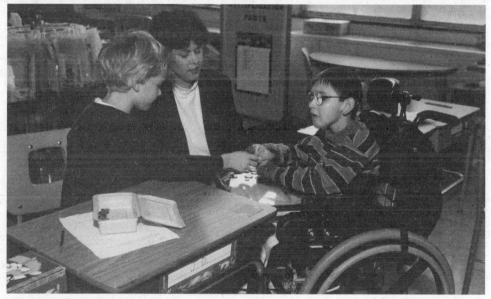

Anthony Magnacca/Merrill

Scott Cunningham/Merrill

What Do I Need to Know to Use Teacher Talk and Questioning as Effective Instructional Tools?

Visual Chapter Organizer and Overview

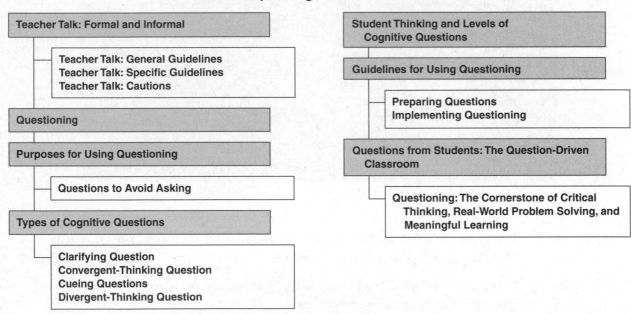

Teacher Talk: Formal and Informal

 Teacher Talk: General Guidelines
 Teacher Talk: Specific Guidelines
 Teacher Talk: Cautions

Questioning

Purposes for Using Questioning

 Questions to Avoid Asking

Types of Cognitive Questions

 Clarifying Question
 Convergent-Thinking Question
 Cueing Questions
 Divergent-Thinking Question

Student Thinking and Levels of Cognitive Questions

Guidelines for Using Questioning

 Preparing Questions
 Implementing Questioning

Questions from Students: The Question-Driven Classroom

 Questioning: The Cornerstone of Critical Thinking, Real-World Problem Solving, and Meaningful Learning

---

LOOKING AT TEACHERS I

Integrated Technology, Digital Camera

Consider, what might be done to improve instruction through the use of questions and teacher talk with students' experiential learning on a farm for hands-on education? With this question in mind, think about this partnership: At Holly Hill Farm in Cohasset (Boston area), schools develop partnerships with the nonprofit farm (a supporter of educational programs) to have their students learn in an outside classroom with the motto, "No child left inside." The education director at the farm, and others, have developed a curriculum guide for the elementary schools and the farm titled *A Growing Relationship: The School Garden, Classroom, and Organic Farm* (South Attleboro: Frances R. Dewing Foundation). The guide has over a dozen lesson plans that use gardens for teaching about earth science, plants, and the soil—all linked to the state's science requirements. Teachers and students interact in the following ways:

- Working on science requirements, special needs students from South Shore Educational Collaborative (Hingham), grades 1–3, visit the farm and use what they learn to tend a garden at their own school. Questions and teacher talk center on when to plant food items, on building farm beds, calculating measurements, and related math. Once, when a farm rabbit unfortunately passed away, the questions and teacher talk dealt with loss.

- The South Shore Charter Public School sends its students through the year to a separate area where they grow a duplicate garden of what's planted at the farm. Questions and teacher talk focus on growing beans, herbs, kale, potatoes, and pumpkins through the months of the year. In June, the students discuss ingredients to prepare a salad party, while in the September October period, they talk about what to take back to the classroom so they can have a feast from the harvest, for example, beets to roast, ingredients for making ratatouille, and items for making a sauce for pasta.

- In another school, Jenkins Elementary, students have discussions, questions, and teacher talk about art lessons, creative writing, science experiments, their own school garden, and harvest days. To help out, the school's cafeteria composts its garbage and the results are tilled back into the garden. Foods that are harvested are served often during school lunch time and favorites are kale chips and tomatillo salsa.

- Further connected to the curriculum, the students take a farm tour to observe the gardens at different times through the year. For more information about the relationship between the school programs and the farm, contact the educational director at Holly Hill Farm in Cohasset at www.hollyhillyFarm.org.

To integrate technology further, you could use a digital camera, take photos of students, what they do, and points of interest about what's going on. Back in the classroom, you could plug the digital camera into the classroom TV and begin an instant replay of the photos to initiate a review of what was learned, and engage in a related Earth science activity of "Twenty Questions" (and answers) or another related activity of your choice.

A Focus on English Language Learners

Since the students have been studying gardens and farms and harvesting, a student or teacher can begin the word-addition activity with the words, I went to Holly Hill Farm and I saw _____. The person who starts the activity names one item that he or she saw at the farm (such as garden or harvest). The next person in the row (or circle) repeats the sentence and adds another item. The third person repeats the sentence and adds still another item. To keep a student in the activity, a student may "call out to a class friend" for help a certain number of times (one, two, etc.) determined by the teacher. If a student has already used up the number of help times available, the game is over and the students tally up the number of items their group has correctly remembered. They can keep the tally to see if the next time their group plays the word-addition activity, they beat their own previous score. This is in keeping with suggested ELL strategies that include thematic unit design, use of primary source materials, collaborative learning, personalizing information, and use of questions (Misco and Castaneda, 2009).

Strategies that are of fundamental importance to any mode of instruction are teacher talk, and its related twin, questioning. You will use teacher talk and questioning for so many purposes that you must be skilled in the use of teacher talk and effective questioning. Because teacher talk is so important and because it is so frequently used and abused, as is questioning, this chapter is devoted to assisting you in the development of your skills in teacher talk generally and, specifically, in using questioning as an instructional tool.

Perhaps no other strategies are used more by teachers than teacher talk and questioning. Teachers need to be able to use teacher talk and ask questions effectively. Questions by a teacher that can be answered "yes" or "no" require very little thinking on the part of the students. In contrast to yes-no questions, open-response questions allow students to reflect on their prior knowledge and generate exploration to find answers. Related to finding answers, Melvin and Gilda Berger's book, *Where Did the Butterfly Get Its Name?* (Scholastic, 2003), allows students to brainstorm possible reasons and then verify their predictions. It gives them a topic to research and utilize their data for oral or written presentations. In the end, students learn that people used to believe that this winged insect flew into kitchens because it was attracted to butter and milk. They may be surprised to learn that butterflies taste with their feet, that some can make sounds, and that the biggest butterflies can grow to be almost twelve inches across! All of this started with one question.

CHAPTER OBJECTIVES

Specifically, as you construct your understanding of the use of teacher talk and questioning, upon the completion of this chapter, you should be able to:

1. Describe when and how to use teacher talk for instruction.

2. Describe the value, purpose, and types of advance mental organizers used when using teacher talk as an instructional strategy.
3. Recognize various levels/types of questions.
4. Develop your skill in raising questions from one level to the next.
5. Understand the importance of well-worded questions and allowing students time to think.

TEACHER TALK: FORMAL AND INFORMAL

Teacher talk encompasses both lecturing to students and talking with students. For purposes of our presentation in this resource guide, a lecture is considered formal teacher talk, whereas a discussion with students is considered informal teacher talk.

Teacher Talk: General Guidelines

First, you realize that certain general guidelines are appropriate whether your talk is formal or informal. Related to this, you should begin the talk with an advance organizer. Advance organizers are introductions that mentally prepare students for a study by helping them make connections with materials already learned or experienced—a **comparative organizer**—or by providing students with a conceptual arrangement of what is to be learned—an **expository organizer.**[1] The value of using these advance organizers is well documented by research.[2]

Further, an advance organizer can be a brief introduction or statement about the main idea you intend to convey and how it is related to other aspects of the students' learning (an expository organizer), or it can be a presentation of a discrepancy to arouse curiosity (a comparative organizer, in this instance, causing students to compare what they have observed with what they already knew or thought they knew). Preparing an organizer helps you plan and organize the sequence of ideas, and its presentation helps students organize their own learning and become motivated about it. An advance organizer can also make students' learning meaningful by providing important connections between what they already know and what is being learned. Figure 8.1 is a checklist for reviewing some of the other general guidelines for formal and informal teacher talk.

Teacher Talk: Specific Guidelines

Some specific guidelines for using teacher talk are presented in Figure 8.2, and discussed briefly in the following text.

More on Specific Guidelines

Understand the Various Purposes for Using Teacher Talk

Teacher talk, formal or informal, can be useful to discuss the progress of a unit of study, explain an inquiry learning situation, or introduce a unit of study. Your talk can present a problem, promote student inquiry learning, or encourage critical thinking. It can provide a transition from one unit of study to the next, provide information otherwise unobtainable to students, and where appropriate, share your experiences. With teacher talk, you can announce your thoughts about steps in an investigation, introduce a problem or process, or summarize a unit of study. And you can teach a thinking skill by thinking "out loud" to model what can be done in a thinking situation to the students, including ELLs and English-speaking students with learning problems. This would be an example of scaffolding, or providing support that can be removed when it is no longer needed.

Clarify the Objectives of the Teacher Talk

Your talk should center around one idea. The learning target objectives, which should not be too numerous for one talk, should be clearly understood by the students.

Choose between Formal and Informal Talk

Long lectures are not appropriate for most, if not all, elementary school teaching; spontaneous interactive informal talks of 5 to 12 minutes are preferred. You should never give long lectures with no teacher-student interaction. If during your student teaching, you have doubts or questions about your selection and use of a particular instructional strategy, discuss your concern with your host teacher or your university supervisor, or both. When you have doubts about the appropriateness of a particular strategy, trust your instincts: without some modification, the strategy probably is inappropriate.

Remember also, today's young people are of the media generation; they are accustomed to highly stimulating video interactions and commercial breaks. For some lessons (especially those that are teacher-centered), student attention is likely to begin to stray after about 10 minutes. For that eventuality, you need elements planned to recapture student attention. These planned

When considering Teacher Talk, I will respond to the following:

1. First, when appropriate, I will begin my talk with an advance organizer.

   Done _____   Somewhat done _____   Needs work _____

   My comments:

2. Second, my talk will be planned so that it has a clear beginning and a distinct end, with a logical order in between.

   Done _____   Somewhat done _____   Needs work _____

   My comments:

3. During my talk, I will reinforce my words with visuals. These visuals can include writing unfamiliar terms on the board (to help my students learn new vocabulary), visual organizers, and prepared graphs, charts, photographs, media support, and various other audiovisuals.

   Done _____   Somewhat done _____   Needs work _____

   My comments:

4. Next, I realize that my pacing will be important. My talk will move briskly, but not too fast. My ability to pace the instruction may be difficult to do because some beginning teachers talk too fast and too much; but this is a skill that I want to develop with experience.

   Done _____   Somewhat done _____   Needs work _____

   My comments:

5. I will constantly remind myself during lessons to slow down and provide silent pauses (allowing for think time) and allow for frequent checks for student comprehension.

   Done _____   Somewhat done _____   Needs work _____

   My comments:

6. Specifically, my talk will:
   - Be energetic, though not so fast that the students cannot understand what I am saying; I'll have occasional slowdowns to change the pace and to check for student comprehension; I will allow students time to think, ask questions, and make notes.

     Done _____   Somewhat done _____   Needs work _____

     My comments:

   - Have a time plan. I realize that a talk planned for 10 minutes (if interesting to students) will probably take longer. If not interesting to them, it will probably take less time.

     Done _____   Somewhat done _____   Needs work _____

     My comments:

(Continued)

Figure 8.1
Teacher talk general guidelines: A checklist.

- Be planned with careful consideration of the characteristics of the students. For example, if I have a fairly high percentage of English learners or students with special needs, then my talk may be less brisk, sprinkled with even more visuals and repeated statements, and with even more frequent checks for student comprehension.

  Done _____ Somewhat done _____ Needs work _____

  My comments:

- Have questions that I want to ask (as comprehension checks) and will include questions that the students ask during the lesson as well as various kinds of checklists.

  Done _____ Somewhat done _____ Needs work _____

  My comments:

- Have questions that I want to ask that reflect various degrees of difficulty.

  Done _____ Somewhat done _____ Needs work _____

  My comments:

7. Next, I will encourage student participation. I realize that active participation by the children enhances their learning. I can plan this encouragement through the questions that I ask, through the time allowed for students to comment and ask questions, or through a visual or conceptual outline or other activity that children can complete during the talk.

   Done _____ Somewhat done _____ Needs work _____

   My comments:

8. Last, I will plan a distinct ending or closure. I want to be sure that my talk will have a distinct ending, maybe followed by another activity (during the same or next class period) that will help reinforce and secure the learning further. As for all lessons, I want to strive to plan a clear and interesting beginning, an involved lesson, and a firm and meaningful closure. I realize that proper preparation prevents poor performance.

   Done _____ Somewhat done _____ Needs work _____

   My comments:

Figure 8.1

Teacher talk general guidelines: A checklist. *(Continued)*

elements can include a temporary strategy and modality shift such as more student interaction that can include a teacher demonstration or a student inquiry. You can:

- Ask students to turn to students on their right and tell them what they learned so far about _____ (topic) in no more than three sentences.
- Use analogies to help connect the topic to students' life experiences.
- Use verbal cues such as voice inflections.
- Use pauses to allow reflection about the information.
- Use humor and visual cues such as media presentations, slides, overhead transparencies, charts, board

drawings, excerpts from videodiscs, real objects (realia), or body gestures.

- Use sensory cues, such as eye contact and proximity (as in moving around the room, or casually standing close to a student without interrupting your talk).
- Ask students to show their points of view by putting their thumbs up if they agree with X.

Vary Strategies and Activities Frequently

For the teacher, perhaps most useful as a strategy for recapturing student attention is the strategy of changing to an entirely different activity or learning modality. For example, from teacher talk (a teacher-centered strategy)

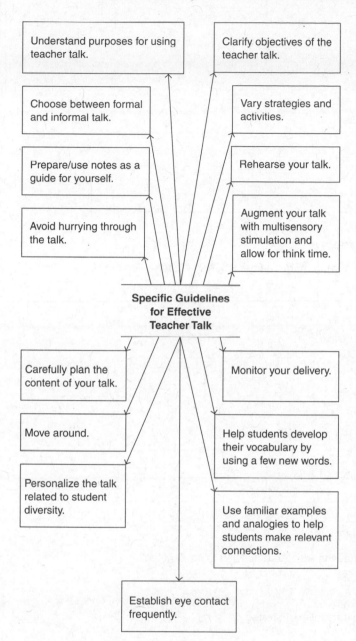

Figure 8.2
Specific guidelines for effective teacher talk.

the grade level of the students, the number of students in the class, the subject being taught—math? art? reading?), generally this means that in a 60-minute time block, you can plan from three to five sequenced learning activities, with one or two activities that are teacher-centered and others that are more student-centered. In exemplary grade K–6 classrooms, some teachers often have several activities being performed concurrently by children as individuals, in dyads, and in small groups—that is, they are using multilevel (multitasking) instruction. Multitasking is, as we have mentioned in this resource guide, highly recommended as a viable strategy when teaching a classroom of 15 or more students. An example of multitasking is shown in Chapter 2.

Prepare and Use Notes as a Guide for Yourself during Your Talk

Planning your talk and preparing notes to be used during formal and informal teacher talk is important—just as important as implementing the talk with visuals. There is absolutely nothing wrong with using notes during your teaching. As you move around the room, your notes can be carried on your eye-catching neon-colored clipboard. Your notes for a formal talk can first be prepared in narrative form; whenever appropriate, though, for class use, try to use an outline form. Talks to students should always be from an outline, so your words never sound as read directly from prose. The only time that a teacher's reading from prose aloud to students is appropriate is when reading a story or a poem or portions of the selections or when reading a brief published article from a newspaper or a magazine. Also, on rare occasions, a teacher might read aloud carefully formulated questions from his or her lesson plan notes.

In your outline (perhaps a computer-generated outline), consider using coding with abbreviated visual cues to yourself. You will eventually develop your own coding system; whatever coding system you use, keep it simple so you will always remember what the codes are for in your outline. Consider these examples of coding: Where transition of ideas occurs or you want to pause or to allow students a silent moment for the students to reflect on the idea, mark *P* for *pause*, *T* for a *transition*, or *S* for a moment of *silence*; where a computer presentation, the school's slide projector, or other visual aid will be used, mark *C* for *computer* or *AV* for *audiovisual*; where you intend to stop and ask a question, mark *TQ* for teacher question, and mark *SQ* or *?* where you want to stop and allow time for student questions; where you plan to have a *discussion*, mark *D*, or mark *SG* when you plan *small-group* work and use *I* or *L* where you plan to switch to an *investigation* in a *laboratory* simulated approach; for *reviews* and *comprehension checks*, mark *R* and *CC*, respectively.

Share your note organization with the students. Teach them how to take notes and what kinds of things they should write down. If you wish, use colored chalk or

you would change to a student activity (a student-centered strategy). Notice that changing from a lecture (mostly teacher talk) to a teacher-led discussion (mostly more teacher talk) would not be changing to an entirely different modality. Figure 8.3 provides a comparison of different changes.

As a generalization, when using teacher-centered direct instruction, with most groups of children, you will want to change the learning activities about every 10 to 12 minutes. (That is one reason that in the sample lesson plan format in Chapter 7, you found space for at least four activities, including the introduction and closure). Although this will vary due to several variables (such as

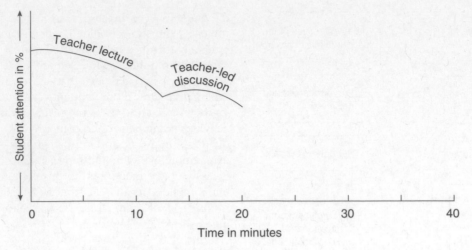

Example 1: Changing from teacher talk (lecture) to more teacher talk (e.g., teacher-led discussion).

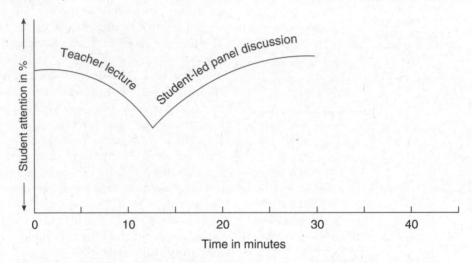

Example 2: Changing from teacher talk (teacher-centered activity) to student-led panel discussion (student-centered activity).

Figure 8.3
Comparison of recapturing student attention by changing the instructional strategy.

marking pens on an overhead transparency, the writing board, or classroom chart to outline and highlight your teacher talk. If it is part of your instructional design, have your students use colored pencils for taking notes so their notes can be color-coded to match your writing board notes.

Rehearse Your Talk

Rehearsing your planned talk is the mark of a professional teacher and is important: you want to be good at what you do, especially giving a talk to your students. Using your lesson plan as your guide, rehearse your talk using a camcorder or while talking into a mirror or to a friend or roommate. Is the pacing proper . . . not too fast and not too slow? Are you speaking clearly? Are your

choice of words, voice tone, and body language conveying professionalism and your thorough preparation and confidence? Do you want to include a time plan for each subtopic to allow you to gauge your timing during implementation of the talk?

Avoid Racing through the Talk Solely to Complete It by a Certain Time

It is more important that students understand some of what you say than that you cover it all and they understand none of it. If you do not finish, continue it later. For ELLs and students with learning problems, you may have to slow down the pace of talking about a new skill and include role-playing practice of the skill or task. Ask the rest of the group to first observe you

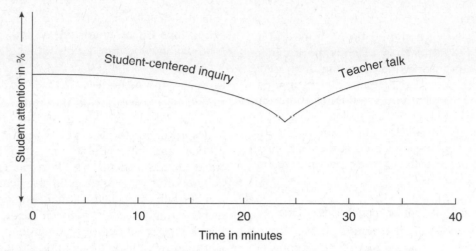

Example 3: Changing from inquiry (student-centered) to teacher talk fueled by student questions from inquiry.

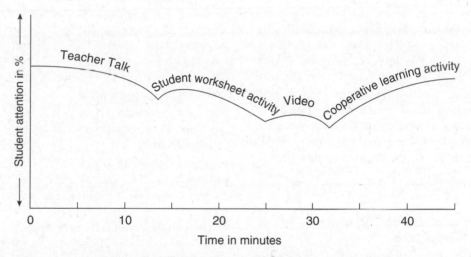

Example 4: Changing from teacher talk (teacher-centered activity) to cooperative learning activity (student-centered activity).

Figure 8.3 *(Continued)*

starting the new skill/task and then observe a student do the same.

Augment Your Talk with Multisensory Stimulation and Allow for Think Time

Your presentation should not overly rely on verbal communication. When using visuals, such as photographs, computer screen projections, video excerpts, or overhead transparencies, do not think that you must be constantly talking; after clearly explaining the purpose of a visual, give the students sufficient time to look at it, to think about it, and to ask questions about it. If the visual is new to the students, give them time to take it in. Also, be sure you're not blocking their view of the visual. Be sure the visual is large enough for students in the back of the classroom/group to see clearly. Varying concrete

materials and visuals helps you guide instruction for students with English language/learning problems.

Carefully Plan the Content of Your Talk

The content of your talk should supplement and enhance the material found in the student textbook rather than simply rehash information from the textbook. Students may never read their book if you tell them in an interesting and condensed fashion everything they need to know from it. Break up your talk with modeling, with questions, and with explanations about concepts. When asking questions of ELLs and students with learning problems, you can encourage them to respond to answers to questions at the same time (thumbs up for agree, thumbs down for disagree, flash small index cards that say yes or no, or respond as a group).

Monitor Your Delivery

On one hand, your voice should be pleasant and interesting to listen to rather than a steady, boring monotone or a constantly shrieking, irritating, high pitch. On the other hand, it is a positive teaching attribute to show enthusiasm for what you are talking about during teaching and learning. Occasionally, use dramatic voice inflections to emphasize important points and meaningful body language to give students a visual focus. Practice these skills so they become second nature.

Avoid Standing in the Same Spot for Long Periods of Time

As is always the case when teaching, move around (circulate) and consider that standing for 10 minutes in the same spot may be too long. You want to monitor student behavior during explicit instruction. Use proximity (moving closer to a student) and signal intervention cues (e.g., eye contact, body language, smiles or frowns, have students move response cards up or down with words showing to agree or disagree, or use other forms of Every Pupil Response [EPR]), such as showing green cards (small green flags, right hands up) to agree and yellow cards (small yellow flags, left hands up) to disagree, as means of keeping students focused. It is especially during extended periods of explicit instruction that a beginning teacher's skills in withitness and overlapping behaviors are likely to be put to the test.

View the Vocabulary of Your Talk as an Opportunity to Help Students with New Vocabulary

The children should easily understand the words you use, though you can still model professionalism and help the students develop new vocabulary further. During your lesson planning, predict when you are likely to use a word that is new to most students, and plan to stop to ask a student to help explain its meaning and perhaps demonstrate its derivation. Some teachers use the "Define It Four Ways" activity, as follows:

- In this activity, steps 1 and 2 are "define" and "demonstrate." To do this, you first invite students to explain the way the students' textbook (or dictionary, glossary) defines the word and then define the word another way by demonstrating something about it. They can work in pairs if appropriate; for example, ELLs can pair with other first-language speakers.
- Steps 3 and 4 are "describe" and "display" an illustration. To do this, students define the word by describing something about the word, and last, further the definition of the word by displaying an illustration that helps show something about the definition of the word (or part of it). When you help students with word meanings and define words in various ways, as

in this activity, students tend to remember the relationships among words, ideas, and concepts that you are talking about in the lesson.

Remember That All Teachers Are Language Arts Teachers

Knowledge of words and their meanings is an important component of skilled reading and includes the ability to generate new words from roots and adding prefixes and suffixes. For some students, nearly every subject in the curriculum is like a foreign language. That is certainly true for some English learners, for whom teacher talk, especially formal teacher talk, should be used sparingly, if at all. Every elementary school teacher has the responsibility of helping children learn how to learn, and that includes helping students develop their word comprehension skills, reading skills, thinking and memory skills, and their motivation for learning. As resources, see *The English Language Arts*, 2nd ed., by J. Flood, D. Lapp, J. R. Squire, and J. M. Jensen, and *Handbook of Reading Research, Volume III* by M. L. Kamil, P. B. Mosenthel, P. D. Pearson, and R. Barr (both Newark, DE: International Reading Association, 2003 and 2000 respectively).

Give Thoughtful and Intelligent Consideration to Student Diversity

During the planning phase, while preparing your talk, consider the children in your classroom who are culturally and linguistically different and those who have special needs. Personalize the talk for them by choosing your vocabulary carefully and appropriately, speaking slowly and methodically, repeating often, and by planning meaningful analogies, giving examples, and having relevant audio and visual displays.

Use Familiar Examples and Analogies to Help Students Make Relevant Connections (Links, Bridges)

While this sometimes takes a great deal of creative thinking as well as action during the planning phase, it is important that you attempt to connect the talk with ideas and events with which the students are already familiar (such as the names of events, places, and people from their neighborhood and community). The most effective teacher talk is talk that makes frequent and meaningful connections between what students already know and what they are learning.

Establish Eye Contact Frequently

Your primary eye contact should be with your students—always! That important point cannot be overemphasized. Only momentarily should you look at your computer screen, your notes, your visuals, the projection screen, the writing board, the bulletin board, and other adults or objects in the classroom. While you will probably raise your eyebrows when you read this, it is true and it is important that with practice, you can learn to scan a classroom of 30 students, establishing eye contact with each student at least once a minute. To establish eye contact means that the student is aware that you are looking at him or her. Frequent eye contact can have two major benefits. First, as you "read" a child's body posture and facial expressions, you obtain important clues about that student's attentiveness and comprehension. Second, eye contact helps to establish rapport between you and a student. A look with a smile or a headshake from the teacher to a child can say so much! Be alert, though, that for children who are from cultures where eye contact is infrequent or even unwanted, this could have negative consequences.

Frequent eye contact is easier when using an overhead projector than when bending down to look at the computer screen or using the writing board. When using a computer screen, you have to bend your head down and when using a writing board, you have to turn at least partially away from your audience, and you may also have to pace back and forth from the board to the students to be able to retain that important proximity to them.

While talking to the children you must be alert and demonstrate your withitness; that is, you must stay aware of and attentive to everything that is happening in the classroom (that is, aware of student behavior as well as of the content of your talk). No one ever said that good teaching is easy, or if they did, they didn't know what they were talking about. But don't dismay: with the knowledge of the preceding guidelines, the cautions that follow, and with practice, experience, and intelligent reflection, you will quickly develop the skills important to being recognized as an accomplished teacher.

Teacher Talk: Cautions

Whether your talk is formal or informal, there are certain cautions that you need to be mindful of when teaching. Perhaps the most important caution is that of talking too much. If a teacher talks too much, the significance of the teacher's words may be lost because some students will tune the teacher out.

Another caution, we repeat, is to avoid talking too fast. Your students can hear faster than they can comprehend what they hear. It is also important to remember that your one brain is communicating with the brains of your students, each of which responds to the sensory input (auditory in this instance) at different rates. Because of this, you will need to pause to let the students reflect on the words and you will need to repeat important ideas and you will need to pause during transitions from one point or from one activity to the next to allow each of those students to make the necessary shift in their thinking. It is a good idea to remind yourself to talk slowly and

to check frequently for student comprehension of what you are talking about. We want you to recall one student who said the following to the teacher after a teacher talk: "You were telling me more than I wanted to know."

A third caution is to be sure you are being heard and understood. Sometimes, teachers talk in too low a pitch or use words that are not understood by many of the students, or both. You should vary the pitch of your voice, and you should stop and help students with their understanding of vocabulary that may be new to them.

A fourth caution is to remember that just because students have heard something before does not necessarily mean that they understand it or that they learned it. From our earlier discussions of learning experiences (such as the learning experiences ladder in Chapter 7), remember that although verbal communication is an important form of communication, because of its reliance on the use of abstract symbolization, it is not always a very reliable form of communication. Teacher talk relies on words and on skill in listening, a skill that is not mastered easily by many children (or for that matter, even many adults). For that and other reasons, to ensure student understanding, it is good to reinforce your teacher talk with either explicit or simulated learning experiences.

A related caution is to resist believing that children have attained a skill or have mastered content that was taught previously by you or by another teacher. During any discussion, rather than assuming that your students know something, you should ensure they know it. For example, if the discussion and a student activity involve a particular thinking skill, then you will want to make sure that students know how to use that skill (thinking skills are discussed in Chapter 9).

Our last caution is to avoid talking in a humdrum monotone. Children need teachers whose voices exude enthusiasm and excitement (though not to be overdone) about the subject and about teaching and learning. A voice that demonstrates enthusiasm for teaching and learning is more likely to motivate children to learn. Enthusiasm and excitement for learning are contagious.

QUESTIONING

A strategy that is of fundamental importance to any mode of instruction is questioning. You will use questioning for so many purposes that you must be skilled in its use to teach effectively. Because it is so important, and because it is so frequently used and abused, the rest of this chapter is devoted to assisting you in the development of your skills in using questioning as an instructional tool.

PURPOSES FOR USING QUESTIONING

You can adapt the type and form of each question to the purpose for which it is asked. The purposes that questions can serve can be separated into five categories, as shown in Figure 8.4 and discussed, with examples, in the next paragraphs.

1. **To politely give instructions.** Examples are: "Are we ready to move on to the next problem, now?" and, "Lupe, would you please turn out the lights so we can show the slides?" Although they probably should avoid doing so, teachers sometimes use rhetorical questions for the purpose of regaining student attention and maintaining classroom control—for example, "Chris, would you please attend to your work?" Rhetorical questions such as this one can sometimes backfire on the teacher. In this situation, for instance, Chris might say, "No"; then the teacher would have a problem that could perhaps have been avoided if the teacher at first had been more explicit and simply told Chris to attend to his work instead of asking him if he would.

   Consider the vignette at the end of this chapter in the *Looking at Teachers II* section. The kindergarten teacher, Tara, seems to have a purpose in transitioning from the reading lesson to the mathematics lesson. If Tara is indeed planning to ask the question ("Shall we do our math lesson, now?"), then she must be prepared to deal with student responses and not ignore what they say back to her question. An improved

transition in this instance might be simply to say, "It is time for us to do our math lesson" and follow that with a transition statement, "So it's time to put away our reading materials and get out our math papers (books, ruler, etc.)." The teacher can then follow that with a question, such as "Who can review for us one thing that we learned (or did) yesterday in math?"

2. **To review and remind students of classroom procedures.** For example: If students continue to talk when they shouldn't, you can stop the lesson and say, "I think we need to review the procedure for listening when someone else is talking. Who can tell me the procedure for listening that we agreed upon at our class meeting?" Perhaps refer to a class chart about procedures for your community of learners during the discussion.

3. **To gather information.** Examples are: "How many of you are ready to raise your hand to show that you have finished the assignment?" or to find out if a student has knowledge about the topic, "Joe, can you please explain to us the difference between a synonym and antonym?"

4. **To discover student knowledge, interests, or experiences.** Examples might be: "Where do you think our drinking water comes from?" or "How many of you have visited the local water treatment plant?" or "How many of you (raise your hands or put thumbs up) think you know the process by which water in our city is made drinkable?"

5. **To guide student thinking and learning.** It is this category of questioning that is the primary focus here. Questions in this category to help guide student thinking and learning can be used for the following:

   • **To build the curriculum.** It is the students' questions that provide the basis for the learning that occurs in an effective program that is based on inquiry learning and is project centered. More on this subject follows in the next two chapters.

   • **To develop appreciation.** Here's an example: "What do you understand about the water cycle we've been talking about?" . . . or "Why is the water cycle valuable to us?"

   • **To develop student thinking.** An example: "When standing water is sprayed with an insecticide that kills mosquito larvae, what do you suppose are the effects to the environment?"

   • **To diagnose learning difficulty.** For example, "What part of the problem don't you understand, Eric?"

   • **To emphasize major points.** Example: "If no one has ever been to the Sun, how do we know what it is made of?"

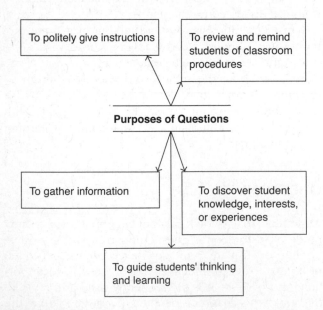

Figure 8.4
Purposes of questions.

- **To encourage students.** Here's an example: "OK, so you didn't remember the whole process. What really impressed me in your writing is what you did understand about photosynthesis. Do you know what part impressed me?"

- **To establish rapport.** An example: "Do you think we have a conflict here? Do you think we can resolve it if we put our heads together? What do you think ought to be our first step?"

- **To evaluate learning.** For example, "Sean, what is the effect when two rough surfaces, such as two slices of toasted bread, are rubbed together?"

- **To give practice in expression.** Here's an example, "Yvonne, would you please share with us the examples of Impressionism that you found?"

- **To help students in their metacognition (that is, their thinking about thinking).** An example: "Yes, something did go wrong in the experiment. Do you still think your original hypothesis is correct? If not, then where was the error in your thinking? Or if you still think your hypothesis is correct, then where might the error have been in the design of your experiment? How could we find out?"

- **To help students interpret information and materials.** For example, "Something seems to be wrong with this compass. How do you suppose we can find out what is wrong with it? For instance, if the needle is marked N and S in reverse, as suggested by Hannah, how can we find out if that, in fact, is the problem?"

- **To help students organize information and materials.** Here's an example: "If you really want to carry out your proposed project, then we are going to need certain information and materials. We are going to have to deal with some questions here, such as, what information and materials do we think we need? Where can we find those things? Who will be responsible for getting them? and How will we store and arrange them?"

- **To provide drill and practice.** An example: "Research Team A has prepared some questions that they would like to use as practice questions for our test at the end of the unit; they are suggesting that we use them to play the game of Educational Jeopardy on Friday. How many of you are okay with their suggestion?"

- **To provide review.** For example, "Today in your groups, you are going to study the unit review questions that I have prepared. After each group has studied and prepared its answers to

these written questions, your group will choose another group and ask them your set of review questions. Each group has a different set of questions. Members of Research Team A are going to keep score, and the group that has the highest score from this review session will receive a free slice of pizza at tomorrow's lunch. Ready?"

- **To show agreement or disagreement.** Example: "Some people believe that stricter gun control laws would reduce acts of violence. With evidence that you have collected from recent articles from newspapers, magazines, and the Internet, do you agree with this conclusion? Explain why or why not."

- **To show relationships, such as cause and effect.** Here's an example: "What do you suppose would be the worldwide effect if just one inch of the entire Antarctic ice shelf were to melt during this year?"

Questions to Avoid Asking

Before going further in reviewing some types of cognitive questions in the next section, take a minute or two to consider the following kinds of questions a teacher should avoid asking in the classroom, as shown in Figure 8.5.

Rhetorical and No-Thinking-Required Questions

While it is important to avoid asking rhetorical questions, that is, questions for which you do not intend or even want a response, you should also avoid asking questions that call for little or no student thinking, such as those that can be answered with a simple yes or no or some other sort of alternative answer response. Unless followed up with questions calling for clarification, questions that call for simple responses, such as yes or no, have little or no diagnostic value; they encourage guessing and allow inappropriate student response that can cause classroom control problems for the teacher.

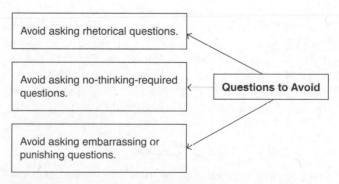

Figure 8.5
Questions to avoid in the classroom.

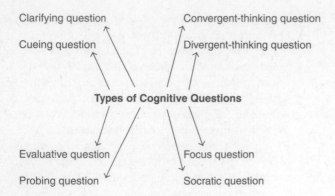

Figure 8.6
Types of cognitive questions.

TYPES OF COGNITIVE QUESTIONS

In this section, we define, describe, and provide examples for each of the different types of cognitive (a process of knowing) questions that you will use in teaching. Although we refer to these types as cognitive questions, we realize that any question type could relate to any of the three domains of learning (cognitive, affective, or psychomotor). In addition, the types of questions are not exclusive or categorically pure. For an example, a question that is classed as a divergent-thinking-type question might also be classed as a focus question, and vice versa. In the discussion that follows, your attention is centered on the levels of cognitive questions. Let's start by looking at Figure 8.6.

Clarifying Question

The clarifying question is used to gain more information from a student to help the teacher and classmates better understand a student's ideas, feelings, and thought processes. Often, asking a student to elaborate on an initial response will lead the student to think more deeply, restructure his or her thinking, and while doing so, discover a fallacy in the original response. Examples of clarifying questions are "What I hear you saying, John, is that you would rather work alone than in your group. Is that correct? What interests you about working alone?" "So, Mary, you think the poem is a sad one, is that right? Which parts are sad to you?" Research has shown a strong positive correlation between student learning and the development of metacognitive skills and the teacher's use of questions that ask for clarification.[3] In addition, by seeking clarification, you are likely to be demonstrating an interest in the child as a person and in that child's thinking.

Convergent-Thinking Question

Convergent-thinking questions, also called **narrow questions,** are low-order thinking questions that have a single correct answer (such as recall questions, discussed

further in the next section). Examples of convergent questions are "How is the Earth classed—as a star or a planet?" "If the radius of a circle is 20 meters, what is its circumference?"

"What is the name of the person who was first president of the United States?" Sometimes, like with the first example, it is good to come back with follow-up questions to move the student's thinking beyond simple recall. With this example, a follow-up question could be "Why is Earth classed as a planet?" or "What characteristics are necessary for a celestial body to be classified as a planet?"

Cueing Question

If you ask a question and wait sufficient wait time (longer than 2 seconds) and no students respond (or their responses indicate they need more information), then you can ask a question that cues the answer or the response you are seeking.[4] In essence, you are going backward in your questioning sequence to cue the students. For instance, in the preceding example, if there is no response then the teacher could ask, "Who can name a characteristic that distinguishes stars and planets?"

As an introduction to a lesson on the study of prefixes, a teacher might ask the students, "How many legs each do crayfish, lobsters, and shrimp have?" If there is no accurate response, then the teacher might cue the answer with the following information and question, "The class to which those animals belong is class Decapoda. Does that give you a clue about the number of legs they have?" If that clue is not enough, and after allowing sufficient wait time for students to think (remember, it's longer than 2 seconds), then the teacher might ask, "What is a decathlon?" or "What is the Decalogue?" or "In what way does the term the *decimal system* give you a clue or hint?" or "What is a decimeter?" or "What is a decibel?" or "What is a decade?"

When questioning students about reading material in particular, consider using the question-answer relationship (QAR) strategy. QAR involves asking a question, and if a student is unable to respond, providing one of three types of cues or responses. The cues are related to the level of thinking required. "Right there" is a cue used for responses to questions where the answer can be found explicitly stated in the sentence or paragraph. "Search and think" means the answer is not directly stated and therefore must be inferred. "On your own" is a cue used for highest-level critical thinking questions for which the answers are neither explicit nor inferred in the text.[5] You'll want to practice giving "right there" cues, "search and think" cues, and "on your own" cues.

Divergent-Thinking Question

Divergent-thinking questions (also known as **broad,** *reflective*, *open-ended*, or *thought* questions) usually having no singularly correct answer. These high-order thinking questions require analysis, synthesis, or evaluation. Students must think creatively, leave the comfortable confines of the known, and reach out into the unknown. Examples of questions that require divergent thinking are, "What measures could be taken to improve safety in our community?" "What might be done to improve school spirit?" and "Who would like to tell us why they believe there are (or are not) any yet undiscovered planets in our solar system?"

Evaluative Question

Whether convergent or divergent, some questions require students to place a value on something or to take a stance on some issue; these are referred to as **evaluative questions.** If the teacher and the students all agree on certain premises, then the evaluative question would also be a convergent question. If the original assumptions differ, then the response to the evaluative question would be more subjective, and therefore, that evaluative question would be divergent. Examples of evaluative questions are "Should the United States allow clear-cutting in its national forests?" "Should school officials have the right to search student lockers?" and "Is the president of the United States or any other person above the law?"

Focus Question

A focus question is any question that is designed to center and focus student thinking. For example, the first question of the preceding paragraph is a focus question when the teacher asking it is attempting to focus student attention on the economic issues involved in clear-cutting. Deliberately constructed focus questions, such as "What reasons support the idea that every citizen has the right to own a gun?" are especially useful for stimulating student interest at the beginning of a unit of instruction such as a unit on the U.S. Constitution.

Probing Question

Similar to a clarifying question, a probing question requires student thinking to go beyond superficial first-answer or single-word responses. Examples of probing questions are "Why, Sean, do you think it to be the case that every citizen has the right to have (not have) a gun?" Always be cautious, though, and not probe so far that the question embarrasses the student. If a student seems embarrassed, give the student time to think further.

Socratic Question

In the fifth century B.C.E., Socrates used the art of questioning so successfully that to this day we still hear of the Socratic method.[6] What, exactly, is the Socratic method?

Well, Socrates' method or strategy was to ask his students a series of leading questions that gradually took them up to the point where they had to look carefully at their own ideas and to think rigorously about themselves. The questions focused on challenging assumptions (I want to challenge your assumption that . . .), exposing contradictions (I want to point out your own contradiction about . . .), questioning the question (I want to question your question . . .), and answering a question with further questions (Why do you ask about that . . .?). Today, that strategy is referred to as the Socratic method.

Socratic discussions were informal dialogues taking place in a natural, pleasant environment. Although Socrates sometimes had to go to considerable lengths to ignite his students' intrinsic interest, their response was natural and spontaneous. In his dialogues, Socrates, pretending to know nothing about the subject, tried to aid students in developing ideas. He did not impose his own notions on the students. Rather, he asked questions to help them find out the truth independently and encouraged them to develop their own conclusions and draw their own inferences. Of course, Socrates may have had preconceived notions about what the final learning should be and carefully aimed his questions so that the students would arrive at the desired conclusions. Still, his questions were open-ended, causing divergent rather than convergent thinking. The students were free to go mentally wherever the facts and their thinking led them.

Throughout history, teachers have tried to adapt the methods of Socrates to the classroom. A coaching guide for starting Socratic seminars and give students ownership over text discussions is available in *Socratic Circles* (Portland, ME: Stenhouse Publishers, 2005) by M. Copeland. However, we must remember that Socrates used this method in the context of a one-to-one relationship between the student and himself. Some teachers have adapted it for whole-class explicit instruction by asking questions first of one student and then of another, moving slowly about the class. This technique may work for you, but it is difficult because the underpinning of the Socratic method is to build question upon question in a logical fashion so that each question leads the student a step further toward the understanding sought. When you spread the questions around the classroom, you may find it difficult to build up the desired sequence and to keep all the students involved in the discussion. Sometimes, you may be able to use the Socratic method by directing all the questions at one student volunteer—at least for several minutes to demonstrate the method—while the other students look on and listen in. That is how Socrates did it. When the topic is interesting enough, this technique can be useful, successful, and even fun, but in the long run, the Socratic method works best when the teacher is working in one-on-one coaching situations or with small groups of children, or when older students get in pairs and take turns directing questions to one another for a few minutes.

STUDENT THINKING AND LEVELS OF COGNITIVE QUESTIONS

Thinking Is the Quintessential Activity

In using Socratic questioning, the focus is on the questions, not answers, and thinking is valued as the quintessential activity.[7] As one way to conduct Socratic questioning, have the student or group identify a problem (either student- or teacher-posed) and then ask the students a series of probing questions designed to cause them to examine critically the problem and potential solutions to it. The main thrust of the questioning and the key questions must be planned in advance so that the questioning will proceed logically. To think of quality probing questions on the spur of the moment is too difficult. With guidance from your instructor, you can decide to use the Socratic method in Application Exercise 8.1 later in this chapter.

Remember, the questions you pose are cues to your students to the level of thinking expected of them, ranging from the lowest level of mental operation, requiring simple recall of knowledge (convergent thinking), to the highest, requiring divergent thought and application of that thought. It is important that you are knowledgeable about the levels of thinking, that you understand the importance of attending to student thinking from low to higher levels of operation, and that you understand that what for one child may be a matter of simple recall of information, may for another, require a higher-order mental activity, such as figuring something out by deduction.

You should structure and sequence your questions (and assist students in developing their skills in structuring and sequencing questions) in a way that is designed to guide students to higher levels of thinking and to connect their understandings. For example, when children respond to your questions in complete sentences that provide supportive evidence for their ideas, it is fairly safe to assume that their thinking is connected to their knowledge and experiences and is at a higher level than if the response were an imprecise and nondescriptive single-word answer.

To help your understanding further, three levels of questioning and thinking are described in the following paragraphs.[8] You should recognize the similarity between these three levels of questioning and Bloom's new version of the six levels of thinking—remembering, understanding, applying, analyzing, evaluating, creating—in Bloom's revised taxonomy of cognitive objectives

(Chapter 5). For your daily use of questioning, you will find it just as useful and more practical to think and behave in terms of these three levels, rather than of six.

1. **Lowest level (the data input phase): Remembering and understanding information.** At this level, questions are designed to solicit from the students, some concepts, information, feelings, or experiences, that were gained in the past and stored in memory. Related to remembering, you want to know if the student can recall or repeat information. Related to understanding, you want to know if a student can explain ideas or concepts. This is the level where you focus on the following key words and desired behaviors:

   For remembering, ask students to *define, describe, duplicate, list, memorize, recall, repeat, reproduce, state; also name, recall, and recite.*
   Question example for remembering: *Please recall and describe at least three organic food items we grew in our garden.*
   For understanding, ask students to *classify, discuss, explain, identify, locate, recognize, report, select, summarize, translate, paraphrase; also complete, count, define, list, match, observe, and select.*
   Question example for understanding: *Summarize what happened during our Fall Harvest day this semester.*

   Thinking involves receiving data through the sensory receptors (the senses), followed by the processing of those data. Inputting without processing is brain-dysfunctional. Information that has not been processed is stored only in short-term memory.

2. **Intermediate level (the data-processing phase): Applying and analyzing (processing) information.** At this level, questions are designed to draw relationships of cause and effect, to synthesize, analyze, summarize, compare data (find similarities), or contrast data (find differences). Regarding applying information, you want to know if the student can use the information in a new way. Regarding analyzing information, you want to know if a student can distinguish between different parts. This is the level where you ask the students to respond to the following key words and desired behaviors:

   For applying, ask students to *choose, construct, demonstrate, dramatize, employ, illustrate, interpret, operate, schedule, sketch, solve, use, and write.*
   Question example for applying: *Construct a theory (speculation, best guess) as to why we should grow (or should not grow) organic food items in the garden.*
   For analyzing, ask students to *appraise, compare, contrast, criticize, differentiate, discriminate, distinguish, examine, experiment, question, and test; also explain, group, infer, organize, plan, synthesize and make analogies.*

Question example for analyzing: *Differentiate between how organic food items are grown and how inorganic food items are grown.*

Thinking and questioning that involve processing of information can be conscious or unconscious. When students observe you, the teacher, modeling your thinking aloud, and when you urge them to think aloud, to think about their own thinking, and to analyze it as it occurs, you are helping them in the process of developing their intellectual skills.

At the processing level, this internal analysis of new data may challenge a student's preconceptions (and misconceptions—also called **naive theories**) about a phenomenon. The student's brain will naturally resist this challenge to his or her existing beliefs. The greater the mental challenge, the greater will be the brain's effort to draw upon data already in storage. With increasing data, the mind will gradually examine existing concepts and ultimately, as necessary, develop new mental concepts.

If there is a match between new input and existing mental concepts, no problem exists. Piaget called this process **assimilation.**[9] If, however, in processing new data there is no match with existing mental concepts, then the situation is what Piaget called **cognitive disequilibrium.** The brain is "discontented" about this disequilibrium and will drive the search for an explanation for the discrepancy. Piaget called this process **accommodation.**

Although learning is enhanced by challenge, in situations that are threatening, the brain is less flexible in accommodating new ideas. As discussed in Chapter 4, that is why each student must feel welcomed in the classroom and the classroom environment must be perceived by the student as challenging but nonthreatening—what is referred to as an environment of **relaxed alertness.**[10]

Questions and experiences must be designed to elicit more than merely recall memory responses. Many teachers find it useful to use strategies that create cognitive disequilbrium, such as to demonstrate discrepant events in order to introduce lessons and concepts. Hearing about or especially seeing a discrepancy stirs the mind into processing and into higher mental activity, without which mental development does not occur. (See the example in Figure 8.7 and Figure 8.8).

3. **Highest level (the data output phase):** *Evaluating and creating.* At the highest level of thinking, questions are designed to encourage learners to think intuitively, creatively, and hypothetically, to use their imagination, to expose a value system, or to make a judgment. In evaluating, you want to know if a student can justify a stand or a decision. In creating, you want to know if a student can create a new product or a point of view. This is the level at which you encourage the students to get involved with the following key words and desired behaviors:

For evaluating, ask students to *appraise, argue, defend, judge, select, support, value, and evaluate.*
Question example for evaluating: *Assess whether or not you think you have learned three things about math while tending our garden this semester.*
For creating, ask students to *assemble, compose, conduct, create, design, develop, formulate, and write; also apply a principle, build a model, extrapolate, forecast, generalize, hypothesize, imagine, predict, and speculate.*

Combustible Won't Burn

Practice this first. Wrap a dollar bill (or a $20 if you are confident) around a drinking glass. While holding the bill tightly around the glass, try to ignite the bill with a match or lighter. The paper bill will not ignite because the glass conducts the heat away too rapidly, maintaining the paper below its kindling/ignition point. After removing the bill from the glass, you may (if you wish and are wealthy), ignite the bill for a moment to prove to the students that it will indeed burn.

Figure 8.7
Example of a discrepant event demonstration.

Instead of	Say
"How else might it be done?"	"How could you *apply* . . .?"
"Are you going to get quiet?"	"If we are going to hear what Joan has to say, what do you need to do?"
"How do you know that is so?"	"What evidence do you have?"
"What do you think might happen?"	"What do you *predict* might happen?"

Figure 8.8
Examples of questions that use cognitive terminology.

Question example for creating: *Compose a brief mini-book, poem, rap, sentences in alliteration, skit, song, artistic presentation, or another format to tell others what you learned during your gardening experience.*

You must use questions at the level best suited for the purpose, use a variety of questions at different levels, and structure questions in a way intended to move student thinking to higher levels. When teachers use higher-level questions, their students tend to score higher on tests of critical thinking and on standardized tests of achievement.[11]

With the use of questions as a strategy to move student thinking to higher levels, the teacher is facilitating the students' intellectual development. Developing your skill in using questions requires attention to detail and practice. The guidelines and exercises that follow in this chapter will provide that detail and some initial practice to check your comprehension of the levels of questions.

GUIDELINES FOR USING QUESTIONING

As emphasized many times in several ways throughout this resource guide, the goals for instruction extend far beyond merely filling students' minds with bits and pieces of information that will likely last only a brief time in their short-term memory. You must help your students learn how to solve problems, to make intelligent decisions, and value judgments, to think creatively and critically, and to feel good about themselves, their school community, and their learning. How you construct your questions and how you implement questioning is important to the realization of these goals.

Preparing Questions

When preparing questions, consider these two important tenets:

- Key questions should be planned, thoughtfully worded, and written into your lesson plan.
- Match questions with their target purposes.

Key Questions Should Be Planned, Thoughtfully Worded, and Written into Your Lesson Plan

Thoughtful preparation of questions helps to ensure that they are clear and specific, not ambiguous, that the vocabulary is appropriate for the children's understanding, and that each question matches its purpose. Incorporate questions into your lessons as instructional devices, welcomed pauses, attention grabbers, and as checks for student comprehension. Thoughtful teachers even plan questions that they intend to ask specific students, targeting questions to the readiness level, interest, or learning profile of a student.

Match Questions with Their Target Purposes

Carefully planned questions allow them to be sequenced and worded to match the levels of cognition expected of students. To help students in developing their thinking skills, you need to demonstrate how to do this. To demonstrate, you must use terminology that is specific and that provides students with examples of experiences consonant with the meanings of the cognitive words. Explicitly using cognitive terms with students—terms such as *apply, interpret,* and *predict*—encourages the construction of new mental concepts.[12] Again, refer to the examples in Figure 8.8.

Implementing Questioning

Careful preparation of questions is one part of the skill of questioning. Implementation is the other part. Figure 8.9 presents a checklist of teaching behaviors that you should reflect upon related to effective implementation of questioning.

QUESTIONS FROM STUDENTS: THE QUESTION-DRIVEN CLASSROOM

Student questions can and should be used as springboards for further questioning, discussions, and inquiry learning. Indeed, in a constructivist learning environment, student questions often drive content. Children should be encouraged to ask questions that challenge the textbook, the process, the Internet source, or other persons' statements, and they should be encouraged to seek the supporting evidence behind a statement.

Being able to ask questions may be more important than having the right answers. Knowledge is derived from asking questions. Being able to recognize problems and to formulate questions is a skill and the key to problem solving and critical-thinking skill development. You have a responsibility to encourage children in your classroom to formulate questions and to help them word their questions in such a way that tentative answers can be sought. That is the process necessary to build a base of knowledge that can be drawn upon whenever necessary to link, interpret, and explain new information in new situations.

Now, to better understand the art of questioning, the importance of well-worded questions, and well-prepared and clear instructions, and the importance of allowing students time to think (wait time), refer to Application Exercise 8.1.

Questioning: The Cornerstone of Critical Thinking, Real-World Problem Solving, and Meaningful Learning

Real-world problem solving usually offers no absolute correct answers. Rather than "correct" answers, some are

After implementing questioning in your teaching, respond and reflect on the following:

1. I always ask a well-worded question *before* calling on a student for a response.
   Always _____   Sometimes _____   Forgot _____
   My comments:

2. I avoid bombarding my students with too much teacher talk.
   Always _____   Sometimes _____   Forgot _____
   My comments:

3. Before I ask a question, I provide students with adequate time (wait time) to think.[13]
   Always _____   Sometimes _____   Forgot _____
   My comments:

4. I can give the same minimum amount of wait time (think time) to all students.
   Always _____   Sometimes _____   Forgot _____
   My comments:

5. I practice gender equity.*
   Always _____   Sometimes _____   Forgot _____
   My comments:

6. I practice calling on all students.
   Always _____   Sometimes _____   Forgot _____
   My comments:

7. I ask that the students raise their hands to be called on.
   Always _____   Sometimes _____   Forgot _____
   My comments:

8. I actively involve as many students as possible in any question–answer discussion session.
   Always _____   Sometimes _____   Forgot _____
   My comments:

9. I can carefully gauge my responses to students' responses to the questions.
   Always _____   Sometimes _____   Forgot _____
   My comments:

10. I use strong praise sparingly.
    Always _____   Sometimes _____   Forgot _____
    My comments:

---

*Some teachers use the term, *gender equality*, in the classroom with clear statements such as "I have just called on two boys—so to practice gender equality, I will call on a girl now." When a girl answers a question, the teacher can ask the student to call on a boy to answer the next question and vice versa, thus involving the students in efforts to include girls and boys equally.

Figure 8.9
A reflection list after implementing questioning.

better than others. The student with a problem needs to learn how to (a) recognize the problem, (b) formulate a question about the problem (e.g., Should I hang out with this person or not? Should I tell what I know or not? Should I join the gang or not? Should I use illegal drugs or not?), (c) collect data, and (d) arrive at a temporarily acceptable answer to the problem, while realizing that at some later time, new data may indicate a review of the former conclusion. For instance, if a biochemist believes that she has discovered a new enzyme, there is no textbook or teacher or any other outside authoritative source to which she may refer to find out if she is correct. Rather, on the basis of her self-confidence in problem identification, asking questions, collecting sufficient data, and arriving at a tentative conclusion based on those data, she assumes that, for now, her conclusion is safe.

Can You Encourage Students to Ask Questions About Content and Process?

Question asking often indicates that the inquirer is curious, puzzled, and uncertain; it is a sign of being engaged in thinking about a topic. And yet, in too many classrooms, too few students ask questions.[14] Students should be encouraged to ask questions. Actually, children are naturally curious and full of questions. Their natural curiosity should never be stifled. After all, we learn in school that what is called knowledge is in reality the answers to other peoples' prior questions.

From children, there is no such thing as a "dumb" question. Sometimes, though, in a classroom situation, students, like everyone else, ask questions that could just as easily have been looked up or are seemingly irrelevant or show lack of thought or sensitivity. Those questions can consume precious class time. For a teacher, they can be frustrating (but we remind you of an anonymous saying we've heard, "The fool wonders while the wise person asks.") A teacher's initial reaction may be to quickly and mistakenly brush off that type of question with sarcasm, while assuming that the student is too lazy to look up an answer. In such instances, you are advised to think before responding and to respond kindly and professionally, although in the busy life of a classroom teacher, that may not always be so easy to remember to do.

Some teachers keep blank slips of paper on their desks and when faced with such questions, they (sparingly) hand a blank slip to the student, ask the student to write the question down for their "teacher homework,"

and say they'll return the paper with their response to the student the next day (the paper is often returned at the end of the next day as the student leaves the classroom to allow for student reflection in the afternoon and evening). Other teachers ask the students to monitor themselves and their questions by considering if their questions are on track with the discussion. If a question is not, then the students are handed a "Hold That Thought" slip of paper (sometimes, small pieces of art paper) from a container or holder on the wall. The students write their questions on the paper slips, the teacher collects them, reads them, and answers them during the last five minutes of the class, or the end of the school day, or during a pause in the lesson.

Be assured, there is a reason for a student's question. It may be the student is signaling a need for recognition or simply demanding attention. In a large school, it is sometimes easy for a child to feel alone and insignificant (though this seems less the case with schools where teachers and students work together in teams, and, as in looping, where one cadre of teachers remains with the same cohort of children for two or more years).[15] When a child makes an effort to interact with you, this can be a positive sign, so gauge carefully your responses to these efforts. If a child's question is really off the topic, off the wall, out of order, and out of the context of the lesson, consider this as a possible response: "This is an involved question (or comment), and I would very much like to talk with you more about it. Could we talk at lunch or recess time?"

Will You Avoid Bluffing an Answer to a Question for Which You Do Not Have an Answer?

Nothing will cause you to lose credibility with children any faster than faking an answer. There is nothing wrong with admitting that you do not know. It helps children realize that you are human. It helps them maintain an adequate self-esteem, realizing that they are okay. What *is* important is that you know where and how to find possible answers and that you help children develop that same knowledge and those same process skills. There is nothing wrong in walking over to the desk, picking up a dictionary or encyclopedia, or searching Google later to model the process of searching for information that one does not readily have available. To reinforce your understanding of questioning, you can always refer to this chapter's Application Exercise 8.1.

APPLICATION EXERCISE 8.1

Practice in Raising Questions to Higher Levels

———————

Instructions: The purpose of this exercise is to develop your skill in raising questions from one level to the next higher level. Remove this perforated page and complete the blank spaces with questions at the appropriate levels. In cooperative groups, share your work and discuss your responses with your classmates.

Recall Level	Processing Level	Application and Evaluation Level
1. How many of you read a newspaper today?	Why did you read a newspaper today?	What do you think would happen if nobody ever read a newspaper again?
2. What was today's newspaper headline?	Why was that topic important enough to be a headline?	Do you think that news item will be in tomorrow's paper?
3. Who is the vice president of the United States?	How does the work the vice president has done compare with that done by the previous vice president?	
4. Has the United States had a woman president?		
5. (Create your own questions.)		

FOR YOUR NOTES

LOOKING AT TEACHERS II

Integrated Technology, Board, DVD

Consider: What might be done to improve instruction through the use of questions and teacher talk? With this in mind, think about the following classroom anecdote: At the completion of an opening reading lesson, Tara, a kindergarten teacher, asked the children, "Shall we do our math lesson now?" One of the children in the class, Mario, answered, "No, I don't like math." Ignoring Mario's response, Tara began the math lesson.

Could (or should) Tara have done anything differently here? What lesson, if any, did Mario learn from the teacher's response or lack of response? What do you believe was the intention of Tara's question? What was the lesson intended by Tara when she asked the question? Explain whether you believe the question was planned and written in Tara's lesson plan.

To integrate technology into this scenario, the teacher can consider the following:

- For group hands-on experience with math, the teacher could use an interactive whiteboard and connect it to a desktop computer and use a projector to show a math image from the computer on a screen or board. Using an electronic pointer, the teacher is able to highlight math images or write math notes or incorporate math graphics. As further interactions, students could match math problems and vocabulary words, visit websites that feature math, or arrange videoconferences with other classes to discuss math.

- For individual recognition, the teacher might mention that when a student finishes his or her regular assignment (and shows some improvement in academic work performance), the teacher will make arrangements for the student to work on a portable DVD player in the classroom (as a motivator). If appropriate, the student can give the teacher a report on the information gained from the DVD educational material. To aid in this, the teacher can give the student a teacher-constructed DVD information form for completion while watching the information. After interacting with the DVD material, the student hands the form back to the teacher so the teacher can review the student's notes to determine the educational value of what was learned at the DVD player.

SUMMARY

This chapter presented guidelines about formal and informal teacher talk and another significantly important teaching strategy, questioning—both of these are perhaps the two most important in your strategy repertoire. It's possible that no other strategy is used more by teachers than is teacher talk, and questioning is the cornerstone to meaningful learning, thinking, communication, and real-world problem solving. You reviewed the purposes for using questions, questions to avoid asking, and different types of cognitive questions. After the review, you practiced raising questions to higher levels. You realize that the art of the use of teacher talk and questioning as instructional devices and as learning tools is something you will continue to develop throughout your teaching career.

What's to Come. In the following two chapters, your attention is directed to the selection and implementation of specific instructional strategies to further facilitate students' meaningful learning of skills and content of the curriculum. For instance, you will see how teachers group children in the classroom. At the end of the next two chapters, you'll be asked to continue extending your competencies in the section Extending My Professional Competency, by discussion, observing a video, or through any of the other interactions that you select.

EXTENDING MY PROFESSIONAL COMPETENCY

With Discussion

Levels/Types of Questions. What would I reply if a teaching colleague asked, "Have you ever noticed that some teachers seem to anticipate a lower-level response to their questions from particular students? What do you think about that interaction? **To do:** Research HOTS (higher-order thinking skills) and the program's effectiveness by reading Stanley Pogrow's article "HOTS Revisited: A Thinking Development Approach to Reducing the Learning Gap After Grade 3" (*Phi Delta Kappan*, 87,(1), 64–75 (2005)) or his earlier writing, "HOTS: Helping Low Achievers in Grades 4-8" in *Principal* (November 1996 accessed 11/11/08 at www.hots.org/article_helping.html.) With your peers, discuss your thoughts about anticipating low-level responses from students to a teacher's questions.

With Video

Video Activity: Teacher Talk and Questioning. How would I explain to parents the importance of well-worded questions to students?

myeducationlab

Go to the Video Examples section of Topic #7: Strategies for Teaching in the MyEducationLab for your course to view the video entitled "Listening during Literature Read Aloud."

In the video, determine an example of questioning that shows raising questions from one level to the next or find an example of *not* raising questions from one level to another. In your example, you can point out any place where you think the teacher raised a question level or where the teacher missed an opportunity to raise a question level. You'll see a teacher read aloud *Mufaro's Beautiful Daughters* to the fourth-grade students and then ask questions to measure their listening skills. Give your example about raising the level of questions to a classmate and talk about it. Discuss your evaluation of the teacher's skill in using questions for instruction in this video.

With Portfolio

Portfolio Planning. How can I continue my professional portfolio and show my knowledge of teacher talk and questioning as effective instructional tools in connection with Principles 3, 4, and 5 of INTASC and Standards 2, 3, and 4 of NBPTS as seen on the inside of the front cover of this book? **To do:** To continue your portfolio, you can develop and write a one- to two-page paper describing your competency in determining when and how to use teacher talk and questioning for instruction. Label your paper Teacher Talk and Questioning. After reading and interacting with Chapter 8 in this text, you can summarize your point of view about one or two of this chapter's objectives in your paper:

- How I can use teacher talk for instruction in a brief lesson of my choice.
- How I can use at least two different types of advance mental organizers because I know their value and purpose as an instructional strategy.
- How I can identify at least three various levels/types of questions.
- Refer to the front of this chapter for other objectives.

Place your paper in your portfolio folder or in your computer file for future reference before taking a teacher test or going to a job interview.

With Teacher Tests Study Guide

Teacher Tests for Future Licensing and Certification. If I want to prepare for taking a state teacher test to qualify for my teaching certificate/license and study the area of effective teacher talk and questioning, how could I begin? **To do:** For this chapter, the constructed-response-type question, similar to those found on state tests for teacher licensing and certification, is found in Appendix A. The question helps you take another look at the classroom vignette *Looking at Teachers II*, in this chapter. Write your response and, if you wish, discuss it with another teaching candidate as one way to initiate changes in your response. If appropriate, use one or two of your colleague's suggestions to help you change your response to the question. Place your response in a Teacher Test Study Guide folder or type/scan into a computer file. Plan to review your response and reread it for study purposes before taking a teacher test.

With Target Topics for Teacher Tests (TTTT)

If I wanted a source to prepare for taking a state teacher test to qualify for licensing and certification, what could I use? **To do:** You'll recall that if you are preparing to take a teacher test, you can review subject matter by locating Target Topics for Teacher Tests in the subject index at the end of this book. The topics are called out with bullets (•) that are placed by selected word entries. The selected word entries identify core subject matter—teacher talk, questioning, and other topics—that the authors suggest reviewing to prepare for taking a teacher test exam for licensing and certification similar to your state's test.

WITH READING

Costa, A., and Garmston, R. (2001). Five Human Passions: The Source of Critical and Creative Thinking. In A. Costa (Ed.), *Developing Minds, a Resource Book for Teaching Thinking*. Alexandria, VA: Association for Supervision and Curriculum Development.

Cross, C. T., and Rigden, D. W. (2002). Improving Teacher Quality. *American School Board Journal, 189*(4), 24–27.

Davis, M. R. (2007). Whiteboards Inc. See www.edweek.org/dd/articles/2007/09/12/02board.h01.html.

Gauthier, L. R. (2000). The Role of Questioning: Beyond Comprehension's Front Door. *Reading Horizons, 40*(4), 239–252.

Good, T. L., and Brophy, J. E. (2003). *Looking in Classrooms* (9th ed., Chap. 9). New York: Addison Wesley/Longman.

Landers, D. M., Maxwell, W., Butler, J., and Fagen, L. (2001). Developing Thinking Skills through Physical Education. In A. Costa (Ed.), *Developing Minds: A Resource Book for Teaching Thinking*. Alexandria, VA: Association for Supervision and Curriculum Development.

Misco, T., and Castaneda, M. E. (2009). "Now, What Should I Do for English Language Learners?" Reconceptualizing Social Studies Design for ELLs. *Educational Horizons, 87*(3), 182–189.

National Association of State Directors of Teacher Education and Certification. (2000). *NASDTEC Manual 2000: Manual on the Preparation and Certification of Educational Personnel* (5th ed.). Dubuque, IA: Kendall/Hunt), Table E-2.

WITH NOTES

1. See D. P. Ausubel's classic work, *The Psychology of Meaningful Learning* (New York: Grune & Stratton, 1963).

2. T. L. Good and J. E. Brophy, *Looking in Classrooms*, 9th ed. (New York: Addison Wesley/Longman, 2003), pp. 252–253.

3. A. L. Costa, The Thought-Filled Curriculum, *Educational Leadership, 65*(5), 20–24 (2008).

4. T. Kwame-Ross, In Just a Minute: Teaching Students the Skills of Waiting, *Responsive Classroom, 15*, 1, 4–5 (2003). Studies in wait time were supported with the classic work of M. B. Rowe, Wait Time and Reward as Instructional Variables, Their Influence on Language, Logic and Fate Control: Part I. Wait Time, *Journal of Research in Science Teaching, 11*(2), 81–94 (1974).

5. D. Guan Eng Ho, Why Do Teachers Ask the Questions They Ask? *RELC Journal, 36*, 297–310 (2005); M. E. McIntosh and R. J. Draper, Using the Question-Answer Relationship Strategy to Improve Students' Reading of Mathematics Texts, *Clearing House, 69*(3), 154–152 (1996); see also T. C. Barrett's early work about 4 levels in Taxonomy of Reading Comprehension, in *Reading 360 Monograph* (Lexington, MA: Ginn, 1972).

6. Socratic questioning, which includes challenging assumptions, exposing contradictions, and responding to all questions with a further question, can be a performance assessment and is a main feature of Paideia schools. For information and a current listing of Paideia schools, contact the National Paideia Center, 140 Friday Center Drive, Chapel Hill, NC 27517; 919-962-3128, www.paideia.org.

7. Focus on the suggestions for middle school students in M. Copeland, *Socratic Circles: Fostering Critical and Creative Thinking in Middle and High School* (Portland, ME: Stenhouse Publications, 2005).

8. This three-tiered model of thinking has been described in different ways by other authorities. For a comparison of thinking models, see Costa, note 3.

9. J. Piaget's early writing, *The Development of Thought: Elaboration of Cognitive Structures* (New York: Viking, 1977) and J. Piaget and B. Inhelder's earlier classic, *The Psychology of the Child* (New York: Basic Books, 1969).

10. T. S. Smyth, Respect, Reciprocity, and Reflection in the Classroom: Gateways to Experience. *Kappa Delta Pi, 42*(1), 38–41 (Fall 2005).

11. L. W. Anderson and D. R. Krathwohl (Eds.), *A Taxonomy for Learning, Teaching, and Assessing: A Revision of Bloom's Taxonomy of Educational Objectives: Complete Edition* (New York: Longman, 2001), pp. 67–68.

12. See discourse about "How does being a constructivist make your teaching different from someone who is not a constructivist?" by E. G. Rozycki, Preparing Teachers for Public Schools: Just More Cannon Fodder? *Educational Horizons, 81*(3) (2003); also see articles in "Constructivist Suggestions," the issue theme in *Educational Horizons, 86*(3) (Spring 2008).

13. See Kwame-Ross, note 4.

14. Ideas for teaching and learning available from regional laboratories include Education Northwest formerly known as Northwest Regional Educational Laboratory, Portland, or retrieved from http://educationnorthwest.org/resources; R. Beltranena, *Leading School Improvement: What Research Says* (Atlanta, GA: Southern Regional Education Board, 2001); and School Size, School Climate, and Student Performance (Portland, OR; Northwest Regional Educational Laboratory) by K. Cotton, retrieved from www.apexsql.com/-brian/SchoolSizeMatters.pdf.

15. Our definition of a "large" elementary school is one with a population of 400 or more children. For more information about school size, see A. P. Barker, Making a Big School "Small," *Educational Leadership, 63*(8), 76–77 (May 2006); also E. W. Eisner, The Kind of Schools We Need, *Phi Delta Kappan, 84*, 579 (2002); and P. A. Ertmer, C. Hruskocy, and D. Woods, *The Worldwide Classroom: Access to People, Resources, and Curriculum Connections* (Upper Saddle River, NJ: Merrill/Prentice Hall, 2003).

9

What Guidelines Assist My Use of Demonstrations, Thinking, Inquiry Learning, and Games?

Visual Chapter Organizer and Overview

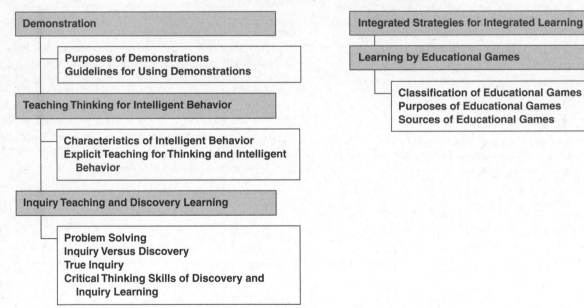

Demonstration

> Purposes of Demonstrations
> Guidelines for Using Demonstrations

Teaching Thinking for Intelligent Behavior

> Characteristics of Intelligent Behavior
> Explicit Teaching for Thinking and Intelligent
> Behavior

Inquiry Teaching and Discovery Learning

> Problem Solving
> Inquiry Versus Discovery
> True Inquiry
> Critical Thinking Skills of Discovery and
> Inquiry Learning

Integrated Strategies for Integrated Learning

Learning by Educational Games

> Classification of Educational Games
> Purposes of Educational Games
> Sources of Educational Games

LOOKING AT TEACHERS I

Integrated Technology, GenYES Clubs

In a school district on the West Coast, several middle schools have initiated GenYES (sounds like genius) clubs—groups where students learn technology and related troubleshooting skills and work one-to-one with teachers in their schools to help them integrate technology in their classes. In this way, GenYES students give tech support to tech-evasive and have-no-time teachers and help them become familiar with the classroom technology that they want/need. The GenYES program is available to all teachers. Teachers who are reluctant to use technology can request student help. The GenYES program also is available to all students—even low performers, disinterested students, at-risk students, and younger students. Students are trained and learn to use graphic design programs, video software, and hardware as needed.

As one example of student involvement, one teacher, an adult advisor of GenYES, assigned an indifferent student (grieving for her mother who had recently passed away and who disliked coming to school), to be a partner with an English teacher who was trying to help her students understand the Accelerated Readers' reading assignment process. After discussion, the student and the teacher decided that a video would be very helpful. To assist in this, the student learned to use a graphic design program and video software and created a video showing students how to check books out of the library and work through the assessments. The student's video was so successful that all English teachers began using it. With this success, the adult teacher-advisor noted that the GenYES student now had a reason to come to school. The student realized she was part of the GenYES team and was valued for her contribution.

To support GenYES clubs (no matter how small) in other schools, the teacher-advisor suggests the following:

- With school administration and staff support, appoint an adult teacher-advisor to monitor, recruit, and supervise the training of new members.
- Continually accept students into the club; let experienced students mentor new recruits (and accept even the younger students).
- Give students access to training, hardware, and software as needed for the teachers in the classrooms.
- Where possible, provide for long-term interest in later academic years in middle school or high school by making the GenYES club a credit-bearing independent study, a credit-bearing internship, a class that counts toward graduation, or a class that gives service-learning credits.[1]

A Focus on English Language Learners

Consider a planned infusion approach with students, such as those in a GenYES group, where important real-life topics relate and can be integrated into instruction (Rossman, 1983). This happens when the elementary school teachers are very aware of specific content that is being taught in their classrooms and can identify material that relates to the real-life topics of the students in the GenYES group. For instance, the skills needed in real life for a GenYES student who disliked coming to school can begin with a positive relationship with a teacher. In the example mentioned previously about the students' reading assignments, the GenYES student and the teacher decided that a video would be very helpful and the student created a video showing students how to check books out of the library and work through

assignments and assessments. The GenYES student's video was successful, which gave her a reason to come to school. Real-life skills, such as working together to create a successful video, could be integrated by an astute teacher into a language arts/reading lesson where the story's main idea is cooperation. A discussion can follow with questions such as, What are some ways you can say your feelings about _____? About concerns over _____? And how does this make you feel? In what ways have you cooperated with someone?

Just as the GenYES student and the English teacher provided tech assistance to the class, students also can accept assistance to study a topic in other ways that include using demonstrations, inquiry learning, and educational games. To be more specific, they can study underlying ideas as well as related knowledge from various disciplines—and what the disciplines have to offer—on an ongoing basis. This happens when students are involved in activities, lessons, and units, especially interdisciplinary thematic units. The teacher, sometimes with the help of students and other teachers and adults, introduces experiences designed to illustrate ideas and skills, just as the GenYES student introduced information in the video she designed about library skills and assessment skills.

In a related example, the teacher could introduce communication skills further through creative writing and other literacy projects. As a sample of creative writing, David Lubar's children's book *Punished!* (New York: Lerner, 2006) introduces students to puns. It gives students an example of a writer's creativity and shows the communication skills of the author. It explains language concepts and gives examples of related word play. It allows students to see problem solving and gives them a topic to consider further. It allows them to think of puns that they can share with others and encourages them to use their puns for oral and written presentations. It demonstrates self-reliance because it allows students to brainstorm possible ways to solve a problem and verify their predictions of problem solving. In this story, students learn that the main character, Logan, realizes that he was in the wrong when he played tag in the library and crashed into an elderly professor. Logan hears the professor say that he will be "pun"-ished and when the boy begins speaking in puns nonstop, he takes the professor's words seriously—that he has only three days to collect some oxymorons, anagrams, and palindromes or he'll speak puns forever. Logan becomes involved with inquiry learning and dictionary use, with demonstrations (but friends think he's just being "smart"), and with games of educational value (e.g., Scrabble). And to think, all of his problem solving began with a quick game of library tag.

CHAPTER OBJECTIVES

Specifically, upon completion of this chapter, you should be able to:

1. Discuss relationships among thinking, problem solving, inquiry learning, and discovery.
2. Describe characteristics of an effective demonstration and effective use of inquiry learning.
3. Analyze an inquiry learning lesson and text information about integrating strategies to form a

synthesis of information for use in your own teaching.

4. Create and demonstrate a brief lesson for a specific grade level or subject and ask your peers for narrative evaluations.
5. Compare/contrast the seven categories of games for learning.
6. Describe at least two ways of integrating strategies for integrated learning.

This chapter begins with a presentation of guidelines for using demonstrations as a vital instructional strategy. Other important strategies, namely, thinking, educational games, and inquiry learning and discovery, have additional guidelines. These instructional strategies can be integrated and combined to establish additional teaching-learning experiences for the students.

DEMONSTRATION

Children enjoy demonstrations because the demonstrator is actively engaged in a learning activity rather than merely verbalizing about it. Demonstrations can be used in teaching at any grade level for a variety of purposes. For example, during a social studies lesson, the teacher uses role play to demonstrate violation of First Amendment rights, and in a math lesson, a teacher presents the steps in solving a mathematical problem. As part of a language arts lesson, the teacher demonstrates ways to write attention-getting opening lines to students ready for a creative writing assignment, and during a science lesson, the teacher shows the effect of the absence of light on a plant leaf. Further, in a physical education session, the teacher demonstrates the proper way to serve in volleyball.

Purposes of Demonstrations

A demonstration can be designed to serve any of the following purposes that help give students an opportunity for vicarious participation in active learning: to introduce a lesson or unit of study in a way that grabs the students' attention; to review; to illustrate a particular point of content; to assist in recognizing a solution to an identified problem or to set up a discrepancy recognition; to demonstrate a skill, for example, thinking skills or conflict resolution skills; to reduce potential safety hazards; to save time and resources (as contrasted to the entire class doing that which is being demonstrated); and to bring an unusual closure to a lesson or unit of study.

Guidelines for Using Demonstrations

When planning a demonstration, you should consider the checklist shown in Figure 9.1. It allows a teacher to consider variables for safety, effectiveness, the audience, visibility, preparation, assembling needed objects, a teachable moment, Plan B when something goes wrong, and for pacing, closure, and detractors.

TEACHING THINKING FOR INTELLIGENT BEHAVIOR

Pulling together what has been learned about learning and brain functioning, teachers are encouraged to integrate explicit thinking instruction into daily lessons, to teach children the skills necessary for intelligent behavior.

A SPECIAL MOMENT IN TEACHING: ADVICE TO BEGINNING TEACHERS

We share with you this brief teaching vignette that we find to be both humorous and indicative of creative thinking. A sixth-grade teacher began a social studies lesson with the question, "What comes to mind when you hear the words 'Caesar' and 'Gladiator'?" Without hesitation, a rather quiet student voice from the back of the room answered, "Salad and a movie." To us, that represented one of those rare and precious moments in teaching, reaffirming our belief that every teacher is well advised to maintain throughout his or her teaching career a journal in which such intrinsically rewarding moments can be recorded so to be reviewed and enjoyed again years later.

1. I can decide on the most effective way to conduct the demonstration. I can consider these variables: Will it be a verbal or a silent demonstration? Will the demonstration be done by a student or by me? Will I have a student assistant helping me?

   Done _____   Somewhat done _____   To do _____

2. I can decide if the demonstration will be shown to a small group or to the whole group. Will the demonstration have some combination of these suggestions, such as, first, I will do the demonstration and second, it will be followed by a repeat of the demonstration by a student (or several students)?

   Done _____   Somewhat done _____   To do _____

3. I will be sure that the demonstration is visible to all students. I will consider the use of special lighting to highlight the demonstration. Students may need to move their seats for better vision.

   Done _____   Somewhat done _____   To do _____

4. I can set up a slide or overhead projector to be used as a spotlight or I can use an overhead projector when the materials of the demonstration are transparent, for example, clear plastic bowls of water.

   Done _____   Somewhat done _____   To do _____

5. I will practice with the materials and procedure before demonstrating to the students. During my practice, I will try to prepare for anything that could go wrong during the live demonstration; if I don't prepare, then as Murphy's Law says, if anything can go wrong, it will. But, if something does go wrong during the live demonstration, I can use that as an opportunity for a teachable moment.

   Done _____   Somewhat done _____   To do _____

6. I can engage the children in working with me to try to figure out what went wrong or if that isn't feasible, I can go to Plan B, which I have planned with the use of the aids and media resources mentioned throughout this text.

   Done _____   Somewhat done _____   To do _____

7. I will consider my pacing of the demonstration, and allow for enough student wait-see and thinking time. At the start of the demonstration, I will explain its purpose and the learning objectives. I will remember this adage: "I'll tell them what I am going to do, do it and show them, and then tell them what they saw."

   Done _____   Somewhat done _____   To do _____

8. As with any lesson, I'll plan my closure and allow time for questions and discussion. During the demonstration, I'll use frequent pauses to check for student understanding.

   Done _____   Somewhat done _____   To do _____

9. I'll be sure that the demonstration table and area are free of unnecessary objects that could distract or be in the way.

   Done _____   Somewhat done _____   To do _____

10. If the planned demonstration will pose a safety hazard to the children or to me, or both, then I won't do it. I will select a safe alternate demonstration.

    Done _____   Somewhat done _____   To do _____

Figure 9.1
Planning checklist for a demonstration.

Characteristics of Intelligent Behavior

Characteristics of intelligent behavior that you should model, teach for, and observe developing in your students, as identified by Costa,[2] are shown in Figure 9.2 and described in the subsequent paragraphs.

Applying Knowledge to New Situations

A major goal of formal education is for students to apply school-learned knowledge to real-life situations. To develop skills in drawing on past knowledge and applying that knowledge to new situations, children must be given opportunity to practice doing that very thing. Project-based learning (discussed in Chapter 10), problem recognition, and problem solving (discussed next in this chapter), are ways of providing that opportunity.

Cooperative Thinking and Social Intelligence

Humans are social beings. Real-world problem solving in our current social milieu has become so complex that

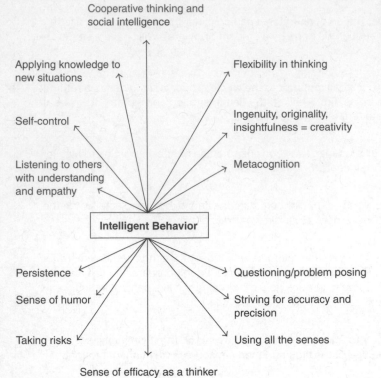

Figure 9.2
Characteristics of intelligent behavior.

seldom can any one person go it alone. Not all students come to school knowing how to work effectively in their classroom societal groups. They may exhibit competitiveness, narrow-mindedness, egocentrism, ethnocentrism, or criticism of others' values, emotions, and beliefs. Altruism, consensus seeking, giving up an idea to work on someone else's, integrating the ideas of others, knowing how to handle disagreements, knowing how to support group efforts, listening, and sharing—those are behaviors indicative of intelligent human beings, and they can be learned by children at school and in the classroom.

Self-Control

Impulsive behavior can create or worsen conflict and can inhibit effective problem solving.[3] In contrast, students with impulse control think before acting. Students can be taught to think before shouting out an answer, before beginning a task, and before arriving at conclusions with insufficient supporting information. As we have emphasized before in this resource guide (Chapters 4 and 8 and on our Companion Website), one reason teachers should usually insist on students raising their hands before a student is acknowledged to respond or to question, is to help students develop control over any impulsive behavior—including shouting out in class.[4]

Flexibility in Thinking

Sometimes called lateral thinking,[5] flexibility in thinking is the ability to approach a problem from a new angle, using a novel approach. With modeling by the teacher,

children can develop this behavior as they learn to consider alternative points of view and to deal with several sources of information simultaneously.

Ingenuity, Originality, Insightfulness = Creativity

All children should be encouraged to say "I can" and discouraged from saying "I can't." Students should be taught in such a way as to encourage intrinsic motivation rather than reliance on extrinsic sources. Teachers must be able to offer criticism/feedback so the student understands that the criticism is not a criticism of the student's self. In exemplary elementary school programs, children learn the value of feedback. They learn the value of their own intuition, of guessing, of risking—and as an integral part of this, they learn the value of "I can."

Listening to Others with Understanding and Empathy

Some psychologists believe that the ability to listen to others, to empathize with and to understand their point of view, is one of the highest forms of intelligent behavior. Empathic behavior is an important skill for conflict resolution. Piaget refers to this behavior as *overcoming egocentrism*. If appropriate, point out to students that in class meetings, brainstorming sessions, think tanks, town meetings, advisory councils, board meetings, and legislative bodies, people from various walks of life convene to share their thinking, to explore their ideas, and to broaden their perspectives by listening to and considering the ideas and reactions of others.

Metacognition

Metacognition (learning to plan, monitor, assess, and reflect on one's own thinking) is another characteristic of intelligent behavior. Cooperative learning groups, journals, portfolio conferences, self-assessment, and thinking aloud in dyads are strategies that can be used to help children develop this intelligent behavior.[6] Also, your thinking aloud is good modeling for your students and your modeling helps them develop their own cognitive skills of thinking, learning, and reasoning.[7]

Persistence

Persistence is the act of sticking to an idea or a task until it is completed. Here are some examples:

- *Thomas Edison.* Persistent in his efforts to invent the electric light bulb, Edison tried approximately three thousand filaments before finding one that worked.
- *Wilma Rudolf.* Because of childhood diseases, Rudolf, at age 10, could not walk without the aid of leg braces. Only ten years later, having won three gold medals in the 1960 World Olympics, she was declared to be the fastest running woman in the world.
- *Babe Ruth.* For years, Ruth was recognized for having not only the highest number of home runs in professional baseball, but also the highest number of strikeouts.
- *Margaret Sanger.* Nearly single-handedly and against formidable odds, Sanger founded the birth-control movement in the United States, beginning in 1914 with her founding of the National Birth Control League. In 1953, she was named the first president of the International Planned Parenthood Federation.

Questioning/Problem Posing

Children are usually full of questions, and unless discouraged, they do ask them. We want students to be alert to, and recognize, discrepancies and phenomena in their environment and to freely inquire about their causes. In exemplary school programs, students are encouraged to ask questions (see Chapter 8) and then use those questions as a basis from which they develop a problem-solving strategy to investigate their questions.

Sense of Efficacy as a Thinker

Wonderment, inquisitiveness, curiosity, and the enjoyment of problem solving all contribute to a sense of efficacy as a thinker. Young children express wonderment, an expression that should never be stifled. Through effective teaching, all students can recapture that sense of wonderment as a facilitating teacher guides them into a feeling of "I can" and into an expression of "I enjoy."

Sense of Humor

The positive effects of humor on the body's physiological functions are well established: a drop in the pulse rate, an increase of oxygen in the blood, the activation of antibodies that fight against harmful microorganisms, and the release of gamma interferon, a hormone that fights viruses and regulates cell growth. Humor liberates creativity and supports high-level thinking skills, such as anticipation, finding novel relationships, and visual imagery.[8] The acquisition of a sense of humor seems to follow a developmental sequence similar to that described by Piaget[9] and Kohlberg.[10] Initially, young children may find humor in all the wrong things—human frailty, ethnic humor, sacrilegious riddles, ribald profanities. Later, creative children thrive on finding incongruity and will demonstrate a whimsical frame of mind during problem solving. Remember, however, that to be most effective as a tool for teaching and learning, the humor used should not be self-degrading or offensive to anyone.

Striving for Accuracy and Precision

Teachers can observe children growing in this behavior when students take time to check over their work. Teachers observe students as they review procedures, avoid drawing conclusions prematurely, and use concise and descriptive language.

Taking Risks: Venturing Forth and Exploring Ideas beyond the Usual Zone of Comfort

Such exploration, of course, must be done with thoughtfulness; it must not be done in ways that could put the child at risk psychologically or physically. Using the analogy of a turtle going nowhere until it sticks its neck out, teachers should explain this behavior and provide opportunities for children to develop this intelligent behavior of risk taking by using techniques such as brainstorming strategies, divergent-thinking questioning, think–pair–share activity, cooperative learning, inquiry learning, and project-based learning.

Using All the Senses

As discussed previously in this and other chapters (especially Chapters 2 and 7), children should be encouraged to learn to use and develop all their sensory input channels—that is, the verbal, visual, tactile, and kinesthetic channels—for learning. We should strive to help our own students develop these characteristics of intelligent behavior. In Chapter 3, you learned about specific teacher behaviors that facilitate this development. Additionally, you probably recalled some of the specific teacher behaviors found in classroom interaction in Chapter 8. To continue, we ask you to take a look now at some additional research findings that offer important considerations in the facilitation of student learning and intelligent behavior.

Explicit Teaching for Thinking and Intelligent Behavior

The curriculum of any school includes the development of skills that are used in thinking, skills such as classifying, comparing, concluding, generalizing, inferring, and others. Because the academic achievement of children increases when they are taught thinking skills directly, many researchers and educators concur that explicit/direct instruction should be given to all children on how to think and behave intelligently.[11]

Several research perspectives have influenced today's interest in the direct/explicit teaching of thinking. One perspective is the cognitive view of intelligence that asserts that intellectual ability is not fixed but can be developed. A second perspective is the constructivist approach to learning that maintains that learners actively and independently construct knowledge by creating and coordinating relationships in their mental repertoire. Another perspective is the social psychology view of classroom experience that focuses on the learner as an individual who is a member of various peer groups in our society. Still another perspective that has influenced educators' interest in thinking about thinking relates to information processing and acquiring information, remembering, and problem solving.[12]

Rather than assuming that children have developed thinking skills, teachers should devote classroom time to teaching them explicitly/directly. When teaching a thinking skill directly, the subject content becomes the vehicle for thinking. For example, a teacher involved in a social studies lesson can teach children how to distinguish fact and opinion; a teacher guiding a language arts lesson instructs children how to compare and analyze; and a teacher leading a science lesson can teach children how to set up a problem for their inquiry.

Inquiry teaching and discovery learning are both useful tools for learning and for teaching thinking skills. For further insight and additional strategies, as well as for the many programs concerned with teaching thinking, see the resources in this chapter's footnotes and the list of readings at the end of this chapter.[13]

INQUIRY TEACHING AND DISCOVERY LEARNING

Intrinsic to the effectiveness of both inquiry and discovery is the assumption that students would rather actively seek knowledge than receive it through information delivery (i.e., traditional expository) methods such as demonstrations, lectures, and textbook reading. While inquiry teaching and discovery learning are important instructional tools, there is sometimes confusion about exactly what inquiry teaching is and how it differs from discovery learning. The distinction should become clear as you study the following description of these two important tools for teaching and learning.

Problem Solving

Perhaps a major reason why inquiry and discovery are sometimes confused is that, in both, students are actively engaged in problem solving. By *problem solving*, we mean the intellectual ability to accomplish the following: (a) recognize and define or describe a problem, (b) specify a desired or preferred outcome, (c) identify possible solutions, (d) select a procedure to resolve the problem, (e) apply the procedure, (f) evaluate outcomes, and (g) revise these steps where necessary.

Inquiry versus Discovery

Problem solving is *not* a teaching strategy but a high-order intellectual behavior that facilitates learning. What a teacher can do, and should do, is to provide opportunities for students to identify and tentatively solve problems. Experiences in inquiry and discovery can provide those opportunities. With the processes involved in inquiry and discovery, teachers can help students develop the skills necessary for effective problem solving. Two major differences between discovery and inquiry are (a) who recognizes and identifies the problem and (b) the percentage of decisions that are made by the students. Table 9.1 shows three levels of inquiry, each level defined according to what the student does and decides.

It should be evident from Table 9.1 that what is called *Level I inquiry* is actually traditional, didactic teaching, where both the problem and the process for resolving it are defined for the student. The student then works through the process to its inevitable resolution. If the process is well designed, the result is inevitable, because the student *discovers* what was intended by the writers of the program. This level is also called *guided inquiry* or *guided discovery*, because the students are carefully guided through the investigation to (the predictable) discovery.

Table 9.1 Levels of Inquiry

Skill	Level I	Level II	Level III
Problem identification	By teacher or textbook	By teacher or textbook	By student
Process of solving the problem	Decided by teacher or textbook	Decided by student	Decided by student
Identification of tentative solution	Resolved by student	Resolved by student	Resolved by student

Level I is, in reality, a strategy within the delivery mode, the advantages of which were described in Chapter 7. Because Level I inquiry learning is highly manageable and the learning outcome is predictable, it is probably best for teaching basic concepts and principles. However, students who never experience learning beyond Level I are missing an opportunity to engage their highest mental operations, and they seldom (or never) get to experience more motivating, real-life problem solving. Furthermore, those students may come away with the false notion that problem solving is a linear process, which it is not. As illustrated in Figures 9.3 and 9.4 about the inquiry cycle, true inquiry is cyclical rather than linear. For that reason, Level I is not true inquiry learning because it is a linear process. Real-world problem solving is a cyclical rather than a linear process. One enters the cycle whenever a discrepancy or problem is observed and recognized, and that can occur at any point in the cycle.

Figure 9.3
The inquiry cycle.

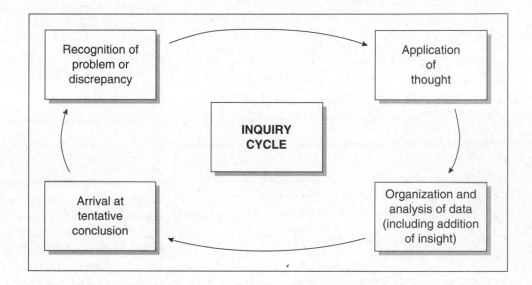

Figure 9.4
Inquiry cycle processes.

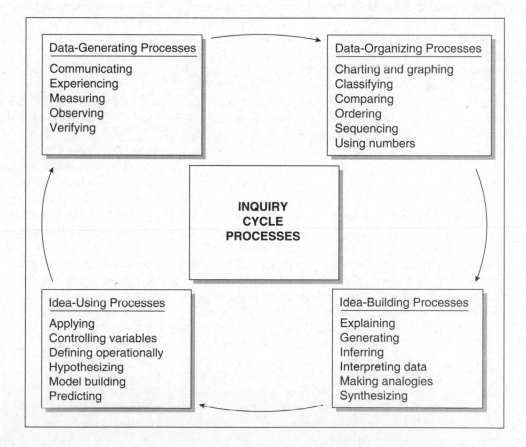

True Inquiry

By the time children are in the upper elementary school grades, they should be provided experiences for true inquiry learning, which begins with *Level II,* where students actually decide and design processes for their inquiry learning. True inquiry emphasizes the tentative nature of conclusions, which makes the activity more like real-life problem solving, in which decisions are always subject to revision if and when new data so prescribe.

At *Level III inquiry,* students recognize and identify the problem, decide the processes, and reach a conclusion. In project-centered learning, students are usually engaged at this level of inquiry learning. By the time students are in the middle grades, Level III inquiry should be a major strategy for instruction, which is often the case in schools that use cross-age teaching and interdisciplinary thematic instruction. But it is not easy: like most good teaching practices, it is a lot of work. But also like good teaching in general, the intrinsic rewards make the effort worthwhile. As exclaimed by one teacher using interdisciplinary thematic instruction with student-centered inquiry, "I've never worked harder in my life, but I've never had this much fun, either."

Critical Thinking Skills of Discovery and Inquiry Learning

In true inquiry, students generate ideas and then design ways to test those ideas. The various processes used represent the many critical thinking skills. Some of those skills are concerned with generating and organizing data; others are concerned with building and using ideas. Figure 9.4 provides four categories of thinking processes and illustrates the place of each within the inquiry cycle. You'll notice that some processes in the cycle are discovery processes and others are inquiry processes. Inquiry processes include the more-complex mental operations, including all those in the idea-using category. Project-based learning provides an avenue for doing that, as does problem-centered teaching.

Inquiry learning is a higher-level mental operation that introduces the concept of the discrepant event, something that establishes cognitive disequilibrium (using the element of surprise to challenge prior notions) to help students develop skills in observing and being alert for discrepancies. Such a strategy provides opportunities for students to investigate their own ideas about explanations. Inquiry, like discovery, depends upon skill in problem solving; the difference between the two is in the amount of decision-making responsibility given to students. Experiences afforded by inquiry help students understand the importance of suspending judgment and also the tentativeness of answers and solutions. With those understandings, students eventually can better deal with life's ambiguities. When children are not provided these important educational experiences, their education is incomplete.

One of the most effective ways of stimulating inquiry learning is to use materials that provoke students' interest. These materials should be presented in a nonthreatening, noncompetitive context, so students can think laterally and hypothesize openly and freely. Your role as the teacher is to encourage the students to form as many hypotheses as possible and then support their hypotheses with reasons. After the students suggest several ideas, your role is to move on to higher-order, more abstract, questions that involve the development of generalizations and evaluations.

We want to point out that true inquiry problems have a special advantage in that they can be used with almost any group of students. Members of a group can approach the problem as an adventure in thinking and apply it to whatever background they can muster. Background experience may enrich a student's approach to the problem, but it is not crucial to the use or understanding of the evidence presented to the student. As an example, Locating an Early Settlement Community Farm (Figure 9.5) is a Level II inquiry learning situation. With the members of your group, follow the instructions of that inquiry if you want to see how this inquiry learning was organized for small groups of students. To extend the idea of farmers seeking fertile, workable land as a criteria in this inquiry learning situation, discuss the example of a thinking process map about farm crops shown in Figure 9.6. What, if anything, would you and the students add to the map about farm crops?

INTEGRATED STRATEGIES FOR INTEGRATED LEARNING

In today's exemplary elementary school classrooms, instructional strategies are combined to establish the most effective teaching-learning experience. For example, in an integrated language arts program, a teacher is interested in his or her students' speaking, reading, listening, thinking, study, and writing skills. These skills (and not textbooks) form a holistic process that is the primary aspect of integrated language arts. In the area of speaking skills, oral discourse (discussion) in the classroom has a growing research base that promotes methods of teaching and learning through oral language. These methods include cooperative learning, instructional scaffolding, and inquiry teaching.

In cooperative learning groups, students discuss and use language in a way that benefits both their content learning and skills in social interaction. Working in heterogeneous groups, students participate in their own learning and can extend their knowledge base and

Presentation of the Problem: Locating a Community Farm

Give the following information to students as they get ready to work in groups of four or five.

What you Need to Know: Background

As a member of an early settlement in your present-day area, you must decide, with others, where the community farm is to be located. Some in your community want to farm near the closest water in your area. Others want to farm on the richest, most workable land. Still others want a farm in a location that can be defended from thieves and invaders.

Directions: Steps to Take

First: Members of your group are to select a location on a map of your area that you feel is best suited for a community farm. Your choice of location needs to satisfy the different views (that is, the criteria stated in the background) in your settlement. On the map of your area, select your town or city as the site of your settlement. (For example, if you live in Sacramento, rename your settlement the Sacramento Colony, Fort Sacramento, or another name your group chooses.) Study the map showing your settlement's area to discuss the possible locations for the community farm. Is the location near water? Does it have rich, workable land? Is it in a location that can be defended? When your group has selected the farm site, list and explain at least three reasons for your choice. When each group has arrived at its decision, get ready to share the decision with the whole class.

Second: After each group makes its presentation with reasons for the choice of the site, arrange needed materials for a whole-class debate. Show a transparency of the map of your area on an overhead projector (or on computer projection or draw a map outline on the whiteboard or poster or on a chalkboard). Let a volunteer in each group mark the farm's site they selected. Discuss pros and cons of each site. Then, take a secret student vote (one student, one vote) to determine a single favorite location. If the majority of the students favor one location, then that is the solution to the problem of locating a community farm.

To the Teacher: Further Discussion

Encourage a discussion with students that can include the point of view that there are no completely right answers in real-world problems—but some answers may seem better than others. Emphasize that (a) working together in problem solving is important to reach an answer, (b) having confidence in one's abilities to solve problems is essential, (c) understanding some answers to problems may be tentative and this understanding will make it easier for us to accept an answer we didn't select, and (d) we need to realize that the answer may have to be changed in the future.

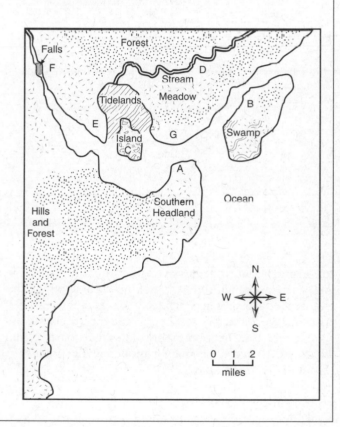

Figure 9.5
Locating an early settlement community farm: A Level II inquiry.

cultural awareness with students of different backgrounds. When students share information and ideas, they are completing difficult learning tasks, using divergent thinking and decision making, and developing their understanding of concepts—all part of their instructional scaffolding. As issues are presented and responses are challenged, student thinking is clarified. Students assume the responsibility for planning within the group and for carrying out their assignments. When needed, the teacher models an activity with one group in front of the class, and when integrated with student questions, the modeling can become inquiry teaching. Activities can include any from a variety of heuristics (a heuristic is a tool used in solving a problem or understanding an idea), such as those discussed next.

Brainstorming

Students generate ideas related to a key word/concept and record them. Clustering (or chunking), mapping, and a Venn diagram are variations of brainstorming. All

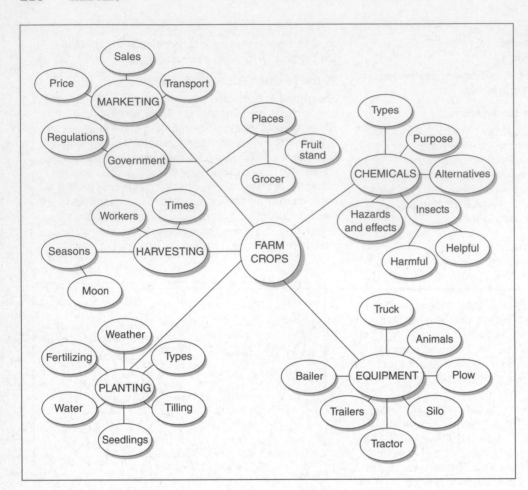

Figure 9.6
Thinking process map
about farm crops.

are instructional strategies used to create a flow of new ideas, during which *judgments* of the ideas of others are not needed and not acceptable. Students orally respond to a question and the teacher, a student, or classroom aide writes their responses on the white board, chalk board, chart, or transparency without making judgments about the responses.

Comparing and Contrasting

Similarities and differences among items are found and recorded. Comparing and contrasting are considered parts of the intermediate level of questioning, that is, drawing relationships of cause and effect, to synthesize, to analyze, to summarize, and to classify data.

Chunking or Clustering

Groups of students apply mental organizers by clustering information into chunks for easier manipulation and remembering. An aid to introducing clustering is a graphic organizer similar to the one shown in Figure 9.6. This is where students write down in a graphic format (or in a list) their ideas about a topic before (or after) discussing it or writing about it. As an example of an aid to introducing chunking, consider the book *There's an*

Ant in Anthony (New York: HarperCollins, 1992) by B. Most. In the story, a boy learns to spell his name when he finds a word chunk, *ant*, in Anthony.

Memory Strategies

The teacher and students model the use of acronyms, mnemonics, rhymes, or the clustering of information into categories to promote learning. Sometimes, such as in memorizing one's Social Security number, one must learn by rote information that is not connected to any prior information. To do that, it is helpful to break the information to be learned into smaller chunks, such as dividing the nine-digit Social Security number into smaller chunks of information (in this instance, with each chunk separated by a hyphen). Learning by rote is also easier if one can connect that which is to be memorized to some prior knowledge. Strategies such as these are used to bridge the gap between rote learning and meaningful learning and are known as mnemonics.[14] Sample mnemonics are:

- The ABCDs of writing instructional objectives (see Chapter 5), and CASE for using classroom bulletin boards

- The notes on a treble staff are FACE for the space notes and EGBDF (Empty Garbage Before Dad Flips or Every Good Boy Deserves Fudge) for the line notes. The notes on the lower staff are All Cows Eat Granola Bars and Grizzly Bears Don't Fly Airplanes).
- The order of the planets from the Sun can be remembered by My Very Educated Mother Just Served Us Nuts (Mercury, Venus, Earth, Mars, Jupiter, Saturn, Uranus, and Neptune).
- The names of the Great Lakes: HOMES for Huron, Ontario, Michigan, Erie, and Superior.
- To recall multiplication tables or grammar rules, consider singing songs as a memory strategy; for example, the words of "The Farmer in the Dell" can be different and instead of "the farmer takes a wife" the words can be "two times two are four, two times two are four, hi, ho, the derry-o, two times two are four."
- To recall the order of operations when solving algebraic equations, remember **P**lease (parentheses) **E**xcuse (exponents) **M**y (multiply) **D**ear (divide) **A**unt (add) **S**ally (subtract).

Think–Pair–Share

Students, in pairs, examine a new topic or concept about to be studied. They discuss what they already know or think they know about the concept and present their perceptions to the whole group. (Refer to Chapters 5 and 10.)

Visual Tools

A variety of terms for the visual tools useful for learning have been invented—some of which are synonymous—terms such as brainstorming web, mind-mapping web, spider map, cluster map or graphic, cognitive map, generalization map, idea map, mental image map, opinion map, semantic map, thought map, Venn diagram, visual scaffold, graphic organizers, and concept map.[15] Hyerle's early work separates these visual tools into three categories according to purpose: (a) brainstorming tools (such as mind-mapping, webbing, and clustering) for the purpose of developing one's knowledge and creativity; (b) task-specific organizers (such as life-cycle diagrams used in biology, decision trees used in mathematics, and text structures used in reading); and (c) thinking process maps (such as visual mapping) for encouraging cognitive development across disciplines.[16] It is the latter with which we are interested here. Some teachers use the computer program *Inspiration* to create graphic organizers.

Based on Ausubel's theory of meaningful learning,[17] thinking process mapping has been found useful for helping learners in changing prior notions—their misconceptions, sometimes referred to as naive views. It can help students in their ability to organize and represent their thoughts, as well as help them connect new knowledge to their past experiences and precepts.[18] Simply put, concepts can be thought of as classifications that attempt to organize the world of objects and events into a smaller number of categories. In everyday usage, the term **concept** means *idea*, as when someone says, "My concept of love is not the same as yours." Concepts embody a meaning that develops in complexity with experience and learning over time. For example, the concept of love that is held by a second-grader is unlikely to be as complex as that held by the child's teacher. Thinking process mapping is a graphical way of demonstrating the relationship between and among concepts.

Typically, a thinking process map refers to a visual or graphic representation of concepts with bridges (connections) that show relationships. Figure 9.6 shows a thinking process map where students have made connections of concept relationships between fruit orchards, farming, and marketing. The typical procedure for thinking process mapping is to have the students (a) identify important concepts in materials being studied, often by circling those concepts, (b) rank order the concepts from the most general to the most specific, and (c) arrange the concepts on a sheet of paper, connect related ideas with lines, and define the connections between the related ideas. For young children, pictures may be used in each of the circles rather than words. Meaningful learning can occur in other ways, also, as discussed next.

Inferring

For instance, students assume the roles of people (real or fictional) and infer their motives, personalities, and thoughts.

Multiple Sources

Students use multiple texts to demonstrate the interpretive nature of historical events.[19] This use is also called using text sets.

Outlining

Each group of students completes an outline that contains some of the main ideas but has the subtopics omitted.

Paraphrasing

In a brief summary, each student restates a short selection of what was read or heard.

Reciprocal Teaching

In classroom dialogue, students take turns at generating questions, summarizing, clarifying, and predicting.[20]

Study Strategies

Important strategies that should be taught explicitly include vocabulary expansion, reading, and interpreting graphic information, locating resources, using advance organizers, adjusting one's reading rate, and skimming, scanning, and study reading.[21]

Textbook Study Strategies

Students use the SQ4R approach or related study strategies (see Chapter 5).

Vee Mapping

This is a road map completed by the students as they learn to show the route they follow from prior knowledge to new and future knowledge.

Venn Diagramming

This is a technique for comparing two concepts, or, for example, two countries, two stories, two personas, to show similarities and differences. Using stories as an example, a student is asked to draw two circles that intersect and to mark the circles *one* and *two*, and the area where they intersect *three*. In circle one, the students lists the characteristics of one story, and in circle two, they list the characteristics of the second story. In the area of the intersection, marked three, the students list characteristics common to both stories.

Visual Learning Log (VLL)

This variation of the road map is completed by the students showing the route they follow from prior knowledge to new and future knowledge, except that the VLL consists of pictograms (free-form drawings) that each student makes and that are maintained in a journal. To review inquiry teaching and integrated learning, return to Figure 9.5.

LEARNING BY EDUCATIONAL GAMES

Devices classified as educational games include a wide variety of learning activities, such as simulations, role play, sociodrama activities, mind games, board games, computer games, and other types, all of which provide valuable learning experiences for participants. These experiences tend to involve several senses and involve several learning modalities to engage higher-order thinking skills and to be quite effective as learning tools.

Of all the arts, drama involves the learner-participant most fully—intellectually, emotionally, physically, verbally, and socially. Interactive drama, a form of role playing, is a simplified form of drama. This is a method by which children can become involved with literature. Studies show that children's comprehension increases and they are highly motivated to read if they are involved in analyzing and actively responding to the characters, plot, and setting of the story being read.[22]

Simulations, a more complex form of drama, serve many of the developmental needs of children. They provide for interaction with peers and allow children of different backgrounds and talents to cooperatively work on a common project. They engage children in physical activity and give them opportunity to try out different roles, which help them to better understand themselves. Simulations also can provide concrete experiences that help children to understand complex concepts and issues, and they provide opportunities for exploring values and developing skill in decision making.[23]

Simulated real-world experiences for use in grades K–8 are available in a program called MicroSociety. This program gives children authentic economic experiences and is used in more than 200 schools in at least 40 states. In collaboration with parents and guardians, community members, and teachers, students build a miniature community in the school, and establish a center of commerce and governance where they earn wages, pay taxes, resolve issues in court, and operate businesses.[24]

Classification of Educational Games

What are educational games? Six types of games fall under the general heading of educational games. Table 9.2 shows the six types, with characteristics and examples of each. Certain types have greater educational value than do others. Games that do not emphasize the element of competition—that are not contests—are particularly recommended for use in the academic classroom (see types 1, 3, and 5 in Table 9.2).

Purposes of Educational Games

Educational games can play an integral role in interdisciplinary teaching and serve as valuable resources for enriching the effectiveness of students' learning. As with any other instructional strategy, the use of games should follow a clear educational purpose, have a careful plan, and be congruent with your school's instructional objectives and the stated mission.

Games can be powerful tools for teaching and learning. A game can serve one or more of the purposes shown in Figure 9.7. Since we trust you are familiar with several games, take a few minutes, recall *one* of your favorites, and write in *one* example for *one* purpose that you select.

Sources of Educational Games

Sources for useful educational games include teacher-created materials, publishers, and journals (see Figure 9.8). Next, turn your attention to the end of this chapter and do Application Exercise 9.1.

Purposes: Recall one of your favorites for each.

(a) add change of pace   Favorite example:

(b) assess student learning   Favorite example:

(c) teach content   Favorite example:

(d) offer opportunity for deductive thinking   Favorite example:

(e) enhance student self-esteem   Favorite example:

(f) focus on process   Favorite example:

(g) provide experiences   Favorite example:

(h) help reinforce convergent thinking   Favorite example:

(i) introduce skill development and motivation through media usage   Favorite example:

(j) provide skill development in inductive thinking   Favorite example:

(k) use of kinesthetic and tactile modality   Favorite example:

(l) learning through skill development in verbal communication and debate   Favorite example:

(m) motivate students   Favorite example:

(n) encourage learning through peer interaction   Favorite example:

(o) offer a break from the usual rigors of learning   Favorite example:

(p) provide problem-solving situations   Favorite example:

(q) offer questioning opportunity   Favorite example:

(r) reinforce real-life issues through simulation and role-playing   Favorite example:

(s) review selected subject matter   Favorite example:

(t) offer divergent and creative thinking   Favorite example:

(u) use of computer   Favorite example:

(v) offer variety   Favorite example:

(w) offer wait time for critical thinking   Favorite example:

(x) can introduce new and (perhaps unfamilar) vocabulary—i.e., *xebec* (Mediterranean vessel with three masts and long bow and stern), *xylem* (a complex tissue in higher plants; woody tissue), and *xylophone* (a percussion instrument)   Favorite example:

(y) yield results of students' time and efforts   Favorite example:

(z) add zip/vigor to gaining information with a brisk, snappy game   Favorite example:

Figure 9.7
Educational games: ABCs of purposes.*

*For grades 5–6 and up, you can consider some updated board games (2008) that encourage critical thinking and support instruction: *Amun-Re* (Rio Grande Games) for concepts of an ancient civilization; *Oregon* (Rio Grande Games) for westward expansion integrated with math coordinates; *Pandemic* (Z-Man Games) for cooperative work, inquiry; *Shadows over Camelot* (Days of Wonder) for teamwork with Knights of the Round Table; and *10 Days In* (Out of the Box) for geography knowledge as students chart courses across the United States and other areas.

Table 9.2 Classification of Educational Games

Type	Characteristics and Examples
1. Pure game*	Fun *Ungame, New Games*
2. Pure content	Stimulates competition; built-in-inefficiency** *Political Contests*
3. Pure simulation*	Models reality in *Toddler Play;* Kingdom's conflicts resolved in nonviolent ways in *Princes' Kingdom.* Reinforces literacy concepts through experiences traveling the Underground Railroad; See www2.scholastic.com/browse/lessonplan.jsp?id=887
4. Content/game	Stimulates competition; fun; built-in inefficiency *Golf**, Trivial Pursuit;* Teaches grammar use in *Hammer the Grammar,* www.hammerthegrammar.com
5. Simulation/game*	Models reality; fun *Puritan Day: A Social Science Simulation*
6. Contest/simulation	Stimulates competition, models reality, built-in inefficiency *Boxcar Derby* of Akron, OH
7. Simulation/game	Models reality; fun, stimulates competition; sometimes built-in inefficiency *Monopoly, Life, Careers*

* These game types do not emphasize competition and thus are particularly recommended for use in the classroom as learning tools. Note that *Princes' Kingdom* is available from http://crngames.com/the_princes_kingdom/ and *Puritan Day: A Social Science Simulation* is attributed to J. B. Schur, *Social Education, 71*(7), 348–353 (2007).

** Rules for accomplishing the game objective make accomplishment of that objective less than efficient. For example, in golf, the objective is to get the ball into the hole with the least amount of effort, but to do that, one has to take a peculiarly shaped stick (the club) and hit the ball, find it, and hit it again, continuing that sequence until the ball is in the hole. Yet, common sense tells us that the best way to get the ball into the hole with the least amount of effort would be simply to pick up the ball and place it by hand into the hole.

Ampersand Press, 750 Lake St., Port Townsend, WA 98368; *www.ampersandpress.com*

Aristoplay, 8122 Main Street, Dexter, MI 48130; 800-634-7738; *www.aristoplay.com*

Carolina Biological Supply Company, P.O. Box 6010, Burlington, NC 27216; 800-334-5551; *www.carolina.com*

Creative Teaching Associates, 5629 E. Westover Ave., Fresno, CA 93727; 800-767-4282

Dawn Publications, 12402 Bitney Springs Road, Nevada City, CA 95959; 800-545-7475; *www.dawnpub.com*

Education Place, *www.eduplace.com/edugames.html*

Fun Brain, *www.funbrain.com*

Harcourt School Publishers, 6277 Sea Harbor Dr., Orlando, FL 32887; 800-225-5425; *www.harcourtschool.com*

Leapfrog, 6401 Hollis St., Suite 100, Emeryville, CA 94608-1071; 510-596-3333; *www.leapfrog.com*

Nobel Prize Educational Games, *http://nobelprize.org/educational_games/*

Other Worlds Educational Enterprises, P.O. Box 6193, Woodland Park, CO 80866-6193; 719-687-3840; *www.otherworlds-edu.com*

Summit Learning, 755 Rockwell Ave., P.O. Box 755, Fort Atkinson, WI 53538-0755; 800-777-8817; *www.summitlearning.com*

Teacher Created Materials, 5301 Oceanus Dr., Huntington Beach, CA 92649; 800-858-7339; *www.teachercreatedmaterials.com*

Young Naturalist Company, 717 42nd St., West, Des Moines, IA 50265; 515-745-4942; *www.youngnaturalistcompany.com*

References for Current Board Games

    BoardGameGeek, online catalog; *www.boardgamegeek.com*

    Games for Educators, information, reviews; *www.gamesforeducators.com*

Figure 9.8
Sources and references of educational games.

APPLICATION EXERCISE 9.1

Developing a Lesson Using Different Approaches: Inquiry
Learning Level II, Thinking Skill Development, a Demonstration,
or an Interactive Lecture—Peer Teaching

Instructions: The purpose of this application exercise is to provide an opportunity for you to create a brief lesson (about 20 minutes of instructional time [actual time to be specified by your instructor] designed for a specific grade level and subject). You will try it out on your peers for their feedback in a cooperative, collaborative, informal peer teaching demonstration. Join your colleagues in one of four groups. Your task, along with the other members of your group, is to prepare lessons individually that fall into one of four categories: (a) Level II inquiry, (b) thinking level, (c) demonstration, or (d) interactive lecture. To structure your lesson plan, use one of the sample lesson plan formats presented in Chapter 7; however, each lesson should be centered around one major theme or concept and be planned for the specified amount of instruction time.

Group 1: Each develops a Level II inquiry lesson.

Group 2: Each develops a lesson designed to raise the level of student thinking.

Group 3: Each develops a lesson that involves a demonstration.

Group 4: Each develops a lesson that is an interactive lecture.

Other Responsibilities:

1. Help schedule your lessons as class presentations so that each member has the opportunity to present his or her lesson and receive feedback.

2. Review the following scoring rubric with your whole group and, if needed, make modifications to it with the class's input.

3. Be sure that each presenter/teacher obtains *your* feedback on the assessment rubric about the lesson after the lesson (make the number of copies that you will need). For feedback, as part of the audience for the presenter/teacher, you can complete the assessment rubric shown by circling one of the three choices for each of the 10 categories. You should give your completed form to each presenter/teacher for his or her use in self-assessment and analysis.

Peer and Self-Assessment Rubric for Use with Application Exercise 9.1

For: Group:

	1	0.5	0
1. Lesson beginning	effective	less effective	not effective
Comment:			
2. Sequencing	effective	less effective	rambling
Comment:			
3. Pacing of lesson	effective	less effective	too slow or too fast
Comment:			
4. Audience involvement	effective	less effective	none
Comment:			
5. Motivators (e.g., analogies, verbal cues, humor, visual cues, sensory cues)			
Comment:	effective	less effective	not apparent
6. Content of lesson	well chosen	interesting	boring or inappropriate
Comment:			
7. Voice of teacher	stimulating	minor problem	major problems
Comment:			
8. Vocabulary used	well chosen	appropriate	inappropriate
Comment:			
9. Eye contact	excellent	average	problems
Comment:			
10. Closure	effective	less effective	unclear/none
Comment:			

OTHER COMMENTS:

LOOKING AT TEACHERS II

Integrated Technology, Computer Searches

A teacher's sixth-grade class considered the fact-finding and decision-making approach of public officials in one state when confronted with the task of making decisions about projects proposed for watersheds in their state. The students knew that while gathering information, the officials consulted with a state hydrologist. The hydrologist led the officials into the field to demonstrate specific ways that efforts had helped control erosion and rehabilitate damaged streams. The officials were escorted by the hydrologist to a natural creek, where they donned high waders and were led down the stream to examine various features of that complex natural stream. The hydrologist pointed out evidence of the creek's past meanders, patterns that had been incorporated into rehabilitation projects. In addition to listening to this scientist's point of view, the public officials listened to other experts to consider related economic and political issues before making final decisions about projects that had been proposed for watersheds in that state.

- The students integrated technology: To study as the state public officials did, the students studied erosion and its underlying ideas as well as related knowledge from various disciplines with computer searches—for example, How can our experience with erosion help us understand how people live (anthropology)? How

has geography influenced erosion? How has erosion study changed over time in America (history)? The students got involved in other disciplines through daily lessons in an interdisciplinary thematic unit about—for example, erosion, What work in the economy, done by people we know, is related to erosion (economics)? How can we express what we know about erosion through math (mathematics)? How have scientists from diverse heritages contributed to our knowledge of erosion (science)? How have people organized themselves to provide information about erosion (political science)? In what way can we participate to resolve a real problem related to erosion (sociology)?

- The teacher integrated technology with a flat-screen monitor and a desktop panel that projected the questions about disciplines on a screen. Using a stylus, the teacher (or a student) drew on an overlay and recorded responses, notes, ideas, and drawings on the screen for the students to see and discuss. Just on the public officials worked toward an integrated view of their project by accepting the hydrologist-introduced information along with views from economic and political experts, the teacher guided the students in accepting data from different disciplines and integrating their knowledge about erosion.

SUMMARY

Central to your selection of instructional strategies should be those strategies that encourage students to become independent thinkers and skilled learners who can help in the planning, structuring, regulating, and assessing of their own learning and learning activities. Important to helping students construct their understanding are the cognitive tools that are available for their use. You have considered the selection and implementation of specific instructional strategies to facilitate students' meaningful learning of skills and content of the curriculum. Additionally, there are many useful and effective aids, media, and resources in this guide from which to draw as you plan your instructional experiences.

What's to Come. In Chapter 10, your attention is directed to how teachers group children in the classroom and provide learning from assignments. You'll review equality in the classroom along with different grouping arrangements.

EXTENDING MY PROFESSIONAL COMPETENCY

With Discussion

Educational Games for Learning. What will I say if a parent expresses his or her concern about games and does not approve of the use of educational games for learning in the classroom? **To do:** Research the cautions that teachers need to be aware of when using educational games for teaching and learning. If there are some cautions that you identify, explain to a colleague what you would say to the parent who is concerned about this issue.

With Video

Video Activity: Use of Demonstrations, Inquiry Learning, and Games. How can I explain how I would use inquiry learning to a colleague? View the video with a colleague and take notes about the following: (a) the problem-based learning simulation you see, (b) inquiry learning as a process, and (c) activities of the students, (i.e., investigating, questioning, and responding based on the students' own experiences).

myeducationlab

Go to the Video Examples section of Topic #11: Inquiry Models in the MyEducationLab for your course to view the video entitled "Inquiry Learning."

View the video again if needed. If time permits, discuss your notes with a colleague and form an explanation of how you would use inquiry learning in your teaching.

With Portfolio

Portfolio Planning. How can I further develop my professional portfolio and show my knowledge of using demonstrations, inquiry learning, and educational games? This activity will support Principles 4 and 5 of INTASC and Standards 1, 3, and 5 of NBPTS and Praxis II teacher test content (as seen on the inside of the front cover of this book). **To do:** To continue your portfolio, you can develop and write a one- to two-page paper explaining your knowledge of using demonstrations, inquiry learning, and educational games. Label your paper Demonstrations, etc. After reading and interacting with this chapter, you can state how you have developed your competency in one or two of this chapter's objectives:

- I can state one or two relationships among thinking, problem solving, inquiry learning, and discovery.
- I can list at least three characteristics of an effective demonstration and effective use of inquiry learning.
- I can analyze an inquiry learning lesson (and text information about integrating strategies) to get information to use in my own teaching.
- Please return to the front of this chapter for the rest of the objectives. Place your paper in your portfolio folder or in your computer file. Go to www.MyEducationalLab.com/general methods to find portfolio templates.

With Teacher Tests Study Guide

Teacher Tests for Future Licensing and Certification. If I wanted to prepare for taking a state teacher test to qualify for my teaching certificate/license, how could I begin? **To do:** For this chapter, the constructed-response-type question similar to those found on state tests for teacher licensing and certification is found in Appendix A. The question helps you take another look at the classroom vignette found in the *Looking at Teachers II* section at the end of this chapter. Write your response and, if you wish, discuss it with another teaching candidate. If appropriate, use one or two of your colleague's suggestions to help

you change your response to the question. Place your response in a Teacher Test Study Guide folder or type/scan into a computer file. Plan to reread it for review purposes before taking a scheduled teacher test.

With Target Topics for Teacher Tests (TTTT)

If I wanted to start early and prepare for taking a state teacher test for licensing and certification and review subject matter content about demonstrations, inquiry learning, and educational games, how could I begin? **To do:** Consider reviewing key words, also known as Target Topics for Teacher Tests (TTTT), in the subject index. Find the key words you are interested in studying from the visual organizer at the opening of this chapter, from the narrative, and from the headings in this chapter. To assist you as you prepare to take a teacher test, bullets (•) have been placed by selected key word entries in the subject index. The bullets highlight core subject matter—such as demonstrations, inquiry learning, and educational games—that the authors suggest can be reviewed to prepare to take a teacher test similar to your state's test.

WITH READING

Bondy, E. (2000). Warming Up to Classroom Research in a Professional Development School. *Contemporary Education, 72*(1), 8–13.

Borich, G. (2003). *Observational Skills for Effective Teaching* (4th ed.). Upper Saddle River, NJ: Merrill/Prentice Hall.

Brisk, M. S., and Harrington, M. M. (2000). *Literacy and Bilingualism: A Handbook for ALL Teachers.* Mahwah, NJ: Erlbaum.

Brown, H. D. (2000). *Principles of Language Learning and Teaching.* New York: Addison Wesley/Longman.

California State Department of Education. (1997). *Descriptions of Practice.* Sacramento: California Standards for the Teaching Profession.

Camp, D. (2000). It Takes Two: Teaching with Twin Texts of Fact and Fiction. *The Reading Teacher, 53*(5), 400–408.

Costa, A., and Garmston, R. (2001). Five Human Passions: The Source of Critical and Creative Thinking. In A. Costa (Ed.), *Developing Minds: A Resource Book for Teaching Thinking.* Alexandria, VA: Association for Supervision and Curriculum Development.

Costa, A., and Garmston, R. (2002). *Cognitive Coaching: A Foundation for Renaissance Schools.* Norwood, MA: Christopher-Gordon.

Dong, Y. R. (2005). Getting at the Content. *Educational Leadership, 62,* 14–19.

Hinman, L. A. (2000). What's the Buzz? A Classroom Simulation Teaches Students about Life in the Hive. *Science and Children, 37*(5), 24–27.

Kellough, R. D. (2006). *A Resource Guide for Teaching: K–12* (4th. ed.). Upper Saddle River, NJ: Pearson/Merrill/Prentice Hall.

Landers, D., Maxwell, W., Butler, J., and Fagen, L. (2001). Developing Thinking Skills through Physical Education. In A.

Costa (Ed.), *Developing Minds: A Resource Book for Teaching Thinking.* Alexandria, VA: Association for Supervision and Curriculum Development.

Morgan, R. R., Ponticell, J. A., and Gordon, E. E. (2000). *Rethinking Creativity* (Fastback 458). Bloomington, IN: Phi Delta Kappa Educational Foundation.

National Research Council. (2000). *Inquiry and the National Science Education Standards: A Guide for Teaching and Learning.* Washington, DC: National Academy Press.

National Science Foundation. (2000). *Foundations, Volume 2: Inquiry—Thoughts, Views, and Strategies for the K–5 Classroom.* Alexandria, VA: Division of Elementary, Secondary and Information Education.

Perkins, D. N. (2000). Schools Need to Pay More Attention to "Intelligence in the Wild." *Harvard Education Letter, 16*(3), 7–8.

Polya. G. (1954). *Induction and Analogy in Mathematics.* Princeton, NJ: Princeton University Press.

Roberts, P. L., and Kellough, R. D. (2008), *A Guide for Developing Interdisciplinary Thematic Units.* Upper Saddle River, NJ: Pearson/Merrill/Prentice Hall.

Rossman, M. (1983). The Cheese: An Essay on Method in Science Teaching. *Phi Delta Kappan, 64,* 632–634.

Sternberg, R., and Grigorenko, E. (Eds.). (2001). *The Evolution of Intelligence.* Mahwah, NJ: Erlbaum.

Tower, C. (2000). Questions That Matter: Preparing Elementary Students for the Inquiry Process. *The Reading Teacher, 53*(7), 550–557.

Wittrock, C. A., and Barrow, L. H. (2000). Blow-by-Blow Inquiry. *Science and Children, 37*(5), 34–38.

WITH NOTES

1. K. Egan, Learning in Depth, *Educational Leadership, 66*(3), 58–79 (November, 2008).

2. A. L. Costa and B. Kallick (Eds.) *Habits of Mind* (Alexandria, VA: Association for Supervision and Curriculum Development, 2000).

3. T. Armstrong, *The Multiple Intelligences of Reading and Writing: Making the Words Come Alive* (Alexandria, VA: Association for Supervision and Curriculum Development, 2003).

4. L. Baines, *A Teacher's Guide to Multisensory Learning: Improving Literacy by Engaging the Senses* (Alexandria, VA: Association for Supervision and Curriculum Development, 2008).

5. J. Willis, *Brain-Friendly Strategies for the Inclusive Classroom* (Alexandria, VA: Association for Supervision and Curriculum Development, 2007).

6. L. Burmark, *Visual Literacy: Learn to See, See to Learn* (Alexandria, VA: Association for Supervision and Curriculum Development, 2008).

7. Costa and Kallick, see note 2.

8. J. Rightmyer, *A Funny Thing about Teaching: Connecting with Kids through Laughter . . . and Other Pointers for New Teachers* (New York: Cottonwood Press, 2008); R. Rosenblum-Lowden and F. L. Kimmel, *You Have to Go to School . . . You're the Teacher! 300+ Classroom Management Strategies to Make Your Job Easier and More Fun,* 3rd ed. (Los Angeles: Corwin, 2007).

9. J. Piaget's early writing, *The Psychology of Intelligence* (Totowa, NJ: Littlefield Adams, 1972).

10. K. Englander, Real Life Problem-Solving: A Collaborative Learning Activity, *English Teaching Forum,* 8–11 (February 2002); See also L. Kohlberg's early writing, *The Meaning and Measurement of Mind Development* (Worcester, MA: Clark University Press, 1981).

11. J. Willis, *Research-Based Strategies to Ignite Student Learning: Insight from a Neurologist and Classroom Teacher* (Alexandria, VA: Association for Supervision and Curriculum Development, 2006).

12. T. Armstrong, *The Best Schools: How Human Development Research Should Inform Educational Practice* (Alexandria, VA: Association for Supervision and Curriculum Development, 2006).

13. For products for teaching thinking, contact The Critical Thinking Company, P.O. Box 1610, Seaside, CA 93955-1610; (800) 458-4849; See www.criticalthinking.com.

14. H. H. Jacobs, *Getting Results with Curriculum Mapping* (Alexandria, VA: Association for Supervision and Curriculum Development, 2004); Also see earlier writing by D. Raschke, S. Alper, and E. Eggers, Recalling Alphabet Letter Names: A Mnemonic System to Facilitate Learning, *Preventing School Failure, 43*(2), 80–83 (Winter 1999).

15. Jacobs, see note 14.

16. J. Haynes, *Getting Started with English Language Learners: How Educators Can Meet the Challenge* (Alexandria, VA: Association for Supervision and Curriculum Development, 2007). See also D. Hyerle's earlier work, *Visual Tools for Constructing Knowledge* (Alexandria, VA: Association for Supervision and Curriculm Development, 1996).

17. R. J. Marzano, *A Six-Step Process for Teaching Vocabulary* (Alexandria, VA: Association for Supervision and Curriculum Development, 2005); Also D. P. Ausubel's earlier writing, The Facilitation of Meaningful Verbal Learning in the Classroom, *Educational Psychologist, 12,* 162–178 (1977).

18. Jacobs, see note 14.

19. L. D'Acquisto, *Learning on Display: Student-Created Museums That Build Understanding* (Alexandria, VA: Association for Supervision and Curriculum Development, 2008).

20. R. W. Cole, *Educating Everybody's Children* (Alexandria, VA: Association for Supervision and Curriculum Development, 2008).

21. Willis, see note 5. Also see A. Herrell and M. Jordan, *Fifty Strategies for Teaching English Language Learners,* (Upper Saddle River, NJ: Pearson Education, 2004); I. Alanis, Effective Instruction: Integrating Language and Literacy, in C. Salinas (Ed.), *Scholars in the Field: The Challenge of Migrant Education* (Charleston, WV: Appalachian Regional Education Laboratory, 2004), pp. 211–224.

22. I. L. Beck, M. G. McKeown, and L. Kucan, *Bringing Words to Life: Robust Vocabulary Instruction* (New York: Guildford, 2002).

23. Englander, see note 10.

24. For information about MicroSociety and school sites using different programs, contact MicroSociety at 13-15 S. Third St., Suite 500, Philadelphia, PA 19106; See www.microsocicty.org.

10

What Guidelines Assist My Use of Groupings and Assignments to Promote Positive Interaction and Quality Learning?

Visual Chapter Organizer and Overview

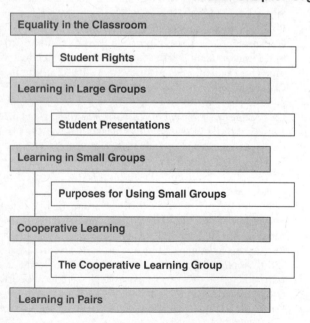

Equality in the Classroom

    Student Rights

Learning in Large Groups

    Student Presentations

Learning in Small Groups

    Purposes for Using Small Groups

Cooperative Learning

    The Cooperative Learning Group

Learning in Pairs

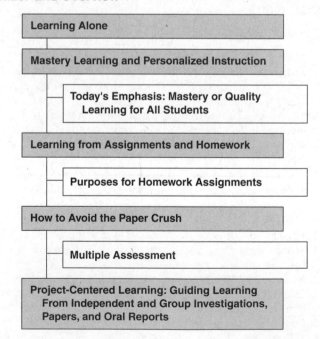

Learning Alone

Mastery Learning and Personalized Instruction

    Today's Emphasis: Mastery or Quality Learning for All Students

Learning from Assignments and Homework

    Purposes for Homework Assignments

How to Avoid the Paper Crush

    Multiple Assessment

Project-Centered Learning: Guiding Learning From Independent and Group Investigations, Papers, and Oral Reports

LOOKING AT TEACHERS I

Integrated Technology, Interdisciplinary Study

In support of future teachers, some educators in Australia, Japan, and the United States suggest that classrooms can become collections of student experts who get involved in learning in depth about topics such as alternative energy, birds, bullet trains, climate change, and others, as well as studying the regular curriculum. As one example of how a student can become an expert, the academic life of a student, Sara, is recapped in the following paragraphs.

- In first grade, Sara receives a topic she will study throughout her schooling for the next twelve years. After a student interview and parent conference, a decision is made: Sara's topic is apples. Through the year, the teacher meets with Sara once a month to contribute to her portfolio that will show the development of her expertise and introduce her to the computer in the classroom. With the teacher's guidance, Sara decides to buy apples, list names of apples to show the variety available, and collects data about taste from her classmates at an apple taste table. She draws apples—sketching size and shape and showing color—and learns stories and poems about apples to share with others. She reads about the growth of apples, places sayings about apples on posters, and decorates the poster borders for a display. Through the year, she joins a peer group in periodic meetings to report on the progress of the study of her topic.
- In second through seventh grades, Sara continues adding to her portfolio (now completely on the computer) about apples that has divisions/computer files for different kinds of information, such as the apple-rose connection, facts about apples, for example, why an apple floats, and a family apple tree that Sara has constructed to show the development from early apples to current varieties. She searches the Internet and locates information about people such as John Chapman (Johnny Appleseed), William Tell, Isaac Newton, and others.

- By the end of secondary school, Sara's interdisciplinary study has developed her expertise. Sara has read the history of apples (history), memorized poems about apples, and knows where apples have significance in selected literature, especially the Greek myths (literacy, literature). Sara participates in active projects such as campaigns to preserve rare apple varieties (service learning). She collects facts about the production of apples in different countries (economics). She calculates proportions of apple production in other countries and tracks the prices (mathematics). She notes the locations of orchards around the world, their owners, the cost of production in their area, the cost of transportation to market, profits made, and information about owner's problems in growing apples (crop diseases, economics, geography). Sara has become an expert through her interest in her topic, apples—and now is a lifelong learner who continues to be stimulated by information and by technology and motivated by her "hobby."[1]

A Focus on English Language Learners

Consider using learning logs that can be used at all grade levels since writing in logs supports the idea of having students think about their learning. Thinking about their learning will assist the students in becoming more successful in the use of English and the knowledge of selected content. For example, consider Sara and what she might have written in her learning logs as she specialized in learning about the topic of apples through her academic years (Echevarria and Graves, 1998).

CHAPTER OBJECTIVES

Specifically, upon completion of this chapter, you should be able to:

1. Describe your knowledge about using a whole-class discussion as a teaching strategy.
2. Contribute to a list of guidelines for using whole-class discussion as a teaching strategy.
3. Explain how the classroom teacher can personalize the instruction (differentiated/tiered instruction) to ensure success for each student.

4. Present your persuasive argument in favor or against providing recovery options for students who don't do an assignment or who don't do well on it.
5. Describe your view about how to effectively use one or more of these instructional strategies: assignments, homework/responsibility papers, journal writing, written and oral reports, cooperative learning groups, learning centers, problem-based learning, and student-centered projects.

Because educators believe in the learning potential of every student, exemplary schools and accomplished teachers are able to effectively modify the key variables of time, methodology, and grouping to help individual students achieve mastery learning of the planned curriculum rather than dilute standards and expectations. Related to this, you'll recall in Chapter 1 we discussed ways in which time is modified. Throughout other chapters in this resource guide, we talk of ways of varying the methodology. In this chapter, we focus on ways of grouping students to enhance positive interaction and quality learning.

In the most effective instructional environments, during any given week or day of school, a student will likely experience a succession of group settings. Ways of grouping children for instruction is the initial topic of this chapter, beginning with large-group instruction, small groups, and dyads, and then individualized instruction. You also will learn how to ensure equality in the classroom, ways to use assignments and homework, and how to coordinate various forms of independent and small-group project-based study.

EQUALITY IN THE CLASSROOM

Especially when using explicit/direct instruction and when conducting whole-group discussions, it is easy for a teacher to develop the habit of interacting with only "the stars," or with only those in the front of the room or on one side, or only the most vocal and assertive. You must exercise caution and avoid falling into that habit. To ensure a psychologically safe and effective environment for learning for every student in your classroom, whatever the grouping arrangement, you must attend to all students and try to involve all students equally in the class activities. Look at Figure 10.1.

You should avoid any biased expectations about certain children, and you must avoid discriminating against students according to their gender, ethnicity, or any orher personal characteristic. Discrimination is not only unfair, it is illegal.

Student Rights

You probably already know that as a result of legislation that occurred three decades ago—federal law Title IX of the Educational Amendments of 1972, P. L. 92-318—a teacher is prohibited from discriminating among students on the basis of their gender. In all aspects of school, male and female students must be treated the same. This means, for example, that a teacher must not put boys against the girls in a quiz game—or for any other activity or reason. Further, no teacher, student, administrator, or other school employee should make

K. S. Berger, Update on Bullying at School: Science Forgotten? *Developmental Review, 27*(1), 90–126 (2007).

L. M. Crothers, J. B. Kolbert, and W. F. Barker, Middle School Students' Preferences for Anti-Bullying Interventions. *School Psychology International, 27,* 475–487 (2006).

J. Dufresne, Keeping Students and School Safe, *Reclaiming Children and Youth, 14*(2), 93 (2005).

M. Franek, Foiling Cyberbullies in the New Wild West, *Educational Leadership, 63*(4), 39–43 (2006).

G. Gladstone, G. B. Parker, and G. S. Malhi, Do Bullied Children Become Anxious and Depressed Adults? A Cross-Sectional Investigation of the Correlates of Bullying and Anxious Depression. *Journal of Nervous and Mental Disease, 194*(3), 201–208 (2006).

L. Lumsden, *Preventing Bullying*, ERIC Clearinghouse on Educational Management Document, No. ED 463563 (2002).

J. S. Peterson and K. E. Ray, Bullying and the Gifted, *Gifted Child Quarterly, 50,* 148–168 (2006).

S. Shariff, Cyber-Dilemmas in the New Millennium: School Obligations to Provide Student Safety in a Virtual School Environment, *McGill Journal of Education, 40,* 467–487 (2005).

N. Willard, Flame Retardant: Cyberbullies Torment Their Victims 24/7: Here's How To Stop the Abuse, *School Library Journal, 52*(4), 54 (2006).

Figure 10.1
Resources on harassment in schools and cyberbullies.

sexual advances toward a student (i.e., touching or speaking in a sexual manner). Students should be informed by their schools of their rights under Title IX, and they should be encouraged to report any suspected violations of their rights to the school principal or other designated person. Review Figure 10.1 again for additional resources on harassment in schools and cyberbullying. Many schools or districts have a clearly delineated statement of steps to follow in the process of protecting students' rights.

Gender Discrimination

Even today, research identifies the unintentional tendency of teachers of *both* sexes to discriminate on the basis of gender. For example, teachers, along with the rest of society, tend to have lower expectations for girls than for boys in mathematics and science. They tend to call on and encourage boys more than girls. They often let boys interrupt girls but praise girls for being polite and waiting their turn. To avoid such discrimination may take special effort on your part, such as observing

National Women's History Month (see www.nwhp.org/whm/index.php or using resources from the National Women's History Project www.nwhp.org). No matter how aware of the problem you may be, some researchers believe the problem is so insidious that courses about it are needed in teacher education.[2]

Ensuring Equity

To ensure equity in interaction with students, many teachers have found it helpful to ask someone quietly to tally classroom interactions between the teacher and students during a class discussion. After an analysis of the results, the teacher arrives at decisions about his or her own attending and facilitating behaviors.

In addition to the advice given in our previous chapter about using teacher talk and questioning, many other strategies can help ensure that children are treated fairly in the classroom, including the following:

- Encourage students to demonstrate an appreciation for one another by applauding all individual and group presentations. Some teachers make a point of shaking hands with a student who has finished a presentation and saying "Thank you."
- Have and maintain high expectations, although not necessarily identical expectations, for all students.
- Insist on politeness in the classroom. For example, a student can be shown appreciation with a sincere remark such as "I appreciate your contribution," or with a genuine smile for the student's contribution to the learning process.
- Insist on students finishing sentences, without being interrupted by others. Be certain that you model this behavior yourself.
- During whole-class instruction, insist that students raise their hands and be called on by you before they speak.
- Keep a stopwatch handy to unobtrusively control the wait time given for each student. While at first this idea may sound impractical, it works.
- Use a seating chart (perhaps attached to a clipboard) and next to each student's name, make a tally for each interaction you have with a student. This also is a good way to maintain records to reward students for their contributions to class discussion. The seating chart can be laminated and then used day after day by simply erasing the marks of the previous day, which should be made with nonpermanent markers.

Now look ahead to Application Exercise 10.1. Consider that this application exercise can be modified to include responses and their frequencies according to a teacher-student interaction you select. Interactions can include (1) your calling on all students equally for responses to your questions, (2) your calling on students equally to assist you with classroom helping jobs, (3) your reminding students about appropriate or inappropriate behavior, or (4) other interactions you select.

LEARNING IN LARGE GROUPS

Large groups are those that involve eight or more students, usually the entire class. Most often, they are teacher directed. Student presentations and whole-class discussions are two techniques that involve the use of large groups.

Student Presentations

Students should be encouraged to be presenters for discussion of the ideas, opinions, and knowledge obtained from their own independent and small-group study. Several techniques encourage the development of certain skills, such as studying and organizing material, discovery, discussion, rebuttal, listening, analysis, suspending judgment, and critical thinking. Possible forms of discussions involving student presentations include the following:

- *Debate*. The debate is an arrangement in which members of two opposing teams, on topics preassigned and researched, make formal speeches supporting their points of view. The speeches are followed by rebuttals from each team.
- *Jury (Mock) Trial*. The jury trial is a discussion approach in which the class simulates a courtroom, with class members playing various roles of judge, attorneys, jury members, bailiff, and court recorder.
- *Panel*. The panel is a setting in which from four to six students, with one designated as the chairperson or moderator, discuss a topic they have studied, followed by a question-and-answer period involving the entire class. The panel usually begins with each panel member giving a brief opening statement.
- *Research Report*. For research reporting, one or two students, or a small group of students, will give a report on a topic that they investigated, followed by questions and discussion by the entire class. Review Figures 10.2 through 10.4 for guidelines about copyrighted material.
- *Roundtable*. The roundtable is a small group of three to five students who sit around a table and discuss among themselves (and perhaps with the rest of the class listening and perhaps later asking questions) a problem or issue that they have studied. One member of the panel may serve as moderator.

Similar to when students are involved in cooperative learning groups, students may need coaching from you to develop some of the skills necessary to use the previously mentioned techniques effectively. Individually, in small groups, or in whole-class sessions, the students may need coaching on how and where to gather information; how

PERMITTED USES—*You May Make:*

1. Single copies of:
   - A chapter of a book; a portion of a book for a class, such as graphs, images, and maps (facts are not protected by copyright).
   - An article from a periodical, magazine, or newspaper.
   - A short story, short essay, or short poem, even from a collected work.
   - A cartoon, chart, diagram, drawing, graph, a character from a reading book to use in a one-time reading lesson.
   - An illustration from a book, magazine, or newspaper.
2. Multiple copies for classroom use (not to exceed one copy per student in a course) of:
   - A complete poem if less than 250 words.
   - An excerpt from a longer poem, but not to exceed 250 words.
   - A complete article, story, or essay of less than 2,500 words.
   - An excerpt from a larger printed work not to exceed 10 percent of the whole or 1,000 words.
   - One cartoon, chart, diagram, graph, or picture per book or magazine issue.
   - Digital copies of analog works for display or performance in a digital classroom at an accredited nonprofit educational institution that meets all of the requirements of the TEACH provisions, including copying a tape at the time a teacher actually plans to use a digital version (Copyright Act, Section 110[2]).

PROHIBITED USES—*You May Not:*

1. Copy more than one work or two excerpts from a single author during one class term (semester or year).
2. Copy more than three works from a collective work or periodical volume during one class term.
3. Reproduce more than nine sets of multiple copies for distribution to students in one class term.
4. Copy to create, replace, or substitute for anthologies or collective works.
5. Copy "consumable" works, for example, workbooks, standardized tests, answer sheets, or game boards, especially those with logos, symbols, or short phrases since these marks are registered trademarks. Be aware that trademark law does not have a fair-use exemption and is much more rigid than copyright law.
6. Copy the same work year after year.

Figure 10.2
Guidelines for copying printed materials that are copyrighted.
(*Source:* Section 107 of the 1976 Federal Omnibus Copyright Revision Act)

PERMITTED USES—*You May:*

1. Make a single back-up or archival copy of the computer program.
2. Adapt the computer program to another language if the program is unavailable in the target language.
3. Add features to make better use of the computer program.
4. Use videos *directly related to the curriculum in the teaching environment* (that even includes tour buses with TVs and VCRs when students are on the way to a site for real-place education); The term *fair use* allows teachers to show videos directly related to the curriculum (and not for entertainment purposes) to their students in the teaching environment, one time, without the prior permission of the copyright holder.
5. Section 110(1) of the copyright law allows nonprofit, educational institutions to publicly show works. It is allowable for educators to use rented films, one time use, in the classroom.
6. Regarding copyright infringement, post an appropriate sign at or near your class computers: "Materials found on the Internet may be protected by copyright law. Any reproduction of copyright-protected materials may be an infringement of the copyright law."

PROHIBITED USES—*You May Not:*

1. Make multiple copies.
2. Make replacement copies from an archival or back-up copy.
3. Make copies of copyrighted programs to be sold, leased, loaned, transmitted, or given away.
4. Make or share files from file-sharing services (such as Streamcast) since this may constitute copyright infringement (U.S. Supreme Court, June 2005).
5. Make video or DVD copies of some of your older filmstrips to update your collection since this could be considered an infringement of the copyright law.

Figure 10.3
Copyright law for use of computer software/videos.
(*Source:* December 1980 Congressional Amendment to the 1976 Copyright Act)

You Should:
1. Follow normal copyright guidelines (e.g., the limitations that apply on the amount of material used, whether it be motion media, text, music, illustrations, photographs, or computer software) for portions of copyrighted works used in your own multimedia production for use in teaching.
2. Obtain permissions from copyright holders before using any copyrighted materials in educational multimedia production for commercial reproduction and distribution or before replicating more than one copy, distributing copies to others, and for use beyond your own classroom.

You May:
1. Display your own multimedia work using copyrighted works to other teachers, such as in workshops.
2. Use your own multimedia production for instruction over an electronic network for education (e.g., distance learning) provided there are limits to access and to the number of students enrolled.
3. The Technology, Education, and Copyright Harmonization (TEACH, 2002) Act now permits accredited, nonprofit educational institutions that *have copyright policies* available to teachers, students, and staff to make a digital copy of an analog work without prior permission if that single copy is made solely for classroom use and kept only as long as is necessary to meet the teaching objective. Thus, TEACH allows teachers and students to show a DVD and art slides, without prior permission, in the physical classroom and in a virtual classroom that is received by students through digital transmission on a network. TEACH also allows the fair use of parts of a nondramatic work such as articles, books, charts, maps, and poetry. Smaller portions of dramatic works such as videos, films, operas, and dramas can be used in the *digital* classroom. Any work that would be used in the physical classroom and is central to the teaching goals of the class can be used in digital form or on digital networks.
4. You may make one copy of a DVD, to be destroyed later, if a replacement exemption applies, if a teaching exemption applies, or if fair use applies.*

You May Not:
1. Distribute your own multimedia production using copyrighted works over any electronic network (local or wide area) without expressed permission from copyright holders.
2. Make and distribute copies to colleagues of your own multimedia work using copyrighted works without obtaining permission from copyright holders.
3. Share files from file-sharing services.

---

*Millennium Copyright Act [DMCA] Sections 110, 108, and 107, and TEACH Act, 2002.

Figure 10.4
Fair use guidelines for using multimedia programs.
(*Source:* Millennium Copyright Act [DMCA] Sections 110, 108, and 107 and TEACH Act, 2002)

to listen, take notes, select major points, organize material, present a position succinctly and convincingly, play roles; and how to engage in dialogue and debate with one another without creating conflict.

Whole-Class Discussion

Teacher-directed whole-class discussion is a teaching technique used frequently by most teachers. On this topic, you should consider yourself an expert. Having been a student in formal education for many years, you are undoubtedly knowledgeable about the advantages and disadvantages of whole-class discussions, at least from your personal vantage point. Explore your knowledge further and share your experiences by responding to Application Exercise 10.1, to assist in generating guidelines for whole-class discussions.

FOR YOUR NOTES

APPLICATION EXERCISE 10.1

Whole-Class Discussion as a Teaching Strategy:
Building upon What I Already Know

Instructions: The purpose of this exercise is to generate a list of guidelines for using whole-class discussion as a teaching strategy. Individually answer the first two questions. Then, as a group, use the first three questions to guide your small group as you generate a list of five general guidelines to contribute to the whole-class discussion. Work cooperatively and collaboratively with your group and help share your group's guidelines with the entire class. Then as a class, derive a final list of general guidelines. Respond to the final questions as you reflect about this discussion strategy.

1. What will you contribute to a list of five general guidelines for a whole-class discussion as a strategy in teaching? (individual response)

   _____
   _____
   _____
   _____
   _____
   _____

2. What do you think allows for (or inhibits) the effectiveness of whole-group discussions? (individual response)

   _____
   _____
   _____
   _____
   _____
   _____

3. General guidelines generated from your discussion (small-group response)

   _____
   _____
   _____
   _____
   _____
   _____

4. General guidelines (final list) derived from whole group (whole-group response)

   _____
   _____
   _____
   _____
   _____

My Reflection About This Discussion

5. How effective was my small-group discussion in generating a list of five general guidelines? (individual response)

_____

_____

_____

_____

_____

_____

6. What allowed for (or inhibited) the effectiveness of my small-group discussion? (individual response)

_____

_____

_____

_____

_____

_____

7. What was the overall effectiveness of my small-group discussion? What helped? What hindered? (individual response)

_____

_____

_____

_____

_____

_____

8. What did I learn to help me in leading discussions in my own classroom?

_____

_____

_____

_____

_____

LEARNING IN SMALL GROUPS

Small groups are those involving three to eight students, in either a teacher- or a student-directed setting. Using small groups for instruction enhances the opportunities for students to assume greater control over their own learning, sometimes referred to as *empowerment*.

Purposes for Using Small Groups

Small groups can be formed to serve a number of purposes that might be useful for a specific learning activity, for example, reciprocal reading groups as demonstrated by Figure 5.3, Sample Multitext Reading Guide and Children's Books That Promote Global Awareness/Understanding, in Chapter 5. Groups might be formed to complete an activity that requires materials that are in short supply or to complete a science experiment or a project, with the understanding that the groups will last only as long as the project does. These are just a few examples of the various rationales teachers have for assigning students to temporary in-class groups. Groups can be formed by grouping children according to (a) personality type (e.g., sometimes a teacher may want to group less-assertive children together to give them an opportunity for greater management of their own learning); (b) social pattern (e.g., sometimes it may be necessary to break up a group of rowdy friends, or it may be desirable to broaden the association among students); (c) common interest; (d) learning styles (e.g., forming groups of either mixed styles or similar styles in common); or (e) their abilities in a particular skill or their knowledge in a particular area.

A teacher we know uses a wheel diagram to organize getting the students into groups by randomly selected students. To use the categories listed previously as an example, the teacher makes a wheel based on any one of the five categories (a. personality type, b. social pattern . . .). Once the teacher assesses where students fit in a category, the teacher places their names on the outside edge of one of three or four wheels stacked upon one another and attached in the center with a paper brad/clasp. To randomly create new groups, the teacher spins one of the wheels one space and a second wheel two spaces, and so on, then records the new groups. Once the groups have been selected, some teachers initiate a specific and well-known type of small-group instruction—the cooperative learning group.

COOPERATIVE LEARNING

Lev Vygotsky (1896–1934) studied the importance of a learner's social interactions in learning situations. Vygotsky argued that learning is most effective when learners cooperate with one another in a supportive learning environment under the careful guidance of a teacher. Cooperative learning, group problem solving, problem-based learning, and cross-age tutoring are instructional strategies used by teachers that have grown in popularity as a result of research evolving from Vygotsky's work.

Although cooperative learning is a genre of instructional strategies for which there are several models, they all share two key components: interdependence among members of the group and individual accountability for learning.[3]

The Cooperative Learning Group

The **cooperative learning group (CLG)** is a heterogeneous group (i.e., mixed according to one or more criteria, such as ability or skill level, ethnicity, learning style, learning capacity, gender, and language proficiency) of two to six students who work together in a teacher- or student-directed setting, emphasizing support for one another. Oftentimes, a CLG consists of three to four students of mixed ability, learning styles, gender, and ethnicity, with each member of the group assuming a particular role (see discussion of roles that follows). Teachers usually change the membership of each group several times during the year.

The Theory and Use of Cooperative Learning

The theory of cooperative learning is that when small groups of students of mixed backgrounds and capabilities work together toward a common goal, members of the group increase their friendship and respect for one another. As a consequence, each individual's self-esteem is enhanced, students are more motivated to participate in higher-order thinking, and academic achievement is accomplished.[4]

Of special interest to teachers are general methods of cooperative learning, such as these:

- *Student team achievement divisions (STAD)*. The teacher presents a lesson, students work together in teams to help each other learn the materials, individuals take quizzes, and team rewards are earned based on the individual scores of the quizzes.
- *Teams-games-tournaments (TGT)*. Tournaments (rather than quizzes) are held during which students compete against others of similar academic achievements and then winners contribute toward their team's score.
- *Group investigations (GI)*. Students form two-to-six-member groups, select subtopics from a broader whole-class unit of study, and produce group reports, followed by each group making a culminating presentation.[5]

The primary purpose of each is for the groups to learn—which means, of course, that individuals within a group must learn. Group achievement in learning, then, is dependent upon the learning of individuals within the group. Rather than competing for rewards for achievement, members of the group cooperate with one another by helping one another learn, so that the group reward will be a good one. This is the interdependence component of cooperative learning.

Normally, the group is rewarded on the basis of group achievement, though individual members within the group can later be rewarded for individual contributions. Because of peer pressure, when using CLGs the teacher must be cautious about using group grading.[6] For example, a student's report card should clearly represent that student's achievement and not be lower than it can be because of whom the student works with in groups. For grading purposes, bonus points can be given to all members of a group; individuals can add to their own scores when everyone in the group has reached preset standards. The preset standards must be appropriate for all members of a group. Lower standards or improvement criteria could be set for students with lower ability so everyone feels rewarded and successful. To determine each student's semester or term grades, that is, the grades that go on reports to the child's home, individual student achievement is measured later through individual students' results on tests and a variety of other criteria, including each student's performance in the group work.

Roles within the Cooperative Learning Group

To structure the interdependent nature of cooperative learning, it is helpful to assign roles (specific duties) to each member of the CLG. These roles should be rotated, either during the activity or from one time to the next. Though titles are discretionary, five typical roles are:

- *Group facilitator.* Role is to keep the group on task.
- *Materials manager.* Role is to obtain, maintain, and return materials needed for the group to function.
- *Recorder.* Role is to record all group activities and processes and perhaps to periodically assess how the group is doing.
- *Reporter.* Role is to report group processes and accomplishments to the teacher and/or to the entire class. When using groups of four members, the roles of recorder and reporter can easily be combined.
- *Thinking monitor.* Role is to identify and record the sequence and processes of the group's thinking. This role encourages metacognition (thinking about one's own thinking) and thus the development of thinking skills.

It is important that students understand and perform their individual roles, and that each member of the CLG performs his or her duties as expected. This is the individual accountability component. No student should be allowed to ride the coattails of the group.

To emphasize the significance of roles in the group and reinforce the importance of each role and to be able to readily recognize the role any student is playing during CLG activity, one teacher made a trip to an office supplier and had permanent badges made for the various CLG roles. During CLGs, each student attached the appropriate badge to her or his clothing. Some teachers we know use index cards (often laminated) and yarn to create "necklaces" or "slings" for the students to wear to identify their roles. This is useful if funds aren't available to get badges from the office supplier.

What Students and the Teacher Do When Using Cooperative Learning Groups

Actually, for learning by CLGs to work, each member of the CLG must understand and assume two roles or responsibilities: the role he or she is assigned as a member of the group and the role of a facilitator, that is, seeing that all others in the group are performing their roles. Sometimes, to teach children what it means to work cooperatively, some teachers teach cooperation by what it looks and sounds like. For example, cooperation looks like two heads close together and sounds like "What a great idea!" They place charts in their classrooms that reinforce this instruction.

At other times, roles and responsibilities of group work require interpersonal skills that children have yet to learn or to learn well. This is where the teacher must assume additional responsibility. Simply placing children into CLGs and expecting each member and each group to function and to learn the expected outcomes may not work. In other words, skills of cooperation must be taught. These are the skills of altruism, consensus seeking, giving up an idea to work on someone else's, integrating the ideas of others, knowing how to handle disagreements, knowing how to support group efforts, listening, and sharing. If all of your students have not yet learned these skills, and they probably have not, then you will have to teach them. This doesn't mean that if a group is not functioning you immediately break up the group and reassign members to new groups. Part of group learning is learning the process of how to work out any conflicts.

A group may require your assistance to work out a conflict. With your guidance, the group should be able to discover what the problem causing the conflict is, identify some options, and mediate at least a temporary solution. If a particular skill is needed, then with your guidance (and perhaps a class meeting), the students can identify and learn that skill.

When to Use Cooperative Learning Groups

CLGs (cooperative learning groups) can be used for experiments, inquiry learning, opinion surveys, problem solving, project work, reviewing, test making, or almost any other instructional purpose. Just as you would organize for small-group work in general, you can use

CLGs for most any purpose at any time; but as with any other type of instructional strategy, it should not be overused, and in the early grades, the group work should be highly structured, pleasant, and scheduled for relatively brief periods of time. As students' skills in group processing develop, they can be given gradually longer and more demanding group tasks.[7]

Outcomes of Using Cooperative Learning Groups

When the process is well planned and managed, the outcomes of cooperative learning include (a) improved communication and relationships of acceptance among students of differences, (b) quality learning with fewer off-task behaviors, (c) improved ability to perform four key thinking strategies—problem solving, decision making, critical thinking, and creative thinking—and (d) increased academic achievement. In the words of Good and Brophy,

> Cooperative learning arrangements promote friendships and prosocial interaction among students who differ in achievement, gender, race, or ethnicity, and they promote the acceptance of mainstreamed handicapped students by their nonhandicapped classmates. Cooperative methods also frequently have positive effects, and rarely have negative effects on affective outcomes such as self-esteem, academic self-confidence, liking for the class, liking and feeling liked by classmates, and on various measures of empathy and social cooperation.[8]

Why Some Teachers Have Difficulty Using CLGs

For the use of CLGs to work well, advanced planning and effective management are musts. As emphasized by Tomlinson, "the nest of strategies we call cooperative learning . . . [sometimes] have fallen short of expectations not because of a deficiency in the strategies themselves but because teachers apply them shallowly."[9] Sometimes, when using CLGs, teachers have difficulty and either give up trying to use the strategy or divide children into groups for an activity and call it cooperative learning when it is simply group work. For the strategy to work, each student must be given *a responsibility of helping others learn* and acquire basic skills in interaction and group processing and must realize that individual achievement rests with that of their group.

Also, as is true for any other strategy, the use of CLGs must not be overused—teachers must vary their strategies.[10] Some teachers monitor cooperative learning groups, such as the Jigsaw groups (where tasks are shared), and note cooperative behaviors that are occurring, and then these are shared in a debriefing/class meeting at the end of the work period or the school day—with students perhaps writing a self-evaluation: "I helped someone learn today when I _____. _____ would help me work better next time. _____ worked well."

Children should be instructed in the necessary skills for group learning. Each student can be assigned a responsible role within the group and be held accountable for fulfilling that responsibility. When a CLG activity is in process, groups must be continually monitored by the teacher for possible breakdown of this process within a group. In other words, while children are working in groups, the teacher must exercise withitness. When a potential breakdown is noticed, the teacher quickly intervenes to reset the group back on track. See Figure 10.5 for additional resources.

LEARNING IN PAIRS

It is sometimes advantageous to pair students (dyads) for learning. Some ways of doing this are described next as we discuss peer tutoring, mentoring, cross-age coaching, team learning, think–pair–share, and a learning center.

- Center for Research on the Education of Students Placed at Risk, Johns Hopkins University, 3003 N. Charles St., Suite 200, Baltimore, MD 21218; 410-516-8810; www.csos.jhu.edu/crespar/
- Cooperative Learning Center at the University of Minnesota, 60 Peik Hall, University of Minnesota, Minneapolis, MN 55455; 612-624-7031; www.co-operation.org
- Kagan Publishing, P.O. Box 72008, San Clemente, CA 92673-2008; 800-933-2667; Kagan Professional Development, P.O. Box 72008, San Clemente, CA 92673-2008; 800-266-7576; www.kaganonline.com

Figure 10.5
Resources on the use of cooperative learning.*

*Classes with students with learning problems/English language learners can engage in groups in collaborative reading where they predict and share what they might read, then read, find words they know, and find words they don't know to discuss in the group. In addition, they can ask questions about what is read (who, what, where, when, and why) and then write questions about the main ideas in the reading before discussing what they have learned.

Peer Tutoring, Mentoring, and Cross-Age Coaching

Peer tutoring, mentoring, or peer-assisted learning (PAL) is a strategy whereby one student tutors another. It is useful, for example, when one student helps another who has limited proficiency in English or when a student skilled in math helps another one who is less skilled. For years, it has been demonstrated repeatedly that peer tutoring is a significant strategy for promoting active learning. Furthermore, peer tutoring increases academic achievement not only for those being tutored but of those students doing the tutoring.[11]

Cross-age coaching is a strategy where one student is coached by another from a different, usually higher, grade level. This is similar to peer tutoring, except the coach is from a different age level than the student being coached.[12] As discussed previously in Chapter 1 and in the final section of this chapter, many schools have service learning projects that involve older students mentoring younger children.[13]

Paired Team Learning

Paired team learning is a strategy where students study and learn in teams of two. Students identified as gifted work and learn especially well when paired. Specific uses for paired team learning include drill partners, reading buddies, book report pairs, summarizing pairs, homework partners/responsibility paper partners, project assignment pairs, and elaborating partners or relating pairs.

Think–Pair–Share

Think–pair–share is a strategy where students, in pairs, examine a new concept or topic about to be studied. Then if a learning extension is appropriate, the students pair again to share again with another student to examine the material further. After the students discuss what they already know or think they know (misconceptions) about the concept, they present their perceptions to the whole group. This is an excellent technique for this type of discovery learning about a topic. To support this further, the think–pair–share–pair again strategy can be combined in use with the K–W–L strategy. For more support, a writing step may be introduced where the modification of *think–write–pair–share* is engaged by pairs where the students think and write ideas or conclusions before sharing their work with the larger group.

The Learning Center

Another significantly beneficial way of pairing students for instruction (and for individualizing the instruction and learning or for integrating the learning) is by using the learning center (LC) or learning station (*Note*: Whereas each learning center can be distinct and unrelated to others, the work at learning stations can be sequenced or in some way linked to one another.) Further, the LC is a special place in the classroom where one student (or two, if student interaction is necessary or preferred at the center) can quietly work, explore, and learn at his or her own pace about a particular topic or to improve specific skills. All materials needed are provided at the center, including clear instructions for the operation of the center. Familiar classroom examples of learning centers are the personal computer station and the reading corner.

The value of learning centers as instructional devices undoubtedly lies in the following facts:

- LCs can provide instructional diversity.
- While working at a center, the student can be giving time and quality attention to the learning task (learning toward mastery) and is likely to be engaging the student's preferred learning modality or integrating several or all modalities.
- To adapt instruction to students' individual needs and preferences, it is possible to design a classroom learning environment that includes several **learning resource centers,** each of which incorporates a different medium and modality or focuses on a special aspect of the curriculum.
- Students can work at the various learning centers according to their needs and preferences.

Learning centers are of three types—direct-learning center, open-learning center, and skill center. In the *direct-learning center*, performance expectations for cognitive learning are quite specific and the focus is on mastery of content. In the *open-learning center*, the goal is to provide opportunity for exploration, enrichment, motivation, and creative discovery. In the *skill center*, as in a direct-learning center, performance expectations are quite specific but the focus is on the development of a particular skill or process.

In all instances, the primary reason for using a learning center is to individualize—to provide collections of materials and activities adjusted to the various readiness levels, interests, and learning profiles of students. Other reasons to use an LC are to provide (a) a mechanism for learning that crosses discipline boundaries, (b) a special place for a student with special needs, (c) opportunities for creative work, enrichment experiences, and multisensory experiences, and (d) an opportunity to learn from learning packages that use special equipment or media of which only one or a limited supply may be available for use in your classroom (e.g., science materials, a microscope, a computer, a videodisc player, or some combination of these).

LEARNING ALONE

Some elementary schoolchildren learn well in pairs (dyads); others learn well with their peers in groups—collaboratively, cooperatively, or competitively—or collaboratively with adults; others learn well in combinations of these patterns; and some students learn best alone. Children who best learn alone usually are gifted, nonconforming, able to work at their own pace successfully, and are independently comfortable using media. Or they may be seemingly underachieving but potentially able students for whom unconventional instructional strategies, such as contract learning packages or multisensory instructional packages, encourage academic success.[14] Agreements can be made between you and individual students so they can proceed with certain tasks appropriate to their readiness, interests, or learning profiles; they can proceed in a sequence and at a pace that they select.

MASTERY LEARNING AND PERSONALIZED INSTRUCTION

Learning is an individual or personal experience. Yet, as a classroom teacher, you will be expected to work effectively with children on an individual basis as well as in a group—perhaps 30 or more students at a time. Much has been written about the importance of personalizing the instruction for learners. Virtually all the research concerning better instructional practice emphasizes greater individualization, or personalization, of instruction.[15] We know of the individuality of the learning experience, and while some elementary schoolchildren are primarily verbal learners, many more are primarily visual, tactile, or kinesthetic learners. As the teacher, though, you find yourself in the demanding position of simultaneously "treating" many separate and individual learners with individual learning capacities, styles, and preferences.

Common sense tells us that student achievement in learning is related to both the quality of attention and the length of time given to learning tasks. From the 1960s, educators have been interested in the concept of individualized instruction called **mastery learning,** saying that students need sufficient time on task (i.e., engaged time) to master content before moving on to new content.[16] Instructional plans have been developed, often called a Personalized System of Instruction (PSI), which involves the student's learning from printed modules of instruction (which today, would likely be presented as computer software programs). This material allows the student greater control over the learning pace. The instruction is mastery oriented; that is, the student demonstrates mastery of the content of one module before proceeding to the next.

Today's Emphasis: Mastery or Quality Learning for All Students

Emphasis today is on working toward mastery of content, which is also called *quality* learning, rather than just coverage of content or *quantity* of learning. Mastery of content means that the student demonstrates his or her use of what has been learned. Because of the emphasis and research that indicates that quality learning programs positively affect achievement, the importance of the concept of mastery learning has resurfaced. For example, in today's efforts to restructure schools, two approaches—Results-Driven Education (RDE), also known as Outcome-Based Education (OBE), and the Coalition of Essential Schools (CES)—use a goal-driven curriculum model with instruction that focuses on the construction of individual knowledge through mastery and assessment of student learning against the anticipated outcomes.[17]

In some instances, unfortunately, attention may only be on the mastery of minimum competencies; thus, in this situation, students may not be encouraged to work and learn to the maximum of their talents and abilities.

Assumptions About Mastery or Quality Learning

Today's concept of mastery, or quality, learning is based on six assumptions:

1. Mastery learning can ensure that students experience success at each level of the instructional process. Experiencing success at each level provides incentive and motivation for further learning.
2. Mastery of content, or quality learning, is possible for all students.
3. Although all students can achieve mastery, to master a particular content, some students may require more time than others. The teacher and the school must provide for this difference in time needed to complete a task successfully.
4. For quality learning to occur, instruction must be modified and adapted, not the students.
5. Most learning is sequential and logical.
6. Most desired learning outcomes can be specified in terms of observable and measurable performance.[18]

Components of Any Mastery Learning Model

Any instructional model designed to teach toward mastery (quality) learning will contain the following five components: (a) clearly defined instructional objectives, (b) a preassessment of the extent of the learner's present knowledge, (c) an instructional component with choices and options for students, (d) practice, reinforcement, frequent comprehension checks (both diagnostic and formative assessment) and corrective instruction at each step of the way to keep the learner on track, and

(e) a summative assessment to determine the extent of student mastery of the objectives.

Strategies for Personalizing the Instruction: Working Toward Quality Learning

You can immediately provide personalized instruction by

1. Starting the study of a topic from where the students are in terms of what they know (or think they know) and what they want to know about the topic. The strategies of K–W–L and think–pair–share are examples of doing this.
2. Providing children with choices from a rich variety of learning pathways and hands-on experiences to learn more about the topic.
3. Providing multiple instructional approaches, that is, using multilevel instruction in a variety of settings, from explicit whole-class instruction to learning alone and mastery learning.
4. Empowering students with responsibility and multiple opportunities for decision making, reflection, and self-assessment.

LEARNING FROM ASSIGNMENTS AND HOMEWORK

An assignment is a statement of what the student is to accomplish and reflects one or more instructional objectives. Assignments, whether completed at home or at school, can ease student learning in many ways, but when poorly planned they can discourage the student and ongoing learning and negatively affect an entire family. *Homework* or *responsibility papers* can be defined as any out-of-class task that a student is assigned as an extension of classroom learning. Like all that you do as a teacher, it is your professional responsibility to think about and plan carefully all homework assignments that you give to students. Before giving students any assignment, consider how you would feel if you were given the assignment and how you would feel if your own child were given the assignment. Think about how much out-of-class time you expect the assignment to take, and to what extent, if any, the parents and guardians should or could be involved in assisting the child in doing the assignment.

The time that a student needs to complete assignments beyond school time will vary according to grade level and school policy. There seems always to be some debate about the value of homework for the elementary grades. Recently, 85 percent of parents surveyed indicated that their children are doing the right amount of homework and say homework is important because it helps the children learn more in school and will help them reach their goals after high school, and three-quarters of the students say they have enough time to complete their assignments.[19] Perhaps the issue is, or should be, not with the value of homework per se but with the quality of the homework that is assigned. Having said that, very generally, children in grades K–3 may be expected to spend from none to about 15 minutes each school night on homework, while children in grades 4–6 may spend 40 minutes to an hour or more. Some parents and teachers point out that the amount of time spent on homework may be increased by the time students spend "IM"ing (instant messaging) their friends when parents can't see what's going on.

Purposes for Homework Assignments

Purposes for giving homework assignments or assigning responsibility papers can be any one or more of the following that are reflected in the word **PRIDE:**

P To personalize, to practice, and to provide learning opportunities,—that is, to personalize the learning for students, to practice and review what has been learned, and to provide a mechanism by which students receive constructive feedback;

R To reinforce, to review, and to reach family members,—that is, to reinforce classroom experiences, review content, and to reach parents or guardians and other family members and get them involved in their children's learning;

I To individualize learning,—that is, to increase personal learning by individuals;

D To develop skills,—that is, to increase students' research skills, study skills, and organization skills; and

E To extend the time that students are engaged in learning.

Parent/Guardian Homework

As a useful strategy to increase home–school communication, we suggest to teachers that one homework assignment each week necessitate adult involvement. This could be an interview, shared reading, and so on. This keeps parents aware of what their children are doing. We know of one teacher who not only gives the students homework, but gives parents brief homework, too. The teacher uses letter writing as a teaching tool that teaches the students to write a weekly letter and increases weekly communication with parents. Each week, the teacher writes brief notes telling what the class has been working on during that week to the parents of her students and then gives her notes to the students to read. To follow up after reading the teacher's note, each student also writes a letter about what was learned each week to his or her parent. The letters are sent home every Friday afternoon. The parents are encouraged to reply in writing to the teacher and to their child, too, in an activity the students call *parent/guardian homework*; this is a term that the students enjoy because they like the idea of their parents/guardians doing homework just as they do. The letters from the parents sent back to school are kept through the year in a binder with covers featuring artwork by the students. In addition to the idea of parent/guardian homework, there are other parent activities that can be done at home with a child to reinforce the child's classroom learning; see Figure 10.6.

Activities

A child is likely to perform well in school when one or more members of a child's family are involved in and supportive of the child's learning. Here are just a few activity suggestions that a family member can do with a child to reinforce the child's learning.

General

- Ask questions about things the child is learning and doing and encourage lengthy answers.
- Expect the child to succeed in school. Encourage the child with praise for hard work and a job well done.
- Have a special place for studying that is quiet and free of distractions.
- Have paper, pencils, crayons, and washable markers handy. Encourage children to write.
- Keep a variety of reading materials in the home. Use them yourself to show you value reading and learning, too.
- Turn a cardboard box (big enough for notebooks) into a special school box to hold all school things when the child comes home. Have the child decorate the box with pictures, words, and artwork.
- Watch television with the child and talk about the things you like and don't like about the shows. Limit the viewing time.

The Arts

- Keep simple art supplies available around the house; encourage self-expression. Pictures don't have to be something that you recognize.
- Help the child make connections between art and other subjects. Look at and talk about book illustrations when you are reading together.
- Display the child's art and music in the home.
- Encourage the child to sing and to sway and dance to music.
- Encourage the child to learn to play a musical instrument, homemade or otherwise.

Geography

- Where are we? Teach the child your address. Look at maps together to see where you live and where the school is. How close or far are you from the school?
- What makes a place special? List some things about where you live. What is the climate like? What kinds of plants and animals share your environment?
- What impact have people had on where you live?
- What does it mean to live in a global society? Make a chart of the things that are happening in other parts of the world that affect you.
- When you talk with the child, use words that indicate direction: "We are going north to New York to visit Grandma," or "The school is three blocks west of our apartment."

History

- Get to know the history of the town or city or place where you live.
- Read with the child about people and events that have made a difference in the world.
- Select a photo of a person in your family or someone else you admire or respect. Tell the child what the person did. Why do you admire this person? Talk about the results of the person's actions.
- Share family history with the child.
- When you celebrate holidays, explain to the child what is being celebrated and why.

(Continued)

Figure 10.6
Activities that can be done at home with a child to reinforce the child's classroom learning.
(*Source:* Adapted from U.S. Department of Education publication, *Learning Partners: A Guide to Educational Activities for Families*, retrieved from www.pueblo.gsa.gov/cic_text/family/lpartner/lpartner.htm)

Mathematics

- From the time the child is very young, count everything. When you empty a grocery bag, count the number of apples. Count the number of stairs to your home.
- Help the child do math in his or her head with lots of small numbers; ask questions: "If I have 4 cups and I need 7, how many more do I need?" or "If I need 12 drinks for the class, how many packages of 3 drinks will I need?"
- Put objects into groups. When you do laundry, separate items of clothing: all the socks in one pile, shirts in another, and pants in another. Divide the socks by color and count the number of each. Draw pictures and graphs of clothes in the laundry: 4 red socks, 10 blue socks, 12 white socks.
- Show the child that you like numbers. Play number games and think of math problems as puzzles to be solved. Tell the child that anyone can learn math. Point out numbers in the child's life in terms of weight, measurements involving food preparation, temperature, and time.

Reading

- Go to the library together and check out books, especially books recommended by the teacher or the librarian.
- If the child has difficulty with a word, you can help in several ways: have the child skip the word, read the rest of the sentence, and then ask what word would make sense in the sentence; have the child use what is known about letters and the sounds that they make to "sound out" the word; or supply the words and keep reading—enjoyment is the main goal.
- Listen to your child read homework or a responsibility paper to you.
- Point to the words on the page when you read aloud. Move your finger from left to right.
- Read aloud to your child: books, newspaper and magazine articles, words on the cereal box, labels on canned goods, road signs.

Science

- Ask the child questions: How do you suppose a clock works? Why does a bird make a nest and what is the nest made of? How does electricity help us every day?
- Ask the child to make predictions about the weather or how fast a plant will grow or how high a piece of paper will fly with the wind. Have the child then test to see if the predictions were correct. Remind the child that it may take several tries before obtaining an answer, and even then it may only be tentative. Keep trying; keep testing.
- Have the child start collections of shells, rocks, or bugs, so that the child can see similarities and patterns.
- Help the child look at what causes things to change. What happens when a plant doesn't have water or sunlight?
- Watch ants in an anthill or around spilled food. Explain that when an ant finds food, it goes back to its "home" to "tell" others. As it goes, it leaves a trail that other ants in the nest can smell. The ants find the food by smelling their way along the trail.

Writing

- Encourage the young child to get ready to write by scribbling, drawing, and making designs with letters.
- Have the child interview a family member or neighbor.
- Play writing and spelling games.
- Show that you write often to make lists, take down messages, send cards, write letters, or write e-mail messages.
- Write often to the child. Put a note in the lunch bag/box; make a birthday poster; or send a postcard or brief note from work.

Figure 10.6
Activities that can be done at home with a child to reinforce the child's classroom learning. (*Continued*)

Opportunities for Recovery

While it is important to encourage good initial efforts by students, sometimes, for a multitude of reasons, a student's first effort is inadequate or is lacking entirely. Perhaps the student is absent unexcused from school or the student does poorly on an assignment or fails to turn in an assignment on time or at all. While accepting late work from students is extra work for you, many educators report that it is worthwhile to give students opportunity for recovery and a day or so to make corrections and resubmit an assignment for an improved score. We realize that allowing the resubmission of a marked or tentatively graded paper increases the amount of paperwork for you. However, out of regard for the students who do well from the start, you should consider carefully before allowing a resubmitted paper to receive an A grade (unless, of course, it was an A paper originally).

Students sometimes have legitimate reasons for not completing an assignment by the due date. At times, the student may have a perfectly justifiable, although officially unexcused, reason for being absent from school. It is our opinion that you should listen and exercise professional judgment in each instance. As others have said before, there is nothing democratic about treating unequals as equals. Providing recovery options for students who are educational works in progress seems a sensible, humanly, scholarly, and professionally responsible approach.

HOW TO AVOID THE PAPER CRUSH

A "Waterloo" for some beginning teachers is that of being buried under mounds of student work to be read, marked, and graded, leaving less and less time for effective planning. To keep this from happening to you, consider the following suggestions.

While in our opinion you should read everything that your students write or draw, papers can be read with varying degrees of intensity and scrutiny, depending on the purpose of the assignment. For assignments that are designed for learning, understanding, and practice, you can allow students to check papers themselves using either self-checking or peer-checking (but see the caution that follows). During the self- or peer-checking, you can monitor the activity and record the extent to which the student did the assignment, or, after the checking, you can collect the papers and do your recording. Besides reducing the amount of paperwork for you, student self- or peer-checking provides other advantages: It allows students to see and understand their errors, it encourages productive peer dialogue, and it helps students develop self-assessment techniques and standards. If the purpose of the assignment is to assess mastery learning and competence, then the papers should be read, marked, and graded only by you, the teacher.

Multiple Assessment

To avoid the paper crush, you can also consider multiple assessment of one piece of writing. To do this, engage your students in writing paragraphs, essays, or responses to open-ended questions. You mention to the students just a few specific skills that you want to target in the written work. For example, you might assign essay writing to students based on an autobiography or biography they have read and mention as part of the specifications that you will grade just on their abilities in the category of mechanical skills—spelling, punctuation, and so on. After evaluating a student's writing on these skills, file the work in the student's portfolio and use it again later for the student's self-editing and mention that this time as part of the specifications, you will grade on a previously unaddressed category of skills. Then select one category—the student's style, use of paragraph structure, including a topic sentence, use of relevant details, logical sequence, or writing a conclusion. Conduct your second evaluation/feedback

and again, file the work and use it still another time for self-editing by the student; mention that this time you will assess the student's use of still another category of skills. This time, you announce that you are assessing one of these features—the students' use of content with emphasis on details, good descriptions, or the inclusion and accuracy of cited references. In this multiple assessment approach, a student's written work might be self-edited by the student several times and then examined by you several times and assessed in different categories at different times.

Peer-Checking: Use with Caution

Peer-checking can be a problem. For instance, children might spend more time watching the person checking their paper than accurately checking the one given to them. Further, the use of peer-checking does not necessarily allow the student to see or understand his or her mistakes.

Of even greater concern is the matter of privacy. When student A becomes knowledgeable of the academic success (or lack thereof) of student B, student A, the "checker," could cause emotional or social embarrassment to student B. Peer-checking of papers should perhaps be done only for the editing of the classmates' drafts of stories or research projects, and for making suggestions about content and grammar, but definitely not assigning a grade or marking answers right or wrong. To protect students' rights to privacy, the use of peers *grading* each other's papers (along with the public/electronic posting of grades) should be avoided. Perhaps names on papers should be marked out and numbers assigned privately to students who write their numbers on the papers, mix their papers in a stack on a table, then receive a paper at random for peer checking. Returning the papers to a table and placing them in a wide spread allows students to retrieve their numbered papers as they return to class from recess. Harassment and embarrassment from knowledge of one's academic success through peer-checking have no place in an elementary school classroom; they do not provide for a safe learning environment.

PROJECT-CENTERED LEARNING: GUIDING LEARNING FROM INDEPENDENT AND GROUP INVESTIGATIONS, PAPERS, AND ORAL REPORTS

For the most meaningful student learning to occur, independent study, individual writing, student-centered projects, and oral reports should be major features of your instruction. There will be times when the children will be interested in an in-depth inquiry learning about a topic and will want to pursue a particular topic for study. This undertaking of a learning project can be flexible—an individual student, a team of two, a small group, or the entire class can do the investigation. The **project** should be a relatively long-term investigative study from which students produce something called the **culminating presentation.** It is a way for students to apply what they are learning. The culminating presentation is a final presentation that usually includes three aspects: (a) it involves an oral report; (b) it involves a hands-on item of some kind (e.g., a display, play or skit, book, song or poem, video, multimedia presentations, a website, diorama, poster, maps, charts, computer webquests, and so on); and (c) it involves a written report. The latter two are usually given to the teacher for the teacher's review and assessment and sometimes contributed or loaned to a long-term display in the classroom or elsewhere in the school.

Values and Purposes of Project-Centered Learning

The values and purposes of encouraging project-centered learning for students, either individually or in groups, are shown in Figure 10.7. As has been demonstrated time and again, when students work together on projects, integrating knowledge as the need arises, motivation and learning follow naturally.[20]

Guidelines for Guiding Students in Project-Centered Learning

Choosing the Project

In collaboration with you, your students can select a topic for the project. You can stimulate ideas and provide an opportunity for the students to see the results of other students' projects (sometimes called anchor projects or studies). For example, as mentioned earlier in *Looking at Teachers I* (Chapter 7), a group of third-grade students from Spring Street School (Shrewsbury, MA) created and produced a podcast of an audio walking tour of the historic part of their town.[21] Such a project as that could be shown year after year to other groups of students as an anchor study. In addition, you can motivate students to share ideas in the following other ways:

- By providing lists of things students might do
- By mentioning each time an idea comes up in class that this could be a good idea for an independent, small-group, or class project
- By having former students visit your class and tell about their projects

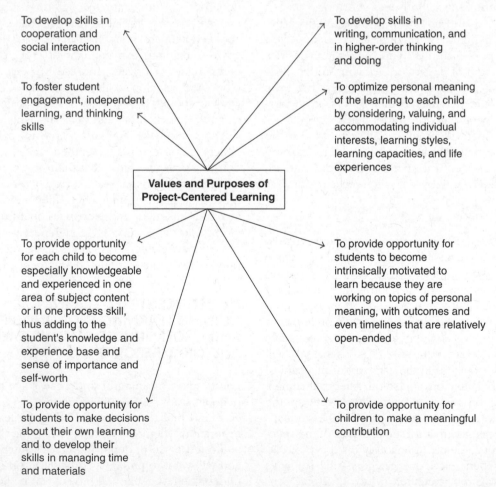

Figure 10.7
Values and purposes of project-centered learning.

- By showing anchor studies as previously mentioned
- By suggesting Internet resources and readings that are likely to give students ideas
- By holding class discussions to brainstorm ideas

Collaborating with the Students

Sometimes, you can write the general problem or topic in the center of a graphic web (perhaps designed as the hub of a wheel) and ask the students to brainstorm some questions. The questions (written on spokes that radiate from the hub of the wheel) can be "reserved" by students and lead to ways for them to investigate, draw sketches, construct models, record findings, predict items, compare and contrast, and discuss understandings. In essence, brainstorming such as this is the technique often used by teachers in collaboration with the students for the selection of a theme, topic, or subtopics of an interdisciplinary thematic unit of study.

Establishing Groups

Allow students to individually choose whether they will work in small groups, in pairs, or work alone. If they choose to work in groups, then help them delineate job descriptions for each member of the group. For instance, you can help the students keep the following role descriptions in mind: facilitator, recorder, reporter, materials manager, and thinking monitor. For project work, groups of five or fewer children usually work better than groups of more than five. Even if the project is one the whole class is pursuing, the project should be divided into parts with small groups of students or partners or individuals undertaking independent study of these parts.

Keeping Track of the Students' Progress

You can do this by reviewing periodic (daily or weekly) updates of their work, perhaps as maintained in their journals (see a later discussion in this chapter). Set deadlines with the groups. Meet with the groups daily (perhaps a class meeting at the end of the day) to discuss any questions or problems they have. Based on their investigations, the students can prepare to present their findings in culminating presentations.

Providing Coaching and Guidance

You can work with each student or student team in topic selection, as well as in the processes of written and oral reporting. To do this, allow students to develop their own procedures, but guide their preparation of work outlines and preliminary drafts, giving them modeling, constructive feedback, and encouragement along the way. Without frequent progress reporting by the students and guidance and reinforcement from the teacher, a student can get frustrated and quickly lose interest in the project. Guide students in their identification of potential resources and in the techniques of research. Your coordination with the library and resource locations is central to the success of project-centered teaching. Frequent drafts and progress reports from the students are a must. At each of these stages, provide students with constructive feedback and encouragement. Provide written guidelines for students who legitimately need negotiations. You can negotiate timelines for their outlines, drafts, and the completed projects.

Promoting Sharing

You can plan to have the students share both the progress and the results of their study with the rest of the class. The amount of time allowed for this sharing will, of course, depend upon any of many variables. The value of this type of instructional strategy comes not only from individual contributions but also from the learning that results from the experience and the communication of that experience with others.

Advising and Guiding Students

Without careful teacher planning, and steady guidance for students, project-based teaching can be a frustrating experience for both the teacher and the students. This is true especially for a beginning teacher who is inexperienced in such a complex instructional undertaking. Students should do projects because they want to and because the projects seem meaningful. Therefore, with guidance from you, the students should decide *what* project to do and *how* to do it. As part of this guidance, your role is to advise and guide students so they experience success. If you lay out a project in too much detail, that project is a procedure rather than a student-centered project. There must be a balance between structure and opportunities for student empowerment via choices and decision making.

Writing Should Be a Required Component of Project-Centered Learning

You can provide options but insist that writing (or drawing) be a part of each student's work. You realize that research has examined the links among writing, thinking, and learning, and this has helped emphasize the importance of writing. Writing is a complex intellectual behavior and process that helps the learner create and record his or her understanding—that is, to construct meaning. Because of this understanding, insist that writing be a part of the student's work (see the section that follows).

When teachers use project-centered teaching with upper-grade elementary students, a paper and an oral presentation are usually automatically required of all students. It is recommended that you use the **I-Search paper** approach rather than the traditional research paper approach. Under your careful guidance, the students (a) list queries/phrases/statements—information they would like to know, and from the list select one that can become the research topic, (b) conduct the study while maintaining a log of their activities and findings, which, in fact, becomes a process journal, (c) prepare a booklet of paragraphs and visual representations that present their findings, (d) prepare a written summary of the findings including the significance the study and their personal thoughts, and (e) share the project as a final oral report with the teacher and classmates. You may want to make available a reference that addresses the needs of young researchers, such as Jean Dreher's *Easy Steps to Writing Fantastic Research Reports* (New York: Scholastic, 2000).

Assess the Final Product

The final product of the project, including papers, oral reports, and presentations, should be assessed and graded. The method of determining the grade should be clear to students from the beginning, along with the weight of the project grade toward the term grade. You can provide the students with clear descriptions (scoring guides/rubrics) of how assessment and grading will be done. The final grade for the study should be based on four criteria: (a) organization, including meeting draft and progress report deadlines; (b) the quality and quantity of both content and procedural knowledge gained from the experience; (c) the quality of the student's sharing of that learning experience with the rest of the class; and (d) the quality of the student's final written and/or oral report. A sample scoring guide/rubric for the oral presentation of a project is shown in Figure 10.8. A rubric for a primary grade (Figure 10.9) has a visual system attached to it to help young children grasp their achievement. Sometimes this is a series of faces with different expressions. For other grades, it has rating scales, or levels of proficiency with paragraphs describing factors that results in that level, or levels of criteria. More on preparing and using rubrics was discussed in Chapter 6.[22]

Project Presentation Scoring Guide/Rubric

Clear understanding of the project and organized in delivery

Score 5. Excellent presentation
- Made eye contact throughout presentation.
- Spoke loudly enough for all to hear.
- Spoke clearly and distinctly.
- Spoke for time allotted.
- Stood straight and confidently.
- Covered at least five pieces of important information.
- Introduced project.

Well thought out and planned in delivery

Score 4. Well-planned presentation
- Made eye contact throughout most of the presentation.
- Spoke loudly enough and clearly most of the time.
- Spoke for most of time allotted.
- Covered at least four pieces of important information.
- Introduced project.

Mostly organized in delivery

Score 3. Adequate presentation
- Made eye contact at times.
- Some of audience could hear the presentation.
- Audience could understand most of what was said.
- Spoke for about half of allotted time.
- Covered at least three pieces of important information.
- Project was vaguely introduced.

Disorganized and unprepared; incomplete information

Score 2 to 1. Unprepared presentation
- Poor eye contact during presentation.
- Most of audience was unable to hear presentation.
- Information presented was unclear.
- Spoke for only a brief time.
- Covered less than three pieces of information.
- Project not introduced or only vaguely introduced.

Figure 10.8
Sample scoring rubric for oral presentation of project.

Soaring High! (4)
—I followed directions.
—I read the example carefully.
—I added words to the sentence that made sense.
—I used my best handwriting

Taking Off (3)
—I followed most directions.
—I read the example.
—I added words to the sentence.
—I need to practice forming my letters.

Getting Ready (2)
—I followed some directions.
—I added some words, but I had trouble thinking of them.
—My letters don't look like the ones on my alphabet strip.
—I asked for help when I needed it.

Still on the Ground (1)
—I didn't follow directions.
—I didn't fill in all the spaces.
—I need to redo my work.
—I need to ask for help.

Figure 10.9
Scoring guide/rubric for writing: completing a sentence frame.

WRITING ACROSS THE CURRICULUM

Because writing is a discrete representation of thinking, every teacher should consider himself or herself to be a teacher of writing. A student should experience a variety of kinds of writing rather than the same form year after year.

Kinds of Writing

Perhaps most important to you as a teacher is that writing should be emphasized as a process that illustrates one's thinking, rather than solely as a product completed as an assignment. During any school day, writing and thinking develop best when a student experiences various forms of writing to express his or her ideas. Consider the following types of writing.

Analysis and Speculation About Effects. The writer conjectures about the causes and effects of a specific event.

Autobiographical Incident. The writer narrates a special event in his or her life and states or implies the significance of the event.

Character Assumption. The writer writes a story or maintains a diary of his or her reading in the first person, assuming the persona of a character in a book being read or a figure in history being studied.

Evaluation. The writer presents a judgment on the worth of an item—artwork, a book, consumer product, educational film, movie—and supports this with reasons and evidence.

Eyewitness Account. The writer tells about an event, a group, or person that was objectively observed from the outside.

Firsthand Biographical Sketch. Through incidents and descriptions, the writer characterizes a person he or she knows well.

Problem Solving. The writer describes and analyzes a specific problem and then proposes and argues for a solution.

Report of Information. The writer collects data from observation and research and chooses material that best represents a phenomenon or concept.

Story. Using dialogue and description, the writer shows the conflict between characters or between a character and the environment.

Student Journals

Many teachers have their students maintain **student journals** in which the students keep a log of their activities, findings, and thoughts (i.e., *process journals*, as discussed previously) and write their thoughts about what it is they are studying (*response journals* are commonly used). Actually, there are two types of response journals: dialogue journals and reading-response journals. *Dialogue journals* are used by students to write anything that is on their minds—usually on the right side of a page—while peers, teachers, and parents or guardians respond on the left side of a page, thereby "talking with" the journal writer. *Response journals* are used by students to write—and perhaps draw a "visual learning log"—to present their reactions to what is being studied.

Purpose and Assessment of Student Journal Writing

Normally, academic journals are *not* the personal diaries of the writer's recollection of daily events and the writer's thoughts about the events. Rather, the purpose of journal writing is to encourage students to write, to think about their writing, to record their creative thoughts *about what they are learning*, and to share their written thoughts with an audience—all of which help in the development of their thinking skills, in their learning, and in their development as writers. Students are encouraged to write about experiences, both in school and out, that are related to the topics being studied. They should be encouraged to record their thoughts about what and how they are learning.

Journal writing provides practice in expression and should not be graded by the teacher. Negative comments and evaluations from the teacher will often discourage creative and spontaneous expression by the students. As the teacher, you should read the journal writing and then offer constructive and positive feedback; but we suggest you avoid negative comments or grading the journals. For grading purposes, you can simply record whether or not a student does, in fact, maintain the required journal and, perhaps, meets due dates. As mentioned earlier, turn to Figure 10.8 and 10.9 for examples of scoring rubrics.

You'll be interested to know that the National Council of Teachers of English (NCTE) has developed guidelines for journal writing. For a copy, contact NCTE directly or via the Internet. Resources on writing across the curriculum, including the NCTE, are shown in Figure 10.10. See also the readings at the end of this chapter.[23, 24, 25]

- The American Literacy Council, 1441 Mariposa Ave., Boulder, CO 80302; (303) 440-7385; www.americanliteracy.com

- International Reading Association, P.O. Box 8139, 800 Barksdale Road, Newark, DE 19714-8139; www.reading.org

- National Council of Teachers of English, 1111 Kenyon Road, Urbana, IL 61801; (217) 328-3870; www.ncte.org

- National Writing Project (NWP), 2105 Bancroft Way, #1042, University of California, Berkeley, Berkeley, CA 94720-1042; www.nwp.org

- Whole Language Umbrella; Affiliated with NCTE; www.ncte.org/wlu

Figure 10.10
Resources for writing across the curriculum.*

*Ask students to be partners and write cooperatively about content, realizing that ELLs/students with learning problems have different degrees of knowledge about the English language, vocabulary, word use, grammar, and writing expectations.

LOOKING AT TEACHERS II

Integrated Technology, Desktop Publishing

Let's suppose that the students from your class have been working nearly all year on an interdisciplinary thematic unit entitled *Surviving Natural Disasters* (referring back to the example in Chapter 5 regarding ITU themes). As a culmination to the students' study, they used desktop publishing to publish a document entitled *Natural Disaster Preparation and Survival Guide for* _____ (community name). They proudly distributed the guide to their parents and other members of the community.

Long before preparing the guide, however, the students had to do research. You guided them in this process. To learn about the history of various kinds of natural disasters that had occurred or might occur locally and about the sorts of preparations a community should take for each kind of disaster, students searched sources on the Internet. They found federal documents, scientific articles, and articles from newspapers from around the world where natural disasters had occurred. They also searched in the local library for informational books such as *Dangerous Planet: Natural Disasters That Changed History* (Crown, 2003) by Bryn Barnard. They read local newspapers' archives to learn about floods, tornadoes, and fires that had occurred during the past 200 years. Much to their surprise, they also learned that their community is located very near the New Madrid Fault and did, in fact, experience a serious earthquake in 1811, although none since that time. As a result of that earthquake, the Mississippi flowed in reverse, and its course changed and even caused the formation of a new lake in Tennessee.

In class meetings, the students decided on different projects to support the publication of their guide and the teacher made a professional effort to ensure equity in interaction with the students (see Figure 10.1). Among the students' projects were the following:

- *Chat meeting.* The students were encouraged to use their favorite (parent-approved) chat source or to use some free chat space available through ParaChat (www.parachat.com) to organize a chat session with other students to discuss natural disasters and the consequences, to learn what others did to prepare for disasters, and to learn some survival techniques that were used during and after a disaster. After the chat sessions, the students made recommendations to the class about material they wanted to include in the guide based on the content of their chat discussions.

- *Newsletters through e-mail.* The students were invited to use their favorite bulk e-mail software, or with district permission, use the software available in the school district. The students gathered e-mail addresses (with parent permissions) and advertised their newsletter to other students. They gathered news about their research for the guide, wrote a newsletter about what they were learning, determined their publication schedule, and later, distributed the newsletter through e-mail.

- *Use of copyrighted sources.* From published and copyrighted sources, including websites, the students also found many useful photographs, graphics, and articles, which they included in whole, or in part, in their Natural Disaster Guide. They cited the sources but did so without obtaining permission from all of the original copyright holders where they used whole materials.

You and the other members of your teaching team and other people were so impressed with the students' work that they were encouraged to offer the document for publication on the school's website. Additionally, the document was received with so much acclaim that the students decided to sell it in local stores. They wanted to help defray the original cost of duplication and enable them to continue the supply of guides to people who wanted to purchase them.

Caution About Copyrighted Sources

Related to the teaching scenario discussed here, there is a positive aspect as well as a negative aspect. The positive aspect is that the students used a valuable technological tool, the Internet, to research a variety of sources, including many primary ones. The negative aspect is that when they published their guidebook on the Internet and when they made copies of their guide to be sold, they did so without the permission from some of the original copyright holders. Unknowingly, they were infringing on copyright law. Students need to be aware that unless there is a clear statement that materials taken from the Internet are in the public domain, it is best for a teacher and students to assume that the materials are copyrighted and should not be used without expressed permission. Figures 10.2, 10.3, and 10.4, mentioned earlier, provide guidelines for using copyrighted printed materials, computer software, and multimedia programs.

SUMMARY

This chapter has continued the development of your repertoire of teaching strategies. As you know, young people can be quite peer-conscious, can have relatively short attention spans for experiences in which they are uninterested, and prefer active experiences that engage many or all of their senses. Most are intensely curious about things of interest to them. You have found that cooperative learning, student-centered projects, and teaching strategies that emphasize shared discovery learning and inquiry learning within a psychologically safe environment encourage the most positive aspects of thinking and learning for children. Central to your strategy selection should be those strategies that encourage children to become independent thinkers and skilled learners who can help in the planning, structuring, regulating, and assessing of their own learning and learning activities. In addition, there is a large variety of useful and effective aids, media, and resources from which to draw as you plan your instructional experiences; this is the purpose of www.MyEducationLab.com that contains video assignments and other resources to support this resource guide.

What's to Come. In the next chapter (Chapter 11), your attention is directed to techniques designed to help you assess the development of your teaching skills and continue your professional growth, a process that is now only beginning but will continue throughout your teaching career.

When you finish reading the next chapter, you'll be ready to complete a Final Self-Check Reflection Guide in Appendix B to assess your competencies up to this point. You'll note that your reflection of your Final Self-Check means (a) you'll give careful thought to the items on the self-check, (b) you'll take time to pay attention to those you're not sure about, (c) you'll reconsider any previous actions, events, or decisions you've made related to the items, (d) you'll take steps to research information you need related to the items, and (e) you'll confer with a colleague if you wish.

EXTENDING MY PROFESSIONAL COMPETENCY

With Discussion

Grouping. What would I say to a parent who inquires about the values of cooperative learning groups? **To do:** Describe, to a colleague, any research that you can find on the use of cooperation versus competition in teaching in the elementary classroom. If you have some concerns, explain to a colleague what they are.

With Video

Video Activity: Use of Groupings and Assignments. How can I explain how I would use cooperative learning to an educator interviewing me for a teaching job?

PEARSON
myeducationlab

Go to the Video Examples section of Topic #9: Group Interaction Models in the MyEducationLab for your course to view the video entitled "STAD Model of Cooperative Learning."

View the video with a colleague and take notes about one of the following: (a) the steps you see that implement cooperative learning and (b) any assignments given. If you don't see the teacher giving assignments on the video, discuss how an assignment could be incorporated into the video. View the video again if needed. If time permits, discuss your notes with a colleague and state what you could say about cooperative learning at a later date in a job interview.

With Portfolio

Portfolio Planning. How can I further develop my professional portfolio and show my knowledge of grouping and assignments? This activity will support Principles 3, 4, and 9 of INTASC and Standards 2, 3, 4, 6, and 7 of NBPTS and Praxis II teacher test content (as seen on the inside of the front cover of this book). **To do:** To add to your portfolio, you can develop and write a one- to two-page paper explaining your knowledge of using groupings and assignments. Label your paper "My Use of Groupings and Assignments." After reading and interacting with this chapter, you can state how you have developed your competency in one or two of the following objectives:

- I can describe my knowledge about using a whole-class discussion as a teaching strategy
- I can contribute to a list of guidelines for using whole-class discussion as a teaching strategy
- I can explain how I can personalize the instruction (differentiated/tiered instruction) to ensure success for each student
- Return to the front of this chapter for more objectives.

Place your paper in your portfolio folder or in your computer file.

With Teacher Tests Study Guide

Teacher Tests for Future Licensing and Certification. How can I prepare for taking a state teacher test to qualify for my teaching certificate/license by practicing my responses about teaching questions? **To do:** For this chapter, the constructed-response-type question, similar to those found on state tests for teacher licensing and certification, is found in Appendix A. The question helps you take another look at the classroom vignette, *Looking at Teachers II*, at the end of this chapter. Write your response and, if you wish, discuss it with another teaching candidate. After the discussion, make changes in your response. If appropriate, use one or two of your colleague's suggestions to help you change your response to the question. Place your response in a Teacher Tests Study Guide folder or type/scan into a computer file. Plan to review your response and reread it for study purposes before taking a teacher test.

With Target Topics for Teacher Tests (TTTT)

If I wanted a source to study specific subject matter as a way to prepare for taking a state teacher test to qualify for licensing and certification, what could I use? **To do:** You'll recall that if you are preparing to take a teacher test, you can review subject matter by locating Target Topics for Teacher Tests in the subject index at the end of this book. The topics are called out with bullets (•) by selected word entries. The selected word entries identify selected core subject matter—such as groupings, assignments, and others—that the authors suggest reviewing to prepare for taking a teacher test exam for licensing and certification similar to your state's test or to the Praxis II Principles of Learning and Teaching exam.

WITH READING

Brisk, M. E., and Harrington, M. M. (2000). *Literacy and Bilingualism: A Handbook for ALL Teachers.* Mahwah, NJ: Erlbaum.

Childers-Burpo, D. M. (2002, Spring). Mirrors and microscopes: The promise of national board certification in the era of accountability. *Contemporary Education, 72*(1), 14–17.

Cooper, J. (2003). *Classroom Teaching Skills,* (7th ed.). New York: Houghton Mifflin.

Danna, Stephen (2003, Feb./Mar.). Pursuing National Board Certification. *Pi Lambda Theta Educational Horizons* (Bloomington, IN), 5.

Duncan, D., and Lockhart, L. (2000). *I-Search, You Search, WE All Learn to Research: A How-To-Do-It Manual for Teaching Elementary School Students to Solve Information Problems.* Norwich, CT: Neal-Schuman.

Dunn, M. A. (2000). Staying the Course of Open Education. *Educational Leadership, 57*(7), 20–24.

Echevarria, J., and Graves, A. (1998). *Sheltered Content Instruction: Teaching English-language Learners with Diverse Abilities.* Boston: Allyn & Bacon.

Greenwood, C. M., and Walters, C.E. (2005). *Literature-Based Dialogue Journals: Reading, Writing, Connecting, Reflecting.* Norwood, MA: Christopher-Gordon.

Hofstadter, D. R. (2000). Analogy as the Core of Cognition. In J. Gleick, (Ed.), *The Best American Science Writing 2000.* New York: Ecco Press.

Marzano, R. J., Pickering, D. J., and Pollock, J. E. (2001). *Classroom Instruction That Works.* Chapter 7, Cooperative Learning, pp. 84–91. Alexandria, VA: Association for Supervision and Curriculum Development.

Smith, J. A. (2000). Singing and Songwriting Support Early Literacy Instruction. *The Reading Teacher, 53*(8), 646–649.

Thomason, T., and York, C. (2000). *Write on Target: Preparing Young Writers to Succeed on State Writing Achievement Tests.* Norwood, MA: Christopher-Gordon.

WITH NOTES

1. K. Egan, Learning in Depth, *Educational Leadership, 66*(3), 58–63 (November 2008).

2. For information about how to identify equity problems and develop programs to help schools achieve academic excellence for all students, contact EQUITY 2000, 1233 20th St. NW, Suite 600 Washington, DC 20036-2304; 202-822-5930.

3. L. S. Walters, Putting Cooperative Learning to the Test, *Harvard Education Letter, 16*(3), 1–6 (May/June 2000); See also M. S. Leighton in J. Cooper's *Classroom Teaching Skills,* 7th ed. (Boston: Houghton Mifflin, 2003).

4. L. S. Walters, see note 3.

5. For developing understandings in groups/individuals, productive helping, and students explaining their thinking and reasons for their answers, see N. Webb, S. Farivar, and A. Mastergeorge, Productive Helping in Cooperative Groups, *Theory into Practice, 41*(1) (2002); for more details about CLG strategies and support of student thinking, see M. Keefer, C. Zeitz, and L. Resnick, Judging the Quality of Peer-Led Student Dialogues, *Cognition and Instruction, 18*(1), 53–61 (2000); also P. Meter and R. Stevens, The Role of Theory in the Study of Peer Collaboration, *Journal of Experimental Education, 69*(1), 113–227 (2000).

6. N. Webb, S. Farivar, and A. Mastergeorge, see note 5.

7. T. L. Good and J. E. Brophy, *Looking in Classrooms,* 9th ed. (New York: Addison Wesley/Longman, 2003).

8. T. L. Good and J. E. Brophy, *op. cit.,* see note 7.

9. For more about tiered instruction, see C. A. Tomlinson, Differentiating Instruction for Academic Diversity, in J. Cooper, *Classroom Teaching Skills* (Boston: Houghton Mifflin, 2003); or C. A. Tomlinson's earlier writing, *The Differentiated Classroom* (Alexandria, VA: Association for Supervision and Curriculum Development, 1999), p. 61.

10. See note 2.

11. R. Ryan and E. Deci, Intrinsic and Extrinsic Motivations: Classic Definitions and New Directions, *Contemporary Educational Psychology, 25,* 54–67 (2000). Also see T. Loveless, *The Brown Center Report on American Education* (Washington, DC: Brookings Institute and Brown Center on Education Policy, 2003), which found that, overall, the numbers in surveys from 1984 to 1999 from the National Assessment of Educational Progress did *not* support the popular misconception about excessive homework.

12. For strategies for one-to-one sessions and for ways to adapt assignments, see R. Barr, Research on the Teaching of Reading, in J. Richardson (Ed.), *Handbook of Research on Teaching*, 4th ed., Washington, DC: American Educational Research Association, 2001), pp. 390–415.

13. See the story of a project that involved sixth-grade students learning Spanish and making books to send to kids in a school with few resources in Guatemala in S. Levy, The Power of Audience, *Educational Leadership* (November 2008), pp. 75–76.

14. B. Honchell (Ed.) with M. Schulz, *Literacy for Diverse Learners: Finding Common Ground in Today's Classrooms* (Norwood, MA: Christopher-Gordon, 2007), p. 15.

15. N. Allison, *Supporting Independent Readers: Strategies to Increase Proficiency and Engagement* (Norwood, MA: Christopher-Gordon, 2007); see also R. J. Swartz, A. L. Costa, B. K. Beyer, R. Reagan, and B. Kallick, *Thinking-Based Learning: Activating Students' Potential* (Norwood, MA: Christopher-Gordon, 2008).

16. B. Beers, *Learning-driven Schools: A Practical Guide for Teachers and Principals* (Alexandria, VA: Association for Supervision and Curriculum Development, 2006).

17. Information about Coalition of Essential Schools (CES), and a directory of participating schools, can be obtained from www.essentialschools.org.

18. S. J. Zepeda, *Real-World Supervision: Adapting Theory to Practice* (Norwood, MA: Christopher-Gordon, 2008).

19. See disc and viewing guide by K. Gallagher, *Twenty Questions Homework* (Portland, ME: Stenhouse Publishers, 2006); D. Viadero, "Survey on Homework Reveals Acceptance, Despite Some Grips" (Eye on Research in *Education Week*, February 20, 2008, p. 10).

20. K. Checkley, *Priorities in Practice: The Essentials in Social Studies* (Alexandria, VA: Association of Supervision and Curriculum Development, 2007); also L. Torp and S. Sage, *Problems as Possibilities: Problem-Based Learning for K–16 Education*, 2nd ed. (Alexandria, VA: Association for Supervision and Curriculum Development, 2002); see A. S. Posamentier, *Math Wonders to Inspire Teachers and Students* (Alexandria, VA: Association for Supervision and Curriculum Development, 2003).

21. A. M. Dlott, (Pod)cast of Thousands, *Educational Leadership* (April, 2007), pp. 80–82.

22. J. Glickman-Bond, *Creating and Using Rubrics in Today's Classrooms: A Practical Guide* (Norwood, MA: Christopher-Gordon, 2006); See also H. G. Andrade, Using Rubrics to Promote Thinking and Learning, *Educational Leadership, 57*(5), 13–18 (February 2000); See C. Danielson, *Enhancing Professional Practice: A Framework for Teaching*, 2nd Ed. and *Electronic Forms and Rubrics for Enhancing Professional Practice* (Alexandria, VA: Association for Supervision and Curriculum Development, 2007).

23. R. Beach, C. Anson, L. A. Breuch, and T. Swiss, *Teaching Writing Using Blogs, Wikis, and Other Digital Tools* (Norwood, MA: Christopher-Gordon, 2009).

24. C. Tomlinson, *How to Differentiate Instruction in Mixed Ability Classrooms*, 2nd ed. (Alexandria, VA: Association for Supervision and Curriculum Development, 2001).

25. T. Palardy, The Rank Book: Forum on Education and Academics, *National Forum: Phi Kappa Phi Journal* (Summer 2001), 3–9.

How Can I Assess My Teaching Effectiveness and Continue My Professional Development?

Michael Newman/Photoedit

Visual Chapter Organizer and Overview

Teaching Effectiveness

- Through Student Teaching and Interning
  Student Teaching *IS* the Real Thing
  Getting Ready for Student Teaching
  First Impressions
  Comments from the University Supervisor

**Teaching Effectiveness Through E-Teaching:
An Emergency E-Teaching Kit**

- Purposes of E-Teaching with an Emergency
  E-Teaching Kit
  Developing an E-Teaching Kit with a
  Multidisciplinary Emphasis

Finding a Teaching Position

- Guidelines for Locating a Teaching Position
  Through a Professional Career Portfolio
  Resources for Locating Teaching Jobs
  The Professional Résumé
  The In-Person Interview

Professional Development

- Through Reflection
  Through Self-Assessment
  Through Journals or Logbooks
  Through Self-Reflection and
  Self-Assessment

Professional Development Through Mentoring

**Professional Development Through Inservice
and Study**

**Professional Development Through Professional
Organizations**

**Professional Development Through
Communications with Other Teachers**

**Professional Development Through
Peer Teaching**

LOOKING AT TEACHERS I

Integrated Technology, Related to Literature

At Green Oaks Fundamental School (San Juan Unified School District, Sacramento County, CA), fourth-grade students always are excited to see what will arrive in the daily mail. They hope it will be Aranea, a large colorful drawing of one of Charlotte's daughters that chooses to live with Wilbur, the pig, on the farm in the children's book *Charlotte's Web*. Aranea is the literary character used by the students to send out into the world and meet some of the people who live beyond their area. Periodically, Aranea goes to meet someone along with a journal entry and a letter from the students who ask that Aranea be allowed to visit for some time. The students suggest that Aranea be shown around and come back with her completed journal entry and anything else that Aranea's part-time caretaker would like to send back to the class. When Aranea returns through the technology of the U.S. postal service, the students show the state and place she just visited on a map, and the returned material is placed in a book or computer file to record Aranea's travels. Who has Aranea visited? Well, she visited former President Bush and his wife, Laura Bush. During her visit, Aranea had breakfast with them and the then–First Lady wrote to the students to say that Aranea had excellent table manners. Aranea has visited college and professional sports teams around the United States, including the Texas Longhorns football team, the Los Angeles Lakers, and the Sacramento Kings basketball team. Also, Aranea has visited places of business—Domino's Pizza, McDonald's—and one government agency, NASA. Further, Aranea has journeyed to visit authors of well-known children's books and traveled to meet senators and state governors in their offices. She has watched famous actors, actresses, and celebrities as they worked on their sets and relaxed in their homes. Some of these famous persons have even sent autographed photographs of themselves with Aranea along with a personal note back to the students.

From each person and place that Aranea has visited, the fourth-grade students have learned something. They mention that they have learned (1) that people care about their school and class, (2) that people like visiting with Aranea, (3) that they work hard to make Aranea's visit fun for the students, (4) about different parts of the United States and what you can do in those states, (5) about different people and their kindness when they meet Aranea, (6) where all the states are, (7) the postal service technology needed to ensure her safe return to the students, and (8) that people throughout the nation care about public education and the students at their school.[1]

Integrating technology involves discussing technology use related to Aranea, her travels, and the postal service, as shown in these questions:

- What technology is involved in sending and delivering the daily mail that was Aranea's way of traveling? What guest speaker from the post office could visit the class and discuss this? Who might talk to us about this via a computer camera?

- What discussion can take place? Perhaps a student will say something such as, "My brother says Aranea travels by snail mail" or "My sister in high school says e-mail is energy-hog mail and job-loser mail since it takes jobs away from postal workers." Such labeling can open a discussion about the technology used by the postal service as well as what postal workers do to provide individualized service and door-to-door delivery. What are the students' opinions of someone who labels the work of postal employees *snail mail*? Is it possible that this label belittles them and hurts anyone's feelings? Is it possible that such labeling seems to denigrate the hard work the student knows a family member or friend does at the post office?

- What further discussion can happen? Perhaps a student will mention that a relative or a family friend works for the postal service. This statement can begin a discussion about being respectful about the work of others and about ways people can support the mail service for its important delivery of birthday cards and gifts, birth announcements, important documents, overnight packages, three-day express mail, registered mail, certified mail, and first class mail; for memorializing history with its stamp issues; for providing private mail boxes for the people who need them (a law enforcement suggestion); for delivering purchases (especially prescriptions) for incapacitated people; and other services.

- Who wants to talk about feelings of others? Does any student have comments about this name-calling related to the feelings of relatives or friends who work for the postal service? Do the students think a snail-mail labeler is sensitive or insensitive to those who work for the postal service? In what ways can such labeling hurt or demean or sound derogatory to the students' relatives or other people they know? Do the students think such labeling shows respect for the ongoing work one does for the postal service (or other delivery and mail services)?

- Who has a positive comment? In what ways has the postal service assisted people that the students know? Delivering medications? Delivering valuable documents?

One student we know tells how the postal service hired his dad part-time after he had been laid off from his regular job during the latest recession and then cites how the postal service job helped the family survive an economic hardship at that time.

- What else could we find on the web to help us learn more about the current technology used by the postal service? Anyone interested in learning what supportive/nonsupportive remarks were made about an earlier postal service—America's historic pony express?
- What messages can we send to one another to talk about the use of tone and language in the latest personal note that arrived with Aranea? Why do you think the writer of the note considered us as the audience for his or her message?
- Who will be first to copy their message on the writing board so that the rest of us can translate the words into an instant text message? Who will discuss the difference between a complete sentence and an incomplete sentence when we compare two language forms (instant text message/non-standard English and standard English)?
- What messages can we send to each other to brainstorm ideas for writing assignments about Aranea's latest travel? Who will write the idea in the messages on the board so we can discuss them?
- Turning away from the postal service and moving to publishing technology, ask, "What technology is needed to produce a book such as *Charlotte's Web?*" and "What information on which website could help us understand more about this?"
- What technology will help us find out more about the last person and latest place that Aranea visited? Which websites would be most useful? How can we locate the sites?
- How could technology help us thank the people who corresponded with us?

A Focus on Diverse Learners

Now that Aranea has returned, what do we need to do? Encourage all students, and if appropriate, English language learners paired with native-language peers, to discuss that, first, they will show the state and mark the place she just visited on a map. Second, the returned material is read, discussed, and placed in a book or into a computer file to add to the record of Aranea's travels. Next, they can plan the place where Aranea will go next and who she should meet. Since she travels along with a journal entry and a letter from the students who ask in the letter that Aranea be allowed to visit for some time, the journal entry and the letter need to be discussed, dictated, and written. To help achieve what needs to be done, each student can use the MARKER strategy, a series of certain steps that include students having something to work toward (a goal and self-reward) and a tracking plan of the students' progress (Van Reusen and Bos, 1990): **M** means to make a list of goals, order, and a date to accomplish this (this means discuss, dictate, and write journal entry and letter for Aranea; then plan where Aranea will go next and who she should meet); **A** means arrange a plan and work for success; **R** means run your plan and adjust if needed; **K** means keep records; **E** means evaluate your progress; and **R** means reward yourself when you reach a goal.

Just Clicking Around

Consider the students' use of clicking on the computer to study Aranea's travels and the people she met—and imagine you find yourself in a situation where you think that too many students are wasting time on the web by just clicking around without any focus from location to location. We encourage you to research information about this from the point of view of educators and others who are concerned about students spending too much time looking for glossy media and driving back and forth on the cyber road to find barely linked facts on the web. We encourage you to give students time to *think* about what they have found. You may want to have the students give you some evidence that they understand the content or that they have given the subject some individual thought. Ask your instructor for a recommended source on this topic or read *The Flickering Mind: The False Promise of Technology in the Classroom and How Learning Can Be Saved* (Random House, 2003) by Todd Oppenheimer.

CHAPTER OBJECTIVES

Specifically, upon completion of this eleventh chapter, you should be able to:

1. Assess your teaching effectiveness; record self-assessment in student teaching/interning; assess with standards.
2. Prepare for a job interview.
3. Write a résumé.
4. Develop a portfolio for professional growth and development.
5. Self-assess, reflect on what you have done, and evaluate your developing competencies with a final self-check found in Appendix B of this resource guide.

TEACHING EFFECTIVENESS

Through Student Teaching and Interning

You are excited about the prospect of being assigned as a student teacher or intern to your first classroom, but you are also concerned. Questions linger in your mind. Will your cooperating (host) teacher(s) like you? Will you get along? Will the children accept you? Will you be assigned to the school and grade level that you prefer? What curriculum programs will you be expected to use? What will the children be like? Will there be many classroom management problems? How many diverse students and English language learners will be in the class? Your questions will be unending.

Indeed, you *should* be excited and concerned, for this experience of student teaching/interning/mentoring is one of the most significant facets of your program of teacher preparation. In some programs, this practical field experience is planned as a co-experience with the college or university theory and methods classes. In other programs, this practical field experience is the culminating experience. Different sequences are represented in different programs. For example, at some colleges, field teaching extends over two or three semesters. In other programs, teacher candidates first take a theory-class-first arrangement, which includes a full second semester of student teaching. Regardless of when and how your student teaching occurs, the experience is a bright and shining opportunity to hone your teaching skills in a real classroom environment. During this experience, you will probably be supported by an experienced college or university supervisor and by one or more carefully selected cooperating teachers, who will share with you their expertise.

Everyone concerned in the teacher preparation program—your cooperating teacher, your university instructors, school administrators, and your university supervisors—realize that this is your practicum in learning how to teach. As you practice your teaching, you will no doubt make errors, and with the understanding, wisdom, and guidance of those supervising your work, you will benefit and learn from those errors. Sometimes your fresh approach to motivation, your novel ideas for learning activities, and your energy and enthusiasm make it possible for the cooperating teacher to learn from you. We recall one of our student teachers who attended our seminar in student teaching and had been introduced to an approach to grouping students for a social studies project based on social interaction in the classroom (identifying, privately, which students see themselves as wanting to be friends with certain students). In her assigned elementary classroom, the student teacher saw that the elementary students needed to work in groups and talked to her cooperating teacher about grouping. The cooperating teacher admitted to her that she didn't know how to group her elementary students based on social interactions. The student teacher offered to organize the grouping and later, at the university, told us she was feeling great because "I finally had a teachable moment." After all, teaching and learning are always reciprocal processes—even teacher to teacher. What is most important to you at this time is that the children who are involved with you in the teaching-learning process will benefit from your role as the precredentialed teacher in the classroom. The following guidelines are offered to help make this practical experience beneficial to everyone involved.

Student Teaching *IS* the Real Thing

On one hand, because you have a classroom setting for practicing and honing your teaching skills with active, responsive children, your student teaching *is* the real thing. On the other hand, student teaching is *not* real in the sense that your collaborating teacher, not you, has the ultimate responsibility and authority for the classroom and the students' learning.

Getting Ready for Student Teaching

To prepare yourself for student teaching or interning, you must study, plan, practice and reflect. You should become knowledgeable about your students and their developmental backgrounds. In your theory and methods classes, you learned a great deal about children and teaching them. Review your class notes and textbooks from those courses or select some readings from the chapters in Part I of this resource guide. Perhaps some of the topics will have more meaning for you now.

In addition to the aforementioned preparation, you will need to be knowledgeable about your assigned school and the community from which the students come. Review the subject areas you will be teaching and the curriculum content and standards in those areas. Carefully discuss with your cooperating teacher (or teachers, as you may have more than one) and your university supervisor all of the responsibilities that you will be expected to assume. Since it is unlikely that you will assume all the responsibilities at once, there should be discussion of and agreement upon an approximate timeline or schedule showing dates by which you should be prepared to assume various responsibilities.

As a student teacher/intern, you may want to run through each lesson verbally, perhaps in front of a mirror or a camcorder, the night before teaching your lesson. Some student teachers read through each lesson, record the lesson, play it back, and evaluate the extent to which the directions are clear, the instruction is interesting, the sequence is logical, and the lesson closure is concise. Rehearsing a lesson will enable you to ask yourself some of the questions on a brief prelesson rehearsal check shown in Figure 11.1.

Figure 11.1
Brief prelesson rehearsal check.

- In what ways are my voice and body language conveying thorough preparation?
Comments:

- In what ways am I conveying confidence (or uncertainty and confusion)?
Comments:

- Are my directions clear?
Comments:

- Is the instruction interesting?
Comments:

- Are the materials/resources ready?
Comments:

- Is the sequence logical?
Comments:

- Is the lesson closure concise?
Comments:

- In what way am I ready for a Plan B if Plan A turns out to be inappropriate?
Comments:

First Impressions

First impressions are often lasting impressions. You have heard that statement before, and now, as you get ready for this important phrase of your professional preparation, you hear it again. Heed it—for it is crucial to your success. Remember it as you prepare to meet your school principal and cooperating/collaborating teacher for the first time; remember it as you prepare to meet your students for the first time; remember it as you prepare to meet parents and guardians for the first time; and remember it as you prepare for your university supervisor's first observation of your teaching. Remember it again as you prepare for your first teaching job interview. In each case, you have only one opportunity to make a favorable first impression.

Lindfors Photography

For your consideration, locate information about your student teaching/interning from the viewpoint of a cooperating or mentoring teacher from one of the readings at the end of this chapter. Take notes, and if appropriate, share some of the information with your cooperating teacher.

Comments from the University Supervisor

When is the supervisor coming? Is the supervisor going to be here today? Do you see a supervisor's observation of your student teaching as a helpful experience or a painful one? Do you realize that classroom observations of your teaching continue during your beginning years of teaching? Being observed and evaluated does not have to be a painful, nerve-wracking experience for you. You don't have to become a bundle of raw nerve endings when you realize the supervisor is coming to see you. Whether you are a student teacher being observed by your university/college supervisor or an intern or probationary (untenured) teacher being evaluated by your principal (or by a committee of peers as is the case in some schools), some of the professional suggestions in the readings at the end of this chapter may help you turn an evaluating observation into a useful, professionally gratifying experience. Turn to these writings for suggestions for what to do *before* an observation, *during* an observation, and *after* an observation.

As your successful student teaching experience draws to a close, you may be asked to respond to a culminating student teaching experience evaluation. If you haven't seen a culminating evaluation yet, ask your instructor if your group can look at a copy of the evaluation that is used at your college or university. For example, you may be asked to use identified performance evaluation criteria, collect evidence about the performance, and make comments following each performance section related to your state's teaching performance expectations/ standards. Identified criteria could include points such as the following:

4: Consistently demonstrates ability to work collegially with faculty and other school personnel and community members (participates/exhibits the competency)

3, 2: Occasionally demonstrates ability to work collegially with faculty and other school personnel (participates/ exhibits the competency)

1, 0: Little or no participation. Does not demonstrate ability to work collegially with faculty and other school personnel

N/O: Not observed; setting does not apply to demonstration of competency, skill set, knowledge, and/or developmental level.

FINDING A TEACHING POSITION

As your successful student teaching/interning experience draws to a close, you will embark upon finding your first paid teaching job or your first substitute teaching job. The guidelines that follow are provided to help you accomplish your goal.

Guidelines for Locating a Teaching Position

To prepare for finding the position you want or locating a subbing position or interning, focus on the following areas:

1. Obtain strong letters of recommendation from your cooperating teacher(s), your college or university supervisor, and, in some instances, the school principal.
2. Hone your professional preparation as evidenced by your letters of recommendation and other items in your professional portfolio, including your résumé.
3. Refine your job interviewing skills. First, consider the recommendations about your teaching. Some colleges and universities have a career placement center where there is probably a counselor who can advise you how to open the job placement file that will hold your professional recommendations. This enables prospective personnel directors or district personnel who are expecting to employ new teachers to review your recommendations. It is your responsibility to request letters of recommendation and, when appropriate, to supply the person writing the recommendation with the required form and an appropriately addressed, stamped envelope. Sometimes, the job placement files are confidential, so the recommendations will be mailed directly to the placement office. The confidentiality of recommendations may be optional, and, when possible, you may want to maintain your own copies of letters of recommendation and include them in your professional portfolio.

Your Letters of Recommendation

The letters of recommendation from educators at the school(s) where you did your interning or student teaching should include the information mentioned in the brief paragraphs that follow.

Your Preparation

Next, consider your preparation as a teacher. Teachers, as you have learned, represent a myriad of specialties. Hiring personnel will want to know how you see yourself—for example, as a primary-grade teacher, as a specialist in sixth-grade core, or as an elementary school physical education or music teacher. Perhaps your interest is in teaching children at any level of elementary school or only science in grades 4 through 6. You may indicate a special interest or skill, such as competency in sign language or in teaching English to limited-English learners. Or, perhaps, in addition to being prepared to teach elementary school core subjects, you also are musically talented or are bi- or multilingual and have had rich and varied cross-cultural experiences. The hiring personnel who consider your application will be interested in your sincerity and will want to see that you are academically and socially impressive.

Your In-Person Interview

Last, consider your in-person interview with a district official or representatives from a school faculty or both. Sometimes, you will have several interviews or you will be interviewed simultaneously with a small group of candidates. There may be an initial screening interview by a panel of administrators and teachers from the district, followed by an interview by a school principal or by a school team composed of one or more teachers and administrators from the interested school or district. In all interviews, your verbal and nonverbal behaviors will be observed as you respond to various questions, including (a) factual questions about your interning or student teaching or about particular curriculum programs with which you would be expected to work, and (b) hypothetical questions such as "What would you do if . . .?" Often these are questions that relate to your philosophy of education (that you began writing in an earlier chapter), your reasons for wanting to be a teacher, your approach to handling a particular classroom situation, and perhaps specifically, your reasons for wanting to teach in this district at this particular school.

Sometimes, you need to be prepared for a behavioral interview. This means there will be an emphasis on your competencies, that is, your knowledge, skills, and abilities. This means giving specific examples from your past experience to let the interviewer(s) know that *you have done what they are asking about*. At times, the questions may focus on a lesson plan that did not go well and how you handled the situation or a lesson plan that went well and why you think it worked so well. Sometimes, the questions will ask you about a conflict with a parent or guardian and how you handled it or about a collaboration with a parent or colleague or student that helped you better understand a particular situation. Still other times, the questions may ask you to tell when you identified a student's special needs and modified a lesson for the student or when you gave a homework assignment and what the assignment was (perhaps this is the time to share your guiding thought—"I want to improve a student's learning one teacher at a time," "I want to craft a lesson that connects with a kid," or "I see a problem as a possibility"). To assist you in your interview preparation, we provide more interview guidelines later in this chapter.

Through a Professional Career Portfolio

A way to be proactive in your teaching effectiveness, professional growth, and in your job search is to create a personal professional portfolio (computer-based or hardcopy) to be shared with persons who are considering your application for employment. This is the objective of Application Exercise 11.1.

FOR YOUR NOTES

APPLICATION EXERCISE 11.1
Development of a Professional Portfolio

Instructions: The purpose of this application exercise is to guide you in the creation of a personal professional portfolio (electronic or hardcopy) that will be shared with persons who are considering your application for employment as a credentialed teacher.

Because it would be impractical to send a complete portfolio with every application you submit, you should consider developing a minimum portfolio (Portfolio B) that could be sent with each application, in addition to a complete portfolio (Portfolio A) that you could make available upon request or take with you to an interview. However it is done, the actual contents of the portfolio will vary depending on the specific job being sought; you will continually add to and delete materials from your portfolio. While no one can tell you exactly what type of portfolio will work best for you, invite a cooperative friend to read what you have prepared and give you feedback in a collegial manner. Suggested categories and subcategories, listed in the order that they may be best presented in Portfolios A and B, are as follows:

1. Table of contents of portfolio (brief)—Portfolio A only.

2. Your professional résumé—both portfolios.

3. Evidence of your language and communication skills (evidence of your use of English and other languages including American Sign Language)—Portfolio A. You may state this information briefly in your letter of application. See the résumé section that follows in this chapter.
   a. Your teaching philosophy written in your own handwriting to demonstrate your handwriting. (See Chapter 3.)

   b. Other evidence to support this category of communication skills/language skills.

☞

4. Evidence of teaching skills—Portfolio A.
    a. For planning skills, include instructional objectives and a unit plan. (See Chapters 5 and 7.)

    b. For teaching skills, include a sample plan and a video of your actual teaching. (See Chapters 7 and 11.)

    c. For assessment skills, include a sample personal assessment and samples of student assessment. (See Chapters 6 and 11.)

5. Letters of recommendation and other documentation to support your teaching skills—both portfolios.

6. Other. For example, list personal interests related to the position for which you are applying—Portfolio A.

The professional career portfolio should be organized to provide clear evidence of your teaching skills and to make you professionally desirable to hiring personnel. A profession portfolio is not just a collection of your accomplishments that is randomly placed into an electronic file or a hardcopy folder. Your portfolio should be a deliberate, current, and organized collection of your experiences, attributes, skills, and accomplishments. Perhaps you have been adding to your collection after each chapter of this resource guide and responding to the Extending My Competencies section to add to your portfolio.

You realize it would be impractical to send a complete portfolio with every application you submit (electronically or hardcopy), so it might be advisable to have a minimum portfolio (labeled Portfolio B) that could be sent with each application. This would be in addition to your complete portfolio (labeled Portfolio A) that you could make available through e-mail (or regular mail) upon request or that you would take with you as hardcopy to an interview. However it is done, the actual contents of the portfolio will vary depending on the specific job being sought; you will continually add (and delete) materials from your portfolio. Application Exercise 11.1 suggests categories and subcategories, listed in the order that they may be best presented in Portfolios A and B. If you wish, work cooperatively and collaboratively with a colleague to get started on this.[2]

Resources for Locating Teaching Jobs

Various resources are available for locating teaching and subbing possibilities. See Figure 11.2. Keep notes on this list and track the resources that you have contacted.[3]

Academic Employment Network. A network employment page on the Internet, www.academploy.com/ Contact AEN, 244 Fifth Avenue, Suite R266 New York 10001; 775-546-9421

_____ contacted _____ did not contact

College/University Placement Office. Establish a career placement file at your college or university to begin locating teaching (if applicable) and substitute teaching vacancies.

_____ contacted _____ did not contact

Local School/District Personnel Office. You can contact school personnel offices to obtain information about teaching vacancies and sometimes about job interviews/local job fairs. Here are examples:

- Assistant Superintendent for Human Resources, Barrington Community Unit School District 220, 310 E. James St., Barrington, IL 60010

- Director, Personnel and Human Services, Community Consolidated School District 15, 580 North First Bank Drive, Palatine, IL 60067-8110

- Executive Director for Human Resources, Birmingham Public Schools, 550 West Merrill St., Birmingham, MI 48009

- Director of Personnel, City of Erie School District, Erie, 148 West 21st, Erie, PA 16502

- Human Resources Manager, Lincoln-Sudbury Regional School District, 390 Lincoln Road, Sudbury, MA 01776

- Division of Human Resources, Norwalk-La Mirada Unified School District, 12820 Pioneer Blvd., Norwalk, CA 90650

- White Mountains Schools, NH, Human Resources, 262 Cottage St., Suite 230, Littleton, NH 03561

- Ankeny Community School District, 306 S. W. School St., Human Resources, Ankeny, IA 50023

_____ contacted _____ did not contact

County Educational Agency. Local county offices of education sometimes maintain information about teaching jobs.

_____ contacted _____ did not contact

(*Continued*)

Figure 11.2
Resources for locating teaching or substitute teaching jobs: A checklist.

State Departments of Education. Some state departments of education maintain information about job openings statewide.

_____ contacted _____ did not contact

Independent Schools. Contact non-public-supported schools that interest you, either directly or through educational placement services, such as:

- European Council of Independent Schools, 21B Lavant St., Petersfield, Hampshire, GU32 3EL, England
- Human Resources Dept., St. Labre Indian Catholic School, P.O. Box 77, Ashland, MT 59003
- National Association of Independent Schools, 1620 L St., NW, Suite 1100, Washington, DC 20036-5695; online: www.nais.org)

_____ contacted _____ did not contact

Commercial Placement Agencies. Teaching job listings and placement services are available from such agencies as:

- Carney, Sandoe & Associates, 44 Bromfield St., Boston, MA 02108 617-542-0260

Online Resources. Job search resources available on the Internet include:

- Teachers—various areas—in Albemarle County Public Schools, Charlottesville, Virginia, see www.albemarle.org/jobs
- JobsinSchools.com, www.jobsinschools.com
- Teachers-Teachers.com, www.teachers-teachers.com
- Websites for professional journals/organizations/conferences

Out-of-Country Teaching Opportunities. Information regarding teaching positions outside the United States can be obtained from:

- American Field Services Intercultural Programs, 71 West 23rd St., New York, NY 10010
- Department of Defense Dependent Schools, 4040 N. Fairfax Drive, Arlington, VA 22203
- International Schools Services, P.O. Box 5910, Princeton, NJ 08543
- Peace Corps Recruitment Office, 1111 20th St., NW, Washington, DC 20526
- YMCA of the USA, 101 N. Wacker Drive, Chicago, IL 60606
- ESL Teachers Board, www.eslteachersboard.com

Professional Journals, Other Publications, and Professional Conferences. Professional teaching journals often run advertisements of teaching vacancies as do education newspapers such as *Education Week* (P.O. Box 3005, Langhorne, PA, 19047-9105). Professional conferences (National Education Association and others) often assign representatives to assist in job hunting at their regularly scheduled conferences and also provide ongoing assistance to members who want to move to other locations.

Figure 11.2
Resources for locating teaching or substitute teaching jobs: A checklist. (*Continued*)

State and Territorial Sources for Information About Credential and License Requirements

If you are interested in the credential and licensing requirements for other states and U.S. territories, check at the appropriate office of your own college or university teacher preparation program. At those offices, you can see what information is available about requirements for states of interest to you, and whether the credential or license that you are about to receive has reciprocity with the other states.

The Professional Résumé

Résumé preparation is the subject of how-to books, computer programs, and commercial services, but a teacher's résumé is specific. While no one can tell you exactly what type of résumé will work best for you, a few basic guidelines are especially helpful for the preparation of hardcopy for a teacher's résumé. Do Application Exercise 11.2 about preparing your professional résumé.

APPLICATION EXERCISE 11.2
A Professional Résumé

Instructions: The purpose of this exercise is to prepare a draft of a résumé and a cover letter to accompany your résumé specifically for the position for which you want to apply. Résumé preparation often is the general subject of how-to books, computer programs, and commercial services, but you should remember that a teacher's résumé is specific. While no one can tell you exactly what type of résumé will work best for you, invite a cooperative friend to read what you have prepared and give you feedback in a collegial manner. A few basic guidelines are especially helpful for the preparation for a teacher's résumé and the cover letter. You should consider:

- *Length.* The résumé should be contained on two pages. If it is any longer, you've said too much for a professional résumé.
- *Presentation.* The presentation should be in order and neat.
- *Page size.* Page size should be normal 8 1/2 × 11 inches. Extra-large or small pages can get lost.
- *Page color.* Stationery color should be off-white or white.
- *Personal data.* Do not give information such as your age, height, weight, marital status, number or names of your children, or a photograph of yourself, because including personal data like this may make it appear to some readers that you are trying to influence members of the hiring committee with the data.
- *Clear, concise writing.* Sentences should be understandable and to the point; avoid slang or lingo, a clumsy phrase, an abbreviation, or unusual words.
- *Neatness counts.* The presentation should be neat and uncluttered.
- *Careful organization.* Organize the information carefully, in this order: your name, postal and/or e-mail address, and telephone number (a cell phone number is fine and might be preferable for security reasons), followed by your education, professional experience, credential status, location of placement file, professional affiliations, and honors.
- *Identify experiences.* When identifying your experiences—academic, teaching, and life—do so in *reverse chronological order*, listing your most recent degree or your current position first.
- *Truthfulness.* Be absolutely truthful; avoid any distortions of facts about your degrees, experiences, or any other information that you provide on your résumé.
- *Be current.* Take the time to improve your résumé, and then keep it current. Do not duplicate hundreds of copies; produce a new copy each time you apply for a job so you are keeping it up to date. If you maintain your résumé on a computer disc, then it is easy to make modifications and print the copy you want each time one is needed.
- *Cover letter needed.* Prepare a cover letter to accompany your résumé written specifically for the position for which you are applying. Address the letter personally but formally to the personnel director. Limit the cover letter to one page, and emphasize yourself, your teaching experiences and interests, and reasons that you are best qualified for the position. Show a familiarity with the particular school or district. Again, if you maintain a generic application letter on your computer, you can easily duplicate the original and then modify it to make it specific for each position.

- *Edit material.* Have your résumé and cover letter edited by someone familiar with résumé writing and editing, perhaps a friend who is a secretary or who teaches English. A poorly written, poorly typed, or poorly copied résumé burdened with spelling and grammar errors will guarantee that you will not be considered for the job.
- *Meet deadlines.* Be sure that your application reaches the personnel director by the announced deadline. If for some reason your application will be late, then call the director, explain the circumstances, and request permission to submit your application late.

After reading the résumé that follows, write a draft of your résumé and cover letter and ask someone to edit it for you.

Sample Professional Résumé

Rachel Da Teacher

10 Main St., Weaverville, CA 96093

(9l6) 552-8996; e-mail Lracd@aol.com

CREDENTIALS

2009	California Preliminary Multiple Subject
	Credential BCLAD (Bilingual Culture and Language Academic Development) Certificate *California State University, Sacramento*

EDUCATION

2005	Bachelor of Arts Degree in Liberal Studies
	Saint Olaf College, Northfield, Minnesota

TEACHING EXPERIENCE

2009	(Student Teaching Phase III) **Wooded Oaks Elementary School (Carmichael, CA)** • Planned, developed, and used lessons for second- and third-grade children. Planned and taught a literature unit on *The Courage of Sarah Noble* with a multicultural emphasis.
2009	(Student Teaching Phase II) **Harriet Lee Middle School (Woodland, CA)** • Planned, developed, and used lessons for a diverse group of sixth-grade students.
2008	(Student Teaching Phase I) **Roberson Avenue School (Rancho Cordova, CA)** • Observed and assisted teachers of Title I students in grades K–5. • Prepared bilingual stories and activities; readers' theater presentations.

RELATED EXPERIENCE

2008	• Developed and taught a Summer Writing Workshop for students, grades 3–10. Met with students and parents and guardians to establish goals.
2005	• Reader for Placerville High School English Department; paraprofessional.

PHONE REFERENCES

Dr. Guy Fontasio, Department of Teacher Education, College of Education, California State University, (916) 278-6155

Ms. Shanna Moore, Cooperating Teacher at Wooded Oaks Elementary School, Carmichael, CA (916) 778-8900

The In-Person Interview

If your application and résumé are attractive to the personnel director, you will be notified and scheduled for a personal or small-group interview, although in some instances, the hiring interview may precede the request for your personal papers. Whichever the case, during the interview you should be honest, and you should be yourself. Practice an interview, perhaps with the aid of a video camera. Ask someone to role-play an interview with you and to ask you some tough questions (for examples of questions, see the questions listed at the end of the chapter in each video activity listed in this resource guide). As you view the video, observe how you respond to questions. What is your body language conveying? Are you appearing confident?

Plan your interview wardrobe and get it ready the night before. Leave early for your interview so that you arrive in plenty of time. Dress for success. Regardless of what else currently you may be doing for a living, take the time necessary to make a professional and proud appearance.

If possible, long before your scheduled interview, locate someone who works in the school district and discuss curriculum, classroom management policies, popular programs, and district demographics with that person. If you anticipate a professionally embarrassing question during the interview, think of diplomatic ways to respond. This means that you can think of ways to turn your weaknesses into strengths. For instance, if your cooperating teacher has mentioned that you need to continue to develop your room environment skills (meaning that you were sloppy and left your desk and the room cluttered), admit that you realize that you need to be more conscientious about keeping supplies and materials neat and tidy, but mention your concern about the students and the learning and that you realize you have a tendency to interact with students more than with objects. Assure someone that you will work on this skill, and then do it. The paragraphs that follow offer additional specific guidelines for preparing for and handling the in-person interview. As you peruse these following guidelines, please know that what may seem trite and obvious to one reader is not necessarily the same to another.

- You will be given a specific time, date, and place for the interview. Regardless of your other activities, accept the time, date, and location suggested, rather than trying to manipulate the interviewer around a schedule more convenient to you.
- Avoid coming to the interview with small children. If necessary, arrange to have them taken care of by someone.
- Arrive promptly, shake hands firmly with members of the committee, and initiate conversation with a friendly comment, based on your personal knowledge about the school or district.

- Be prepared to answer standard interview questions. Sometimes, school districts will send candidates the questions that will be asked during the interview; at other times, these questions are handed to the candidate upon arrival at the interview. Some of the questions that are likely to be asked will cover the topics listed in Figure 11.3.

As a part of the interview you may be expected to do a formal but abbreviated (10–15 minutes) teaching demonstration (or present a video of one of your lessons). You may or may not be told in advance of this demonstration. If hiring personnel are interested in seeing a video of your teaching, they will inform you. So, it is a good idea to thoughtfully develop and rehearse a model of your teaching, one that you could perform on immediate request. Just in case it might be useful, some candidates carry to the interview a video (or make electronic arrangements to show a teaching episode) of one of their best teaching episodes made during student teaching.

When the interview has obviously been brought to a close by the interviewer, that is your signal to leave. Do not hang around; this might be interpreted as nervousness or a sign of lacking confidence. Follow the interview with a thank-you letter addressed to the personnel director or the one in charge of interview. Even if you do not get the job, you will be remembered for future reference.[4]

Once you are employed as a teacher, your professional development continues. The sections that follow demonstrate ways in which that can happen.

PROFESSIONAL DEVELOPMENT

Through Reflection

Beginning now and continuing throughout your career, you will reflect on your teaching (reflection is inevitable), and you will want to continue to grow as a professional as a result of those reflections (growth is not so inevitable unless it is self-initiated and systematically planned). The most competent professional is one who is proactive, that is, one who takes charge and initiates a continuing personal professional development.

Through Self-Assessment

One useful way of continuing to reflect, self-assess, and grow professionally is by maintaining a professional journal, much as your students do when they maintain journals reflecting on what they are learning. Another is by continuing to maintain the professional career portfolio that you began assembling early in your preservice program (perhaps electronically as mentioned at the end of some chapters in this guide) and finalized for your job search (as discussed in this chapter).

Possible questions about:

1. *Your experiences with students of the relevant age.* The hiring committee wants to be reasonably certain that I can effectively manage and teach at this level. I can answer questions about this by sharing specific successes that demonstrate that I am a decisive and competent teacher.

   _____ I am prepared   _____ I am working on this

2. *Hobbies and travels.* The committee wants to know more about me as a person to ensure that I will be an interesting and energetic teacher to the students, as well as a congenial member of the faculty.

   _____ I am prepared   _____ I am working on this

3. *Extracurricular interests and experiences.* The committee wants to know about all the ways in which I might be helpful in the school and to know that I will promote the interests and co-curricular activities of students and the school community.

   _____ I am prepared   _____ I am working on this

4. *Classroom management techniques.* I want to convince the committee that I can effectively manage a classroom of diverse learners in a manner that will help the students develop self-control and self-esteem.

   _____ I am prepared   _____ I am working on this

5. *Knowledge of content and standards.* I want to show that I have knowledge of the curriculum standards and the subject taught at the grade for which I am being considered. The committee needs to be reasonably certain that I have command of the subject and its place within the developmental stages of children at this level. This is where I can show my knowledge of national standards and of state and local curriculum standards and documents.

   _____ I am prepared   _____ I am working on this

6. *Knowledge about the teaching of reading.* I want to show the committee my views about teaching reading, and that I am knowledgeable about specific strategies for teaching reading, at any grade level.

   _____ I am prepared   _____ I am working on this

7. *Knowledge of assessment strategies relevant for use in teaching at this level.* I realize that this is my place to shine with my professional knowledge about using scoring guides/rubrics and performance assessment.

   _____ I am prepared   _____ I am working on this

8. *Commitment to teaching at this level.* I want to assure the committee that I am knowledgeable about teaching and learning at this level and committed to the profession (as contrasted with just seeking this job until something better comes along).

   _____ I am prepared   _____ I am working on this

9. *My ability to reflect on experience and to grow from that reflection.* I want to demonstrate that I am a reflective decision maker and a lifelong learner.

   _____ I am prepared   _____ I am working on this

10. *My strengths as a teacher.* I realize that the hiring committee may want to ask me what I perceive as my major strength as an elementary schoolteacher. I will consider my answer carefully so I can be impressive without taking an inordinate amount of time answering the question.

    _____ I am prepared   _____ I am working on this

11. *My perceived weaknesses.* If I am asked about my weaknesses, I have an opportunity to show that I can effectively reflect and self-assess, that I can think reflectively and critically, and that I know the value of learning from my own errors and how to do it. I will be prepared for this question by identifying a specific error that I have made, perhaps while student teaching, and explaining how I was able to turn that error into a profitable learning experience.

    _____ I am prepared   _____ I am working on this

12. *Interacting with the committee.* Throughout the interview, I will maintain eye contact with the person talking to me while demonstrating interest, enthusiasm, and self-confidence. When an opportunity arises, I will ask one or two planned questions that demonstrate my knowledge of and interest in this position and this community and school or district.

    _____ I am prepared   _____ I am working on this

Figure 11.3
Preparing for interview questions: A self-check.

Through Journals or Logbooks

You may want to maintain a **professional logbook,** which will serve you not only as a documentation of your specific professional contributions and activities, but also as documentation of the breadth of your professional involvement. You can maintain a research logbook to record the questions that come up during your busy teaching day and then establish a plan for finding some answers.[5]

The research logbook strategy can be of tremendous benefit to you in actively researching and improving your classroom work, but also can be of interest to colleagues. Working in teams and sharing your work with team members is still another way of continuing to reflect, self-assess, and grow as a teacher.

Through Self-Reflection and Self-Assessment

To assist you in immediate reflection and self-assessment, consider looking at the following self-reflection and the included teaching suggestions in Figure 11.4. This figure offers you a summary of teaching suggestions to consider before, during, and after a lesson. Also, this self-reflection can be used as it is, or you can personalize it now, or at any time during your career.

PROFESSIONAL DEVELOPMENT THROUGH MENTORING

Mentoring, one teacher facilitating the learning of another teacher, can aid in professional development.[6] In what is sometimes called peer coaching, a mentor teacher (sometimes called a consulting teacher) volunteers or is selected by the teacher who wishes to improve or is selected by a school administrator, formally or informally. The mentor observes and coaches the teacher to help the teacher improve. Sometimes the teacher simply wants to learn a new skill. In other instances, the teacher being coached remains with the mentor teacher for an entire school year, developing and improving old and new skills or learning how to teach with a new program. In some districts, new teachers are automatically assigned to mentor teachers for their first year, and sometimes a second year, as a program of induction. Induction is often part of the mentoring process where there is formalized assistance given to beginning teachers by district or university supporters.

PROFESSIONAL DEVELOPMENT THROUGH INSERVICE AND GRADUATE STUDY

Inservice workshops, seminars, and programs are offered for teachers at the school level, by the district, and by other agencies such as a county office of education or a nearby college or university. Inservice seminars and workshops and programs are usually designed for specific purposes, such as to train teachers in new teaching skills, to update their knowledge in content, and to introduce them to new teaching materials or programs.[7]

University graduate study is yet another way of continuing your professional development. Some teachers pursue master's degrees in academic teaching fields, while many others pursue their degrees in curriculum and methods of instruction or in educational administration or counseling. Some universities offer a master of arts in teaching (MAT), a program of courses in specific academic fields that are especially designed for teachers.

PROFESSIONAL DEVELOPMENT THROUGH PROFESSIONAL ORGANIZATIONS

There are many professional organizations, local, statewide, national, and international. Some organizations are discipline-specific, for example, the International Reading Association, the National Council of Teachers of Mathematics, the National Council for the Social Studies, and the National Science Teachers Association (see Chapter 5). Become familiar with the national teachers' organizations such as the National Education Association (NEA),[8] which is the oldest, and more recent ones such as the Association of American Educators (AAE) and the National Association of Professional Educators (NAPE).

Local, district, state, and national organizations have meetings that include guest speakers, workshops, and publishers' displays. Professional meetings of teachers are educational, enriching, and usually fulfilling for those who attend. In addition, many other professional associations, such as those for reading teachers, supply speakers and publish articles in their journals that are often of interest to teachers, including those beyond the targeted audience.

Professional organizations publish newsletters and journals for their members, and these will likely be found in your college or university library. Many professional organizations have special membership prices for teachers who are still college or university students, a courtesy that allows for an inexpensive initial affiliation with a professional organization.

PROFESSIONAL DEVELOPMENT THROUGH COMMUNICATIONS WITH OTHER TEACHERS

Related to your professional development through communications with other teachers, here are some of the valuable experiences available to you: visiting teachers

Before the lesson:

1. Did you write specific objectives, and will you share them with your students?
2. Have you prepared tentative assessment strategies and items to be used to determine if objectives are being achieved?
3. Did you refer to the established course of study for your grade level and review your state and local frameworks, the teacher's manuals, scope and sequence charts, and standards?
4. Are your motivational techniques relevant to the lesson, helping children connect their learning to real-world experiences?
5. Are you taking students' interest in a topic for granted, or does your motivational component of the lesson meet their developmental needs and interests?
6. Did you order media materials and equipment pertinent to your lesson, and did you preview these materials?
7. Did you prepare large-size demonstration materials, and will you display them so that all of the children can see them?
8. Have you planned your lesson transitions from one activity to the next or from one lesson to the next?
9. Do you have the necessary supplies and materials ready for the lesson so time is not wasted looking for them once the lesson has begun?
10. Have you mastered manuscript writing so as to provide a model for the primary grades and mastered cursive writing so as to provide a model for the intermediate and upper grades?
11. Have you established efficient, orderly routines and procedures for your class management tasks, such as collecting homework, taking roll, collecting money, sharpening pencils, distributing and collecting books, obtaining attention, moving around in the classroom, and dismissing students for recess, for lunch, and at the end of the school day?
12. Have you planned your preassessment strategy, perhaps as an advance organizer for the lesson, to discover what the students already know, or think they know, about the concept of the lesson?
13. Have you built into your lesson plans strategies for student reflection, metacognition, and self-assessment of their learning?
14. Have you planned your postassessment strategies to find out whether the children have, in fact, learned that which you intend them to learn?
15. To the best of your knowledge, do your assessment strategies authentically assess the learning objectives?
16. Have you planned for frequent checks for student understanding of the material?
17. Have you considered the needs of individual children in your class, such as children who have disabilities or who have limited proficiency in the English language?
18. Do you have a contingency plan in case something goes wrong with the lesson or there is a major disruption of the learning?
19. Are you planning variation in your instructional strategies so that students not only learn subject content but also develop their thinking skills, study skills, social skills, and sense of self-worth?
20. Have you incorporated multitasking in your instruction?
21. Have you intelligently planned the physical layout of your classroom to match the nature of the instruction and learning needs of the children?

During the lesson:

22. Are you clearing the writing board before you begin a new lesson?
23. Are you remembering that sometimes material is clearer to students if they can read it as well as hear it?
24. Are you remembering to write legibly and boldly, with large letters and in an orderly manner, so all can read your writing on the writing board?
25. Are you being gracious and sympathetic to every student, showing that you have confidence in each child's abilities?
26. Are you allowing your students to participate in discussion (to talk) and be heard, and are you giving each student the individual, private, and specific reinforcement that the student deserves?
27. Are you setting the mental stage for the learning of each new idea?
28. Are you varying your class activities sufficiently to best reach each child's learning capacities and modalities?
29. Are you attempting to build on each student's ideas, questions, and contributions during the lesson?
30. Are you making clear all relationships between main ideas and details for your students, and presenting examples of abstract concepts in simple and concrete ways?
31. Are you explaining, discussing, and commenting on any media materials you use in your lesson?

(Continued)

Figure 11.4
My self-reflection: Teaching suggestions.

32. When asking questions of students, are you remembering to give them time to review the topic, to hear the frame of reference for your questions, to recognize that your questions are on their level of understanding, and to use "think time" before they respond?
33. Are you remembering to avoid answering your own questions?
34. Are you remembering to interact with and to call on the children and to give them tasks equally according to their gender and other personal characteristics?
35. Are you introducing materials (e.g., rulers, protractors, scissors, magnets, media, art supplies, felt boards) to the children *before* they are needed in your lesson?
36. Are you evincing enthusiasm in your speech and mannerisms, maintaining a moderate pace in your classroom, and insisting that all children give you their attention when you begin a lesson?
37. Are you maintaining proximity and eye contact with all the children?
38. Are you checking frequently during the lesson to see whether the children are "getting it"; that is, that they understand the content and processes being taught?

After the lesson:

39. Are you taking time to reflect on how the lesson went and on what might have been "muddy" and what was "clear," and then reteaching all or portions of it if necessary?
40. Are you making notes to yourself as follow-up to today's lesson, perhaps special attention to be given tomorrow regarding specific content or skills for particular students?

Figure 11.4
My self-reflection: Teaching suggestions. (*Continued*)

at other schools; attending inservice workshops, graduate seminars, and programs; participating in teacher study groups[9] and meetings of professional organizations; participating in teacher networks,[10] in video clubs,[11] in teacher book clubs,[12] and sharing with teachers by analyzing one another's teaching videos, or communicating by means of electronic bulletin boards; these are all valuable experiences, if for no other reason than to talk and to share with teachers from across the nation and around the world. Your discussions can be a sharing of "frontline" stories and also a sharing of ideas and descriptions of programs, books, materials, and techniques that work.

As in the other process skills, the teacher practices and models skill in communication, in and out of the classroom. This includes communicating with other teachers to improve one's own repertoire of strategies and knowledge about teaching as well as sharing one's experience with others. Teaching other teachers about your own special skills and sharing your experiences are important components of the communication and professional development processes.

PROFESSIONAL DEVELOPMENT THROUGH THE INTERNET, ADDITIONAL TRAINING, AND WORKSHOPS

In many areas of the United States there are workshop retreats and special programs of short-term employment available to interested teachers. Often these are available especially, though not exclusively, to teachers with special interests in reading and literacy, physical education, mathematics, science, and social studies and are offered by public agencies, private industry, foundations, and research institutes. These organizations are interested in disseminating information and providing opportunities for teachers to update their skills and knowledge, with an ultimate hope that the teachers will stimulate in more students a desire to develop their physical fitness, to understand civic responsibilities, and to consider careers in science and technology. Participating industries, foundations, governments, and institutes provide on-the-job training with salaries or stipends to teachers who are selected to participate. During the program of employment and depending on the nature of that work, a variety of people (e.g., businesspersons, politicians, scientists, social workers, technicians, and sometimes, university educators) meet with teachers to share experiences and discuss what is being learned and its implications for teaching and curriculum development.

Some of the programs for teachers are government-sponsored, field-centered, and content-specific. For example, a program may concentrate on geology, anthropology, mathematics, or reading. At another location, a program may concentrate on teaching methods, using a specific new or experimental curriculum. At still another location, a program may be a part of a distance learning program shown on an identified television station in your area with e-mail backup to the instructor's computer. These programs, located around the country, may have university affiliation, which means that university credit may be available. Registration fees, room and board, travel, and a stipend are sometimes granted to participating teachers.

Sources of information about the availability of programs include professional journals, a neighboring university or college or the local chamber of commerce, and meetings of the local or regional teachers' organization. In areas where there are no organized retreat or work experience programs for teachers, some teachers have had success in initiating their own by grant writing[13] or establishing contact with management personnel of local businesses or companies.

PROFESSIONAL DEVELOPMENT THROUGH PEER TEACHING

Peer teaching (PT) is a skill-development strategy used for professional development by both precredentialed (preservice, prelicensed) and credentialed (inservice, licensed) teachers. Peer teaching (to which you were introduced previously in this resource guide) is a scaled-down teaching experience involving the following characteristics:

- Limited objective(s)
- Brief interval for teaching a lesson
- Lesson taught to a few peers taking the roles as your students (8–10)
- Lesson that focuses on the use of one or several instructional strategies

Peer teaching can be a predictor of later teaching effectiveness in a regular classroom. More importantly, it can provide an opportunity to develop and improve specific teaching behaviors. A videotaped PT lesson allows you to see yourself in action for self-evaluation and diagnosis. Evaluation of a PT session is based on the following criteria:

- The quality of the teacher's preparation and lesson implementation
- The quality of the planned and implemented student involvement
- The extent to which the target objective(s) was reached
- The appropriateness of the cognitive level of the lesson

Whether you are a precredentialed teacher or a credentialed teacher, you are urged to participate in one or more peer-teaching experiences. The PT experience is formatted differently from previous application exercises in this resource guide. Application Exercise 11.3 can represent a summative assessment *performance* for the course for which this book is being used.

Please turn to the final self-check for this resource guide in Appendix B. This final self-check can serve as a summative assessment of *content* and *knowledge* for the course for which this book, *A Resource Guide for Elementary School Teaching: Planning for Competency,* 7th edition, is being used.

APPLICATION EXERCISE 11.3

Pulling It All Together: Peer Teaching

Instructions: The purpose of this exercise is to learn how to develop your own PT experiences. You will prepare and teach a lesson that is prepared as a lesson presentation for your peers, at their level of intellectual maturity and understanding (i.e., opposed to teaching the lesson to peers pretending that they are public school students).

This experience has two components:

1. Your preparation and implementation of a demonstration lesson
2. Your completion of an analysis of the summative peer assessment and the self-assessment, with statements of how you would change the lesson and your teaching of it were you to repeat the lesson.

You should prepare and carry out a 15- to 20-minute lesson to a group of peers. The exact time limit for the lesson should be set by your group, based on the size of the group and the amount of time available. When the time limit has been set, complete the time-allowed entry (item 1) of Form A of this exercise. Some of your peers will serve as your students; others will be evaluating your teaching. (The process works best when "students" do not evaluate while being students.) Your teaching should be videotaped for self-evaluation.

For your lesson, identify one concept and develop your lesson to teach toward an understanding of that concept. Within the time allowed, your lesson should include both teacher talk and a hands-on activity for the students. Use Form A for the initial planning of your lesson. Then complete a lesson plan, selecting a lesson plan format as discussed in Chapter 7. Then present the lesson to the "students." The peers who are evaluating your presentation should use Form B of this exercise.

After your presentation, collect your peer evaluations (the Form B copies that you gave to the evaluators). Then review your presentation by viewing the videotape. After viewing the tape, prepare:

- A tabulation and statistical analysis of peer evaluations of your lesson
- A self-evaluation based on your analysis of the peer evaluations, your feelings having taught the lesson, and your thoughts after viewing the videotape
- A summary analysis that includes your selection and description of your teaching strengths and weaknesses, as indicated by this peer-teaching experience, and how you would improve were you to repeat the lesson.

Tabulation of Peer Evaluations

The procedure for tabulating the completed evaluations received from peers is as follows:

1. **Use a blank copy of Form B for tabulating.** In the left margin of that copy, place the letters N (number) and σ (total) to prepare for two columns of numbers that will fall below each of those letters. In the far right margin, place the word *Score*.

2. **For each item (A through Y) on the peer evaluation form, count the number of evaluators who gave a rating (from 1 to 5) on the item.** Sometimes an evaluator may not rate a particular item, so although there may have been 10 peers evaluating your micro peer

teaching, the number of evaluators giving you a rating on any one particular item could be less than 10. For each item, the number of evaluators rating that item we call N. Place this number in the N column at the far left margin on your blank copy of Form B, next to the relevant item.

3. **Using a calculator, obtain the sum of the peer ratings for each item.** For example, for item A, Lesson Preparation, you add the numbers given by each evaluator for that item. If there were 10 evaluators who gave you a number rating on that item, then your sum on that item will not be more than 50 (5×10). Because individual evaluators will make their X marks differently, you sometimes must estimate an individual evaluator's number rating; that is, rather than a clear rating of 3 or 3.5 on an item, you may have to estimate it as being a 3.2 or a 3.9. In the left-hand margin of your blank copy of Form B, in the σ column, place the sum for each item.

4. **Now obtain a score for each item, A through Y.** The score for each item is obtained by dividing σ by N. Your score for each item will range from 1 to 5. Write this dividend in the column in the right-hand margin under the word *Score* on a line parallel to the relevant item. This is the number your will use in the analysis phase.

Procedure for Analyzing the Tabulations

Having completed the tabulation of the peer evaluations of your teaching, you are ready to proceed with your analysis of those tabulations.

1. To proceed, you need a blank copy of Form C of this exercise, your self-analysis form.

2. On the blank copy of Form C are five items: Implementation, Personal, Voice, Materials, and Strategies.

3. In the far left margin of Form C, place the letter σ for the sum. To its right, and parallel with it, place the word *Average.* You now have arranged for two columns of five numbers each—a σ column and an *Average* column.

4. For each of the five items, get the total score for that item, as follows:
   a. *Implementation.* Add all scores (from the right-hand margin of blank Form B) for the four items a, c, x, and y. The total should be 20 or less (4×5). Place this total in the left-hand margin under σ (to the left of "1. Implementation").

   b. *Personal.* Add all scores (from the right-hand margin of blank Form B) for the nine items f, g, m, n, o, p, q, s, and t. The total should be 45 or less (9×5). Place this total in the left-hand margin under σ (to the left of "2. Personal").

c. *Voice.* Add all scores (from the right-hand margin of blank Form B) for the three items h, i, and j. The total should be 15 or less (3×5). Place this total in the left-hand margin under σ (to the left of "3. Voice").

d. *Materials.* Add all scores (from the right-hand margin of blank Form B) for the item k. The total should be 5 or less (1×5). Place this total in the left-hand margin under σ (to the left of "4. Materials").

e. *Strategies.* Add all scores (from the right-hand margin of blank Form B) for the eight items b, d, e, l, r, u, v, and w. The total should be 40 or less (8×5). Place this total in the left-hand margin under σ (to the left of "5. Strategies").

5. Now for each of the five categories, divide the sum by the number of items in the category to get your peer evaluation average score for that category. For item 1, you will divide by 4; for item 2, by 9; for item 3, by 3; for item 4, by 1; and for item 5, by 8. For each category you should then have a final average peer evaluation score of a number between 1 and 5. If correctly done, you now have average scores for each of the five categories: Implementation, Personal, Voice, Materials, and Strategies. With those scores and evaluator's comments, you can prepare your final summary analysis.

The following table includes three sample analyses of PT lessons based *only* on the scores—that is, without reference to comments made by individual evaluators, although peer evaluator's comments are important considerations for actual analyses.

Sample Analyses of PTs Based Only on Peer Evaluation Scores

Teacher	Category/Rating					Possible Strengths and Weaknesses
	1	2	3	4	5	
A	4.2	2.5	2.8	4.5	4.5	Good lesson, weakened by personal items and voice.
B	4.5	4.6	5.0	5.0	5.0	Excellent teaching, perhaps needing a stronger start.
C	2.5	3.0	3.5	1.0	1.5	Poor strategy choice, lack of student involvement.

FORM A: PT PREPARATION

Instructions: Form A is to be used for initial preparation of your PT lesson. (For preparation of your lesson, study Form B.) After completing Form A, proceed with the preparation of your PT lesson using a lesson plan format as discussed in Chapter 7. A copy of the final lesson plan should be presented to the evaluators at the start of your PT presentation.

1. Time allowed _____

2. Title or topic of lesson I will teach _____

3. Concept _____

4. Specific instructional objectives for the lesson:

   Cognitive _____

   _____

   Affective _____

   _____

   Psychomotor _____

   _____

5. Strategies to be used, including approximate time plan:

   Set introduction _____

   _____

   Transitions _____

   _____

   Closure _____

   _____

   Others _____

   _____

6. Student experiences to be provided (i.e., specify for each—visual, verbal, kinesthetic, and tactile experiences): _____

   _____

7. Materials, equipment, and resources needed:

   _____

   _____

✏ FORM B: PEER EVALUATION

Instructions: Evaluators use Form B, making an *X* on the continuum from 5 to 1. Far left (5) is the highest rating; far right (1) is the lowest. Completed forms are collected and given to the teacher upon completion of the teacher's PT and reviewed by the teacher prior to reviewing his or her videotaped lesson.

To evaluators: Comments as well as marks are useful to the teacher.

To teacher: Give one copy of your lesson plan to the evaluators at the start of your PT. (*Note:* It is best if evaluators can be together at a table at the rear of the room.)

Teacher _____   Date _____

Topic _____

Concept _____

1. Organization of lesson	5	4	3	2	1
a. Lesson preparation evident	very		somewhat		no
b. Lesson beginning effective	yes		somewhat		poor
c. Subject matter knowledge apparent	yes		somewhat		no
d. Strategies selection effective	yes		somewhat		poor
e. Closure effective	yes		somewhat		poor

Comments

_____

_____

_____

_____

_____

_____

_____

_____

_____

_____

_____

_____

_____

2. Lesson implementation	5	4	3	2	1
f. Eye contact excellent	yes		somewhat		poor
g. Enthusiasm evident	yes		somewhat		no
h. Speech delivery	articulate		minor problems		poor
i. Voice inflection; cueing	effective		minor problems		poor
j. Vocabulary use	well-chosen		minor problems		poor
k. Aids, props, and materials	effective		okay		none

FORM B: PEER EVALUATION *(continued)*

l. Use of example and analogies	effective	need improvement	none
m. Student involvement	effective	okay	none
n. Use of overlapping skills	good	okay	poor
o. Nonverbal communication	effective	a bit confusing	distracting
p. Use of active listening	effective	okay	poor
q. Responses to students	personal and accepting	passive or indifferent	impersonal and antagonistic
r. Use of questions	effective	okay	poor
s. Use of student names	effective	okay	no
t. Use of humor	effective	okay	poor
u. Directions and refocusing	succinct	a bit vague	confusing
v. Teacher mobility	effective	okay	none
w. Use of transitions	smooth	a bit rough	unclear
x. Motivating presentation	very	somethat	not at all
y. Momentum (pacing) of lesson	smooth and brisk	okay	too slow or too fast

Comments

_____

_____

_____

_____

_____

_____

_____

_____

_____

_____

_____

FORM C: TEACHER'S SUMMATIVE PEER EVALUATION

See instructions within Application Exercise 11.3 for completing this form.

1. Implementation (items a, c, x, y)   5   4   3   2   1

2. Personal (items f, g, m, n, o, p, q, s, t)   5   4   3   2   1

3. Voice (items h, i, j)   5   4   3   2   1

4. Materials (item k)   5   4   3   2   1

5. Strategies (items b, d, e, l, r, u, v, w)   5   4   3   2   1

Total = _____

Comments

_____

_____

_____

_____

_____

_____

_____

_____

_____

_____

_____

_____

_____

_____

_____

_____

_____

_____

_____

_____

_____

_____

_____

_____

LOOKING AT TEACHERS II

Integrated Technology, PowerPoint

At times, as an elementary schoolteacher, you'll realize that some of the teachers of students in the middle school or high school can provide insight into teaching that reflects on your teaching of elementary school students. To illustrate this, we want to point out one teacher's reflection on his classroom research with high school students and how the use of technology in the teacher's classroom focuses on several ideas that can affect you, your elementary school teaching, and your pedagogical interest. Here's a recap of the teacher's reflections:

• First, the teacher considered that most of his students could *use technology all they wanted at home* (or at their friend's home) with their computers, the Internet, television, VCRs, DVD players, compact discs, CD-ROMs, electronic games, cell phones, handheld personal digital assistants, and their family's assortment of other tech items. He considered the drawbacks of digital books, e-books. He thought it didn't make sense for newspapers to have one e-reader, for bookstores to have another reader, and for magazine publishers to have still another reader. He considered the non-flippable pages, often gray or brown, the clumsy menus, small screen size, and in some cases,

pages that turn from left to right that make an e-book difficult to read. He thought about the idea that too many devices could be too much for some students. So it seemed to the teacher that what his students needed most in his classroom was interaction with a caring, concerned adult (all too often unavailable outside of school from this teacher's point of view).

• Second, no technique seemed to be quite as effective as the teacher himself when he made the lectures/discussion interesting and when he drew his students into what was being learned with an occasional joke, question, or allusion to their own lives.

• Third, the most important piece of classroom equipment seemed to be the professional teacher's attitude—sense of humor, patience, and caring for young people.

• Fourth, the students' PowerPoint presentations as a finale to their unit of study were a success and led this teacher to include this as an assignment in all of the rest of his classes, but the teacher *did not* let it replace human caring, or what could be labeled the concerned touch, in his teaching in the classroom. It seemed that, indeed, teacher "affect" was an effective teaching technique when compared with teaching with technology only.[14]

SUMMARY

Because teaching and learning go hand in hand and the effectiveness of one affects that of the other, the sixth chapter and the last chapter of this resource guide have dealt with both aspects of the *how well* component of teacher preparation—how well the students are learning and how well the teacher is teaching. In addition, in this chapter you have been presented with guidelines about how to obtain your first teaching job and how to continue your professional development. Throughout your teaching career, you will continue improving your knowledge and skills in the many aspects of teaching and learning. To highlight this career improvement, Casbon, Shagoury, and Smith emphasize the words of S. Nachmanovitch, an advocate of improvisation:[15]

> You have to teach each person, each class group, and each moment as a particular case that calls out for particular handling. The teacher's art is to connect, in real time, the living bodies of the students, with the living body of knowledge. In this way, you pass beyond competence to presence.

We wish you the very best in your new career. If you are interested in a children's CD to share on the last day of school, we suggest that you choose one of your musical favorites or play some of the songs on *Camp Lisa* (New York: Redeye Productions, 2008) sung by

folksinger Lisa Loeb. Part of the proceeds from the sale of this CD goes to support the Camp Lisa Foundation that sends underpriviledged children to summer camp. We especially recommend singing along with "Best Friends," "It's Not Good-Bye," and "Make New Friends." Regardless of how you plan to say good-bye to the students or how to close the last day of school to end the year, be the very best teacher that you can be every teaching day and for as long as you can.[16] And be further motivated by reading the "Thumz Zup" article in J. W. Underwood's *Today I Made a Difference* (2009) before your upcoming first day of school. Our nation and our children need you.

—P. L. R.
—R. D. K.
—K. M.

EXTENDING MY PROFESSIONAL COMPETENCY

With Discussion

My Teaching Philosophy. If a principal interviews me for a teaching job and asks me about my philosophy of teaching students, how will I respond? **To do:** You will recall that in Chapter 3 you participated in an exercise during which you developed your first draft of your teaching philosophy. It was mentioned that at the completion of this text, you might want to revisit your philosophical statement and perhaps even to revise it. Do this now. It will be useful for you to have your educational philosophy in mind for your future teaching interviews, so we encourage you to discuss your philosophy with another and to role play an interview with a colleague.

With Video

Video Activity: Teaching Effectiveness and Professional Development. How can I explain how I would improve my teaching effectiveness, especially with technology, as part of my professional development?

myeducationlab

Go to the Video Examples section of Topic #14: Integrating Technology in the MyEducationLab for your course to view the video entitled "Managing Technology in the Classroom."

View the video with a colleague and take notes about the benefits of computers in the classroom that you observe. Discuss your notes. Discuss how changes could be incorporated into the video to make the video more effective from your point of view. View the video again if needed. If time permits, discuss your notes with a colleague and state anything you want to say about the misuse of a computer in a classroom.

With Portfolio

Portfolio Planning. As part of my professional development, how can I further add to my professional portfolio and show my teaching effectiveness? This activity will support Principles 9 and 10 of INTASC and Standards 9, 10, and 11 of NBPTS and Praxis II teacher test content (as seen on the inside of the front cover of this book). **To do:** To add to your portfolio, you can develop and write a one- to two-page paper stating ways you've assessed your teaching effectiveness. Label your paper Teaching Effectiveness and Professional Development. After reading and interacting with this chapter, you can tell how you have developed your competency in one or two objectives. I have

1. Assessed my teaching effectiveness; recorded self-assessment in student teaching/interning; assessed with standards.
2. Prepared for a job interview.
3. Written a résumé.
4. Developed a portfolio for professional growth and development.
5. Self-assessed and evaluated my developing competencies with the Final Self-Check Reflection Guide found in Appendix B. Place your paper in your portfolio folder or in your computer file.

With Teacher Tests Study Guide

Teacher Tests for Future Licensing and Certification. If I wanted to prepare for taking a state teacher test to qualify for my teaching certificate/license and review my knowledge about teaching effectiveness and professional development, how could I begin? **To do:** To support you as you prepare for teaching, you will find constructed-response-type questions similar to those found on state tests for teacher licensing and certification in Appendix A. The question related to this chapter and teaching effectiveness and professional development helps you take another look at the classroom vignette found in *Looking at Teachers II*. Write your response and, if you wish, discuss it with another teaching candidate. If appropriate, use one or two of your colleague's suggestions to help you change your response to the question. Place your response in a Teacher Tests Study Guide folder or type/scan into a computer file. Plan to review and reread for study purposes before taking a scheduled teacher test.

With Target Topics for Teacher Tests (TTTT)

If I wanted to study subject matter to prepare for taking a teacher test for licensing and certification, how could I begin? **To do**: Consider finding selected word entries in the subject index of this book. To assist you as you prepare to take a teacher test, bullets (•) have been placed by certain words in the index that stand for Target Topics for Teacher Tests. The bullets indicate core subject matter such as teaching effectiveness, reflection, self-assessment, professional development, and other topics that you'll find in this chapter. This is material that the authors suggest be reviewed before taking a teacher test similar to your state's test or to the Praxis II Principles of Learning and Teaching exam.

With Final Self-Check Reflection Guide

Final Self-Check Reflection Guide. If I wanted to self-assess and evaluate my competencies as guided by this entire resource guide, how could I begin? **To do**: You can begin with a final self-check of what you know about planning for competency in elementary school teaching. For this final self-check, go to Appendix B to locate the Final Self-Check Reflection Guide for this book. Complete the Reflection Guide for this last self-check and take time to think about your knowledge shown on the self-check. Consider the items that concern you. What are your specific concerns? What content do you want to review about these? If you wish, discuss some of these items with a colleague. Use these items to guide you in improving your competencies for elementary school teaching. What other steps do you plan to take to develop your competencies further? If required for an assessment review for an instructional course linked to this book, give this material to the instructor.

WITH READING

Carlson, A., and Carlson, M. (2005). *Flannelboard Stories for Infants and Toddlers, Bilingual Edition.* Spanish translation by Ana-Elba Pavon et al. Chicago: American Library Association.

Costa, A. L., and Garmston, R. L.(2002). *Cognitive Coaching: A Foundation for Renaissance Schools* (2nd ed.). Norwood, MA: Christopher-Gordon.

Danielson, C., and McGreal, T. (2000). *Teacher Evaluation to Enhance Professional Practice.* Alexandria, VA: Association for Supervision and Curriculum Development.

Ellison, J., and Hayes, C. (2003). *Cognitive Coaching: Weaving Threads of Learning and Change Into the Culture of an Organization.* Norwood, MA: Christopher-Gordon.

Fry, P., and Konopak, B. (2003, Spring). Preparing Teachers for Inclusionary Practices: Action in Teacher Education. *Journal of the Association of Teacher Educators, vxxv,* 1.

Good, T. L., and Brophy, J. E. (2003). *Looking in Classrooms* (9th ed.). New York: Addison Wesley/Longman.

Hurst, C. O., and Otis, R. (2000). *Friends and Relations: Using Literature with Social Themes, Grades 3–5.* Greenfield, MA: Northeast Foundation for Children.

Kellough, R. D. (2009). *Your First Year of Teaching: Guidelines for Success* (5th ed.). Upper Saddle River, NJ: Merrill/Prentice Hall.

Lever-Duffy, J. and McDonald, J. B. (2008). *Teaching and Learning with Technology* (3rd ed.). Boston: Pearson Education.

Lipton, L., and Wellman, B., with Humbard, C. (2001). *Mentoring Matters: A Practice Guide to Learning-Focused Relationships.* Sherman, CT: MiraVia.

Minkel, W. (Ed.). (2003, November). Techknowledge: Rage Against the Machine. *School Library Journal,* p. 34.

Moore, R. A. (2004). *Classroom Research for Teachers.* Norwood, MA: Christopher-Gordon.

NASDTEC Manual 2000: Manual on the Preparation and Certification of Educational Personnel (5th ed.). Dubuque, IA: Kendall/Hunt, Table E-2.

Underwood, J. W. (2009). *Today I Made a Difference: A Collection of Inspirational Stories from America's Top Educators.* Bloomington, IN: Adams Media.

Van Reusen, A. K., and Bos, C. S. (1990). I PLAN: Helping Students Communicate in Planning Conferences. *Teaching Exceptional Children, 22,* 30–32.

WITH NOTES

1. A. Nichols, Fourth Grade Befriends Traveling Spider (*San Juan Scene Online,* p. 8 (April 2006). See www.sanjuan.edu.
2. Internet at www.teachnet.com.
3. *Education Week* (Fall, 2000) launched its test phase of a national online teacher job bank on which districts nationwide may post their job vacancies and on which job-seeking teachers can post their résumés. See www.edweek.org or www.topschooljobs.org.
4. Review this chapter for suggestions for preparing for a teaching job interview.
5. M. Clarke, Reflection: Journals and Reflective Questions: A Strategy for Professional Learning. *Australian Journal of Teacher Education, 29*(2), 1-13 (Nov., 2004)
6. For additional information, see a description of California's Beginning Teacher Support and Assessment (BSTA) Program at www.btsa.ca.gov, and G. L. Good and J. E. Brophy, *Looking in Classrooms,* 9th ed. (New York: Addison Wesley/Longman, 2003).
7. K. S. Shipiro and J. E. Clauss, Freshness in the Mountains, *Educational Leadership, 57*(8), 66–68 (May, 2000).
8. The NEA and the AFT have merged in some states—Minnesota, Montana, Florida, and New York.
9. S. J. Zepeda, Teacher Study Groups, Whole Faculty Study Groups, and Book Studies, in *Professional Development: What works* (chapter 8), (Eye on Education, 2008).
10. Phi Kappa Phi and other education-affiliated organizations offer teacher networks enabling a teacher seeking a job to make contact with a teacher mentor in the area in which the job-seeker wishes to locate. See also M. P. Correia and J. M. McHenry, *The Mentor's Handbook: Practical Suggestions for Collaborative Reflection and Analysis,* 2nd ed. (Norwalk, MA: Christopher-Gordon, 2008); J. G. Gabriel, *How to Thrive as a Teacher Leader* (Alexandria, VA: Association for Supervision and Curriculum Development, 2006); H. B. Price, *Mobilizing the Community to Help Students Succeed* (Alexandria, VA: Association for Supervision and Curriculum Development, 2008);
11. M. G. Sherin, Viewing Teaching on Videotape, *Educational Leadership,* 57(8), 39–41 (May, 2000).
12. S. M. Goldberg and E. Pesko, The Teacher Book Club, *Educational Leadership, 57*(8), 39–41 (May, 2000).
13. K. Chandler, Summer Sustenance, *Educational Leadership, 57*(8), 63–65 (May, 2000).
14. A. Perry, Tech versus the Human Touch: Teacher Affect Is More Effective, *Educational Horizons, 81*(4), 183–185, (Summer, 2003).
15. C. H. Casbon, R. Shagoury, and G. A. Smith, Rediscovering the Call to Teach: A New Vision for Professional and Personal Development, *Language Arts, 82*(5) 359–366 (2005); See also W. Minkel (Ed.), Techknowledge, *School Library Journal,* 34 (November, 2003).
16. Another suggestion for the last day of school is reading aloud *Oh, the Places You'll Go!* (New York: Random House, 1990) by Dr. Seuss. Seuss gives advice about going forward in one's life, especially overcoming a slump (start un-slumping yourself), about facing loneliness (face up to your problems), and moving on (your mountain is waiting. So . . . get on your way).

Appendix A

Teacher Tests Study Guide

Hints for Short-Answer Response Questions

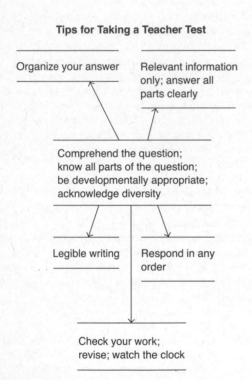

Tips for Taking a Teacher Test

Organize your answer

Relevant information only; answer all parts clearly

Comprehend the question; know all parts of the question; be developmentally appropriate; acknowledge diversity

Legible writing

Respond in any order

Check your work; revise; watch the clock

PLACE-VALUE ARRANGEMENT
(Review Looking at Teachers II, Chapter 1)

Referring back to Chapter 1's ending vignette, consider Rachael and her class of students. You'll recall that Rachael is a fifth-grade teacher in a low-socioeconomic school in a large city on the East Coast. The thirty-four students in her class include twenty English language learners and ten with identified learning problems. Some of the children have skills equivalent to those of first-graders. In any given week, Rachael recycles newspapers and sells snacks to help pay for at least one field

trip because she realizes the value of place-based education/nature-based education and the school and the children's families cannot support field trips financially. At times, with the students, Rachael reviews what money has been made from selling the snacks to help pay for the group's one field trip. During these reviews, she has observed that some of her students with learning problems do not understand the place-value arrangement in counting money from pennies to dimes to dollars.

Hints: Describe two (2) activities that you would use to help Rachael's students with learning problems who do not understand the ones, tens, and hundreds place-value arrangement in mathematics. Give examples of what the students would be doing during the activity. Explain how you, as the teacher, would assess the children's understanding of the place-value arrangement after they have completed the activities.

Activity #1: Use of manipulatives
I would have the children use manipulatives (beans, chips, blocks, paper squares) of different colors and count different numbers of manipulatives separately to see ones, then a group of ten, then ten groups of ten to make one hundred. I would write the numeral that represents the number on the board so the children could see the numeral. I would have the children team up together as math partners and count manipulatives together; I would ask a question such as, "If I gave you two more (name the color) _____ ones, how many would you have? What is your total?" I would have the partners combine their manipulatives, count, and recognize numerals, to participate in a cooperative learning activity.

Activity #2: Real-life example using popcorn

I believe that children learn best through hands-on learning and I would use a real-life example of popped popcorn as manipulatives. I would tell them that they need one kernel of popcorn to feed each bird that lives in the area near their home or to feed to the birds that they saw on one of the field trips. I would have them announce the number of birds they have seen and have them hold the kernels of popcorn, one for each bird. I would tell them that they have just found out that two (three, four) other birds are flying in, and ask, what should they do? I would repeat this activity with different numbers so the children would understand the idea of basic facts (and one-to-one correspondence).

Assessment for both activities: To assess, I would look to see that all of the children are cooperating while doing the activity. I would notice who is listening to find out what to do. I would show numeral cards (or write the numerals on the board) and ask them to show the number of manipulatives that the numeral represents. I would ask questions such as, "If I have the numeral 2 in the ten space and 1 in the ones place, what number is it?" I would use observation as a major assessment tool. I would look for student confusion. At the end of the activity, I would give a written problem, read it aloud, and assess responses to see if the students have improved in their understanding of the ones, tens, and hundreds place value arrangement.

A Focus on English Language Learners. For ELLs, I believe that they can work with a partner who can support language understanding and disccover that manipulatives are a means of overcoming a language barrier.

DESIGNING AND PREPARING GRAPHS
(Review Looking at Teachers II, Chapter 2)

You are asked to describe two (2) different activities that would help the fourth-grade students design and prepare graphs and give a justification of the activities for this age group. **Hints:** Consider explaining clearly two different activities that would help fourth-grade students prepare a graph; Consider discussing the cognitive (or social, emotional, physical) characteristics of these students to justify your choice of activities and write about it.

Activity #1: Favorite healthy snacks graph

After a brief introduction to a line graph (perhaps pointing out to students that a line graph or bar graph is useful for showing differences in choices or showing changes over time), I would have the children play a graph game. To do this, I would divide the children into two (2) groups. With input from the children, I would write the names of five (5) favorite healthy snacks on the board in a left-hand column.

Favorite Healthy Snacks

Favorite Healthy Snacks	Total Tally
Celery	
Carrot sticks	
Cucumber slices	
Broccoli	
Other	
Total Tally for Celery	
Team A	Team B
Total Tally for Carrot Sticks	
Team A	Team B

I would have one student from each group, taking turns, go to the board to make a tally mark beside their favorite healthy snack or beside the term *Other*. I would continue this until all of the children have made their tally marks. Then, I would have one from each group, on my signal, race to the board to write the total adding the tallies for each snack. That is, one pair would race to the board to tally the total for celery snack; the group then counts the tallies for that snack aloud to verify the addition; another pair, on my signal, would race to tally the total for the next snack, and so on. The first member of a team to tally a snack's tallies correctly wins a point. The team with the highest number of points wins the game after all of the totals for all of the snacks have been added correctly. Discuss the use of a line graph and what information it can tell the children—telling differences in choices in this case. If a student asks about a circle graph or pie graph, I will point out that the circle graph and pie graph are best for showing the relationship between the whole and its parts (for example, a pie graph could show the total number of choices and then how many students selected carrot sticks or another snack in a pie wedge on the graph). These two graphs are also useful in showing information about comparing and contrasting items.

Activity #2: Favorite yogurt flavors graph

Discussing the use of a line graph, I would have the children repeat a favorite graph game. To do this, I would divide the children into two (2) groups. With input from the children, I would write the names of five (5) favorite flavors of yogurt (or Jello™, ice cream) on the board in a left-hand column.

Favorite Yogurt Flavors Graph

Favorite Yogurt Flavor	Total Tally
Strawberry	
Vanilla	
Orange	
Peach	
Other	

Total Tally for Strawberry

Team A	Team B

Total Tally for Vanilla

Team A	Team B

I would have one from each group, taking turns, go to the board to make a tally mark beside their favorite flavor or beside the term *Other*. I would ask that if the student is a boy to make a tally mark with the letter B on top of it; If the student is a girl, then she should make a tally mark with a G on the top of it. I would continue this until all of the children have made their tally marks. Then, I would have one from each group, on my signal, race to the board to write the total, adding the tallies for each flavor that the boys liked, then adding the tallies for each flavor that the girls liked. That is, one pair would race to the board to tally the total of boys who liked the strawberry yogurt; the group then counts aloud the tallies for the boys who liked that flavor to verify the addition; another pair, on my signal, would race to tally the total of girls who liked the vanilla yogurt and the group would count to verify the total. Another pair, on my signal, would race to the board to tally the total of boys who liked the next flavor, and so on. The first member of a team to count a flavor's tallies by boys/girls correctly wins a point. The team with the highest number of points wins the game after all of the totals for all of the flavors of yogurt liked by boys and by girls have been added correctly. I would discuss the use of this line graph and the information it can tell us (or the future owner of a grocery store) about preferences that are similar or different between the boys and the girls in their choice of yogurt flavors.

Justification of activities for this age level

Fourth-grade students will become engaged in these two activities because students at this age level prefer active learning experiences; they like interaction with their peers and are willing to learn what they consider to be useful information; They like to use their skills to solve real-life problems (like determining the kind of yogurt flavors an owner should stock in his/her store if the families of this fourth-grade class were to buy yogurt and other items there). They can reason, judge, and apply their experiences and think about their own thinking.

They want to be popular and have a sense of humor. They mature at varying rates and have individual differences. Physically, they have strong appetites and socially, they want group acceptance.

A Focus on English Language Learners. For ELLs, I would ask them to respond to similar activities (i.e., favorite snacks in a selected culture, favorite sweet flavors graph) based on data from newspapers or magazines that give information about people or events that represent other cultures.

CONCEPTS
(Review Looking at Teachers II, Chapter 3)

You are asked to describe two (2) learning activities that you would use to help the third-grade students with learning problems in this class who do not fully understand the concept of transplanting. **Hints:** Activities could include making charts, diagrams, or drawing some planting maps about transplanting tasks. Some students could draw cartoons, tell stories, and make posters to show what they do when they transplant plants. Other students could write invitations to a program they have planned about gardening/transplanting and draw advertisements, write invitations to members in another class, and plan a program that includes speeches about the value of transplanting, a script of a story about gardening, and a planned debate over what to do (or not to do) when considering transplanting a certain type of plant. Still other students can write personal letters to one another about their transplanting experiences, or make daily entries in diaries or journals. For this question, you are to give examples of what the students would be doing and should explain how you would assess the two activities that you choose and the students' understanding of the concept of transplanting after they have completed the two (2) activities.

Activity #1: Planting bean seeds

I would have the students plant three (3) bean seeds—one each in three small clear plastic glasses and water them frequently. When the beans have developed roots and the first two leaves, I would have the students transplant one (1) of the seedlings into a small paper cup that they have decorated to give to different teachers as gifts. With hands-on learning in mind, I would have the students transplant a second seedling to a larger cup to take home and give to someone in the home.

Activity #2: Transplanting to the school campus

Considering the third seedling, I would have the students transplant it to a larger pot, and then eventually have the students transplant the seedlings to a place on the school campus where the students have determined that the transplanted seedlings will receive sunlight and water for future growth.

Assessment for both activities: To assess, I would look to see that all of the children are cooperating with the activity. I would notice who is listening to find out what to do. At the end of the activity, I would ask the students to demonstrate their understanding of the term *transplanting*, and assess it to see if the students have improved in their understanding of the term. As a group activity, I would ask them to demonstrate the meaning of the term in several ways: by reading the definition aloud from a dictionary, by reading some content about transplanting aloud from an information book, by showing an illustration about transplanting from a source of their choice, and by demonstrating with actions (similar to the game of charades) their understanding of the meaning of the word. With hands-on learning in mind, one assessment activity would be for a small group to take turns to draw from a deck of cards (whose faces show stick figure drawings of gardening tasks, i.e., raking leaves, pruning shrubs, cutting flowers)—until they recognize two (2) cards that show transplanting—one (1) card that shows a plant in a pot and on the second card, a plant in the ground beside the same pot now empty.

Another assessment activity would be to give each of the students one of the cards from the gardening deck and ask them to walk around the room until the two transplanting cards are found. I think it is very important for learning to be enjoyed by students so they will want to learn. If not, I suspect some of the children will become disinterested and decide to turn their attention elsewhere. I believe that quite a few children need hands-on learning to further their comprehension.

A Focus on English Language Learners. For ELLs, whenever possible, I would ask the students to use their language throughout the lesson. For example, I would ask them to give a word that means the same as *transplanting* in their native language and then use both words when referring to the concept in the lesson. I would encourage all students to repeat the words in a choral response when I refer to the words. I would repeat this dual-language approach often with different words to show that the class values their language.

PURPOSES OF WRITING ACTIVITIES
(Review Looking at Teachers II, Chapter 4)

First, in the classroom vignette *Looking at Teachers II* at the end of this chapter, you were asked to consider what ways the second-grade students, rather than the teacher, could accept the procedures and rules that the teacher suggested and also assume responsibility for their actions and make their classroom a community of learners. **Hints:** Imagine that you were asked to take the role of a teacher working with older students and focus on rules and procedures. You were asked to begin a unit on the American Revolution for a fifth-grade class and plan one (1) or two (2) writing activities that will help your students pass along the information that they have about the need for laws/procedures/rules and help organize their thinking about the idea that laws should be designed to equally support and value all members of a community, even a community in the time period of the American Revolution. As part of this instruction, you were asked to give the purposes for and describe two (2) writing activities that you might use in your unit on the American Revolution. Some of the activities (related to the letters in the word *activities*) that you can consider are the following:

A is for advertisements related to the period

C is for creating cartoons, making charts, stating comparisons

T is for telling stories

I is for invitations

V is for video programs

I is for individual letters

T is for telling predictions

I is for individual diaries and journals

E is for engaging in debates

S is for speeches and scripts

Consider giving the purposes of both of the writing activities and be sure to be clear about your specific writing examples.

Activity #1: Writing activity and purpose

I would select one of the following writing activities: (1) asking the students to work in dyads to construct informational paragraphs about what was learned about rules in this unit of study, with the *purpose* of developing an understanding of the particular concept of rules; or (2) having the students each write a letter to a friend in the classroom to tell the friend what was learned, with the purpose, of using accurate information and applying it in another situation. For a creative writing activity, I would ask the students to work together in pairs to write a response to the question, "What do you think a colonist during the days of the American Revolution would say if transported to this time period and given a cell phone to communicate with others?" I understand that the letters in the word *purposes* will help me remember examples of the different purposes for learning activities for the students. I could focus on one of the following purposes for selected activities:

P particular concept selected (understanding of); to clarify thinking about a concept

U use of accurate information; to inform/advise

R requiring in-depth learning (to be applied); to record thoughts

P parts contribute to a whole situation (to see how the parts contribute to the whole); to persuade; to predict/hypothesize

O other situations (apply to); to compare to other situations

S synthesis and analysis (use of)

E expansion of the students' thinking

S stressing creativity; to entertain/amuse

Activity #2: Writing activity and purpose

I would engage the students in writing entries in their student learning journals for the *purpose* of expanding the students' thinking, to determine the students' understanding of the particular concept of *rules*, to note the use of accurate information, and to see the students' understanding of how parts (for instance, the making of rules) during the time period contributed to the whole situation of following someone's rules/not following someone's rules during this time period.

A Focus on English Language Learners. I would not expect the same level of accuracy in writing and spelling as from most English speakers but I want to give ELLs opportunities to express themselves in writing and to develop their writing skills. Perhaps their writing topic would be different than the class-assigned topic and instead be about a topic they know or about something they have experienced. I would ask them what ways are helpful to get them started. Perhaps they would work with a partner at a "writing lab table" in the room. I would be interested in seeing their writing first, then conferencing, and later, focusing on selected errors in spelling and punctuation in a mini-lesson or ad hoc lesson.

FANCIFUL/CREATIVE AND REALISTIC WRITING
(Review Looking at Teachers II, Chapter 5)

You are asked, as a sixth-grade teacher, to describe two more writing activities (and the purposes) that you might use after a student brainstorming session about a language arts lesson on listening. And, you are to give examples for the students. **Hints:** Consider a fanciful/creative and a realistic kind of writing activity.

Activity #1: Fanciful/creative writing and purpose

I would ask the students to consider that they were assigned an alien writing partner and they are going to be time travelers back to the time of the American Revolution to see the rules going on there. The student is to write a letter to the alien to explain what was going on. The alien, being from another planet, does not understand what rules are or what is going on. After the letters are written, the students can divide into small groups and take turns reading their letters or excerpts of

their letters aloud and listening to one another. The *purpose* is to stress creativity, to use accurate information about the time period, to apply their learning to a different situation of letter correspondence, to display their listening skills, and to expand the students' thinking about ways to explain the topic to others.

Activity #2: Realistic writing and purpose

I would ask the students to consider writing an informational paragraph about an incident where rules were in evidence during this time period. After the informational paragraphs are written, the students can join together as partners and take turn reading the writing aloud and listening to one another. They can ask for feedback about their use of accurate information. The *purpose* would be to show the students' understanding of the particular concept of rules, to use accurate information, to expand the students' thinking, to demonstrate their listening skills, and to apply their learning to writing an informational-type paragraph.

A Focus on English Language Learners. ELLs can be introduced to stories and books that are culturally relevant and related to a writing purpose. For an example related to Activity #1, stories of cultures that are similar and different from the ones in the class can be read aloud and rules that were in that culture *at the same time* that America's Revolution was happening can be discussed. For an example related to Activity #2, stories of cultures can be read aloud and rules discussed that seem to be in evidence *during any time period.*

HIGHER-ORDER THINKING SKILLS
(Review Looking at Teachers II, Chapter 6)

You are asked to take the role of a middle-school teacher and draft two (2) questions for the students to respond to in short-answer essays. You want the questions to give the students an opportunity to demonstrate their higher-order thinking skills that can include application, analysis, synthesis, and evaluation. **Hints:** You want to give them an opportunity to write about what they have learned on the subject of equality, and so the main focus of the questions should be related to the concept of *equality*, or the statement: *All men/women are created equal.* Tell which higher-order thinking skills the questions would require the students to use and how the questions extend the students' knowledge about the topic.

Question #1: I would offer this question: "In what way can you apply what you have learned to a new situation and describe the effect of equality on people in the _____ society where women and men are considered to be equal?"

Higher-order thinking skills: The students would be required to use these higher-order thinking skills: (a) application; that is, they will use the knowledge that they have learned and apply that knowledge to a new situation (in this case, a different societal group); (b) analysis; that is, the students will analyze the effect on people in a certain societal group so they can describe the effect in writing; and (c) evaluation; that is, the students will make a judgment call about the concept that women and men were considered to be equal in the given society and give examples to support that view.

Question #2: I would offer this question: "In what way can you analyze what you have learned to describe the effect that a *lack* of equality had on the people in the _____ society?"

Higher-order thinking skills: The students would be required to use these higher-order thinking skills: (a) analysis; that is, the students would use what they have learned to describe and consider/analyze the effect of the *lack* of equality on people in a society; (b) evaluation; that is, the students will make a judgment call that there was *lack* of equality in a particular situation and describe its effect on the people.

A Focus on English Language Learners. ELLs could discuss what it is like to take a walk in someone else's shoes. They can tell what they know about equality and lack of equality of people in different cultures motivated by the illustrations in one of the sources in Figure 5.3, Sample Multiple Readings Guide and Children's Bibliography to Promote Global Awareness/Understanding, or in *Feet and Footwear: A Cultural Encyclopedia* (Santa Barbara, CA: Greenwood Press, 2009) by M. DeMello. In this book about cultures, illustrations and words show and discuss beliefs/customs related to the feet, folktales and myths featuring feet/shoes, and important people associated with shoes.

WRITING A RESEARCH REPORT
(Review Looking at Teachers II, Chapter 7)

You are asked to take the persona of a sixth-grade teacher who is teaching a humanities block that integrates language arts, reading, and social studies, and you want to prepare your sixth-graders to write a research report about a topic related to the concept of Manifest Destiny. **Hints:** List the steps that you would take, including prewriting, drafting, editing, and publishing, and briefly explain each step.

Activity #1: Writing a research report
Here are the steps that I would take to guide the sixth-grade students through the writing of their research reports.

First, I would consider several prewriting activities that include discussion of the topic, process of interviewing another person, researching information, taking notes when necessary, and brainstorming about the topic.

Second, I would consider the drafting process. I would encourage the students to record their ideas and, at this step, would not have a great concern about spelling or the mechanics of the language.

Third, I would consider an editing step. I would engage the students in reading a draft aloud to a class partner for discussion, in trading drafts with partners for proofreading. At this step, I would encourage correcting and refining according to spelling and the mechanics of the language.

Fourth, I would consider a publishing step. I would have the students write a final copy and present the final work to others in small groups or to the whole group.

A Focus on English Language Learners. For ELLs, I would assist the students in learning these procedures by taking time to show my own modeling of the steps, giving demonstrations, and providing feedback.

CLASSROOM TRANSITIONS
(Review Looking at Teachers II, Chapter 8)

You are asked to take the role of a kindergarten teacher who wants to make a smooth classroom transition from one lesson to the next. **Hints:** You are asked to draft two (2) questions that the students could respond to at the completion of a reading lesson that would help a transition to the next lesson, a math lesson. You'll recall that classroom transitions are procedures that move student thinking from one idea to the next or that moves their actions from one activity to the next; a transition guides a change in the classroom. Some teachers emphasize decent, responsible behavior by the students, discuss goals, invite student cooperation, help students make good choices, and award reinforcers such as points and tokens. Other teachers self-evaluate to make sure that they are avoiding jerkiness, leaving their words dangling in the verbal air, or starting one activity before another is finished. Still other teachers avoid flip-flopping, that is, stopping one activity, starting another one, and then going back to the first activity the teacher terminated.

Question #1: Aiding transition I would offer this question: "In what way did the ending (or trick ending) make the story more interesting to you?"

Question #2: Aiding transition Then, second, I would offer this question: "Just as stories can be interesting to you, in what way can numbers make a math lesson interesting to you?"

A Focus on English Language Learners. For Question #1, I would encourage the students to talk about what makes a story-ending interesting to them by modeling my own thinking about the ending of a story recently read. For Question #2, I would get the students started by modeling one or two examples of how numbers can be interesting, that is, the price of a desired treat or the amount needed before a snack can be purchased.

MAIN IDEA
(Review Looking at Teachers II, Chapter 9)

This chapter's vignette in *Looking at Teachers II* was about real-life problem solving; you'll remember that the emphasis was on integrated learning and about looking at a problem or subject of study from the point of view of many separate disciplines. Related to this, imagine that you were asked to introduce a unit on reading newspaper articles related to a topic of interest. You want to introduce students to the idea of public officials in the real world using knowledge from various disciplines to help solve one or more of their problems. After a week or two of reading newspaper articles, you discover that some of your students still don't understand a key principle of newspaper articles—the main idea. **Hints:** Describe two activities that might help these students identify main ideas in nonfiction prose. Give specific examples and explain the purpose of the activities. You'll recall that the letters in the word *purposes* help you remember the reasons for activities: **P** for (understanding) a particular concept; **U** for use of accurate information; **R** for recording thoughts; **P** for persuading or predicting; **O** for (applying to) other situations; **S** for synthesis; **E** for expansion of thinking; and **S** for stressing creativity.

Activity #1: What is this article really emphasizing?
I would have the whole group read an article on an overhead transparency and ask, "What is this article really emphasizing?" and "What do you think the main point is?" Record the students' responses and discuss.

Activity #2: Newspaper articles and the main point
I would clip brief articles from newspapers and clip off the accompanying headlines. I would have the students, in partners or triads, study one article, determine the main idea, and write the idea as a headline to later share with the whole group for discussion. I would repeat the activity with different news articles.

Purposes of the activities: The purposes of these activities are: (1) to develop an understanding of the particular concept of *main idea*, (2) to clarify the students' thinking about a *main point* in an article, (3) to use accurate information from a newspaper article, and (4) to record their thoughts about a main idea.

A Focus on English Language Learners. For Activity #1, I would indicate native speakers as partners who can read along together to determine what an article is emphasizing and to talk about the main point. For Activity #2, I would use articles related to different cultures. I would ask native speakers to be partners to study, discuss the main idea, and write it as a headline together.

WRITING PROCESS
(Review Looking at Teachers II, Chapter 10)

You are asked to explain the steps to guide the students through the writing process as they prepare to write a survival guide about natural disasters. **Hints:** You'll recall there are several recommended steps in the writing process: prewriting activities, drafting, editing, and publishing. Here are the steps that I would take to guide the students through the writing of a survival guide about natural disasters:

Step 1: I would plan several prewriting activities and have the students:

Discuss the topic

Interview another person to get information

Research information from sources

Take notes when necessary

Brainstorm about the topic

Step 2: I would plan a drafting process and have the students:

Record their ideas

Basically ignore (for the moment) spelling/mechanics of the language

Focus on writing their ideas

Step 3: I would include an editing step and have the students:

Read their drafts aloud to a class partner for discussion/feedback/evaluation

Trade their drafts with partners for proofreading

After proofreading, start correcting and refining their drafts related to spelling/mechanics of the language

Step 4: I would plan a publishing step and have the students:

Write a final copy

Present their final work to others in a group situation

END-OF-THE-UNIT ACTIVITY
(Review Looking at Teachers II, Chapter 11)

You are asked to select a unit of study of your choice for students of a selected grade and age level. You are asked to describe an end-of-the-unit activity, such as the Power-Point presentation in the vignette, that would be an extension of the study. **Hints:** The activity should demonstrate your understanding of how children learn at this choice of age and grade level.

Activity #1: End-of-the-unit activity

I have selected a unit of study about the American Revolution for fifth-grade students, usually ages 10 or 11. The end-of-the-unit activity that I would select as an extension of this study would be to let each student write his/her own informational narrative about what was learned and share it with the whole group in a culminating program that would extend the information about the topic to all of the students. If appropriate for the instructional time that I had, I would have the students prepare their informational narratives first by working in dyads to construct information paragraphs about what they learned and use the information as references to support the writing of their narratives. As part of the culminating program on this topic, I would have them each write an informative letter to a friend in the class to tell the friend what he/she learned about the topic.

My understanding of how children learn at this age and grade level:

Children in the fifth grade at the ages of 10 or 11, like interaction with their peers (such as participating in a culminating class program about the topic or studying in dyads, or writing personal letters to class friends). They prefer active learning experiences (working with partners, writing letters to friends, preparing for a culminating program) and can use their skills in real-life situations (preparing for culminating programs, letter writing). Related to problems, they can reason, judge, and apply what they have experienced (working in dyads). They can think about their own thinking, that is, metacognition (preassessing what they know through a K–W–L [know, want to know, learn strategy]).

A Focus on English Language Learners. I would want ELLs to preassess what they know through K–W–L. I want them to identify what they want to know; and still later, working with native-speaking partners, or other selected students, to state/identify what they have learned.

FUTURE CONSIDERATION: NATIONAL BOARD CERTIFICATION*

Barone, D. (2002). *The National Board Certification Handbook: Support and Stories from Teachers and Candidates.* Portland, ME: Stenhouse Publishers.

Berg, J. H. (2003). *Improving the Quality of Teaching through National Board Certification: Theory and Practice.* Norwood, MA: Christopher-Gordon.

Danna, S. (2003, Feb./March) Pursuing National Board Certification. *Pi Lambda Theta Educational Horizons,* 5.

*In three or more years after getting your initial teaching certificate, you may decide to seek National Board Certification (an important declaration of accomplished teaching) by going through the required portfolio and assessment process. To do this, you can begin looking for an NBC mentor in your district and turn to one of these handbooks for guidance or to a resource suggested by a mentor or colleague. See www.nbpts.org.

Appendix B

Self-Check Reflection Guides

SELF-CHECK REFLECTION GUIDES

- Midpoint Self-Check Reflection Guide: Checklist of Competencies
- Final Self-Check Reflection Guide: Checklist of Competencies

*Midpoint Self-Check Reflection Guide: Checklist of Competencies**

Instructions: Complete this midpoint reflection guide and checklist of competencies as reviewed through *A Resource Guide for Elementary School Teaching: Planning for Competence, Seventh Edition*, Chapters 1–6. Check yourself on the following competency list.

	Very Aware	Somewhat Aware	Not Aware
1. I am aware of some information about today's elementary schools and can recall some informational sources about students. (Chapter 1)	—	—	—
2. I can recall and reflect on my own elementary school experiences to help me make certain decisions as a beginning teacher. (Chapter 1)	—	—	—
3. I have rehearsed/practiced/used both manuscript and cursive handwriting that I expect to model for elementary students in my classroom. (Chapter 1)	—	—	—
4. I have visited an elementary classroom recently. (Chapter 1)	—	—	—
5. I have identified one or more characteristics of productive teaching. (Chapter 2)	—	—	—
6. I can identify a unit of study for a selected grade level that I might prefer to teach and how the whole unit is divided into parts. (Chapter 2)	—	—	—
7. I am aware of the professional responsibilities of a first-year teacher. (Chapter 3)	—	—	—
8. I am aware of the preactive phase of instruction and can mentally rehearse my teaching actions before meeting the students. (Chapter 3)	—	—	—

*If you are interested in a numerical score, consider 3 points for each item marked *very aware*, 2 points for *somewhat aware*, and 0 points for *not aware*. 87 = Very Aware.

	Very Aware	Somewhat Aware	Not Aware
9. I can find useful Internet sites and share sites with others. (Chapter 3)	—	—	—
10. I am aware of the instructional and the noninstructional responsibilities facing me as a beginning teacher. (Chapter 3)	—	—	—
11. I have prepared a management system that I can explain to my students during the first day or the first week of school. (Chapter 4)	—	—	—
12. I can compose a positive message home to a student's parent or guardian. (Chapter 4)	—	—	—
13. I can learn from observing another teacher's classroom management system. (Chapter 4)	—	—	—
14. I can analyze how an experienced teacher opens a class meeting or begins a school day. (Chapter 4)	—	—	—
15. I can determine which measures of control I would apply in selected situations. (Chapter 4)	—	—	—
16. I am familiar with my state's standards for the K–6 curriculum. (Chapter 5)	—	—	—
17. I am familiar with other curriculum documents published by my state's department of education. (Chapter 5)	—	—	—
18. I am familiar with curriculum documents prepared by a local school district. (Chapter 5)	—	—	—
19. I am familiar with student textbooks and teachers' editions that I may be using in my teaching. (Chapter 5)	—	—	—
20. I can organize my ideas about subject content and the sequencing of content. (Chapter 5)	—	—	—
21. I have considered what I will do about controversial content and issues I might encounter. (Chapter 5)	—	—	—
22. I can recognize verbs that are suitable for use in overt objectives. (Chapter 5)	—	—	—
23. I have practiced my skill in recognizing four components of a criterion-referenced instructional objective: audience, performance, conditions, and performance level. (Chapter 5)	—	—	—
24. I can recognize objectives that are measurable. (Chapter 5)	—	—	—
25. I can identify objectives according to the domain: cognitive, affective, or psychomotor. (Chapter 5)	—	—	—
26. I can prepare different types of assessment items. (Chapter 6)	—	—	—
27. I recognize the importance of teacher comments about student behavior. (Chapter 6)	—	—	—
28. I have prepared my thoughts about participating in parent-teacher conference situations. (Chapter 6)	—	—	—
29. I have reflected about part-to-whole relationships in a subject area that could be taught to students in a selected grade that I might prefer to teach. (Chapter 6).	—	—	—

Final Self-Check Reflection Guide: Checklist of Competencies*

Instructions: Now that you have completed Part III in this resource guide and completed Chapters 7–11, check yourself on this final self-check competency list. In the appropriate space to the right of each item, write in 4 points for each item checked with *definite readiness*, 3 points for each item checked as *comfortable*, 2 points for *still needs work*, and 1 point for *weak* and *needs work*.

4   if you have definite readiness or awareness

3   if you have comfortable readiness or awareness

2   if you still need more work

1   if you are uncomfortable, have little awareness/knowledge about it, and still need more work

N/O write in *no opportunity* if you did not have the assigned time, procedures, or responsibilities to achieve the competency and explain the situation

Share the results with your instructor.

	4 definite readiness	3 comfortable	1 still needs work	0 weak; needs more work
1. I can generate a list of potential topics suitable as interdisciplinary units. (Chapter 7)	—	—	—	—
2. I can use an interdisciplinary theme in the curriculum and provide suggestions for teaching the theme. (Chapter 7)	—	—	—	—
3. I can write questions for a question map related to a theme/topic/grade level for an interdisciplinary thematic unit. (Chapter 7)	—	—	—	—
4. I can connect questions and activities related to a theme for an interdisciplinary thematic unit. I realize that learning activities can be planned around central questions. (Chapter 7)	—	—	—	—
5. I can write a specific teaching plan for a minimum of one day that includes preparing goals, writing objectives, selecting resources, and selecting and planning learning activities. (Chapter 7)	—	—	—	—
6. I can reference selected learning activities to national standards, state frameworks, district documents, and local school curriculum. (Chapter 7)	—	—	—	—
7. I can plan a closure for a unit. (Chapter 7)	—	—	—	—
8. I can analyze information about the implementation of a lesson to predict the success or failure of a lesson based on its planning and structure. (Chapter 7)	—	—	—	—
9. I can follow a model format to prepare a lesson plan and have it evaluated. (Chapter 7)	—	—	—	—
10. I can give at least one example of learning experiences or activities from each of the following categories: verbal, visual, vicarious, simulated, and explicit/direct. (Chapter 7)	—	—	—	—
11. I can use a lesson format that is approved by the instructor and prepare a lesson plan for a grade/course of my choice. (Chapter 7)	—	—	—	—
12. I can evaluate my own lesson plan and the plan of one of my peers. (Chapter 7)	—	—	—	—

*If you are interested in a numerical score, award 4 points for each item checked with *definite readiness*, 3 points for each item checked as *comfortable*, 2 points for *still needs work*, and 1 point for *weak* and *needs work*. Note that 108 = definite readiness and competency demonstrated.

	4 *definite readiness*	3 *comfortable*	1 *still needs work*	0 *weak; needs more work*
13. I can write a teaching plan with goals, objectives, resources, and learning activities. (Chapter 7)	—	—	—	—
14. I can prepare a regular instructional unit (or an interdisciplinary thematic unit) with sequential lesson plans and a closure, one that I can use in my teaching. (Chapter 7)	—	—	—	—
15. I know when and how to use teacher talk for instruction. (Chapter 8)	—	—	—	—
16. I can describe the value, purpose, and types of advance mental organizers used when using teacher talk as an instructional strategy. (Chapter 8)	—	—	—	—
17. I recognize and use various types/levels of questions. (Chapter 8)	—	—	—	—
18. I have developed my skill in raising questions from one level to the next. (Chapter 8)	—	—	—	—
19. I understand the importance of well-worded questions and allowing students time to think. (Chapter 8)	—	—	—	—
20. I have practiced the skill of raising questions to higher levels. (Chapter 8)	—	—	—	—
21. I can discuss some of the relationships among thinking, problem solving, inquiry learning, and discovery learning. (Chapter 9)	—	—	—	—
22. I can describe the characteristics of an effective demonstration and effective use of inquiry learning. (Chapter 9)	—	—	—	—
23. I can analyze an inquiry learning lesson and text information about integrating strategies to form a synthesis of information for use in my own teaching. (Chapter 9)	—	—	—	—
24. I can create and demonstrate a brief lesson for a specific grade level or subject and ask my peers for narrative evaluations. (Chapter 9)	—	—	—	—
25. I can compare/contrast the seven categories of games for learning. (Chapter 9)	—	—	—	—
26. I can describe at least two ways of integrating strategies for integrated learning. (Chapter 9)	—	—	—	—
27. I can develop a lesson using different approaches: inquiry learning level II, thinking skill development, a demonstration, or an interactive lecture—peer teaching II. (Chapter 9)	—	—	—	—
28. I can describe my knowledge about using a whole-class discussion as a teaching strategy. (Chapter 10)	—	—	—	—
29. I am knowledgeable about guidelines for using whole-class discussion as a teaching strategy. (Chapter 10)	—	—	—	—
30. I can explain how the classroom teacher can personalize the instruction (differentiated/tiered instruction) to ensure success for each student. (Chapter 10)	—	—	—	—
31. I can explain my view about being in favor of or against recovery options for students who don't do an assignment or who don't do well on it. (Chapter 10)	—	—	—	—

(continued)

	4 definite readiness	3 comfortable	1 still needs work	0 weak; needs more work
32. I can describe my view about how to effectively use one or more of these instructional strategies: assignments, homework, journal writing, written and oral reports, cooperative learning groups, learning centers, problem-based learning, and student-centered projects. (Chapter 10)	—	—	—	—
33. I can build upon what I already know and use whole-class discussion as a teaching strategy. (Chapter 10)	—	—	—	—
34. I can assess my teaching effectiveness: using self-assessment in student teaching/interning and using standards for assessment. (Chapter 11)	—	—	—	—
35. I can organize my teaching; example: planning for E-teaching with an Emergency Teaching Kit. (Chapter 11)	—	—	—	—
36. I am knowledgeable about preparing for a job interview. (Chapter 11)	—	—	—	—
37. I have written a résumé. (Chapter 11)	—	—	—	—
38. I have started a portfolio. (Chapter 11)	—	—	—	—
39. I have participated in peer teaching for analysis and feedback. (Chapter 11)	—	—	—	—

Glossary

ability grouping   The assignment of students to separate classrooms or to separate activities within a classroom according to their perceived academic abilities. This means matching instruction to the needs of students with similar abilities who are placed in groups; homogeneous grouping is the grouping of students of similar abilities, whereas heterogeneous grouping is the grouping of students of mixed abilities.

access mode   Indicates providing students with access to information by working with the students.

accommodation   The cognitive process of modifying a schema or creating new schemata in response to one's experiences.

accountability   This is a term that refers to the concept that an individual is responsible for his or her own behaviors and should be able to demonstrate publicly the worth of the activities carried out; a student can be asked to show that he/she has met specified standards; a teacher can be asked to demonstrate how he/she has been responsible for the students' performance.

achievement tests   See *standardized tests*.

active learning   Hands-on and minds-on learning.

advance organizer   Preinstructional cues that encourage a mental set, used to enhance retention of materials to be studied.

advisor-advisee   A homeroom or advisory program that provides each student the opportunity to interact with peers about school and personal concerns and to develop a meaningful relationship with at least one member of the school staff.

affective domain   The area of learning related to attitudes, feelings, interests, values, and personal adjustment.

aim   The term sometimes used for the most general educational objectives.

aligned/authentic assessment   An assessment that matches the instructional objectives.

aligned curriculum   A curriculum where teachers prepare specific objectives, teach toward them, and assess students' progress against them. Also known as *performance-based teaching* and *criterion-referenced measurement*.

alternative assessment   Assessment of learning in ways that are different from traditional paper-and-pencil objective testing, such as direct examination on real life tasks, a portfolio, PowerPoint presentation, project, or self-assessment. See *authentic assessment*.

American Federation of Teachers (AFT)   A national professional organization of teachers founded in 1916 and currently affiliated with the American Federation of Labor and Congress of Industrial Organizations (AFL-CIO).

analysis   Dissecting information into its component parts to comprehend their relationships.

anchor assignment   An ongoing assignment that students work on after they have finished their basic work. Also called *transitional activity* or *star activity*.

anticipatory set   See *advance organizer*.

application   Using information.

articulation   The connectedness of the various components of the formal curriculum. *Vertical articulation* is used when referring to the connectedness of the curriculum K–12; *horizontal articulation* refers to the connectedness across a grade level.

assessment   Gathering information; this is a teacher's relatively neutral process of finding out what students are learning or have learned as a result of instruction. Helps a teacher make further decisions about teaching and the students' learning. See *evaluation*.

assignments   A statement telling the student what he or she is to accomplish as a follow-up to a lesson either as homework (responsibility papers) or as in-class work.

assimilation   The cognitive process by which a learner integrates new information into an existing schema.

at-risk   General term given to students who show a high potential for dropping out of formal education.

authentic assessment   The use of evaluation procedures (usually portfolios and projects) that are highly compatible with the instructional objectives. Also referred to as *accurate, active, aligned, alternative, direct*, and *performance assessment*.

behavioral objective   A statement describing what the learner should be able to do upon completion of the instruction, and containing four ingredients: the audience (learner), the overt behavior, the conditions, and the degree (performance level). Also referred to as *performance* and *terminal objective*.

behaviorism   A theory that equates learning with changes in observable behavior.

bias in tests, cultural The bias that happens when the language of an item on a test hinders a response by a student of a particular ethnic or cultural background.

block scheduling The school programming procedure that provides large blocks of time (e.g., two hours) in which individual teachers or teacher teams can organize and arrange groupings of students for varied periods, thereby more effectively individualizing the instruction for students with various needs and abilities.

brainstorming An instructional strategy used to create a flow of new ideas, during which judgments of the ideas of others are forbidden; actions of students as they orally respond to a question and the teacher, a student, or classroom aide writes their responses on the board, chart, or transparency without making judgments about the responses.

broad questions Higher-order thinking questions that require analysis, synthesis, or evaluation. Also known as *reflective, open-ended, thought,* and *divergent-thinking questions.*

CD–ROM (compact disc–read only memory) Digitally encoded information permanently recorded on a compact disc.

character education The transmission of honesty and other values.

charter school It is usually recognized as a school established within the provisions of state charter school laws that becomes an educational campus that operates under a contract/charter that has been negotiated between the operators of the school and the sponsors who oversee the provisions of the contract/charter.

checklist A written description related to a topic that indicates an adequate demonstration/performance of that topic.

classroom assessment A teacher's procedures that he or she uses to make decisions about the learning progress of the students; can include informal assessment strategies such as informal reading inventories, observations by the teacher, oral reports by students, performance samples, work in portfolios, and ongoing records.

classroom control The process of influencing student behavior in the classroom; includes all of a teacher's strategies related to maintaining a safe learning environment.

classroom management The teacher's system of establishing a climate for learning; includes his or her techniques used to prevent and respond to a student's misbehavior.

clinical supervision A nonevaluative collegial process of facilitating teaching effectiveness by involving a triad of individuals: the precredentialed teacher, the collaborating teacher, and the college or university supervisor/ instructor/representative. Sometimes known as *effective supervision*, clinical supervision includes (a) a preobservation conference between the supervisors and the precredentialed teacher to specify and agree upon the specific objectives for an observation visit; (b) a data collection observation; and (c) a postobservation conference to analyze the data collected during the observation and to set goals for a subsequent observation.

closure In a lesson, the means by which a teacher brings the lesson to an end.

coached practice Providing individual attention to students by using in-class times to begin assignments.

coaching See *mentoring*.

cognition The process of thinking.

cognitive dissonance (disequilibrium) The mental state of not yet having made sense out of a perplexing (discrepant) situation.

cognitive domain The area of learning related to intellectual skills, such as retention and assimilation of knowledge.

cognitive psychology A branch of psychology devoted to the study of how individuals acquire, process, and use information.

cognitivism A theory that supports the idea that learning involves the construction or reshaping of mental schemata and that mental processes mediate learning; maintains that learners construct their own understanding of the topics they study. Also known as *constructivism*.

common planning time A regularly scheduled time during the school day when teachers who teach the same students meet for joint planning, parent conferences, materials preparation, and student evaluation.

compact disc (CD) A 4.72-inch disc on which a laser has recorded digital information.

comparative organizer An introduction that mentally prepares students for a study by helping them make connections with materials already learned or experienced. See *advance organizer*.

competency-based instruction Instruction that is designed to evaluate student achievement against specified and predetermined behavioral objectives. The term also indicates instruction referred to as *outcome-based* and *results-driven*. See *performance-based teaching*.

comprehension Also seen as a level of cognition that refers to the skill of *understanding*.

computer-assisted instruction (CAI) Instruction received by a student when interacting with lessons programmed into a computer system; can also refer to the management of information about the performance of students and selections of educational resources that can be prescribed and controlled for individual lessons.

computer literacy The ability at some level on a continuum to understand and use computers.

concept A general idea or thought, based on one's experiences, that classifies or categorizes information or phenomena and that ranges from simple (objects) to complex (perhaps themes); also an abstraction (i.e., each person's concept about phenomena is an abstraction), is unique to that person's experiences; this refers to a group of facts or ideas that can have something in common.

conceptual misunderstanding Faulty understanding of a major idea. See *misconception*.

constructivism See *cognitivism*.

continuous progress Describes the performance of a student who moves at his or her own pace through a sequence of lessons that make up the curriculum.

convergent thinking Thinking that is directed to a preset conclusion.

convergent-thinking questions Low-order thinking questions that have a single correct answer, such as recall questions. Example: How is the Earth classed, as a star or a planet? Also called *narrow questions*.

cooperative learning A genre of instructional strategies that use small groups of students working together and helping each other on learning tasks, with an emphasis on support for one another rather than on competition.

cooperative learning group A heterogeneous group of two to six students who work together that is organized according to one or more criteria, such as ability or skill level, ethnicity, learning style, learning capacity, gender, and language proficiency; a teacher- or student-directed setting, emphasizing support for one another, where each student often takes a particular role such as group facilitator, materials manager, or recorder.

core curriculum Subject or discipline components of the curriculum considered absolutely necessary. Traditionally these are English/language arts, mathematics, science, and social science.

covert behavior A learner behavior that is not outwardly observable.

criterion A standard by which behavioral performance is judged.

criterion-referenced measurement Assessment in which standards are established and behaviors are judged against the preset guidelines, rather than against behaviors of others. Also referred to as *competency-based, performance-based, results-driven,* or *outcome-based* education.

critical thinking The ability of a learner to recognize and identify problems and discrepancies, to propose and to test solutions, and to arrive at tentative conclusions.

cross-age coaching This refers to an instructional strategy that places students, sometimes in different age groups, in a tutorial role in which one student helps another learn.

cues Hints or prompts that can produce student behaviors that a teacher wants to reinforce.

culminating activities The activities that bring the study to a natural close.

culminating presentation This is a way for students to apply what they have learned and is a final presentation/activity that often includes an oral report, a hands-on item of some kind, and a written report.

curriculum Originally derived from a Latin term referring to a race course for the chariots, the term still has no widely accepted definition. As used in this text, *curriculum* is that which is planned and encouraged for teaching and learning. This includes both school and nonschool environments, overt (formal) and hidden (informal) environments, and broad as well as narrow notions of content—its development, acquisition, and consequences.

culturally responsive teaching What teachers should use (cultural knowledge, students' experiences, strengths, and performance styles) to make learning appropriate and effective.

curriculum standards What students should know (content) and should be able to do (process and performance).

data-input phase The lowest level of questioning, that is, gathering and recalling information.

data-output phase The highest level of questioning, that is, to think intuitively, creatively, and hypothetically, and to use imagination.

data-processing phase The intermediate level of questioning, that is, drawing relationships of cause and effect, to synthesize, to analyze, to summarize, to compare/contrast, and to classify data.

deductive learning Learning that proceeds from the general (the whole, looking overall at a particular group, kind, class, topic) to the specifics (a designation of the particular characteristics). See also *expository* (explaining or elucidating) *instruction*.

delivery mode Indicates a delivery of information, often using traditional strategies such as textbook reading, lecturing, questioning, and teacher-centered or teacher-planned discussions; also known as the *didactic, expository,* or *traditional* style of instruction.

demonstration A showing or exhibition of methods or reasoning.

developing activities The activities that make up the majority of the lessons and an ongoing unit.

developmental characteristics A set of common intellectual, psychological, physical, and social characteristics that, when considered as a whole, indicate an individual's development relative to others during a particular age span.

developmental needs A set of needs unique and appropriate to the developmental characteristics of a particular age span.

diagnostic assessment See *informal preassessment*; could be standardized tests that indicate a student's strengths/weaknesses in areas of identified skill sets.

didactic teaching See *explicit* or *direct teaching.*

differentiated learning Teacher use of personalizing the learning for students of various abilities that can include differentiated reading, flexible grouping, tiered assignments, and different tasks for special populations of students; also a synonym for personalized instruction that reflects a concern for learners and a teacher's way of adjusting the teaching and learning environment to enhance the learning needs of individual students. See *multireading approach, personalized instruction,* and *tiered instruction.*

differentiated/tiered instruction Teacher insight of and use of varied methods and content of instruction according to individual student differences and needs. See also *differentiated learning* and *personalized instruction.*

direct experience Learning by doing (applying) that which is being learned.

direct intervention Teacher use of verbal reminders or verbal commands to redirect student behavior, as opposed to nonverbal gestures or cues.

direct teaching Teacher-centered expository instruction.

discipline The process of controlling student behavior in the classroom. This term has been largely replaced by the terms *classroom control* or *classroom management.* It is also used in reference to the subject taught (e.g., language arts, mathematics, social sciences, and so forth).

discovery learning This is learning that proceeds from identifying a problem, developing the hypotheses, testing of hypotheses, and arriving at a conclusion. See *critical thinking.*

divergent thinking Thinking that expands beyond original thought.

divergent-thinking questions High-order thinking questions that require analysis, synthesis, or evaluation. usually have no singularly correct answer and students must think creatively. Example: "What measures could be taken to improve safety in our community?" Also known as *broad, reflective, open-ended,* or *thought* questions.

downshifting Reverting to earlier-learned, lower-cognitive-level behaviors.

early adolescence The developmental stage of young people as they approach and begin to experience puberty. This stage usually occurs between 10 and 14 years of age and deals with the successful attainment of the appropriate developmental characteristics for this age span.

eclectic Utilizing the best from a variety of sources.

educational goal See *goal, educational*

effective school A school where students master basic skills, strive for academic excellence in all subjects, demonstrate achievement, and display good behavior and attendance. Known also as an *exemplary school.*

elective High-interest or special-needs courses that are based on student selection from various options.

electronic teaching portfolio A collection of documents that shows your professional work over periods of time to show ways that your teaching changes; can include reflections and feedback about your teaching.

elementary school Any school that has been planned and organized especially for children of some combination of grades kindergarten through 6. There are many variations; for example, a school might house children of preschool through age 7 or 8 and still be called an elementary school or *grade school.*

ELL cluster model An approach that is similar to the sheltered instruction approach where the class is conducted in English, the teaching aides speak the native languages of the students, and content and language skills are taught concurrently.

empathy The ability to understand the feelings of another person.

English language learners Limited-English-proficient children whose English proficiency is not developed to the point where they can profit fully from instruction in English.

equality Considered to be the same in status or competency level.

equilibration The mental process of moving from disequilibrium to equilibrium.

equilibrium The balance between assimilation (integrating new information) and accommodation (modifying or creating a new schema).

equity Fairness and justice, that is, impartiality.

essay A form of measurement that asks a student to write a response to a problem/question.

evaluation Similar to assessment, but includes making sense out of the assessment results by judging the worth of something, usually based on criteria or a scoring guide/rubric. Evaluation is more subjective than is assessment.

evaluative questions A question that requires a student to place a value on something or to take a stance on some issue.

exceptional student A student who deviates from the average in any of the following ways: his or her ability to communicate, mental characteristics, multiple disabilities, neuromotor characteristics, physical characteristics, and social behavior. Also known as a *special-needs student* and *special education student*.

exemplary school A school where students master basic skills, seek academic excellence in all subjects, demonstrate achievement, and display good behavior and attendance. Known also as an *effective school*.

explicit instruction Teacher-centered instruction, typically with the entire class, and where the teacher controls student attention and behaviors as opposed to permitting students greater control over their own learning and behaviors. Also called *explicit teaching* and referred to as *explicit/direct instruction, expository teaching*, or *teacher-centered instruction*. This mode of instruction is different from implicit/indirect experiences.

exploratory course A course designed to help students explore curriculum experiences based on their felt needs, interests, and abilities.

expository instruction This is a classroom instructional approach that usually is in a sequence: present the information to students, make a reference to selected examples, and apply the information to the students' experiences.

expository organizer An introduction that mentally prepares students for a study by helping them see an arrangement of what is to be learned. See *advance organizer*.

extended-year school Schools that have extended the school year calendar from a designated 180 number of days to a longer period such as 210 days.

extrinsic motivators Motivation of learning by rewards outside of the student such as certificates, gifts, grades, points, stickers, and teacher/parent/guardian expectations.

facilitating behavior Teacher behavior that makes it possible for students to learn.

facilitative teaching See *implicit/indirect teaching*.

family, educational See *school-within-a-school*.

feedback In interpersonal communication, this is information sent from the receiver to the originator that provides disclosure about the reception of the intended message.

flexible scheduling Organization of classes and activities in a way that allows for variation from day to day, as contrasted with the traditional fixed schedule that does not vary from day to day.

formative assessment Evaluation of learning in progress.

full inclusion A commitment to each special-needs student to educate him or her to the maximum extent that is appropriate in the class, school, and district.

full-service community school A school that serves as a community center.

goal, course A broad generalized statement telling the expected outcomes of the course.

goal, educational A statement telling what the instructor intends to do that is often broad and general in scope; can reflect an expected educational outcome. See *instructional goal*.

goal indicator Indicates performance objectives that are parts of larger educational goals that reflect the competencies that the students are expected to achieve.

goal, instructional See *educational goal*.

goal, teacher A statement about what the teacher hopes to accomplish.

grade school See *elementary school*.

hands-on learning Learning by doing or active learning.

heterogeneous grouping A grouping pattern that does not separate students into groups based on their intelligence, learning achievement, or physical characteristics.

high-stakes testing Standardized tests that measure which standards are being met by the students and, in some cases, can be used to make a decision about a student being promoted to the next grade.

holistic learning Learning that incorporates emotions with thinking.

homogeneous grouping A grouping pattern that separates students into groups based on their intelligence, school achievement, or physical characteristics.

house (educational) See *school-within-a-school*.

implicit teaching Student-centered teaching using discovery learning and inquiry learning instructional strategies.

inclusion The commitment to the education of each special-needs learner, to the maximum extent appropriate, in the school and classroom he or she would otherwise attend. See *full inclusion*.

independent study An instructional strategy that allows a student to select a topic, set the goals, and work alone to attain them.

individualized educational program (IEP) An instructional plan/program designed by general education teachers, special education teachers, the parents/guardians, and in some cases, the student and the school/district resource professionals.

individualized instruction See *individualized learning*.

individualized learning A self-paced process whereby individual students assume responsibility for learning through study, practice, feedback, and reinforcement with appropriately designed instructional packages or modules.

inductive learning Learning that proceeds from the specifics to the general.

informal assessment Types of informal and classroom-based assessment strategies that include informal reading inventories, observations by the teacher, oral reports, performance samples, portfolios, and ongoing records.

initiating activities The activities that start with a beginning lesson or start a unit into motion.

inquiry learning An instructional approach that is similar to discovery learning except that the learner designs the processes to be used in resolving a problem. Inquiry learning typically demands higher levels of mental operation than does discovery learning because the students themselves often gather the needed information and use it to investigate problems in real life.

inservice teacher Credentialed and employed teachers.

instruction Planned arrangement of experiences to help a learner develop understanding and to achieve a desirable change in behavior; experiences associated with methods facilitating student learning.

instructional components Denotes the arrangement of the procedures to be used in a lesson plan.

instructional goal See *goal, instructional*

instructional module Any instructional unit that includes these components: rationale, objectives, pretest, learning activities, comprehension checks, posttest.

instructional objectives Statements describing what the student(s) will be able to do upon completion of the instructional experience; also called *learning objectives*.

integrated (interdisciplinary) curriculum This is curriculum reorganization that combines subject matter traditionally taught separately. Other terms for this reorganization are *integrated studies, thematic instruction,* and *multidisciplinary teaching*.

integrated thematic unit Denotes when a unit integrates disciplines and is centered on a central theme.

interdisciplinary team An organizational pattern of two or more teachers representing different subject areas. The team shares the same students, schedule, areas of the school, and the opportunity for teaching more than one subject.

interdisciplinary thematic unit (ITU) A thematic unit that crosses boundaries of two or more disciplines.

intermediate grades Sometimes refers to grades 4–6. An intermediate school, for example, is an elementary school that houses children of grades 4–6.

internalizing The extent to which an attitude or value becomes a part of the learner. That is, without having to think about it, the learner's behavior reflects the attitude or value.

intervention A teacher's interruption to redirect a student's behavior, either by direct intervention (e.g., by a verbal command) or by indirect intervention (e.g., by eye contact or physical proximity).

intramural program Organized activity program that features event between individuals or teams from within the school.

intrinsic motivation The motivation of learning through the student's internal sense of accomplishment.

introduction The section of a lesson plan about preparing the students mentally for the lesson; also referred to as the *set* or *initiating activity*.

intuition Knowing without conscious reasoning.

I-search paper An approach to writing a research paper that differs from the traditional research paper approach and engages the students in listing information they would like to know, conducting a study to find information, keeping a log that is a process journal, and preparing a summary of their findings.

jigsaw This term refers to an instructional approach to facilitate students' metacognitive development where individual students or small groups of students are given responsibilities for separate tasks that lead to a bigger task or understanding; the students put together the separate tasks/parts to make a whole.

journals, student A record, diary, or account of daily learning that includes what students are studying, classroom interactions, free writing, or school events; also called *process journals, response journals,* and *dialogue journals*.

knowledge Recognizing and recalling information.

learning A change in behavior resulting from experience.

learning activity Denotes *how* the students will learn something.

learning center (LC) An instructional strategy that uses activities and materials located at a special place in the classroom and is designed to allow a student to work independently at his or her own pace to learn one area of content; types include direct-learning center, open-learning center, and skill center.

learning modality The way a person receives information. Four modalities are recognized: visual, auditory, tactile (touch), and kinesthetic.

learning objective Denotes what the students will learn as a result of the learning activity. See *instructional objectives*.

learning resource center The central location in the school where instructional materials and media are stored, organized, and accessed by students and staff.

learning station A learning center that is somehow linked or sequenced to another center where each incorporates a different medium or modality or focuses on a special aspect of the curriculum.

learning style The way a person learns best in a given situation.

learning targets Competencies that the students are expected to achieve; also called *educational goals*, which can be divided into performance objectives and sometimes referred to as *goal indicators*.

lesson conclusion The section of the lesson that provides closure and is the planned process of bringing the lesson to an end.

lesson development The section of a lesson plan that details the activities that occur between the beginning and the end of the lesson.

literacy The 2008 NCTE definition of 21st century literacies states that a literate person should possess multiple abilities and competencies with technology, solve problems cross-culturally, meet a variety of purposes with global communities, interact with multiple streams of simultaneous information and multimedia texts, and attend to ethical responsibilities in complex environments.

looping An arrangement in which the cohort of students and teachers remains together as a group for several or for all the years a child is at a particular school. Also referred to as *multiyear grouping, multiyear instruction, multiyear placement*, and *teacher-student progression*.

magnet school A school that specializes in a particular academic area, such as the arts, international relations, mathematics, science, and technology; also referred to as a *theme school*.

mainstreaming Placing an exceptional student in a regular classroom for all (inclusion) or part (partial inclusion) of his or her learning.

manipulatives Objects that can be moved/used with the hands with the goal of demonstrating something.

mastery learning The concept that a student should master the content of one lesson before moving on to the content of the next.

mean The average score in a distribution of scores achieved by test takers.

measurement The process of collecting and interpreting data, most often quantifying information.

median The middle score in a distribution of scores achieved by test takers.

mentoring One-on-one coaching, tutoring, or guidance to facilitate learning.

metacognition The ability to think about, understand, and to develop one's own thinking and learning.

middle grades Schools that typically house grades 5 through 8; based on a movement in the 1980s relying upon research that indicated that the needs and interests of children in the seventh and eighth grades more closely resemble those of elementary schoolchildren than they resemble those of ninth graders.

middle-level education Any school unit between elementary and high school.

middle school A school that has been planned and organized especially for students of ages 10–14 and that generally has grades 5–8, with grades 6–8 being the most popular grade-span organization, although many varied patterns exist. For example, a school might include only grades 7 and 8 and still be called a middle school.

minds-on learning Learning in which the learner is intellectually active, thinking about what is being learned.

misconception Faulty understanding of a major idea of concept. Also known as a *naive theory* and *conceptual misunderstanding*.

mode The most frequent score in a distribution of scores achieved by test takers.

modeling The teacher's explicit/direct and implicit/indirect demonstration, by actions and by words, of the behaviors expected of students.

multicultural education A deliberate educational attempt to help students understand facts, generalizations, attitudes, and behaviors derived from their own ethnic roots as well as others. In this process the students should unlearn racism and biases and recognize the interdependent fabric of our human society, giving due acknowledgment for contributions made by all its members.

multilevel instruction Multilevel teaching means to identify the child's unique needs relative to your classroom, and design lessons that teach to different needs at the same time. See *multitasking*.

multimedia The combined use of sound, video, and graphics for instruction.

multiple intelligences A theory of several different intelligences, as opposed to just one general intelligence; other intelligences that have been described are verbal/linguistic, musical, logical/mathematical, naturalist, visual/spatial, bodily/kinesthetic, interpersonal, and intrapersonal.

multipurpose board A writing board with a smooth plastic surface.

multireading approach Teacher use of different reading and workbook assignments and supplementary sources; students work out of different books and do different exercises and can work toward the same or different objectives. See *multitasking* and *multilevel instruction*.

multitasking The simultaneous use of several levels of teaching and learning in the same classroom with students working on different objectives or different tasks leading to the same objectives. Also called *multilevel teaching*.

naive theories See *misconception*.

narrow questions Lower-order thinking questions, such as recall questions, that have single correct answers. Also called *convergent-thinking questions*.

National Education Association (NEA) The nation's oldest professional organization of teachers; organized in 1857 as the National Teachers Association and changed in 1879 to its present name.

National Network of Partnership Schools (2000) An organization of support for schools with family and community participation.

norm-referenced The assessing process where an individual performance is judged relative to overall performance of the group. It is different from criterion-referenced assessment, which establishes preset standards and judges student behaviors against the preset standards rather than against the behaviors of other individuals.

norms These are standardized test scores from a representative group of students nationally that were used to compare a single student's score in a particular testing situation; the term can also indicate the median (middle score) achievement of a large group.

organizing Placing values into a system of dominant and supporting values.

orientation set See *advance organizer*.

outcome-based instruction This means that instruction is designed to evaluate the achievement of students against specified and predetermined behavioral objectives. The term also indicates instruction that is referred to as *competency-based, results-driven*, and *performance-based instruction*.

overlapping The teacher's ability to attend to several matters at once.

overt behavior A learner behavior that is outwardly observable.

paraprofessional An adult who is not a credentialed teacher but who works with children in the classroom with and under the supervision of a credentialed person.

partial inclusion Placing special-needs students in a regular education classroom part of the day.

partners A student who works with another student in accomplishing a learning task.

peer teaching (PT) A clinical technique of preparing, implementing, and evaluating a teaching demonstration to a small group of peers.

peer tutoring An instructional strategy that places students in a tutorial role in which one student helps another learn.

percent A specified number of parts out of one hundred; can indicate the number of units in proportion to one hundred.

percentile A ranking that compares a child's score with the scores of all the other children who have taken the test (also known as a *percentile rank* [PR or % rank]).

performance assessment See *authentic assessment*.

performance-based teaching Instruction designed around evaluating student achievement against specified and predetermined behavioral objectives. The term also indicates instruction referred to as *competency-based, outcome-based*, and *results-driven*.

performance objective See *behavioral objective*.

personalized instruction A synonym for differentiated or tiered instruction that reflects a concern for learners and a teacher's adjustment in the teaching and learning environment to meet the learning needs of individual students. See *differentiated/tiered instruction*.

plan B Denotes an addition to your lesson plan about what to do if you finish the lesson and time remains.

pod A *school-within-a-school*; sometimes, referred to as a *cluster, family, house*, or *village*; it is a teaching arrangement where a team of teachers is assigned to work with the same group of about 125 students for a common block of time, across grades for the entire school day, or in some instances, for all the years those students are at that school.

portfolio assessment An alternative approach to evaluation that assembles representative samples of the student's work over time as a basis for assessment.

positive reinforcer A means of encouraging desired student behaviors by rewarding those behaviors when they occur.

post-observation conference A visit where the student teacher/intern, the cooperating teacher, and the supervisor/principal discusses the classroom students' performances and the teaching performance.

practice The teacher's follow-up, that is, ways that the teacher intends to have students interact in the classroom, such as individual practice, in dyads, or small groups, to receive guidance or coaching from each other or from the teacher.

Praxis teacher tests Tests required by some states for credentialing and licensing of teachers with the passing scores recommended by panels of educators; includes multiple-choice and constructed-response-type questions.

preassessment Diagnostic assessment of what students know or think they know prior to the instruction.

preobservation conference A visit between student teachers/interns/teachers with supervisors/principals to discuss goals, objectives, teaching strategies, and the evaluation process.

preservice Precredentialed teachers in training, as opposed to inservice teachers or teachers who are employed.

prior knowledge Earlier-acquired facts, information, and ideas that comprise what a student knows before learning something else or before a lesson.

probationary teacher An untenured teacher; after a designated number of years in the same district (usually three years), the probationary teacher, upon rehire, receives a tenure contract.

procedure A statement that indicates to students a way to accomplish a task. It can also indicate the section of a teacher's lesson plan that outlines what a teacher and the students will do during the lesson. See *rules*.

professional logbook A diary-type journal that serves a teacher as a documentation of specific professional contributions and activities and also as documentation of one's breadth of professional experience.

project A relatively long-term investigation or study from which students produce their culminating presentations that show how the students apply what they have learned.

proportion The relation of one thing to another.

psychomotor domain Classification of learning locomotor behaviors that include moving, manipulating, communicating, and creating.

realia Real objects used as visual props in teaching, such as political campaign buttons, plants, memorabilia, etc.

receiving Being aware of the affective stimulus and beginning to have favorable feelings toward it.

reciprocal teaching A form of collaborative teaching where the teacher and the students share the teaching responsibility and all are involved in asking questions, clarifying, predicting, and summarizing.

reflection The conscious process of mentally replaying experiences.

reflective abstraction See *metacognition*.

relaxed alertness A classroom environment that is perceived by the student as challenging and nonthreatening.

reliability In measurement, the consistency with which an item is measured over time.

responding Taking an interest in the stimulus and viewing it favorably.

results-driven instruction See *performance-based teaching*.

rubric A presented, prescribed, or established form or method for assessing a student's work; can also be an outline of the criteria for an accomplishment. See *scoring guide*.

rules In classroom management, rules/procedures are the standards of expectation for classroom behavior. See *procedure*.

sans penalty Without a negative consequence.

scaffolding A system for learning support that can be removed when it is no longer needed. It can include modeling, paired work, graphic organizers, outlining aids, study guides, written questions, outlines for note taking, explicit objectives—oral and written, analogies, examples, repetitions, relating lesson to prior experience and background knowledge, clear explanation of tasks, and examples of responses.

schemata (singular, schema) A mental construct by which the learner organizes his or her perceptions of situations and knowledge.

school-within-a-school Sometimes referred to as a *house, cluster, family, pod*, or *village*, it is a teaching arrangement where one team of teachers is assigned to work with the same group of about 125 students for a common block of time, for the entire school day, or in some instances, for all of the years those students are at that school.

scoring guide A method for assessing a student's work; can also be an outline of the criteria for an accomplishment. See *rubric*.

self-contained classroom Commonly used in the primary grades, it is a grouping pattern where one teacher teaches all or most all subjects to one group of children.

self-paced learning See *individualized learning*.

sequencing Arranging ideas in logical order.

simulation An abstraction or simplification of a real-life situation.

special-needs student A special education student. See *exceptional student*.

standard unit A way to organize a unit into a series of activities built into lessons around a topic, major concept, or block of subject content; also known as a *traditional* or *conventional unit*.

stanine/stanines A term that refers to another term, standard nine, that indicates a student's standardized test performance based on a scale from 1 to 9 points as shown on a normal curve. This performance (stanine) is identified as a specific percentage of the normal curve (stanine score).

statement of mission This is a school's written philosophy or vision that often relates what the school means to the people within the school or district.

structured English immersion program A program to teach students the English language quickly with a goal of being more successful in school. Teachers maximize instruction in English as the main content and integrate focused lessons according to the abilities of the students. Lessons focus on listening skills, pronunciation, sentence structure, reading, writing, and other aspects of English.

student journal A log of student activities, findings, and thoughts; sometimes called *process journals, response journals*, or *dialogue journals*.

student teaching A classroom experience component of teacher preparation, often the culminating experience, where the precredentialed teacher practices teaching students while under the supervision of a credentialed teacher, and in university programs, a university supervisor.

summative assessment The assessment of learning after instruction is completed.

synthesis Putting components of information together to generate new ideas.

teacher's logbook A diary-type journal that documents a teacher's teaching activities with dated entries.

teaching See *instruction.*

teaching observation A visit where the supervisor/principal collects data on the classroom students' performance of objectives and performance of the teaching strategies.

teaching style The way a teacher teaches and includes the teacher's distinctive mannerisms complemented by his or her choices of teaching behaviors and strategies.

teaching team Two or more teachers who work together to provide instruction to the same group of students, either alternating the instruction or team teaching simultaneously.

teaching video A form of alternative authentic assessment that involves the teacher/student teacher/intern in the design and evaluation of teaching future lessons.

team teaching Two or more teachers working together to provide instruction to a group of students.

technology Related to elementary schools, this term includes the students' use of computers, the Internet, television, VCRs, DVD players, compact discs, CD-ROMs, electronic games, cell phones, personal digital assistants, and other high-tech items.

tenured teacher After serving a designated number of years (usually three) in the same school district as a probationary teacher, the teacher, upon rehire, receives a tenure contract, which means that the teacher is automatically rehired each year thereafter unless the contract is revoked by either the district or the teacher and for specific and legal reasons.

terminal behavior That which has been learned as a direct result of instruction.

thematic unit A unit of instruction built on a central theme or concept.

theme school See *magnet school.*

think time See *wait time.*

tiered instruction A teacher's insight about (and use of) varied methods and content of instruction according to individual student differences and needs; different levels of assignments.

timetable A planning and implementation guide for a lesson plan.

total immersion program A program where all of the classroom instruction is in the target foreign language.

tracking The practice of the voluntary or involuntary placement of students in different programs or courses according to their ability and prior academic performance.

traditional teaching Teacher-centered explicit instruction, typically using teacher talk, discussions, textbooks, and worksheets.

transitions In a lesson, the planned procedures that move student thinking from one idea to the next or that move their actions from one activity to the next; a change.

validity In measurement, the degree to which an item or instrument measures that which it is intended to measure.

valuing Showing a tentative belief in the value of an effected stimulus and becoming committed to it.

video teaching Referring to the teacher/student teacher/intern, this is a form of alternative authentic assessment that involves the design and evaluation of teaching future lessons.

village A *school-within-a-school*; sometimes, referred to as a *house, cluster, family,* or *pod.*

wait time In the use of questioning, this is the period of silence between the time a question is asked and the time an inquirer (teacher) does something, such as repeats the question, rephrases the question, calls upon a particular student, asks another question, or answers the previous question him- or herself.

whole language learning A point of view of teaching with a focus on seeking or creating meaning that encourages language production, risk-taking, independence in producing language, and the use of a wide variety of print materials in authentic reading and writing situations.

withitness A teacher's ability to be aware of what is going on in the classroom and, if needed, to intervene and redirect a student's misbehavior in a timely manner.

year-round school A school that operates on a traditional schedule, that is, with the district's designated number of school days, but the days are spread out over twelve months rather than the more traditional ten. Most common is a nine-weeks-on, three-weeks-off format.

young adolescent The 9–14-year-old experiencing the developmental stage of early adolescence.

Children's Literature Index

Name Index

Subject Index

Note — A bullet (•) placed by selected word entries in this subject index highlight the words that are Target Topics for Teacher Tests (TTTT). These bulleted words are subject matter areas that a reader can target when studying for a teacher test. The topics are based on analysis of selected teacher tests, student teaching evaluations, and the Praxis II Exam. Thus, the foci/topics represent core material and it is suggested that the topics be reviewed when preparing to take state teacher tests or the Praxis II Principles of Learning and Teaching exam.